PLACE AND MEMORY

EXCAVATIONS AT THE PICT'S KNOWE, HOLYWOOD AND HOLM FARM, DUMFRIES AND GALLOWAY, 1994–8

PLACE AND MEMORY
EXCAVATIONS AT THE PICT'S KNOWE, HOLYWOOD AND HOLM FARM, DUMFRIES AND GALLOWAY, 1994–8

Julian Thomas

with the editorial assistance of

Matt Leivers, Julia Roberts and Rick Peterson

and contributions by

Patrick Ashmore, Kenneth Brophy, Graeme Brown, Ciera Clark, Kate Clark, Mike Cressey,
Anne Crone, John Crowther, Diane Dixon, Carol van Driel-Murray, Chris Fowler,
B. Andrew Haggart, Fraser Hunter, Penny Johnson, Helen Joyner, Matt Leivers, Grith Lerche,
Gilbert Marshall, Paula Milburn, Jennifer Miller, Ruth Pelling, Rick Peterson, Susan Ramsay,
Julia Roberts, Maggie Ronayne, Mike Roy, Rob Sands, Theo Skinner, Richard Tipping,
Kerry Tyler and Aaron Watson

OXBOW BOOKS

Published by
Oxbow Books, Oxford

© Oxbow Books, Julian Thomas
and the individual authors, 2007

ISBN 978-1-84217-247-6

A CIP record of this book is available from the British Library

This book is available direct from

Oxbow Books, Oxford
(Phone: 01865-241249; Fax: 01865-794449)

and

The David Brown Book Company
PO Box 511, Oakville, CT 06779, USA
(Phone: 860-945-9329; Fax: 860-945-9468)

or from our website

www.oxbowbooks.com

Front cover image:
Reconstruction of Holm post alignments by Aaron Watson

Printed in Great Britain by
Antony Rowe Ltd, Chippenham, Wiltshire

Contents

PART THREE: CONCLUSION

APPENDICES

COLOUR PLATES

Addresses of Contributors

Patrick Ashmore, Historic Scotland, Longmore House, Salisbury Place, Edinburgh EH9 1SH

Kenneth Brophy, Department of Archaeology, The Gregory Building, University of Glasgow, Lilybank Gardens, Glasgow G12 8QQ

Graeme Brown, Department of Archaeology, The University of Edinburgh, Old High School, 12 Infirmary Road, Edinburgh EH1 1LT

Ciera Clark, Centre for Field Archaeology, The University of Edinburgh, Old High School, 12 Infirmary Road, Edinburgh EH1 1LT

Kate M. Clark, Moonrakers, Lockerley Green, Lockerley, Romsey, Hampshire

Anne Crone, AOC Archaeology (Scotland), Edgefield Industrial Estate, Loanhead, Edinburgh EH20 9SY

John Crowther, Department of Archaeology and Anthropology, University of Wales, Lampeter, Ceredigion SA48 7ED

Carol van Driel-Murray, Amsterdams Archaeologisch Centrum, Amsterdam University, Nieuwe Prinsengract 130, 1018 VZ Amsterdam, Netherlands

Chris Fowler, School of Historical Studies, University of Newcastle, Newcastle Upon Tyne NE1 7RU

B. Andrew Haggart, School of Earth and Environmental Sciences, University of Greenwich, Medway University Campus, Chatham Maritime, Kent ME4 4TB

Fraser Hunter, Royal Museum of Scotland, Chambers Street, Edinburgh EH1 1JF

Matt Leivers, Wessex Archaeology, Portway House, Old Sarum Park, Salisbury SP4 6EB

Grith Lerche, Department of Food Science, Food Technology, Rolighedsvej 30, DK-1958 Fredriksberg C, Denmark

Gilbert Marshall, Department of Archaeology, University of Southampton, Avenue Campus, Southampton SO17 1BF

Paula Milburn, Department of Environmental Science, University of Stirling, Stirling FK8 3BX

Jennifer Miller, Glasgow University Archaeological Research Division, The Gregory Building, University of Glasgow, Lilybank Gardens, Glasgow G12 8QQ

Rick Peterson, School of Natural Resources, University of Central Lancashire, Preston PR1 2HE

Susan Ramsay, Glasgow University Archaeological Research Division, The Gregory Building, University of Glasgow, Lilybank Gardens, Glasgow G12 8QQ

Julia Roberts, School of Natural Resources, University of Central Lancashire, Preston PR1 2HE

Maggie Ronayne, Department of Archaeology, National University of Ireland, University Road, Galway, Ireland

Mike Roy, AOC Archaeology (Scotland), Edgefield Industrial Estate, Loanhead, Edinburgh EH20 9SY

Rob Sands, School of Archaeology, University College Dublin, Belfield, Dublin 4, Ireland

Theo Skinner, Royal Museum of Scotland, Chambers Street, Edinburgh EH1 1JF

Julian Thomas, School of Arts, Histories and Cultures, University of Manchester, Oxford Road, Manchester M13 9PL

Richard Tipping, Department of Environmental Science, University of Stirling, Stirling FK8 3BX

Acknowledgements

The excavations at the Pict's Knowe, Holywood and Holm were made possible through the kindness and hard work of numerous people. The author would firstly like to thank the landowners and tenants of the sites concerned for their permission to work on their land: Mrs F. Havard and her land agent Mr N. Pollard of G. M. Thomson and Co. at the Pict's Knowe; Mrs and Mrs Carson at the Twelve Apostles; Captain and Mrs Weatherall, and Mr Hastings, Mr Howie and Mr Whiteford at Holywood and Holm. The entire project was made possible through the encouragement and support (material, financial and moral) of Historic Scotland, and in particular I would liker to thank Patrick Ashmore, Gordon Barclay, Noel Fojut, Rod McCullagh and Richard Welander. Jane Brann (Dumfries and Galloway Regional Authority) provided invaluable local contacts and knowledge, while Theo Skinner and Alison Sheridan of the National Museum of Scotland gave assistance in the field and afterwards, above and beyond the call of duty. Marilyn Brown and Jane Murray gave unstinting help and information. Financial assistance was provided by the Society of Antiquaries of Scotland, the Russell Trust, the Prehistoric Society and the University of Southampton, and is gratefully acknowledged. In the period leading up to publication, support of various kinds has been provided by the University of Manchester.

I would like to thank all of those who dug, supervised, surveyed, drove minibuses and logged finds on the various sites, including Rick Peterson, Matt Leivers, Michael Tierney, Tim Sly, Avril Purcell, Maggie Ronayne, Chris Fowler, Kenneth Brophy, Vicky Cummings, Jayne Gidlow, Emma Clarke, Katherine Edwards, Ian Heath, Dave Robinson, Paul Everill, Gavin Glover, Roy Sykes, Nina Hawkins, Jeb Baker, Julia Murphy, Andy Dunham, Katherine Briggs, Anna Andréasson, Karin Berggren, Katherine Patton, Charlotta Malm, Annika Östlund, Vanessa Balloqui, Olivia Merritt, Nichola Tucker, Tim Havard, Kerry Tyler, Jemma Pyne, David Brown, Danny Bateman, Piers Lewis, Helen Saunders, Anna Hayward, Agnieszka Leszczyń ska, Jane Davies, Joe Hess, Adrian Turgel, Doug Murphy, Jane Martin, Colin Richards and Yvonne Marshall, as well as numerous students from the Universities of Southampton, Lampeter, Cardiff and Gothenburg. Rebecca Davies cooked at the Pict's Knowe, and Tim Walley was site manager. During the excavations at Holywood and Holm, the team stayed at the Barony College, Parkgate, and I would like to thank all concerned for their forbearance, particularly Anne Twiname.

Julian Thomas
June 2006

PART ONE
THE PICT'S KNOWE

1

Introduction

Julian Thomas

This volume is concerned with the investigation of three complexes of prehistoric ceremonial monuments in the immediate environs of Dumfries in the south-west of Scotland, conducted over the period between 1994 and 1998. These were the Pict's Knowe henge, excavated between 1994 and 1997, the Holywood cursus complex, where work took place in 1997, and the post alignments/ cursus at Holm, dug in 1998 (see Fig. 1.1 for locations). These projects were undertaken on a collaborative basis between Historic Scotland and the author's employer at the time, the University of Southampton. The excavations were carried out as training projects using undergraduate students, with professional archaeologists and post-graduates as supervisory staff. At the Pict's Knowe, on-site assistance with conservation was provided by Historic Scotland and the National Museum of Scotland. More recently, the programme of fieldwork in the south-west has continued with excavations at the Neolithic palisaded enclosure and post-defined cursus at Dunragit in Galloway (see Thomas 2004a; 2004b).

Traditionally, there has been a tendency to identify separate traditions of stone and earth-and-timber monuments in different parts of the British mainland during the Neolithic and Bronze Age. Earthen long barrows, causewayed enclosures, cursus monuments and henges have sometimes been presented as characteristic of the 'lowland zone' of the south and east, while megalithic tombs and stone circles have been associated with the highlands of the north and west (e.g. Childe 1940, 62; Fox 1947, 32). To some extent this has been explained in terms of the development of parallel and equivalent traditions of construction which made use of locally available materials. However, the development of aerial reconnaissance in the past few decades has demonstrated that in the south-west of Scotland, conventionally 'lowland' monumental forms can be found alongside stone structures that have been known for much longer. Indeed, prior to the 1970s, the Neolithic archaeology of many parts of Scotland was exclusively focused on stone

monuments (Barclay 2000, 2). Yet it is the juxtaposition of timber and stone ceremonial architectures that makes Dumfries and Galloway a potentially rewarding location for archaeological research. The particular spatial and temporal relationships between monuments within this region can arguably shed light on the significance of structures and the use of landscape in other, quite different contexts. The work described in this book is therefore particularistic at one level, while having more general implications. The field research was designed in such a way as to recognise that prehistoric monuments often have complex and individual sequences of construction and use, while also acknowledging that it will be detailed studies of particular sites and local contexts that will ultimately advance our understanding of the phenomenon of monumentality in prehistoric Europe.

The three sites of the Pict's Knowe, Holywood and Holm have proved especially helpful in addressing questions of how particular places maintained their importance over long periods of time. In each instance, our attention was drawn to the location by features which possess a high degree of archaeological visibility. In the former case it was the upstanding earthwork of the bank and ditch that identified the site as a henge monument, while Holywood and Holm were discovered through aerial photography. However, while the information available in advance of excavation might encourage us to label each as an example of a particular 'type' of site (a henge, a pair of cursus monuments, a post alignment), this morphological approach can occlude the likelihood that each site will have an elaborate structural history. Each of the sites investigated here had complex sequences of development, in which the structural elements that were recognised prior to fieldwork were not necessarily the most important or the most long-lived. Indeed, the impression that arises from these sites is one of locations which held an enduring significance, but where events of construction and performance might be fleeting and sometimes ephemeral. In this monograph, we will con-

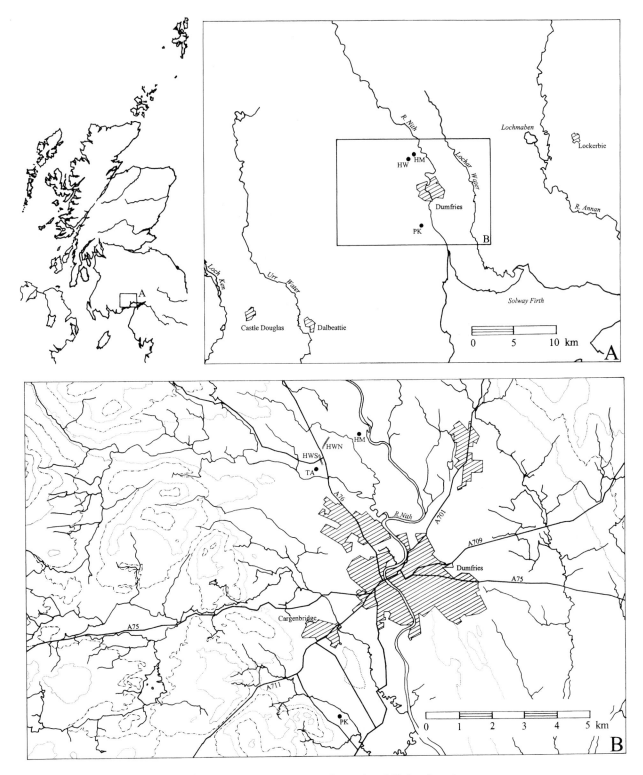

Fig. 1.1 The Pict's Knowe, Holywood and Holm: locations.

sider the details of the excavated features, environmental and artefactual evidence before returning to these more general concerns. In the first part of the volume, we will concentrate on the Pict's Knowe, while in the second, we will turn to the more spatially and typologically related sites of Holywood and Holm.

It will be evident that the structure of this text is a rather traditional one, which departs little from the established format of the excavation report. In recent years, there has been considerable debate over the ways in which we represent archaeological investigation through the written word (Lucas 2001, 202). It has been pointed out that archaeological fieldwork is a collective and collaborative enterprise, in which an understanding of the site emerges from a physical engagement on the part of numerous excavators. It is the context of the physical activity of excavation, 'at the trowel's edge', that interpretations are generated (Hodder 1999, 92). Yet the convention is to separate the description of structures and stratigraphy from the evaluation of the site's significance, giving the impression that archaeological deposits exist in the first instance as inert matter, to which we later bring meaning. This creates the illusion that what happens in the field and the laboratory is purely descriptive, and that the work of interpretation only begins once the site has been verbally and graphically illustrated, and the specialist contributions completed and absorbed. A series of impressive recent works have challenged this hierarchical organisation, mixing description and interpretation to present a more accurate representation of the archaeological process (e.g. Richards 2005). The author is acutely aware that the present volume does not attempt such an exercise. Yet the strategy that has been adopted can be defended on other grounds.

In this text, descriptive passages are separated from those in which the material is contextualised and explained. However, it is recognised that this is an artificial separation, in which an attempt is made to distil the material evidence from an already-existing conception of the site and its significance. In other words, the process is the precise opposite of that which is conventionally understood to constitute good archaeological practice. The description of structures and deposits is recognised as an artifice, and this would be a somewhat perverse way of proceeding were it not for the question of the way in which an excavation report is likely to be used. A large proportion of the potential readership for such a volume is likely to be made up of professional archaeologists, whether fieldworkers, academics, or students. It is to be expected that such an audience will not always be content to accept the author's views on trust, and that they will in some cases wish to re-work the evidence, as far as is possible with a paper record. One of the problems that attends more 'interpretive' accounts of archaeological sites is that they sometimes concentrate on those aspects of the evidence that support the author's account of the material. In this volume, while it is recognised that any purely objective description is a practical impossibility, the attempt has been made to make as much as possible of the evidence directly available to the reader. Context and finds numbers have been preserved from the original field records. All of this should also mean that it will be comparatively easy for the researcher to make use of the archives for these sites, should they require more information than is contained in the report. Stretching the point, we might argue that the disadvantage of some recent excavation reports is that they are 'readerly', promoting a specific view of the evidence and its meaning, while this volme is 'writerly', in that it provides the

reader with the maximum opportunity to develop their own interpretations (Olsen 1990, 184–5). To that end, where the evidence admits more than one reading the attempt has been made to present the alternatives, while still indicating the author's preference.

The site of the Pict's Knowe is situated four kilometres to the south-west of Dumfries (NX 9538 7213), located at around 10m OD in the bottom of the valley of Crooks Pow, some six kilometres inland from the meeting of the River Nith with the Solway Firth. The monument sits on a small eminence that stands proud of the surrounding peat, which cloaks the valley bottom. This natural mound is composed of well-sorted brown to reddish pink silty fine to medium sands, which appear to represent glacial and fluvioglacial deposits reworked by the Late Devensian sea (see Tipping, Haggart and Milburn below). The bank and ditch structure which stands on the hillock was first scheduled as an ancient monument in 1928. Although it was at that time designated a 'fort', the possibility that it might represent a late Neolithic henge was already recognised. This is in itself remarkable, for Kendrick was only to formally define this class of monuments in 1932 (Kendrick and Hawkes 1932, 83). Kendrick's definition was itself a somewhat vague one, referring to prehistoric 'sacred places' that included stone and timber circles. The category of 'henge monument' was refined by Grahame Clark, who emphasised the presence of a central area containing stone or timber uprights, surrounded by a ditch and bank (Clark 1936, 23). Later, Stuart and Margaret Piggott were to place greater stress on the bank and ditch, which provided the basis for their distinction between Class I (one entrance) and Class II (two opposed entrances) henges (1939, 140). In turn, Richard Atkinson insisted that it was the external bank and internal ditch that represented the distinguishing criterion for a henge monument (1951, 82). More recent work has served to recognise the diversity of henges, both in terms of their internal features and the activities that seem to have taken place within them (Burl 1969; Wainwright & Longworth 1971). The large Wessex henges, for instance, produced very large quantities of pottery, lithics, and animal bones on excavation, while smaller sites in other parts of England, Scotland, Wales and Ireland contained very little material culture in either ditches or internal features. Some henges can therefore be argued to have been connected with the conspicuous and large-scale consumption of food and artefacts, and with the formal deposition of cultural residues, while others cannot (Richards and Thomas 1984). This should make us wary of using the term 'henge' as anything but the loosest of classifications, or of jumping from an identification based on morphology to the attribution of a function or significance (Barclay 1989, 261).

Bearing in mind these concerns, the recognition of the Pict's Knowe as a henge was reiterated by Gordon Barclay and Noel Fojut (1990), who carried out an earthwork survey of the site. This attribution confirms the presence of a small group of henge-type enclosures in the general area of Dumfries. The best-known of these is the Class II henge at Broadlea in Annandale. This site is located on a small plateau overlooking a stream, and appears to have had a Roman marching camp built over it (Atkinson 1951, 100). In view of the watery location and later history of the Pict's Knowe, these features are both significant. Another possible henge is known at Newbridge, near the River Nith (Gregory 2000, 18). Barclay and Fojut noted that the Pict's Knowe had undergone considerable damage from cattle trampling, rabbit burrows and tree root disturbance (1990, 69). A visit to the site by the author in the summer of 1993 confirmed that this damage had carried on apace, to the extent that the earthwork could now be judged to be in a terminal state of disrepair. Under these circumstances, the most satisfactory course of action seemed to be to undertake a rescue excavation intended to maximise the amount of information that could still be extracted from the site. The presence of standing water in the ditch, and the existence of beds of peat surrounding the monument, demonstrated that an extensive palaeoenvironmental analysis would form an essential element of the project. This is outlined in the next two sections below, before we proceed to the results of the excavations of 1994–7.

2

The interaction of site and landscape around the Pict's Knowe

Richard Tipping, B. Andrew Haggart and Paula Milburn

Introduction

The Pict's Knowe occupies a low flat knoll just above the valley floor of the Crooks Pow, a small stream draining to the Nith Estuary some 2km to the east (Fig. 2.1). Its position is intriguing, in a central location within the valley and yet in a setting that until drainage in the last two centuries was probably marginal to the agricultural economy. This issue of centrality *versus* marginality engages the archaeologist in evaluating why henges were built where they were, and this problem is key to the palaeoenvironmental reconstruction we describe in this chapter.

The techniques that were applied to explore this were diverse. They had a central focus, to try to establish what the landscape around the Pict's Knowe looked like prior to and during construction of the monument, and then to understand the choices in locating the structure made by the builders. Because of the survival of different sediment types predating and contemporaneous with construction, there was a greater likelihood than at most archaeological sites to reconstruct this past landscape, and thus to define what attracted people to the Pict's Knowe.

2.1a Topographic setting

The Crooks Pow around the Pict's Knowe has an almost featureless valley floor (Plate 2.1). The flat grassy knoll supporting the monument at 10m OD, underlain by fine sands that are so inviting to rabbits (see Chapter 1), is matched by similar surfaces at comparable altitudes to south-east and north-west and forms the Upper Terrace. These knolls used to form a continuous surface, now separated by small embayments and gaps cut by deep gullies, subsequently infilled with peat. One prominent gully called here Bauldie's Brae lies immediately west of the Pict's Knowe (Plate 2.2). Below these knolls is a single fluvial surface, the Floodplain Terrace, formerly marshy and peaty but drained since the 19th century and now rough pasture. The small straightened stream of the

Crooks Pow is incised below this surface. These discrete valley floor landsurfaces have very different ages, and a key concern was to define the processes of sediment deposition, burial and erosion that lead to the partial archaeological record that survives today.

2.1b Sea level change

At just over 10m above present sea level (Ordnance Datum: OD), the Pict's Knowe knoll could be anticipated from past work to have been affected by former changes in sea level (Jardine 1964, 1971, 1975, 1980, 1982; Nichols 1967). A central concern was to establish when and to what extent sea level rise led to the inundation of the Crooks Pow, when the retreat occurred from maximal sea level, what landsurfaces had always lain above the highest sea levels, what landsurfaces had been eroded or buried during sea level change, and how sea level change altered the morphology and environments of the valley floor during henge construction, use and re-use. The implications of sea level change for how we might picture the Crooks Pow in the Neolithic and early Bronze Age were clear and far-reaching. The confirmation of recent work that suggests inundation of valley floors on the Solway Firth by tidal waters into later prehistory (Dawson *et al.* 1999; Wells & Smith 1999; Smith, Cullingford & Firth 2000), would introduce a prehistoric geography radically different to established models.

2.1c Fluvial and floodplain barriers

The theme of isolation and 'specialness' was also pursued by reconstructions of fluvial history. The Crooks Pow is not a major river (Fig. 2.1). It has its headwaters only 4km to the north west, in low hills rising less than 200m OD. The stream gradient is almost imperceptible below Mossside Farm, 2km upstream of the Pict's Knowe. This small catchment and limited stream power suggests that in the past the Crooks Pow would not have presented a significant barrier across the valley. However, changes in

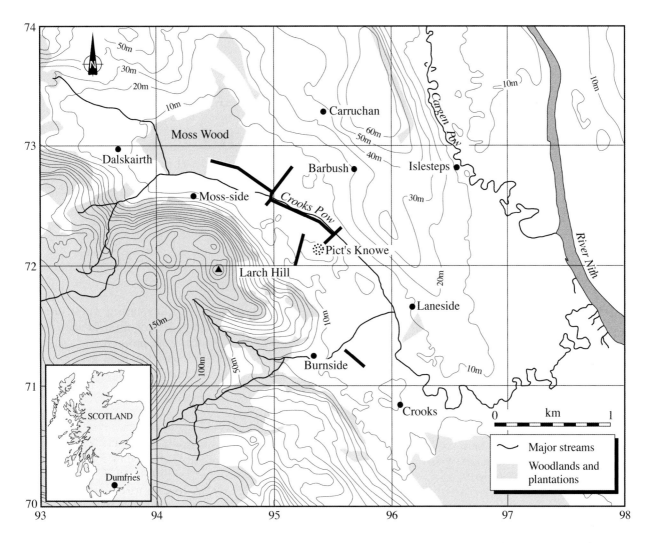

Fig. 2.1 The location of the Crooks Pow on the Solway Firth (inset) and the present landscape of the Crooks Pow between Dalskairth in the north west and the Nith estuary in the east, showing the wooded slopes (Plate 2.1), streams, farms and localities in the valley mentioned in this chapter. Pict's Knowe is at the centre of the map. Also depicted are the along-valley transect of boreholes used in sediment stratigraphic reconstructions from Moss Wood to Pict's Knowe and at Burnside, and the cross-valley transects north west of Pict's Knowe, along the Bauldie's Brae gully and south west of Carruchan.

sediment loads induced through human impacts or through climate change may have led to increases in flood frequency or floodplain development, and these may have introduced significant geomorphic barriers. If used seasonally, the monument at the Pict's Knowe may have proved effectively inaccessible to communities on the north side of the valley by winter flooding.

For a valley in south-west Scotland, the Crooks Pow has a surprising amount of peat. Peat underlies or forms the surface of the Floodplain Terrace and infills the prominent gully of Bauldie's Brae west of the monument (Figs 2.2, 2.3). Peat infilled the ditch of the Pict's Knowe, and upon excavation (see Chapter 4 below) a thin peat was found buried beneath the upcast of the earliest ditch. This last peat bed was formed directly on the well-drained sandy substrate, and this led to speculation during

excavation as to the extent of the former peat cover across the sandy knoll. Any such extensive peat cover has been destroyed by mineralisation on drainage and, possibly, ploughing in the last couple of centuries, but how close to the monument had peat extended in the later prehistoric period? Would this have formed a barrier to access, at least symbolic if not actual? Richards (1996) raised the question of water as boundary and bridge in more specific ways, arguing that ditches of henge monuments may have been designed to contain water which acted as a division between 'inside' and 'outside' and which served as a symbolic inclusion of the natural world, rivers, in archaeological space. An elegant idea though flawed in specifics (Waddington 1999), the thesis could be tested at the Pict's Knowe.

Plate 2.1 The valley floor context of the Pict's Knowe. Viewed from the northern valley side below Barbush Farm (Fig. 2.1) across the wood sheltering St. Queran's Well, the valley floor appears featureless. The fields in the foreground are on both till and sands of the Upper Terrace. The Crooks Pow is barely visible, flowing right to left under the line of bushes towards the centre, and immediately beyond is the rough grazing and marsh of the Floodplain Terrace. The henge of Pict's Knowe, under excavation here, is on the improved pasture of the Upper Terrace, slightly higher than the Floodplain Terrace. The camp site also lies on the Upper Terrace, and shows the large extent of this surface on the south side of the valley. Behind, the bedrock slopes support the woods of Mabie Forest that rise to the skyline.

Plate 2.2 The Pict's Knowe, looking north from the slopes of Bauldie's Brae. The till slope from which the photograph is taken passes under the lane to the sands of the Upper Terrace. The darker bulges of soil are the peats infilling the Bauldie's Brae gully in a broad gash across the Upper Terrace, isolating from the west the surface on which Pict's Knowe stands.

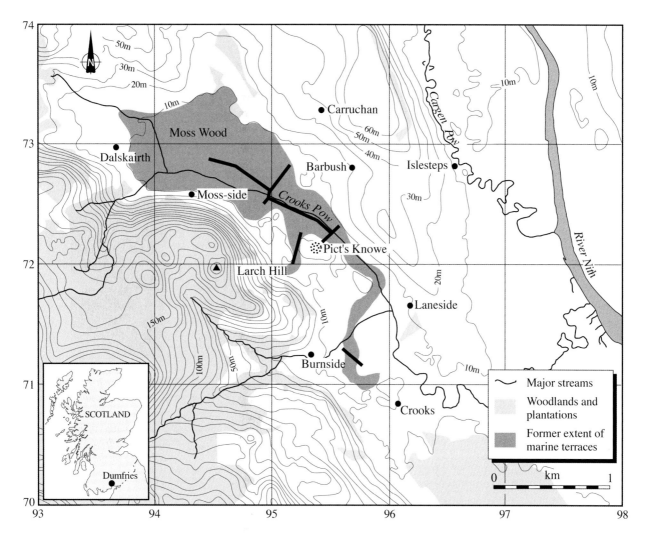

Fig. 2.2 The present distribution of landform units on the Crooks Pow valley floor between Moss Wood in the north-west to Crooks in the south-east, modified and extended from the mapping of Jardine (1975).

2.1d The familiarity of landscapes at the Pict's Knowe

Was the Pict's Knowe constructed in a new place, unfamiliar to human communities? Was the Pict's Knowe different from everywhere else or part of a landscape that was used? Did the day-to-day activities of a farming community go on around the site, integrating the monument with 'ordinary' life, or was the monument seen as outside the daily round? The technique used in this chapter to understand these questions is pollen analysis, which can very effectively identify natural plant communities and the disturbances that relate to a range of anthropogenic activities (e.g. Tipping 1994). The concern at the Pict's Knowe was to depict the development of plant communities on the valley floor, anticipated to be highly complex temporally through the changing effects of sea level, fluvial and groundwater hydrological change. To understand vegetation dynamics at this limited spatial

scale requires analysis of peat or lake sediments in basins of small diameter (Jacobson & Bradshaw 1981; Bradshaw 1991) because these can best exclude pollen from distant regions. In this we were fortunate to identify and sample deep peats from the Bauldie's Brae gully only 200m west of the Pict's Knowe, and to be able to analyse in detail the highly spatially precise depiction of short term changes within the early Bronze Age from the peat bed preserved beneath upcast at the Pict's Knowe itself, a pollen stratigraphy called the Pict's Knowe A (Fig. 2.3).

2.1e The data sets and the synthetic approach taken in environmental reconstruction

The research has generated large and diverse datasets on some of the major environmental changes influencing the small valley of the Crooks Pow. The basic findings of some of this work have been summarised in Haggart (1999) and Milburn and Tipping (1999a, b). The individual datasets collected include:

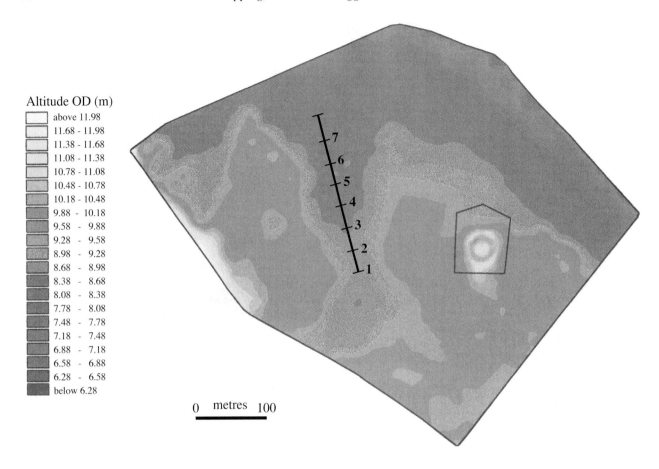

Fig. 2.3 *Detailed contour survey at 30.0cm intervals of the immediate surroundings of the Pict's Knowe, modified from Thomas (this volume). The south west edge of the map is close to the view depicted from the southerly hillslope in Plate 2.2. The surface of the Upper Terrace is red and orange, and the lower Floodplain Terrace is in greens and blues. The survey emphasises the position of the Bauldie's Brae gully in the centre. The line of the sediment stratigraphic transect along the Bauldie's Brae is shown, as is the borehole BB1 from which the record of sediment, vegetation and hydrological change was derived. Also depicted within the polygon defining the archaeological site in yellow is the location of the peat sealed by the bank of the henge, which yielded the pollen sequence called Pict's Knowe A.*

- the geomorphic mapping of valley floor landsurfaces around the Pict's Knowe
- sediment stratigraphic data from borehole logging along the axis of the Crooks Pow and at four cross-valley transects, instrumentally levelled to Ordnance Datum, to record the distribution and stratigraphies of the several metres of sediments infilling the valley to seaward, adjacent to and landward of the Pict's Knowe
- biostratigraphic analyses (diatoms, dinoflagellates, foraminifera, pollen) and geochemical analyses on key horizons from the valley to define depositional environments (marine to estuarine, fluvial, terrestrial) of sediment units
- pollen and microscopic charcoal analyses of a 480cm deep peat sequence infilling the narrow gully of Bauldie's Brae, 200m north west of the Pict's Knowe
- quantitative analyses of groundwater state and mire surface wetness in the Bauldie's Brae peat sequence

using colorimetry
- pollen and microscopic charcoal analyses of the thin (11cm) peat bed excavated from beneath the upcast in the West Cutting at the Pict's Knowe (Thomas: Chapter 4), the sequence here called the Pict's Knowe A.

All of these analyses were supported by a comprehensive ^{14}C dating programme:

- 14 radiometric assays (GU-4645 to -4658 inclusive) defined the chronology of Holocene sediment infilling across and along the valley floor
- 8 radiometric assays (GU-7655 to -7663 inclusive) defined the changes in vegetation, land uses and groundwater state (humification) within the Bauldie's Brae gully
- 2 AMS assays (AA-21249 and -21250) were analysed to define the ages of the lower and upper boundaries to the buried peat, the Pict's Knowe A.

Each of these datasets has been interpreted individually, using the independent ^{14}C chronologies (Haggart 1999; Milburn & Tipping 1999a, b), and each has formed the subject of forthcoming papers for specialist readerships (Smith *et al.* 2003; Tipping *et al.* 2004). However, the crucial element we wish to stress in this presentation is the synthetic, integrated nature of the data. All the analyses assembled focus on one element of this landscape, the valley floor. All are spatially constrained and depict changes through time in components of the landscape, initially treated discretely, that are in reality very closely interlinked. Section 2.2 will describe the individual techniques used in assembling the different datasets in sufficient detail to satisfy colleagues but also, hopefully, in non-technical form. The interpretative section of this chapter (Section 2.3) is chronological in structure, from the earliest established landscape change to the latest, exploring in Section 2.4 the themes outlined above.

Techniques, interpretative principles and presentation of data

2.2a Geomorphic mapping

Landforms on the Crooks Pow valley floor, below c. 15m OD and 1km up and downstream of the Pict's Knowe between Mossside and Laneside Farms, were mapped onto enlarged OS 1:10000 scale base maps. Four landform units are recognised above the river (Fig. 2.2). The modern Crooks Pow, in part at least straightened by ditching and modified by the construction of levees (e.g. Fig. 2.5), lies on the axis of the valley north west of Barbush, but then flows on the north side of the valley. It is a sluggish stream with a very low gradient in this reach, <10m wide and capable of transporting only sands and finer sediment. The stream is incised 2.5 to 3m below the Floodplain Terrace (e.g. Fig. 2.5), the lower of two extensive surfaces. The Floodplain Terrace has no observable gradient over the 2km reach mapped, lying at around 8m OD, and supports peaty soils beneath unimproved rough pasture (Plate 2.1). It occupies a large basin extending to the valley edges around Mossside Farm, but below Carruchan is increasingly and sharply constricted below the surfaces of the Upper Terrace (Fig. 2.2). At Barbush the Floodplain Terrace is around 200m wide and below the Pict's Knowe is very narrow at around 100m. The modern Crooks Pow stays on the north side of the valley but the palaeochannel containing the Floodplain Terrace swings to the south opposite Burnside (Fig. 2.2).

Higher and older than the Floodplain Terrace is the Upper Terrace, bordering the valley floor below the steep drift-covered siltstone bedrock slopes above 10m OD. The Pict's Knowe is on this surface (Plates 2.1, 2.2). Here the Upper Terrace lies at 9.5 to 10m OD (Fig. 2.3). There is no discernible gradient in the reach mapped (Fig. 2.2). This well drained terrace surface supports sandy soils

beneath improved pasture. It is not seen at Mossside, but it forms a laterally extensive series of flat surfaces on both sides of the valley below Carruchan, 250m wide and causing the marked constriction to the Floodplain Terrace width (Fig. 2.2). The terrace is nearly everywhere better developed on the south side of the valley. At the Pict's Knowe the terrace surface is 400m wide (Plates 2.1, 2.2; Fig. 2.3) but it widens still further south-east (Fig. 2.2).

Hillslope landforms were not mapped but one alluvial fan spreading across the valley floor is mapped from the Mabie Burn at Burnside (Fig. 2.2). Its stratigraphic relationship to the terrace surfaces is explored below (Section 2.2d). Shallow channels occur on the hillsides but only one, 200m west of the Pict's Knowe, has dissected the Upper Terrace to flow into the buried channel beneath the Floodplain Terrace (Plate 2.2; Fig. 2.3). It has no name but is called Bauldie's Brae after the hillslope source above it. The gully is younger than the Upper Terrace and older than the sediments underlying the Floodplain Terrace. It is defined best on the high resolution contour survey (Fig. 2.3) where the present peat surface is around 1.5 to 2m below the Upper Terrace, around 25 to 75m wide.

2.2b Sediment stratigraphic transects

The Floodplain Terrace is underlain by several metres of sediment that infill a generally narrow and meandering buried channel. Sediment description of these fills allows interpretation of depositional environment, supported by biostratigraphic and geochemical analyses (below). Blue-grey clays and silty clays, known in Scotland as carse deposits, characterise estuarine or fully marine environments. Peat beds often relate to terrestrial deposition. The stratigraphic relationships between these sediment types can demonstrate the number of incursions into the valley of marine conditions during sea level rise (transgression) and subsequent retreat (regression). Cross-valley transects allow the identification of the buried channel and so the earliest indication of sea level rise. Along-valley transects define the furthest penetration of tidally influenced water. Recording the altitude (OD) of these sediment types can help in approximating, together with biostratigraphic data, contemporaneous water depths.

Boreholes were positioned at varying intervals on transects depending on the complexity of the underlying sediment stratigraphy. The ground surface of each borehole was instrumentally levelled by Electronic Distance Measurer to a benchmark to establish altitude OD. Sediments were sampled in 1.0m sections using a 3.0cm diameter open sided gouge sampler. Stiff sediments were penetrated by using a Stitz power corer. Sediments were logged in the field and texture, sorting, organic content, colours and other features described.

Three cross-valley transects were linked by one along-valley transect (Fig. 2.1). A separate along-valley transect was laid out nearest the coast at Burnside where eight boreholes were cored on a 220m north west – south east

Burnside

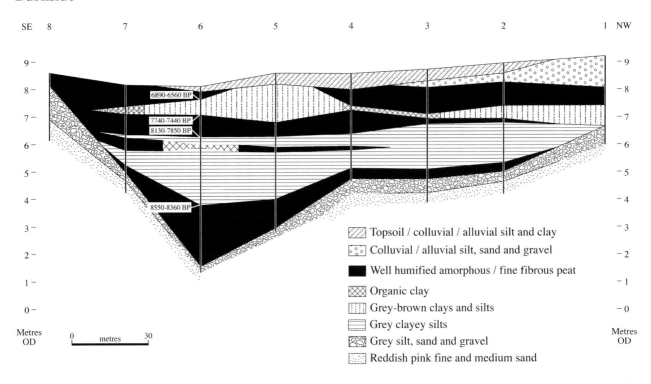

Fig. 2.4 Generalised sediment stratigraphy surveyed to OD for the transect along the valley at Burnside (see Fig. 2.1 for location). Also depicted are the positions of [14]*C assays obtained on sediments in borehole BU6: assays are calibrated in Table 2.3.*

The Pict's Knowe

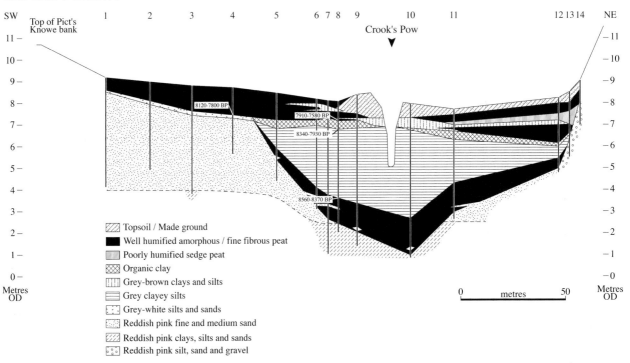

Fig. 2.5 Generalised sediment stratigraphy surveyed to OD for the transect across the valley adjacent to the Pict's Knowe (see Fig. 2.1 for location). Also depicted are the positions of calibrated [14]*C age ranges obtained on sediments in boreholes PK4 and 8: assays are calibrated in Table 2.3.*

Depth (cm)	Description
490.0–480.0	grey-white bedded silts and sands; abrupt to
480.0–376.0	dark brown to black well humified amorphous peat with common well preserved herbaceous plant fragments, with one layer of wood remains (unidentified) at 410.0–400.0cm; gradual to
376.0–270.0	dark brown poorly humified sedge peat; gradual to
270.0–245.0	abundant wood remains within a matrix of dark brown to black well humified amorphous peat; gradual to
245.0–0.0	dark brown well humified amorphous peat with occasional to common herbaceous plant fragments.

Table 2.1 Description of the sediment stratigraphy at Bauldie's Brae (borehole BB1).

Depth (cm)	Description	Interpretation
0.0–7.0	structureless humic fine-medium sand with common fine and medium fibrous roots; gradual boundary to	poorly developed soil
7.0–25.0	uniform structureless medium brown silty fine sand; gradual boundary to	probably bioturbated upcast
25.0–44.0	medium brown silty fine sand with dark brown diffuse organic staining, sharply defined lenses of organic-rich sediment and common open rabbit-holes; sharp irregular boundary to	bioturbated upcast
44.0–55.0	pale bleached sharp silty fine sand with common discrete sub-horizontal and sloping bands (c. 2mm) of amorphous organic matter and high disseminated amorphous organic matter, increasing down-unit; sharp conformable boundary to	non-bioturbated soil upcast with tip-lines preserved in organic matter
55.0–64.0	laminar and finely banded greasy dark brown-black amorphous peat, laminae on mm-scale, sub-horizontal and broadly parallel to upper boundary, comprising dark brown and possibly more minerogenic peat and black peat with no or minimal mineral content; sharp boundary to	*in situ* thin peat with periodic influx of mineral matter in ponds
64.0–68.0	white pale bleached silty fine sand (base not seen)	subsoil to peat

Table 2.2 Description of the sediment stratigraphy in the West Cutting at the point sampled for the Pict's Knowe A peat.

transect (Fig. 2.4: boreholes prefixed 'BU'). At the Pict's Knowe itself (boreholes prefixed 'PK') fourteen boreholes were sunk on a 230m transect across the full width of the valley from the monument to St. Queran's Well (Fig. 2.5). This was linked by boreholes along the valley 0.6km to a 370m cross-valley transect below Carruchan where eleven boreholes were obtained (Fig. 2.6: boreholes prefixed 'CA'). North west of Carruchan, the Moss Wood transect of seventeen boreholes (Fig. 2.1) was laid out along the main axis of the valley (Fig. 2.7: boreholes prefixed 'MW'). A single 220m long sediment stratigraphic transect was laid out with seven boreholes along the axis of the Bauldie's Brae gully (Fig. 2.3) using a hand operated 2.5cm diameter Eijelkamp gouge sampler (Fig. 2.8: boreholes prefixed 'BB'). Interpretation of these sediment sequences is combined in synthesis with other data in Section 2.3.

The peat at the Pict's Knowe A was seen in excavation of the West Cutting (Fig. 4.6: Context 0063). The detailed sediment stratigraphy recorded at the point sampled is given in Table 2.2. This and micromorphological analyses (Crowther: Chapter 10 below) show this peat to have formed *in situ* on the well drained sand of the Upper Terrace, indicated by the delicate laminated structure of the peat, representing rapid alternations of ponds and peats and intermittent deposition of mineral matter.

2.2c Sediment sampling

Sediment samples from the buried channel beneath the Floodplain Terrace and from Bauldie's Brae were sampled for a range of physical and biological analyses and for ^{14}C dating because of their potential resolution in defining environmental conditions and change. Samples were obtained from boreholes in the clay rich sediments of the buried channel with an Atlas Copco percussion corer driving in a 1.0m long, 5.0cm internal diameter Stitz closed chambered piston sampler. At Bauldie's Brae the peat sequence at BB1 was sampled with a hand operated 0.5m long, 12.0cm internal diameter closed chambered Russian sampler. All analyses were derived from the same very large diameter cores. All cores were placed in labelled plastic guttering, sealed with plastic film and stored in the laboratory in cold stores at 3° to 4°C to retard drying and reduce microbial activity. The thin peat bed at the Pict's Knowe A preserved beneath upcast in the West Cutting (Thomas: Chapter 4 below) was subsampled from a cleaned open section by inserting three sets of metal Kubiena tins (10.5 × 5.0 × 4.0cm), which were also sealed and stored as for other samples.

Continuous sediment sequences from cores were obtained from the following sites and boreholes: Burnside B6 (Fig. 2.4), the Pict's Knowe PK4 and 8 (Fig. 2.5), Carruchan CA1 (Fig. 2.6), Moss Wood MW 7 and 10

Carruchan

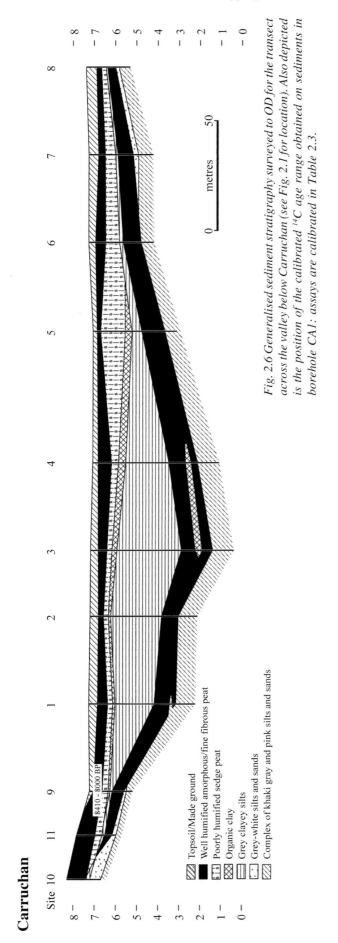

Fig. 2.6 Generalised sediment stratigraphy surveyed to OD for the transect across the valley below Carruchan (see Fig. 2.1 for location). Also depicted is the position of the calibrated ¹⁴C age range obtained on sediments in borehole CA1: assays are calibrated in Table 2.3.

Moss Wood

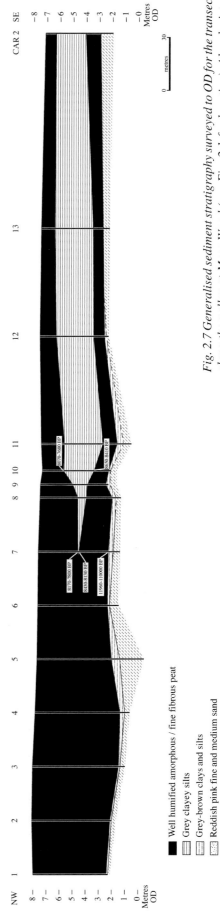

Fig. 2.7 Generalised sediment stratigraphy surveyed to OD for the transect along the valley at Moss Wood (see Fig. 2.1 for location). Also depicted are the positions of calibrated ¹⁴C age ranges obtained on sediments in boreholes MW7 and 10: assays are calibrated in Table 2.3.

Bauldie's Brae

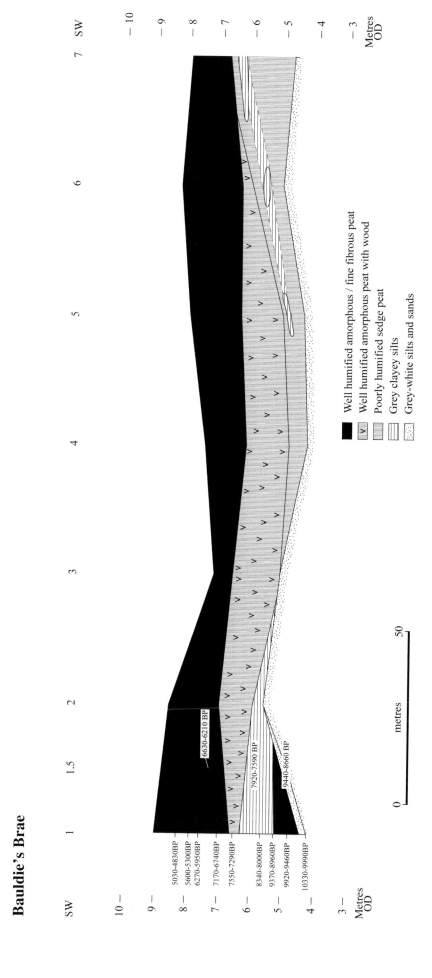

Well humified amorphous / fine fibrous peat

Well humified amorphous peat with wood

Poorly humified sedge peat

Grey clayey silts

Grey-white silts and sands

Fig. 2.8 Generalised sediment stratigraphy surveyed to OD for the transect along the gully at Bauldie's Brae (see Fig. 2.2 and 2.3 for location). Also depicted are the positions of calibrated ^{14}C age ranges obtained on sediments in boreholes BB1 and BB1.5: assays are calibrated in Table 2.4.

(Fig. 2.7) and Bauldie's Brae BB1 (Fig. 2.8). Laboratory analyses on these samples are outlined below and the data are integrated into the discussion in Section 2.3.

2.2d Radiocarbon dating

[14]C dating is used to correlate the stratigraphies. From Burnside, the Pict's Knowe, Carruchan and Moss Wood, sediment slices of, generally, 5.0cm thickness were taken from sediment stratigraphic boundaries and dated by radiometric ^{14}C techniques at the Scottish Universities Research and Reactor Centre (SURRC) of Glasgow University (GU-). The assays in Table 2.3 correct errors in table 1 of Haggart (1999).

At Bauldie's Brae, three 'rangefinder' assays were subsampled for ^{14}C dating (GU-4552 to -4554 inclusive; Table 2.4) using a hand operated 50cm long, 12.0cm diameter Russian corer from a point halfway between boreholes BB1 and BB2, to assess the timespan of sediments prior to sampling for pollen analysis. On confirmation of an early to mid Holocene stratigraphy the gully was revisited and a slightly deeper sequence (borehole BB1) located and sampled. [14]C samples were 1.0cm thick slices removed from the same large diameter cores used for other analyses (Section 2.2e) and dated by radiometric ^{14}C methods at SURRC (Table 2.4).

At the Pict's Knowe A the need to define the ages of lower and upper boundaries to a peat no thicker than 9cm meant that AMS ^{14}C techniques were used. Using a scalpel to shave slices of sediment from frozen sediment blocks (Tipping *et al.* 1994), tightly constrained slices of 0.3 cm and 0.4 cm were submitted for dating at the University of Arizona at Tucson after pretreatment at SURRC (Table 2.4).

All assays reported in Table 2.3, and assays AA-21249 and -21250 in Table 2.4 are on acid washed organic matter. The remaining assays in Table 2.4 were acid washed and the humic acid fraction isolated and analysed: the two fractions should be closely comparable (G. Cook pers. comm.). [14]C assays are calibrated using the program CALIB 3.0.3A (Stuiver & Reimer 1993): calibrated age ranges at 2σ BP in Tables 2.3 and 2.4 are rounded up to the nearest decade.

There are no *a priori* grounds for questioning the validity of the assays since the bedrock and 'drift' do not contain carbonates. The depositional context of all samples is secure with peats being laterally extensive and demonstrably *in situ*. Within the Burnside, the Pict's Knowe, Carruchan and Moss Wood stratigraphies, sediment boundaries where peats underlie carse clays are frequently described (Section 2.2d) as erosional: rip-up clasts of peat reworked by wave action are recorded but these occur within the clays and all assays on these contacts (GU-4658, -4656; -4647; -4653) are from stratified peat. Nevertheless, erosion may imply that these assays are maximal for the age of carse deposition (discussed further in Section 2.3). Transitional boundaries where peat replaces carse sediments are more secure. Reworking of organic matter by wave action in carse sediments and in tidal mudflats at these sites is possible but is not demonstrated. There is little evidence for stratigraphic disturbance or sediment reworking at Bauldie's Brae (Section 2.2j; below) and the sequences here from boreholes BB1 and BB1.5 have strong coherence.

The comprehensive internal consistency of the dated stratigraphies suggests no errors in the assays. In Table 2.3 the assays are arranged by site in ascending altitude OD. Higher samples should be younger and in all but one case they are: at the Pict's Knowe assays GU-4645 and -4648 appear 'reversed' but these are from different boreholes, date the same 'event' and are statistically inseparable at 2σ. There is no internal evidence for error at Bauldie's Brae (Table 2.4). However, the ^{14}C assays strongly suggest that the peat has been truncated: extrapolation of the peat accumulation rate using the mean trend of assays GU-7761 to -7663 inclusive indicates that the peat at the present ground surface has an age of around 4000 cal. BP. At the Pict's Knowe A the dates are also inseparable but this is thought to reflect the rapid rate of sediment accumulation there. Further testing of the veracity of these assays comes from biostratigraphic correlation through pollen analyses with other dated sequences in the region (Section 2.3).

2.2e Sedimentological analyses

Contiguous 4.0cm sediment slices from the sediments at borehole BB1 (Bauldie's Brae) were analysed for their organic content by loss on ignition, measuring weight loss in samples after burning off organic matter in dried subsamples at 550°C for 4hrs. This technique readily identifies increases in mineral content through, for instance, soil inwashing from surrounding slopes. All values were greater than 60% (Fig. 2.9a).

Contiguous 4.0cm sediment slices from BB1 were also analysed by colorimetric techniques for peat humification. Peat is subject to decay by microbial action in arerobic environments, most effectively at and close to the peat surface soon after deposition. Decay leads to humification of the peat, which can be described qualitatively (Section 2.2e: Table 2.1) and can be quantified by determining proportions of humic acid (Aaby & Tauber 1975; Rowell & Turner 1979; Blackford & Chambers 1991). Rates of humification are not constant. They are determined by the effectiveness of bacterial activity. A major control on this is the waterlogging of peat at or close to the ground surface. In this way, the degree of humification becomes a proxy measure of how wet or dry the mire surface was through time: well humified peat typifies a dry peat surface and *vice versa*. Colorimetry measures the proportion of humic acids in a prepared sample by measuring the ability of that sample to transmit light; the lower the % light transmission, the more humified is the peat. Colorimetry was determined on samples prepared by the methods of Blackford (1990; Blackford & Chambers 1993) using a Jenway Colorimeter.

Lab. Code	Site	Borehole	Depth (cm)	Altitude (m OD)	Sediment	^{14}C Age	$\delta^{13}C$	Age Range Probability (±1σ)	Cal. BP (±2σ) (>95%)
GU-4658	Burnside	BU6	478–783	3.31–3.26	well humified amorphous peat	7680 ± 50	-28.5	8550–8360	8520–8360 (0.96)
GU-4657	Burnside	BU6	185–190	6.24–6.19	well humified amorphous peat	7220 ± 70	-28.5	8130–7850	8130–7900 (0.99)
GU-4656	Burnside	BU6	119–124	6.90–6.85	well humified fine fibrous peat	6790 ± 90	-27.7	7740–7440	7770–7430 (1.0)
GU-4655	Burnside	BU6	66–71	7.43–7.38	well humified amorphous peat	5910 ± 70	-27.9	6890–6560	6890–6550 (1.0)
GU-4647	Pict's Knowe	PK8	428–435	3.78–3.71	black amphorous peat with rotted wood fragments	7710 ± 50	-28.7	8560–8370	8550–8380 (1.0)
GU-4646	Pict's Knowe	PK8	124–129	6.82–6.77	grey-brown organic clay with peat	7360 ± 100	-29.1	8340–7930	8340–7950 (1.0)
GU-4645	Pict's Knowe	PK8	104–109	7.02–6.97	grey-brown organic clay with peat	6950 ± 80	-28.4	7910–7580	<95%: not defined
GU-4648	Pict's Knowe	PK8	149–159	7.27–7.17	dark brown amorphous peat	7170 ± 80	-28.5	8120–7800	8120–7800 (1.0)
GU-4654	Carruchan	CA1	115–120	6.05–6.10	poorly humified sedge peat	7460 ± 100	-28.9	8410–8000	8410–8070 (0.95)
GU-4651	Moss Wood	MW7	524–530	2.38–2.32	black amorphous peat	10,010 ± 70	-29.0	11,960–11,000	11,860–11,010 (1.0)
GU-4653	Moss Wood	MW10	393–398	3.38–3.33	black amorphous peat	7770 ± 60	-28.1	8650–8410	8660–8410 (0.99)
GU-4650	Moss Wood	MW7	303–308	4.59–4.54	black amorphous peat	7540 ± 90	-27.4	8430–8130	8440–8130 (0.99)
GU-4649	Moss Wood	MW7	294–299	4.68–4.63	black amorphous peat	7210 ± 100	-27.6	8170–7800	8170–7770 (1.0)
GU-4652	Moss Wood	MW10	149–154	5.82–5.77	black amorphous peat	7090 ± 90	-27.6	8070–7680	8010–7680 (0.98)

Table 2.3 Details of ^{14}C assays and calibrations at Burnside, the Pict's Knowe, Carruchan and Moss Wood.

Series	Lab. Code	Borehole	Depth (cm)	Altitude (m OD)	Sediment	^{14}C Age	$\delta^{13}C$	Age Range Probability ($\pm 1\sigma$)	Cal. BP ($\pm 2\sigma$) (>95%)
Rangefinder	GU-4554	BB1.5	400–405	4.80–4.75	amorphous peat	8160 ± 120	-29.5	9440–8660	9390–8710 (0.98)
	GU-4553	BB1.5	300–305	5.80–5.75	Wood-rich peat	6970 ± 80	-29.6	7920–7590	7920–7620 (1.0)
	GU-4552	BB1.5	150–155	7.30–7.25	brown amorphous peat	5590 ± 90	-28.6	6630–6210	7770–7430 (1.0)
	GU-4655	BU6	66–71	7.43–7.38	well humified amorphous peat	5910 ± 70	-27.9	6890–6560	6570–6230 (0.92)
Palynological	GU-7755	BB1	479–478	4.21–4.22	amphorous peat	9170 ± 70	-29.7	10,330–9990	<95%: not defined
	GU-7756	BB1	422–421	4.78–4.79	amphorous peat	8700 ± 100	-29.4	9920–9460	9900–9490 (1.0)
	GU-7757	BB1	374–373	5.26–5.27	poorly humified peat	8180 ± 60	-28.6	9370–8960	9270–8980 (0.95)
	GU-7758	BB1	333–332	5.67–5.68	poorly humified peat	7420 ± 70	-28.6	8340–8000	8340–8070 (0.94)
	GU-7759	BB1	248–247	6.52–6.53	wood rich amorphous peat	6590 ± 80	-30.3	7550–7290	7550–7330 (0.96)
	GU-7760	BB1	201–200	6.99–7.00	amorphous peat	6080 ± 80	-29.7	7170–6740	<95%: not defined
	GU-7761	BB1	140–139	7.60–7.61	amorphous peat	5320 ± 50	-28.0	6270–5950	<95%: not defined
	GU-7762	BB1	108–107	7.92–7.93	amorphous peat	4710 ± 70	-29.6	5600–5300	5590–5310 (1.0)
	GU-7763	BB1	69–68	8.31–8.32	amorphous peat	4330 ± 50	-28.5	5030–4830	5000–4830 (0.95)

Series	Lab. Code	Location	Depth (cm)	Position	Sediment	^{14}C Age	^{13}C	Age Range Probability (1)	Cal. BP (2) (>95%)
Pict's Knowe A	AA-21249	Trench 2	61.2–61.5	base of peat	finely laminated amorphous peat with sand	3715 ± 80	-29.7	4340–3840	4300–3840 (1.0)
	AA-21250	Trench 2	55.05–55.09	top of peat	finely laminated amorphous peat with sand	3760 ± 60	-30.0	4350–3930	4300–3930 (0.99)

Table 2.4 Details of ^{14}C assays and calibrations at Bauldie's Brae and the Pict's Knowe A.

Humification analysis is most often used to describe changes in mire surface wetness assumed to be driven by climate change, and has been used for this extensively at sites around the Solway Firth (Barber *et al.* 1994a, b; Tipping 1995a; Chambers *et al.* 1997; Mauquoy & Barber 1999; Charman *et al.* 1999; Tipping 1999b: see Tipping 1999a). At Bauldie's Brae the record of mire surface wetness cannot be interpreted as a proxy climate record. Firstly, because the gully is connected to the Crooks Pow valley, sea level change is a major determinant of groundwater hydrology. Secondly, because the gully receives water from surrounding slopes its hydrology can be modified by anthropogenic processes, principally deforestation which generates increased runoff (Bormann & Likens 1979). Accordingly caution is exercised in interpretation as to the causes of mire surface wetness change, but nevertheless this measure is a sensitive way of determining groundwater hydrological change, which is a key determinant of valley floor environmental change (Section 2.1).

Fig. 2.9 presents the data for organic content and humification (% transmission) at Bauldie's Brae (BB1) plotted by depth. The peat is highly organic and has almost no evidence for sediment inwashing. The humification data are more variable, and single sample excursions, preserved in Figure 2.9b, have also been smoothed by a curve derived from the application of 3 point running means through the data. These data are integrated into the synthetic interpretation in Section 2.3.

2.2f Pollen analyses: interpretative principles

Pollen analyses discussed in this chapter were undertaken on sediments from three localities: borehole BU6 at Burnside, borehole BB1 at Bauldie's Brae and from the Pict's Knowe A at the archaeological site. The purpose at each site is to define plant communities and changes in these through time, and from these to interpret the range of depositional environments, soil type and quality, the natural vegetation and disturbances to it including, most importantly, anthropogenic interference and land uses.

The sediments sampled probably reflect different pollen source areas, or rather, there are different degrees of confidence in defining where the majority of the pollen originates. The sediments analysed at all sites are peats (Section 2.2d) which are autochthonous (e.g. formed *in situ*) but they differ in the extent of allochthonous (transported) sediment and pollen. The tidal influences at Burnside introduce sediment from both marine and fluvial sources, and this makes the pollen data least reliable for detailed reconstruction. Wave induced turbulence affects the pollen dispersal of some taxa, and buoyant pollen grains like *Pinus* can easily be overrepresented. This has proved an interpretative problem at similar sites on the Solway Firth (Walker 1966; Nichols 1967: Section 2.1) and at Burnside the pollen analyses are designed only to define specific depositional environment at sediment boundaries.

Peats at Bauldie's Brae and the Pict's Knowe are much more reliable sources of pollen data. They represent continuous vegetation patterns for the time periods represented (Section 2.2h). Here, major controls on pollen source are the effects of different peat forming plant communities. Wooded landscapes around small sites like Bauldie's Brae and the Pict's Knowe restrict the pollen source areas to moderately well defined regions within a few hundred metres of the pollen site because of the abundance of tree (arboreal) pollen and the effects of canopy cover on factors like wind strength. As landscapes become more open the pollen source area increases (Sugita *et al.* 1999). It is assumed that the site characteristics and probable vegetation covers at both Bauldie's Brae and the Pict's Knowe mean that what is being depicted are valley floor plant communities growing on the sandy soils of the Upper Terrace and the accreting, changing surface of the Floodplain Terrace. Plant communities from the hill-slopes above will also be depicted, particularly at Bauldie's Brae, but this source will not be dominant.

2.2g Pollen analyses: techniques and presentation of data

Sediment subsamples of 0.5cm thickness were removed by scalpel from cleaned cores of BU6 at four sediment stratigraphic boundaries at 1.0 or 2.0cm intervals: the probably high variability of sediment accumulation rates at these boundaries means that the temporal resolution of analyses, the time interval between analyses, cannot be calculated.

At BB1 similar thickness subsamples are spaced at 16.0cm intervals below 200.0cm, in sediments known from 'rangefinder' ^{14}C dating (Section 2.2h) to be least relevant to the archaeological record, and at 8.0cm intervals above this. Sediments above 50.0cm were not subsampled because cattle trampling was thought to have disturbed the stratigraphy. The ^{14}C chronology is used to define the temporal resolution of the analyses (Table 2.5): below 200.0cm the 280.0cm of sediment (c. 3200 cal. years) is analysed on average every 180 to 200 years; above 200.0cm the sequence is analysed on average every 125 years.

The Kubiena tins from the Pict's Knowe A were prepared by the fine slicing method of Tipping *et al.* (1994) from frozen blocks, and sixteen slices of an average 0.3 to 0.4cm thickness were then processed (below). The lower and upper boundaries of this peat are indistinguishable in age (Section 2.2h) and so the temporal resolution of pollen analyses cannot be defined: the sequence took between a few years and more than 300 years to accumulate.

Subsamples were processed by standard physical separation and chemical treatments (Moore *et al.* 1991) to remove mineral and extraneous organic matter. Residues were treated with safranin stain to highlight organic matter, including pollen grains, placed in silicon oil, and microscope slides made. Counting was undertaken on Olymus BX40 microscopes.

Slides were traversed at regular intervals to avoid errors induced by counting too close to the edge of the coverslip, normally at magnification ×400 but under oil immersion at magnification ×1000 for problematic grains and all size measurements. Pollen taxonomy (pollen types or taxa) accords with Moore *et al.* (1991) modified to accord with recommendations of Birks (1973): nomenclature follows Bennett (1994) after Stace (1991). Cereal type pollen grains are defined from Andersen (1979). Slides at Burnside and Bauldie's Brae were counted until 300 pollen grains thought to be derived from terrestrial soils were recorded: at the Pict's Knowe A this total was increased to 500 such grains. This total is called a total land pollen (tlp) sum and is designed to emphasise plant communities occupying 'dryland' soils. Percentages of pollen types within this sum are proportions of this total.

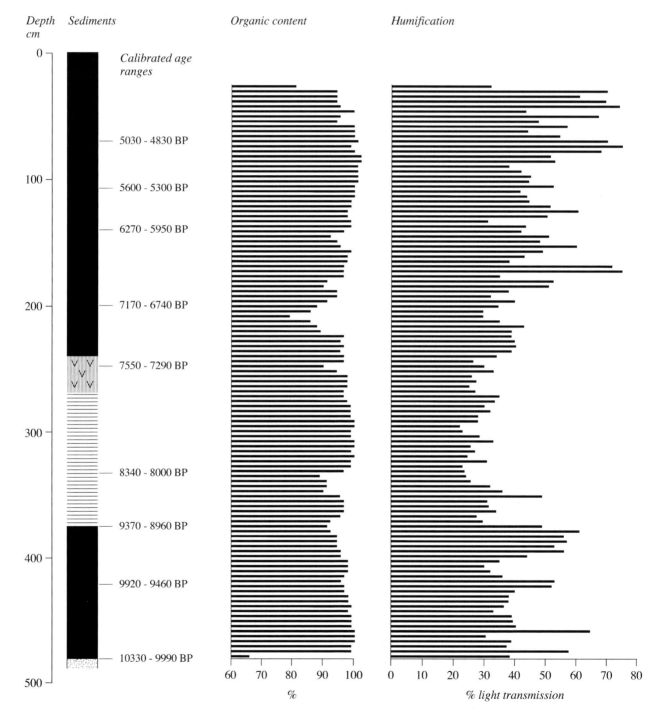

Fig. 2.9 (a) % organic contents and (b) humification (% transmission) values plotted against depth for the sediment stratigraphy at borehole BB1 at Bauldie's Brae. Also depicted are the positions of calibrated ^{14}C age ranges obtained on the sediments: assays are calibrated in Table 2.4.

Depths (cm)	Depth Interval[1] (cm)	Cal. Ages	Age Interval[2]	Mean peat accum. rate[3]	Temporal resolution
69.0–108.0	39.0	4890–5450	560	14.3	115
108.0–140.0	32.0	5450–6120	670	21.0	170
140.0–201.0	61.0	6120–6960	840	13.7	110
201.0–248.0	47.0	6960–7440	480	10.2	165
248.0–333.0	85.0	7440–8215	775	9.11	145
333.0–374.0	41.0	8215–9160	945	23.1	370
374.0–422.0	48.0	9160–9690	530	11.0	180
422.0–479.0	57.0	9690–10160	470	8.2	50

[1] depth interval between ^{14}C assays; [2] mean cal. ages of depth-interval; [3] mean accumulation rate: cal. yrs/cm.

Table 2.5 Temporal resolution of pollen analyses at Bauldie's Brae.

Percentages of pollen types that are thought not to be derived from terrestrial soils (e.g. obligate aquatic or bog plants; algal remains) are calculated as percentages of tlp + other grains. This reduces the percentage proportions of these types.

Fragments of microscopic charcoal were counted at Bauldie's Brae and the Pict's Knowe A (Figs. 2.11, 2.13). These provide a measure of the significance of fire around a pollen site, although it is not possible to define with any clarity differences in magnitude, location or frequency of fires (Tipping & Milburn 2000). Charcoal fragments are black, opaque and usually sharp edged (Patterson *et al.* 1987) and here only those >10mm were counted; partially carbonised brown or incompletely opaque particles were not included.

All pollen data are calculated and depicted using TILIA2 and TILIAGRAPH software (Grimm 1991) (Figs. 2.10 to 2.13). The pollen analyses at Burnside are not zoned (Fig. 2.10). At Bauldie's Brae the percentage (%) based pollen stratigraphy is divided on visual inspection into four zones, local to the site and prefixed BB (referred to as 'local pollen assemblage zones': lpaz) (Fig. 2.11): lpaz Bbd is subdivided further. Similarly, the diagrams from the Pict's Knowe A are zoned into three assemblages (lpaz PKAa to PKAc) which are specific to that sequence (Fig. 2.12).

2.2h Diatom analyses

Diatoms are multicellular subaqueous algae that are sensitive to water conditions. In this study the known relation to salinity gradients of diatom species and assemblages within the marine and freshwater system (Hustedt 1957) is used to interpret the contemporaneous environments of the earliest carse sediments formed at Moss Wood (Fig. 2.13: MW10 392 to 386cm) and within

the two beds of carse clay at Burnside (Fig. 2.14: BU6 250 to 192cm; 120 to 70cm). Subsamples of 0.5cm thickness removed by scalpel at varying depth intervals were treated by standard physical and chemical techniques (Battarbee 1986). Residues were placed on microscope slides and analysed under an Olympus BX40 microscope. During scanning of slides, qualitative observations were made on rarely preserved sponge spicules and foraminifera.

A synthetic interpretation of environmental change in the Crooks Pow Valley

This section will use the independent ^{14}C chronologies from the several sites analysed (Section 2.2h) to link the diverse evidence for environmental change on the Crooks Pow valley floor. It will take a chronological approach which defines time in calibrated or calendrical (cal.) years BP (Before Present). The timing of events is necessarily approximate given that ^{14}C chronologies have age ranges (Tables 2.3 and 2.4). For fluency in discussion, dates are referred to loosely (e.g. *circa* (c.), around or approximately) but we do not seek to disguise the uncertainties in chronology construction or the difficulties in such a temporal framework of defining cause and effect (Section 2.1). The discussion stretches back to the end of the last glaciation in the area and this section will end within the early Bronze Age with the construction and use of the first monument at the Pict's Knowe. This long timescale is necessary to explain the origin, original extent and age of the landsurfaces that prehistoric communities grew familiar with, and because the complexity of lowland valley floor processes necessitates the distinction of natural as well as anthropogenic disturbances. We subdivide the period between around 15000 cal. BP and 4000

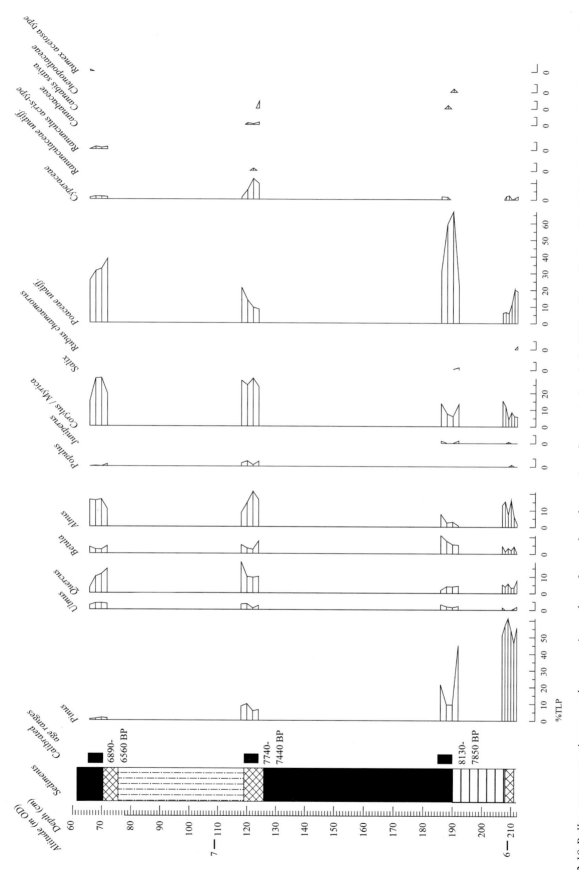

Fig. 2.10 Pollen taxa occurring more than once in analyses from selected organic sediments in borehole BU6 at Burnside (see Fig. 2.1 for location) plotted against depth and showing the positions of calibrated ^{14}C age ranges. Only horizons at the transition from organic to mineral sediment were analysed to define the terrestrial or coastal character of local plant communities. Proportions are calculated as percentages (see figure).

Burnside 6

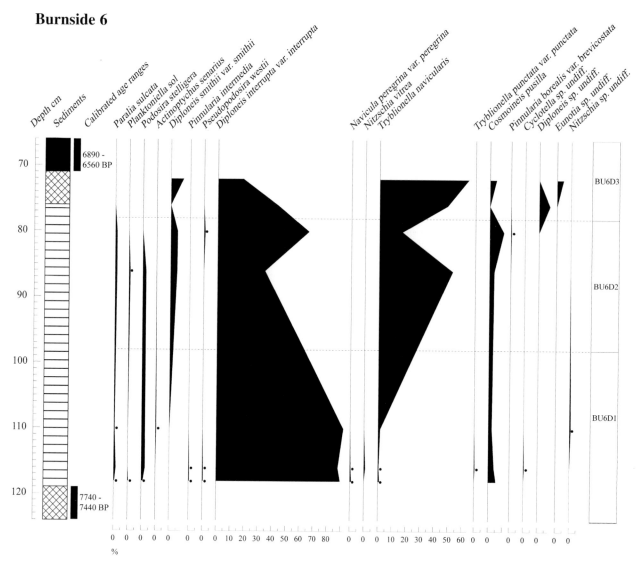

Fig. 2.14 Selected diatom taxa in the carse sediments between 120 and 70cm in borehole BU6 at Burnside (see Fig. 2.1 for location) plotted against depth, showing calibrated ^{14}C *age ranges and the local diatom assemblage zonation (ldaz BU6D1 to 3). Proportions are calculated as percentages of all diatoms. The key to sediment type is in Fig. 2.4.*

cal. BP into different events or processes, and these form the subheadings in this discussion.

2.3a The effects of deglaciation

Till covers as a thin veneer the bedrock slopes but large morainic deposits are absent. There is almost no evidence for gravel deposits from fluvioglacial sources that elsewhere in the region form prominent terrace surfaces above valley floors (May 1981; Gordon & Sutherland 1993). Only at the edge of the valley floor at the Pict's Knowe (PK13 and 14) are gravels probably formed by fluvioglacial rivers found, but at depth, and their stratigraphic relations are unclear. These sediments were either removed in the valley by erosion soon after deposition (Section 2.3b) or were not deposited through, perhaps, glacier ice calving into tidal waters.

2.3b Late Devensian valley floor aggradation and formation of the Upper Terrace

Replacing fluvioglacial sands and gravels across the entire floor, either successively or instead of, were finer grained red to pink clays, silts and sands and overlying very well sorted fine and medium grey to white sands. They are probably Late Devensian in age but how old is not known directly. They predate peat deposited on them at Moss Wood (borehole MW7; Fig. 2.7 and Table 2.3; GU-4651) at c. 11500 cal. BP and were formed prior to gully incision and initial peat accumulation at Bauldie's Brae at 10100 cal. BP (borehole BB1; Fig. 2.8 and Table 2.4; GU-7755), but may be much older.

At the Pict's Knowe (Fig. 2.5) the deepest and oldest sediments, below 2m OD, are homogeneous, structureless pink inorganic clays with rare silt bands. The colour

derives from local Permian rocks. The silt bands imply they are waterlain and the clay dominance suggests quiescent conditions. Their total thickness is unknown and contemporaneous valley floor width and morphology cannot be reconstructed on present data. No biostratigraphic data were obtained. They may represent subaqueous sediments deposited beneath glaciers floating in deep water in the valley at a time of relatively high sea level, perhaps near the glacial maximum of c. 21500 cal. BP, or be later Devensian, cold water estuarine or marine sediments (Errol or Clyde Beds equivalents: Wells 1997).

Above these clays in borehole PK3 are pink well sorted fine to medium grained sands. These underlie all sediment stratigraphic transects (Section 2.2d), but only at the Pict's Knowe are the morphology and full thickness of sediments understood. Here the sands aggrade in a seemingly continuous sequence to c. 10m OD, where they outcrop as the consistently flat surface of the Upper Terrace (Sections 2.2b, d). These terrace fragments were originally deposited across the entire width of the valley floor to this altitude. This surface has no discernible gradient within the valley, and this is likely to reflect deposition in marine or estuarine water. The sands were either deposited in a higher energy environment or clays were winnowed out by flowing or wave agitated water.

The data cannot define the direction of sea level change during deposition of this thick but uniform sediment accumulation: no sedimentological trends are discernible and biostratigraphic data were not obtained. Although clearly aggradational, the sediments need not have accumulated as relative sea level rose to around 10m OD. Relative sea level may instead have initially been much higher than 10m OD. Sands may have been deposited to higher altitudes than they are found now, and during relative sea level fall, the surface at 10m OD would have been truncated by wave erosion during a brief pause. Models developed for other localities in Scotland would suggest a declining relative sea level throughout the Late Devensian (Sutherland 1984): data from the Solway Firth have been absent until now (Jardine 1975; Wells 1999a).

2.3c Incision and buried channel formation

Following formation of the Upper Terrace surface at c. 10m OD, the sands were incised in a major erosional event. This also occurred prior to peat inception at Moss Wood at c. 11500 cal. BP. At Moss Wood this event appears to have excavated the entirety of the Upper Terrace fill in a large basin, to a bevelled surface of around 2m OD. This became a channel, much narrower and flowing between fragments of the Upper Terrace to the south east (Sections 2.2b, d; Fig. 2.2), descending to around 1m OD between the Pict's Knowe (Fig. 2.5) and Burnside (Fig. 2.4). The meandering form of the channel suggests this was a fluvial feature, not marine. Energies were focused on vertical incision in the lower reaches of the valley and not to valley widening, and so extensive surfaces of the Upper Terrace survived.

At Bauldie's Brae several shallow hillslope streams combined to incise a narrow gully through this terrace fill, the only interruption to the Upper Terrace surface on the south side of the valley below Carruchan (Section 2.2b). The gully floor is around 6m below the Upper Terrace surface (Fig. 2.8), deepening as it enters the main buried channel east of Carruchan (Fig. 2.6). No sediments associated with this activity are found in the buried channel or gully: erosion was apparently thorough and sediment transported downstream.

The deepest part of the identified channel, at around 1m OD at both Burnside and the Pict's Knowe, is some 10m below the Upper Terrace surface. The buried channel may continue to deepen east of Laneside (Fig. 2.2). Incision probably occurred through relative sea level fall to below 1m OD at some time in the Late Devensian, in support of most other data in the inner Solway Firth (Bishop & Coope 1977; Wells 1997, 1999a; Wells & Smith 1999: but see Lloyd 1999).

2.3d Early Holocene (11500 to 8000 cal. BP) environments

Peats then infilled the buried channel. At Moss Wood (Fig. 2.7) these are laterally extensive and probably blanket the basin floor. They formed at the beginning of the Holocene Interglacial, at c. 11500 cal. BP (borehole MW7; Fig. 2.7 and Table 2.3; GU-4651), immediately after the abrupt climatic amelioration at the end of the Loch Lomond Stadial. Fluvial activity presumably continued but was much less significant.

The Moss Wood transect is the only point in the buried channel where valley floor peat inception has been directly dated. Within the Bauldie's Brae gully, peat began to form at BB1 (4.2m OD) at c. 10100 cal. BP (GU-7755; Table 2.4), but a few metres away and 1m higher in altitude at BB1.5 (Section 2.2h), peat inception is c. 900 cal. years later (GU-4554; Table 2.4). Peat inception appears to have been site specific. At Bauldie's Brae the basal peat was unsurprisingly probably wet, moderately poorly humified and with % light transmission values around 40% (Section 2.2j; Fig. 2.9b).

Pollen data from Bauldie's Brae are limited before c. 8000 cal. BP because of low sampling resolutions (Section 2.2m; Table 2.5), but when peat began to form at BB1 at around 10100 cal. BP the surrounding soils were already colonised by *Betula* (birch) and *Salix* (willow) (lpaz BBa; Fig. 2.11). The low percentages do not, however, suggest a closed woodland. No other tree had colonised the catchment by this time, and Poaceae (grass) communities were seemingly abundant. The *Betula* woodland was colonised by *Corylus* (*Corylus/Myrica* pollen but here assumed to represent hazel) after 9600 cal. BP (Fig. 2.11; dated by GU-7756: Table 2.4) but soils still appear to have remained open, with tree and tall shrub pollen totalling <60% tlp. These plant communities were subject to burning but little can be said from these data concerning magnitude, frequency or origin of fires in this period.

One reason for the maintenance of open ground plant communities is episodic soil instability. This is not seen at Bauldie's Brae where organic content of the peats remains >95% (Fig. 2.9b). However, at Carruchan (boreholes Ca3 to 4; Fig. 2.6) a more minerogenic clay within the basal peats may represent the river transporting mineral grains, while at the Pict's Knowe at least two bands of well sorted sands, derived from the easily eroded, still high (8m) and steep slopes leading to the Upper Terrace (Section 2.2d; Fig. 2.5) probably represent soil erosion across valley floor peats prior to c. 8400 cal. BP (GU-4646; Table 2.3).

2.3e Pinus *in the Early Holocene*

At Bauldie's Brae at around 9300 cal. BP, at the start of lpaz Bbb (Fig. 2.11), *Pinus* (Scot's pine) pollen is represented at values that almost certainly indicate local growth (cf. Bennett 1984). This is the first ¹⁴C dated sequence in the eastern Solway Firth where this is attested (Tipping 1997, 1999). The sands of the Upper Terrace probably provided base poor, acid but dry soils on which pine competed successfully with birch and hazel, although not displacing them (cf. Bennett 1984). Colonisation by pine may have begun under comparatively wet ground conditions, but at c. 9200 cal. BP an abrupt shift to markedly lower water tables seen in increasingly humified peat (declining % transmission values; Fig. 2.9b) may have given a competitive advantage to pine. Scot's pine seedlings may have spread eastward from the Galloway Hills (Birks 1972; Jones & Stevenson 1993) but local growth at coastal localities here at Crooks Pow and at Brighouse Bay to the west (Wells *et al.* 1999) appears to have been earlier than the brief expansion in the uplands (Section 2.1) and seed sources introduced from Ireland *via* the Irish Sea are possible (Birks 1989).

2.3f *Early to mid-Holocene marine incursion*

At Burnside, peat infilling the buried channel is replaced above 3.26m OD (borehole BU6; Fig. 2.4) by waterlain grey clayey silts at c. 8450 cal. BP (GU-4658; Table 2.3). At the Pict's Knowe a comparable change in sediment across the buried channel at 3.71m OD (Fig. 2.5) is statistically inseparable in age at c. 8460 cal. BP (GU-4647; Table 2.3). A similar contact at Carruchan is at c. 3m OD but is undated. At Moss Wood the intrusion of this wedge of grey clayey silt has an age at borehole MW10 (3.33m OD; Fig. 2.7) of c. 8490 cal. BP (GU-4653), while at its landward extreme and 90cm higher (4.54m OD: MW7; Fig. 2.7) the mean calibrated age is slightly younger at around 8280 cal. BP (GU-4650; Table 2.3).

Limited diatom analyses (Fig. 2.13) of the clayey silts immediately younger than c. 8490 cal. BP at Moss Wood (MW10) indicate a transition from freshwater, with the oligohalobous indifferent forms, *Rhopalodia gibba* and *Epitheia adnata v. porcellus* prominent, to brackish water dominated by *Navicula peregrina* and finally to more marine conditions typified by *Raphoneis amphiceros*,

Podosira stelligera and *Paralia sulcata*. This was a rapid rise in relative sea level, with the buried channel as far as Moss Wood (MW10) inundated over a maximum age range of 200 cal. years (8650-8360 cal. BP). These dates are closely comparable with other studies (Jardine 1975; Haggart 1989; Lloyd 1999; Lloyd *et al.*. 2000; Wells & Smith 1999). Lloyd (1999) suggested an initial sea level rise of around 0.5cm/yr in the inner Solway Firth, but the magnitude need not be great because there are no significant altitudinal differences between Burnside and Moss Wood.

There is little evidence that relatively high sea level drove hydrological changes on the elevated soils of the Upper Terrace. Although only c. 2.5m higher than the basal carse sediments, the peats in the Bauldie's Brae gully at borehole BB1 show no significant increase in mire surface wetness (Fig. 2.9b) and the Upper Terrace surface is 3.5m higher than this. This provides some additional control on the shallowness of tidal waters in the buried channel, with the upper diatom assemblage at MW10 suggesting intertidal conditions, and sea level was probably below 5m OD. Peat had begun to form at the adjacent borehole BB1.5 well before sea level rise, from c. 9100 cal. BP (GU-4554; Table 2.4), probably simply by spreading from borehole BB1.

2.3g *Early to mid-Holocene sea level retreat*

In the Crooks Pow, sea level rise may have been briefly halted and possibly reversed. Furthest inland at Moss Wood (MW7), the organic clay that was deposited at c. 8280 cal. BP was replaced by peat at c. 7970 cal. BP (GU-4649; Table 2.3). The carse at the Pict's Knowe (PK8) was subject to post-depositional iron staining under aerobic conditions at a time after c. 8100 cal. BP. At Burnside (BU6) the carse clay around 210cm, below peat dated to c. 7990 cal. BP, is more organic (Fig. 2.10). There are significant differences in age between this event and others in the inner Solway Firth, such as at Newbie Cottages, near Annan. where Dawson *et al.* (1999) ¹⁴C dated peat to c. 7400 to 6900 cal. BP and at Lochar Moss on the east of the Nith Estuary, where Lloyd (1999; Lloyd *et al.* 2000) recorded falling relative sea level from around 4m OD at c. 7500 cal. BP, and it is unclear whether early to mid-Holocene sea levels fluctuated more than once.

2.3h Alnus *establishment and sea level retreat*

Alnus (alder) pollen is recorded at values >10% tlp at Burnside (Fig. 2.10), probably from trees growing near the sampling site, from around 8000 cal. BP. At Bauldie's Brae, *Alnus* pollen increases rapidly at the start of lpaz BBc to local growth between 8100 and 7900 cal. BP (Fig. 2.11). *Alnus* probably colonised the peats that were by now very extensive in this gully and across the floor of the buried channel, above Moss Wood (MW7) and extending at least to Dalskairth (Fig. 2.2). On this nutrient poor but wet substrate *Alnus* would have outcompeted other trees, but on drier sandy substrates such as the Upper Terrace surface, the birch, hazel and pine woodland need not have been significantly disturbed (Fig. 2.11). The sharp spatial differentiation of soil types in the Crooks Pow provides a setting where competition was more limited. Colonisation by alder of peats may have been enhanced by shortlived relative sea level fall in the Crooks Pow as expanses of freshwater peat increased around Moss Wood and tidal mudflats became less saline between the Pict's Knowe and Burnside.

2.3i Renewed sea level rise

Renewed sea level rise is seen at Burnside (BU6; Fig. 2.10) after c. 7900 cal. BP (Section 2.3f) by the deposition of clayey silts for a short interval not able to be defined by ^{14}C assays: overlying peat indicating terrestrial sediment at 6.24m OD is dated to c. 8000 cal. BP (GU-4657; Table 2.3). At the Pict's Knowe carse sedimentation resumed and relative sea level rose to more than 7.10m OD at PK9, before being replaced at PK8 (6.82m OD) by an organic rich clay at c. 8150 cal. BP (GU-4646; Table 2.3), indistinguishable in ^{14}C age to that at Burnside. At Carruchan a comparable sediment boundary but at 6.10m OD (CA1; Fig. 2.6) is also indistinguishable in age at c. 8200 cal. BP (GU-4654; Table 2.3). At Moss Wood carse deposits continued to accumulate at MW10 (Fig. 2.7) to an altitude of 5.82m OD prior to c. 7840 cal. BP (GU-4652; Table 2.3). The altitudes of the highest carse sediments above Carruchan are up to 1m lower than east of the Pict's Knowe. One interpretation of this (cf. Haggart 1989) is that recent drainage and sediment compaction has lowered sediment in the Moss Wood basin; another is that the tidal range was higher as tides were funnelled through the narrow channel between Burnside and the Pict's Knowe.

At Moss Wood, peat continued to grow and seemingly kept pace with rising sea level (Fig. 2.7). This suggests that this second demonstrable sea level rise was not as rapid as the first. At the Bauldie's Brae gully, peat also accumulated without major incursion of carse deposits except for a thin wedge at around 6.5m OD (Fig. 2.8), suggesting that although the valley floor was once more inundated by sea water there was no significant loss of valley floor peat. The consistently well humified peats at Bauldie's Brae (Fig. 2.9b) and the abundance of wood in this peat (Fig. 2.8) shows that elevated sea levels did not drive significant groundwater movements. The dry soils of the Upper Terrace, by c. 8000 cal. BP still some 3m higher than the infilling valley floor, were unaffected by physical coastal change. In turn there was no apparent displacement of wetland alder communities around Bauldie's Brae (Fig. 2.11).

2.3j Sea level pulses and the maintenance of open ground plant communities

At the early to mid Holocene relative sea level fall (Section 2.3g), most commonly at c. 8000 to 7900 cal. BP, the pollen of open or disturbed ground plants is

recorded at Burnside (BU6; Fig. 2.10), including Chenopodiaceae (fat hen), *Rumex* (sorrels), Ranunculaeae (buttercup), Plantaginaceae (plantains including *Plantago coronopus* (buckshorn)), Compositae (daisies: *Solidago virgaurea* type) and *Pteridium* (bracken). These are not all characteristic of coastal communities, although some can be, and with Poaceae (grasses), grasslands of a more terrestrial character might have developed near the water's edge. Comparable open ground and grassland herbs, including buttercups, Umbellifereae (umbellifers), sorrels and bracken are consistently recorded from around 9100 cal. BP, perhaps more commonly after 8200 cal. BP, at Bauldie's Brae (Fig. 2.11). Grasslands close to Bauldie's Brae contained *Plantago lanceolata* (ribwort plantain). Fluctuations in relative sea level may have forced these grasslands to have expanded and contracted in extent, and the frequent disturbance may have prevented the establishment of a woodland cover, increasing the diversity of valley floor vegetation.

2.3k Sea level fall?

Although valley floor peat replaced carse deposits throughout the Crooks Pow north west of Laneside (Fig. 2.1) at 8200 to 8000 cal. BP, it is not clear that relative sea level fell. The continued growth of peats at Moss Wood and at Bauldie's Brae (Section 2.3g) does not necessarily imply marine regression. Their expansion may have been due to increasing rates of peat growth and not to a fall in sea level. Positive indicators of sea level fall are not available. Pollen analyses across this contact at Burnside (BU6: 192 to 186cm; Fig. 2.10) indicate a Poaceae (grass) dominated grassland but with persistent saltmarsh indicators (e.g. Chenopodiacae, *Glaux maritima* (sea milkwort), *Plantago coronopus*, *Artemisia* type (e.g. sea wormwood)).

2.3l A final sea level rise and fall

At Burnside a subsequent sediment stratigraphic change is recorded when grey to brown clays and silts, with varying organic contents, are developed over peats across almost the entire width of the buried channel at 6.8 to 7.2m OD (Fig. 2.4). The onset is dated to c. 7590 cal. BP (GU-4656; Table 2.3). Clays and silts accumulate in the channel centre (borehole BU5) to an altitude of at least 8.3m OD (Section 2.2d). Away from this point they are replaced by peats at lower altitudes and peat probably accumulated contemporaneously with minerogenic sediments within a much narrower channel. At the Pict's Knowe a thinner but comparable grey to brown clayey silt was deposited over organic clays and peats in the centre and north east of the buried channel (Section 2.2d; Fig. 2.5), above 6.9m OD and up to 7.2m OD, but this surface may have been lowered by later fluvial erosion. The beginning of this event is dated to c. 7700 cal. BP (GU-4645; Table 2.3); the top contact is undated. This unit is not traced north-west of the Pict's Knowe.

The diatom flora at BU6 is sparse (Fig. 2.14) but in the

dominance of *Diploneis interrupta* and *Tryblionella navicularis*, indicates at least a brackish water environment, suggesting a third pulse of sediment from a relative sea level rise to as far upstream as the Pict's Knowe. In borehole BU6, close to but not at the highest altitude reached by clays and silts (Fig. 2.4), peat then replaced minerogenic sediments at c. 6720 cal. BP. This peat (Fig. 2.10) has a pollen assemblage with very few coastal indicators, and the occurrence of freshwater aquatic taxa (*Myriophyllum* sp.; milfoils).

After c. 6720 cal. BP there is no evidence in this reach of the Crooks Pow for sea level change. Fig. 2.15 summarises the changes in altitude of the ^{14}C dated sea level index points for the Crooks Pow. Falling relative sea levels after 6700 cal. BP would be in agreement with findings in other regions (Haggart 1989) and new interpretations in the eastern Solway Firth (Lloyd 1999; Lloyd *et al.* 2000). The Crooks Pow data provide no evidence to support new analyses from the Solway coast for either sustained high relative sea levels, perhaps to around 9.5m OD, until c. 4450 cal. BP (Wells & Smith 1999), or a final transgressive pulse to 7 to 8m OD immediately prior to c. 5500 cal. BP (Dawson *et al.* 1999). Whether local geomorphic changes to the coast downstream of Laneside isolated the Crooks Pow from relative sea level change after c. 6720 cal. BP (e.g. Jardine 1975; Wells 1999b) is unknown. However, later geomorphological and vegetation change have no demonstrable links with relative sea level change.

2.3m The Pinus *decline and increasing mire surface wetness*

Until c. 7400 cal. BP Scot's pine continued to coexist with birch and hazel, whilst alder and, probably, birch colonised and established a dense woody carr on terrestrial peat surfaces. Gradually in lpaz BBc (Fig. 2.11) *Quercus* (oak) and *Ulmus* (elm) invaded dry soils but either not abundantly or not close to Bauldie's Brae, and it may have been that mixed deciduous woodland developed principally on till soils of the slopes above the valley floor (cf. Nichols 1967).

Scot's pine was lost from soils around Bauldie's Brae (250cm; Fig. 2.11) at c. 7440 cal. BP (Table 2.4). As elsewhere in south west Scotland the tree was not able subsequently to recolonise. This decline is some 300 to 400 cal. years later than that recognised in the Galloway Hills by Birks (1972) and Jones & Stevenson (1993) and on the Galloway coast at Brighouse Bay (Wells *et al.* 1999).

Coincident with the decline of pine pollen at Bauldie's Brae is the onset of a marked decrease in humication, signifying increasingly wetter peat in the Bauldie's Brae gully (Fig. 2.9b). This trend was interrupted between 7000 and 6900 cal. BP but then erratically but strongly sustained after c. 6100 cal. BP (below) when the peat surface remained consistently or became increasingly wet. This major rise in the water table is thought to have

driven pine from sandy soils on the valley floor. Pine would not have been able to compete on valleyside soils with deciduous trees, and in any case these soils may also have become wetter and equally intractable to pine. The Bauldie's Brae gully may indeed have become too wet to support trees like alder and birch: wood rich peat in boreholes BB1 and BB1.5 is replaced at this time by a peat lacking wood remains (Fig. 2.8).

This period represents a decisive change at Bauldie's Brae and perhaps across the valley floor. The reason for increased surface wetness is unclear. A third pulse of marine or estuarine sediment to the Pict's Knowe is recorded after c. 7590 cal. BP (Section 2.3l). This may have been a rapid inundation of the lower part of the valley, although this cannot be demonstrated, and carse sediment accumulating in the buried channel to at least 8.3m OD, <3m below the Upper Terrace, could have led to groundwater rise. However, high groundwater levels were maintained long after the probable fall in relative sea level at c. 6720 cal. BP (Section 2.3l). Fig. 2.16 is an interpretation of peat stratigraphic data used as proxy climate indicators in the region (Tipping 1999a), and the increase in the water table at Bauldie's Brae is not seen in these: shifts to wetter mire surfaces occur significantly earlier at Walton and Burnfoothill Mosses, at 8000 to 7700 cal. BP (Tipping 1995a; Hughes *et al.* 2000).

The Crooks Pow pine decline may, given that synchroneity with other sites is not demonstrated and has no independently identifiable climate signal (Section 2.3m), be local to the valley. It is possible that pine woodland was cleared by human communities which in turn induced a rise in groundwater tables. If this happened, clearance seems to be have been selective. No other tree taxa appear to have been affected. Increases in Poaceae (grass) percentages may have derived from greater abundance or productivity of grasses on the peat surface following loss of alder and birch carr, and this is the best explanation for increases in Cyperaceae (sedge) values, but the rise in *Rumex* and reappearance of other open ground herbs (Ranunculaceae, Compositae) suggest an increase in terrestrial grasslands. Losses of pine through 'natural' causes should have been closely followed by colonisation from deciduous trees, but this seemingly did not happen at Bauldie's Brae: gap grasslands persisted, suggesting the maintenance of grazed areas (cf. Buckland & Edwards 1984).

Later Mesolithic woodland disturbance is identified from several sites, upland and lowland, in the region (Tipping 1997, 1999a), but was usually shortlived and resulted in no permanent shift in vegetation composition (e.g. Tipping 1995b). It was also usually associated with high fire frequencies or intensities, but this was not shown at Bauldie's Brae (Fig. 2.11). If anthropogenic in origin, the landscape impact at Bauldie's Brae was much more marked than elsewhere although the duration of the disturbance itself need not have been sustained. The extent of the impact was also not necessarily intentional:

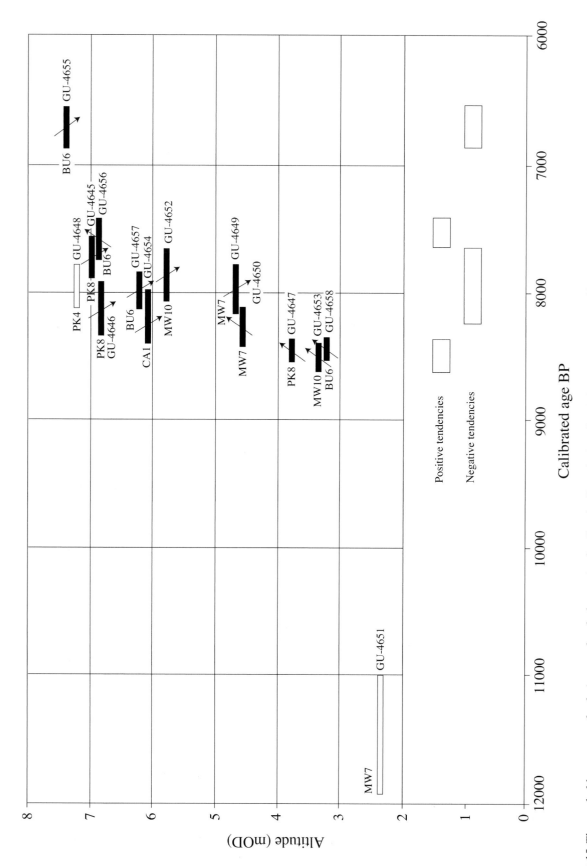

Fig. 2.15 The probable pattern of relative sea level change in the Crooks Pow during the Holocene period. All ¹⁴C dated samples relevant to sea level change in different boreholes are plotted against altitude (mOD). Those which have no information on changing relative sea level are open boxes. The length of each box equates to the calibrated age range at 2s of the sample (Table 2.3). The indications of sea level rise or fall for each point are indicated by ascending or descending arrows. Blocks of time during which index points indicate a relative sea level rise (a positive tendency) or fall (a negative tendency) are also depicted. Modified from Haggart (1999).

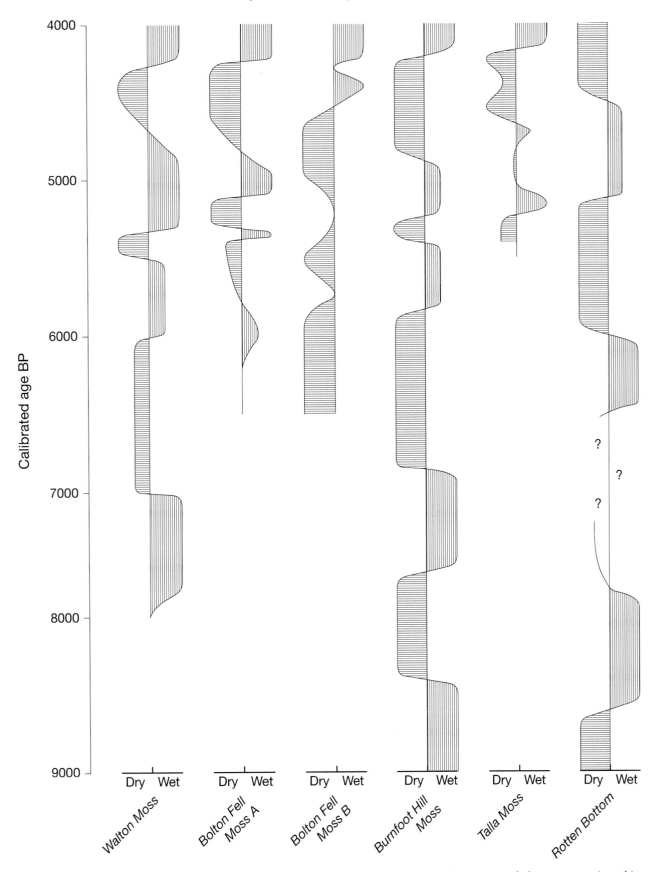

Fig. 2.16 Interpretations of changes in surface wetness in early to mid Holocene proxy climate records from peat stratigraphies in the region plotted against cal. BP: Walton Moss (Hughes et al. 2000); Bolton Fell Moss A (Barber et al. 1994a); Bolton Fell Moss B (Barber et al. 2002); Burnfoothill Moss (Tipping 1995a); Talla Moss (Chambers et al. 1997); Rotten Bottom (Tipping 1999b).

woodland disturbance here is thought to have been magnified by feedback processes in groundwater hydrology, which then drove further woodland decline.

2.3n Adaptations to a waterlogged landscape 7000 to 6100 cal. BP

Pollen data are too limited until above 200cm depth (Fig. 2.11; Table 2.5) to identify in detail competitive adjustments to the removal of pine from the catchment, but as discussed in Section 2.3l, no single tree gained advantage. Grasses and sedges probably expanded on the peat surface at Bauldie's Brae as alder was driven from the gully. This surface was probably increasingly waterlogged, suggested by the occurrence of *Callitriche* (water starwort) (Fig. 2.11), which probably colonised stagnant, unshaded and shallow pools. Humification continues to decrease (% light transmission increases; Fig. 2.9b), and this period is characterised by extreme excursions which may represent brief flooding events.

After c. 6500 cal. BP (170cm; Fig. 2.11) Cyperaceae proportions decline in response to competition from a huge expansion of *Sphagnum* (bog moss) on what was probably by now an intractable gully floor, possibly through increasingly acid stagnant groundwater. This moss dominated assemblage persisted until an abrupt decline at 140cm (c. 6100 cal. BP: GU-7761; Table 2.4). This extraordinary phase emphasises how wet ground conditions had become, at least in the gully but almost certainly across the lower altitude peats that had spread over the buried channel (Floodplain Terrace). The very wet ground conditions on the valley floor persisted until c. 6100 cal. BP. Cause is not clear: the few proxy measures of climate change available (Fig. 2.16) are in agreement that the climate was dry until 6000 to 5800 cal. BP. Human disturbance of woodlands may have continued, but no significant woodland losses are identified, and the near absence of evidence for sediment inwashing into the Bauldie's Brae gully (shown by very high organic contents; Fig. 2.9a), suggests that localised soil erosion did not occur except for one phase at c. 7100 cal. BP.

After c. 6500 cal. BP (170cm) the numbers of microscopic charcoal fragments at Bauldie's Brae increase massively (Fig. 2.11). There are modest increases prior to this, from c. 6800 cal. BP, but after c. 6500 cal. BP for the following c. 600 cal. years, fire was a major part of the landscape, either in frequency, intensity or both. Fire cannot on *a priori* grounds be presumed to be of anthropogenic origin (Tipping 1996). Regional proxy climate records (Fig. 2.16) suggest dry conditions from c. 7000 cal. BP, but although a lag between climate change and fire can be expected because of the need to accumulate a combustible biomass on soils, a lag of c. 500 cal. years (longer than the probable lifespan of trees around Bauldie's Brae) strongly suggests that fire was not triggered by relative aridity. Fire increased at a time when some soils in the catchment are argued to have become increasingly waterlogged (Section 2.3n) and, presumably,

less sensitive to natural triggers like lightning strikes (e.g. Thompson 1971). Fire is, thus, accepted at Bauldie's Brae as most probably anthropogenic in origin, although within the region susceptibility to burning may have been enhanced by a dry climate (Tipping & Milburn 2000). Fire may be linked to the modest pollen analytical evidence for woodland disturbance. If so, this technique of woodland clearance was newly introduced and was not employed within the catchment earlier in the Mesolithic. Whether changes in woodland composition or soils after the pine decline favoured the use of fire is unknown. Microscopic charcoal may also have been associated with settlement (seasonal or sedentary) in the Crooks Pow (cf. Bennett *et al.* 1992).

2.3o The elm decline and the charcoal fall

Within a very short period around 6000 cal. BP several significant environmental changes occurred: a single gradual decline in *Ulmus* (elm) pollen commenced at c. 6100 cal. BP until c. 5450 cal. BP (140 to 110 cm; Fig. 2.11); an abrupt fall to very low numbers of charcoal fragments began at the same time, c. 6100 cal. BP and was completed by 5800 cal. BP (Fig. 2.11); a brief and seemingly modest drying of the peat surface recorded between c. 6100 and 5800 cal. BP (140 to 130 cm; Fig. 2.9b) nevertheless appears to have adversely affected *Sphagnum* growth in the Bauldie's Brae gully (Fig. 2.11). It is assumed that these events are interlinked (Tipping & Milburn 2000), and this assumption will be explored after each element is briefly evaluated.

The elm decline (see Smith (1981) for the best summary) is, of course, much discussed and still unresolved. Here the elm decline will be treated essentially at a site specific scale. Elm was not common in the catchment prior to its decline. It is most likely to have grown with *Quercus* (oak) on drier and less acid soils on till covered slopes above the valley floor and not on the acid sands and peats of the Upper and Floodplain Terraces. The beginning of the elm decline (lpaz Bbdii; Fig. 2.11) is well dated to 6270 to 5950 cal. BP (1.0cm thick sample; 50 yr. error at 1σ: Table 2.4). This is early for this feature at sites in the region (Tipping 1997). *Contra* Tipping (1997), however, the elm decline in the region is now demonstrably diachronous (Tipping 1999a; Tipping & Milburn 2000). At Bauldie's Brae, at the temporal resolution available (Table 2.5), it was a single decline (cf. Oldfield 1963; Hirons & Edwards 1986). It appears to have been selective in that only *Ulmus* (elm) percentages are affected during the decline but at its beginning *Quercus* (oak) values are also sharply reduced (Fig. 2.11). There is no evidence that the local elm decline has an anthropogenic origin: cereal type pollen is not recorded. At the beginning of the elm decline Poaceae (grass) percentages are abruptly doubled, though some grass pollen was probably derived from the peat surface and pollen of grassland herbs like *Rumex* (sorrels) is less common, but as with earlier woodland losses, grasslands rather than trees benefited. The end of the decline (lpaz Bbdiii; Fig. 2.11) is also well dated, to 5600 to 5300 cal. BP, after which elm pollen is not recorded and the tree may have been extremely rare or absent.

The charcoal fall (Edwards 1988, 1990) is less well recorded and is no better understood than the elm decline. From sites in upland western Scotland (Edwards 1988), the North York Moors (Simmons & Innes, 1988, 1996) and lowland southern Scotland (Tipping 1995b), a reduction in the representation of microscopic charcoal is seen to have occurred close to or at the transition from Mesolithic to Neolithic economies. This feature can be seen as a reduction in the purposeful use of fire by human populations as agriculture was adopted (Edwards 1990), but it is not clear why early agriculturalists should have been significantly less reliant on fire: a clear difference in resource management between hunter gatherers and early farmers is less firmly supported today (Thomas 1991). The charcoal fall may not be related to human activity: its apparent synchroneity at sites throughout upland Britain has instead been used to imply a natural, climatic control on fire frequency/intensity (Tipping 1996). However, at three sites within the northern Solway lowlands, including Bauldie's Brae, the charcoal fall was, like the elm decline, demonstrably diachronous between c. 6400 and 5400 cal. BP (Tipping & Milburn 2000). At two of these sites, including Bauldie's Brae, the charcoal fall was synchronous with the elm decline.

Microscopic charcoal values at Bauldie's Brae fluctuate over the period c. 6500 to 6100 cal. BP (Fig. 2.11) but are consistently much more abundant than prior to or after this phase. This pattern suggests that high fire frequency/intensity in the late Mesolithic is the anomalous feature, not its apparent absence in the earliest Neolithic. However, there is no apparent differentiation in how the landscape was used across the charcoal fall. This may say more, however, about pollen analytical resolution of land use than for the continuity of Mesolithic and Neolithic economies (Tipping & Milburn 2000).

By c. 5800 cal. BP *Sphagnum* bog communities had almost disappeared from around borehole BB1 (Fig. 2.11). They were probably replaced by grass and sedge (Poaceae and Cyperaceae) communities. This could have been a response to a drier peat surface. Humification increased for a short period (Fig. 2.9b) but this is a small shift with one single sample anomaly, and *Callitriche* persists within standing water (Fig. 2.11) which makes relative aridity less probable. Maintenance of high groundwater levels is probable. Prior to this the Bauldie's Brae peat did not replicate regional trends in climate but after c. 6000 cal. BP this relation is much closer (below), in turn suggesting an increased sensitivity to externally driven change in hydrology and the likelihood that the peat, like other sites in the region, was affected by wetter conditions at 6000 to 5800 cal. BP (Fig. 2.16). The peat floor did not become drier, and it is unlikely that *Sphagnum* communities drowned, but they may have died through increases in pH

and nutrient status of water from relatively base rich soils on the slopes above the gully. Sediment itself, however, was not transferred from slopes as the continuing very high organic contents indicate (Fig. 2.9a).

Some of these complex changes were probably linked. Incursions of nutrient rich runoff from slopes above the valley floor, which killed *Sphagnum* (bog moss) communities, were probably generated from increased precipitation as climate shifted, but nutrients in solution may have been more easily removed and transferred from soils no longer protected by a continuous canopy cover. Firstly, oak trees had been removed abruptly, and regeneration over the next several hundred years was limited, and at the same time but more gradually, elm trees had begun to die and did not regenerate. The removal of oak trees is likely, in its suddenness, to have been through human activity. For the first time in the record the slopes appear to have become a focus for anthropogenic disturbance. In the apparent absence of cereal type pollen, clearance is assumed to have been for the development of grazing or for settlement. This was a continuation of earlier events, and this disturbance is not seen as an intensification of human impact.

The elm decline occurred with the removal of oak, and because the two were synchronous, is assumed also to be connected with human activities. Clearly, however, the elm population was depleted more slowly, although eventually with greater landscape impact. This pattern suggests a different technique in clearance of elm, perhaps through ring barking. More complex explanations involving the spread of disease within woodlands already open through clearance (Rackham 1980) are unnecessary. This contrast between the declines of oak and elm raises currently untestable questions about spatial patterning in woods.

The charcoal fall may be explained by changes in the way woodlands were manipulated. It is suggested, although this is unclear, that valley side mixed deciduous woodlands were disturbed for the first time after c. 6100 cal. BP. This woodland may have required clearance by techniques other than burning because they are less flammable (Rackham 1980). This model implies that valley floor woods, previously manipulated by fire, were no longer a focus for human communities: this cannot be tested with current data. One reason for abandoning interest in valley floor woods might have been the increasingly intractable nature of the terrain, particularly after climatic deterioration. Climate change itself may, however, have led literally to a dampened response to burning as a clearance tool (Tipping & Milburn 2000), such that fire was of limited effectiveness and was abandoned as a tool.

2.3p Continuity and change in the Crooks Pow Valley after 6000 cal. BP

In many ways the landscape after the elm decline reflects continuity in process and form. The distribution of soils, wet and dry, mineral and organic, had not altered since relative sea level fell over 1000 cal. years earlier. Around Bauldie's Brae and on soils of the Upper Terrace woodland composition remained unchanged following the loss of Scot's pine. Alder remained dominant, with birch and rare willow. Fluctuations in the proportions of the first two occurred, perhaps in response to cyclic climate change (below), and perhaps in woodland regeneration as the impact of human communities on the valley floor became less. However, this damp carr woodland was not cleared around Bauldie's Brae before c. 4000 cal. BP when the record ends (Fig. 2.11). On the slopes, despite sizeable impacts on woodland (below), soil erosion did not occur in response to clearance. There is no evidence for sediment inwashing within the Bauldie's Brae gully (Fig. 2.9a). The peats of the Floodplain Terrace probably continued to accumulate, although this has not been dated, and there are no minerogenic fluvial deposits within these (Figs. 2.4 to 2.7 inclusive). At Burnside (Fig. 2.4) a single alluvial fan postdates c. 6800 cal. BP but is very late in the sequence, and is not directly dated.

In other ways there was change, probably partly concealed by the abundance of carr woodland still screening the pollen site. Oak and elm woodland seems to have been severely modified. The scale and extent of clearance cannot be reconstructed, but may have been substantial. There was no competitive advantage conferred to the major dryland shrub, *Corylus* (hazel), as the tree canopy was opened, and this strongly suggests the significance of grazing impacts in suppressing woodland regeneration. Oak populations appear to have partially recovered, but only after the elm decline at c. 5450 cal. BP (lpaz Bbdiii; Fig. 2.11). Elm pollen is still recorded after c. 5000 cal. BP, but it is not clear whether the tree grew locally.

From being unresponsive to climate driven hydrological change before c. 6000 cal. BP, the Bauldie's Brae gully humification record (Fig. 2.9b) appears to be remarkably well coupled to regional proxy climate records (Fig. 2.16) up to c. 4000 cal. BP. This may have had much to do with the responsiveness of partially deforested slopes and soils above the gully. There is seemingly impressive agreement between these records, and although the Bauldie's Brae peat is predominantly much wetter than in the earlier Holocene, short term fluctuations accord with those seen elsewhere in the region.

2.3q The Pict's Knowe in the early Bronze Age

Within the early Bronze Age, in the topmost 20cm of the truncated peat stratigraphy at Bauldie's Brae (Section 2.2h; Fig. 2.11), dated by assay GU-7763 to 5030 to 4830 cal. BP (c. 4930 cal. BP; Table 2.4), the more abundant records of *Callitriche* and occurrence of *Nymphaea* (water lily) pollen suggest that standing water was probably increasingly common within the gully. Together, *Callitriche* and *Nymphaea* would suggest water depths certainly >25cm and arguably much deeper, in excess of 1m, and estimated pH closer to neutral than acid (Spence

1964) as the gully continued to receive runoff. Flooding only in winter is unlikely because standing water was present when these plants flowered, from May to September, and the probability is that the gully contained standing water throughout the year. The floor of the peat in the gully by now lay <1.5m below the Upper Terrace surface. Much of the Upper Terrace surface could have been inundated. Although the apparent difference in altitude between contemporaneous peats in the Bauldie's Brae gully and under the Floodplain Surface might imply drainage rather than ponding, recent drainage and compaction on the valley floor may have created this difference. High groundwater levels persisted until the end of this sediment record at c. 4250 cal. BP (25.0cm; Fig. 2.9b). Within the region, climate deteriorated very markedly after c. 4250 cal. BP in what may have been the most significant mid late Holocene climate shift (Barber *et al.* 1994a).

Two hundred metres east of Bauldie's Brae, buried by upcast from ditch construction at the Pict's Knowe, is the peat of the Pict's Knowe A (Fig. 2.3; Sections 2.2e–h; k–m). This peat began to develop on well drained sands on the Upper Terrace surface at c. 4100 cal. BP (4340 to 3840 cal. BP; Table 2.4). It is difficult to avoid a correlation with either the exceptionally high groundwater levels at Bauldie's Brae or with the regional trend to increasing effective precipitation at this time. The peat is argued to have formed at the Pict's Knowe in response to rising groundwater levels within the sands of the Upper Terrace. As soils became wetter organic matter decay became less until the soil surface was organic. This water table was elevated by increasing precipitation in addition to runoff from partially cleared slopes. It is a moot point whether this surface could have supported peat earlier in the Holocene which was subsequently oxidised and lost, but if hydrological inputs from both precipitation and runoff were required, this is perhaps unlikely, but the sand beneath the peat was not significantly pedogenically altered. There is some micromorphological evidence for faunal turbation in these sands, indicating a phase of aerobic soil development prior to peat formation (see Crowther: Chapter 10 below).

The peat at the Pict's Knowe is preserved by burial beneath parts of the archaeological site: nowhere else on this extensive terrace surface (Fig. 2.2) is peat preserved. Nevertheless, our model for peat formation probably implies that these sandy soils almost everywhere on this fragment of the Upper Terrace were being lost to peat. This represents a major transformation in the appearance and land use potential of this surface. Any human activities on and around the Pict's Knowe would have had to adapt to a wetter and more nutrient poor soil. The peat at the Pict's Knowe is only thin but probably formed very rapidly (Section 2.2h). It is highly amorphous (Table 2.2) suggesting that here, 1m and more above the Bauldie's Brae gully, waterlogging was seasonal with organic matter breakdown taking place in dry seasons.

The upper part of this peat contains thin laminae of sand, and received this probably from nearby sands that were either not peat covered or were frequently disturbed; the sand may have blown in rather than washed in (Crowther: Chapter 10 below).

Pollen analyses (Fig. 2.12) show several changes in plant communities around the peat despite the rapidity with which peat accumulated. No chronology can be given because the ^{14}C dates are inseparable (Section 2.2h) but the micromorphological description (Crowther: Chapter 10 below) makes it clear that the peat accumulated in a stratigraphically secure context, with horizontal banding discernible. These vegetation changes are probably specific to a few tens of metres around the Pict's Knowe A (Section 2.2k). Initially the sands here (lpaz PKAa; Fig. 2.12) were characterised by a very similar plant community to that persisting at this time around Bauldie's Brae (Fig. 2.11), a woodland of *Alnus* (alder) and *Betula* (birch). *Corylus* (hazel) or *Myrica* (bog myrtle) was a subsidiary element. These data indicate that alder and birch woodland not only grew within and near the gully at Bauldie's Brae, but across the Upper Terrace. These soils did not support *Quercus* (oak) or *Ulmus* (elm). Poaceae pollen is much less significant at the Pict's Knowe A, supporting the interpretations (Section 2.3n) that much grass pollen is derived from the peat surface at Bauldie's Brae itself. It was suggested (Section 2.3o) that from c. 6100 cal. BP, soils of the Upper Terrace had not been a focus for grazing pressures.

Alder populations around the Pict's Knowe A may have been in decline from before peat inception. In lpaz PKAb (Fig. 2.12) around c. 4100 cal. BP, alder was replaced locally by a birch rich *Calluna* (ling) heath. This plant community is not recognised at Bauldie's Brae (Fig. 2.11) and it is most likely that pollen analyses here ceased below sediments of this age (Section 2.2m). Vegetation on the Upper Terrace surface became much more open as the dense alder and birch woodland (tree pollen totals are initially 60 to 70% tlp; Fig. 2.12) was replaced by birch heath. Access across the surface was made easier to human communities. It is not known whether alder was removed by human communities. It may be that *Calluna* replaced alder in response to reductions in nutrient status on the deepening peat. Fire frequency/intensity increases in lpaz PKAb (Fig. 2.12) but this may be related to the greater ease with which *Calluna* is burnt; charred *Calluna* stems are seen in soil thin sections (Crowther: Chapter 10 below).

The final vegetation change is an abrupt, probably very rapid reduction in birch and alder as both were lost from around the site. This may represent the removal by human communities of the remaining trees on site as construction of the monument commenced, because there are no pronounced increases in indicator pollen taxa typical of agriculture. Only *Calluna* proportions rise, perhaps increasing in pollen productivity as canopy cover was removed as much as increasing in extent.

However, immediately prior to burial by upcast from the adjacent ditch, cereal type pollen, of both *Hordeum* group (cf. barley) and *Avena/Triticum* (oats or wheat) are recorded. They may not have been grown on the soils immediately adjacent to the Pict's Knowe since they are unaccompanied by significant numbers of arable 'weed' taxa (Fig. 2.12). Earlier evidence for cereal cultivation around the Pict's Knowe, but still within the early Bronze Age, occurs at Bauldie's Brae (Fig. 2.11) where a number of grains of cereal type are recorded in two contiguous spectra at and after c. 4930 cal. BP, but associated arable weed taxa are not recorded there either. The reconstruction of a damp to wet Upper Terrace surface would suggest that crop growing took place some distance away, probably on valley slopes. The significance of crop growing may thus be underestimated.

Discussion: landscape and site

This section will focus on the questions raised in Section 2.1. These relate to the site and its surrounding landscape, and importantly, why the monument was constructed where it was in the late Neolithic or early Bronze Age. Many other aspects of landscape change have been raised in Section 2.3 and only briefly evaluated, and these will be considered further in more specialist publications, but the key concern here is to use established techniques of environmental reconstruction to forge new links with an archaeology increasingly concerned not with economic explanation but with more subtle social relations. Is environmental archaeology still of relevance? We would argue that landscape scale techniques such as employed here provide a vital context to decision making by prehistoric communities. To presume purely determinist responses to environmental change is nonsensical, but equally to imagine these societies were somehow divorced from nature is equally inadequate.

2.4a The Pict's Knowe in the early Bronze Age: isolation and access

Very considerable parts of the Crooks Pow landscape have survived from well before the early Bronze Age to the present. The valley sides have been unmodified in major ways since the last glaciers (Section 2.3a). Below these, the sandy surface of the Upper Terrace has persisted since the Devensian Lateglacial (Section 2.3b). Archaeological site and find distributions on this surface will be affected by agricultural disturbance, but not by concealment or destruction by natural processes.

Only the peat covered surface of the Floodplain Terrace has formed since the early Bronze Age (Section 2.3p). This thick complex marine and terrestrial sediment stratigraphy accumulated from the earliest Holocene (c. 11500 cal. BP; Section 2.3d), not necessarily continuously, but there is the high potential for buried archaeological sites and very incomplete surface recovery of finds. The Mabie Burn logboat (Mowat 1996), though poorly contexted, is one such find. The Crooks Pow itself, though artificially straightened, can only ever have meandered within the confines of the Floodplain Terrace.

The Upper Terrace, central to reconstruction because this was the surface selected for the Pict's Knowe monument, has been dissected by erosion into a comparatively few fragments, and east of Carruchan is almost continuous along the south side of the valley (Fig. 2.2). Upstream of Carruchan all of this surface was removed during the Devensian Lateglacial, possibly during the Loch Lomond Stadial, replaced by peats of the Floodplain Terrace. West of the Pict's Knowe the Bauldie's Brae gully was cut at the same period, but below this the incised channel was confined to a narrow meander belt between broad and laterally extensive surfaces of the Upper Terrace (Section 2.3c).

Morphologically, there is nothing distinctive about the Pict's Knowe. It is not an isolated knoll. The fragment of the Upper Terrace immediately west of the Bauldie's Brae gully (Figs. 2.2, 2.3) is equally accessible and more constricted: this and the Pict's Knowe fragment share the Bauldie's Brae as a barrier or border. The Pict's Knowe is at the edge of the buried channel occupied by the Floodplain Terrace, which may have been important in access (below) but the visual impact of this channel in the early Bronze Age was not strong. The cross valley transect at the Pict's Knowe (Fig. 2.5) shows that sediment infilling had all but concealed the steeply incised buried channel by the late Mesolithic period (Section 2.3m), and peat growth smoothed out any pronounced topographic contrasts between monument and river valley (Section 2.3n). The Pict's Knowe is also not at the most confined location on this part of the Upper Terrace: this is at the angle between the Floodplain Terrace and the Bauldie's Brae gully 70m north west of the monument (Fig. 2.3).

The Pict's Knowe is, however, central to the valley axis (Fig. 2.1; Plate 2.1). In particular, from the peat covered wastes of Moss Wood and Carruchan, the Pict's Knowe was one of the first (though not the first) extensive terrace surfaces in the later Neolithic period (Section 2.3p). Equally, from the coast the Pict's Knowe was almost the last 'dry' land in the valley until the mass of valley floor peat extending to the low hills rising to the north west some kilometres away. This location, separating the soils of the Upper Terrace from the bogs and mosses of the Floodplain Terrace, at the divide between farmed and wild resources (Section 2.4b, c; below) may have been critical.

The Pict's Knowe was not difficult to access. The role of increased waterlogging of the valley floor is discussed in Sections 2.4c and 2.4d, but access in a broad arc south and east from the south-west to the east was always possible across the flat sands of the Upper Terrace. The detailed topography of the site (Fig. 2.3) shows that a causeway to the site constrained by the physical landscape did not exist, and access is unlikely to have determined the position of the single entrance to the monument (Thomas: Chapter 19 below). The uniformity of this flat surface suggests that

peat formation on this surface in the late Neolithic period was unlikely to have been discontinuous (Sections 2.3p, q). Walking to the Pict's Knowe across the Upper Terrace in the early Bronze Age, across the newly formed peat, would have been mildly irritating rather than demanding. These soils had become peat covered before monument construction, but this peat was only thin. Wet feet at the wrong time of year may have been the worst physical experience, although psychological impacts may have been more significant (Section 2.4c). Valley floor woodland was not by this time a barrier to monument construction (Section 2.3p), and there is no reason to assume that it ever had been (Section 2.3m). The alder and birch woodland across this terrace surface was probably still dense by the later Neolithic period, but these valley floor woods had been utilised and manipulated in the late Mesolithic period (Sections 2.3m, 2.4b), and techniques of woodland clearance were familiar (Sections 2.3m–q inclusive; Section 2.4b), though there is the suggestion (Section 2.3n), drawn out in Section 2.4c, that the valley floor became less attractive in the early Neolithic period. Even so, increasing nutrient depletion through peat formation on the already acid sands probably led to the natural thinning of this dense woodland before monument construction, probably shortly before (Section 2.3q), and this would have made access easier and the Upper Terrace surface more inviting.

Around the site from the south west to the east ground conditions were, however, much more difficult. Open water conditions, possibly with deep pools, had developed over the peats infilling the Bauldie's Brae gully. These had been a landscape feature from the late Mesolithic period (Section 2.3n). This gully may have been further visually enhanced from the valley side by being open, too wet even to have supported alder carr. It is not clear whether the main channel in the Floodplain Terrace was also increasingly waterlogged, because it is more distant from valley side sources of runoff and more efficiently drained by the Crooks Pow, but it too may have been at best unpleasant and probably difficult to cross. These wetland features formed barriers to access, and would have defined the routeways of pedestrian approaches. Access from the north side of the valley in particular would have been problematic.

It is not at all clear whether the Crooks Pow represented a routeway by boat. It is clear that sea level fall had occurred around the Pict's Knowe by 7000 cal. BP (Section 2.3l), and that the idea of high relative sea level persisting into the early Bronze Age here (Smith *et al.* 2000) cannot be supported. It has not been established how low sea level had fallen or how distant the coast was by the early Bronze Age. Though probably waterlogged, areas of open water need not have been connected or continuous, and peat growth may have kept pace with elevated groundwater tables. There is no evidence in any cross-valley transect for river channels (Section 2.3p). Arguably the valley was criss-crossed by numerous small very low discharge anastomosing streams, none of which provided easy access, and without a ^{14}C date for the Mabie Burn boat (Mowat 1996) it is difficult to establish a landscape context for this intriguing find, save that no evidence for an extensive lake (Coles 1893) has been recorded.

2.4b A familiar landscape?

Our interpretation is that people had been familiar with the valley floor, working on and with it, for at least 3000 cal. years before the monument at the Pict's Knowe was erected (Section 2.3m). The several pulses of relative sea level rise that impacted on the valley floor in the early to mid-Holocene (Sections 2.3f–l inclusive) probably allowed the maintenance of grassland communities along the channel edges (Section 2.3j). Some of these were coastal, but terrestrial grasslands are also suggested as tidal waters alternately flooded and drained away from the buried channel. Similar mechanisms of disturbance and temporary creation of land may have driven the establishment of alder on the valley floor (Section 2.3h). These changes are seen as natural: human interference may have contributed but it cannot be distinguished. Such coastal and estuarine settings, of course, have increased faunal diversity (Coles 1971; Bonsall 1981) and are assumed to have attracted Mesolithic communities (cf. Boyd 1982).

It is unclear whether human impact was causal in vegetation change after c. 7300 cal. BP. The decline and removal of Scots pine, probably from the sands of the Upper Terrace, is interpreted as being by anthropogenic clearance (Section 2.3m). Scot's pine had not been a major component of the vegetation, but nevertheless this was a major vegetation change, an apparent impact more substantive than assigned to hunter-gatherer-fisher intervention elsewhere in the region. Selectivity in losses, with seemingly only pine affected, is explained by rising groundwater level affecting the only species on the valley floor sensitive to waterlogging, and hydrological feedback processes are argued in Section 2.3m to have amplified and sustained the initial disturbance so that the effect was not commensurate with the initial impact.

The purpose of disturbance is also unclear, but very quickly grazing pressures on the valley floor are thought to have prevented regeneration from trees like alder or birch (Sections 2.3m, n). Gaps created by dying pines were apparently maintained as glades or more continuous grasslands, probably by coastal grazing animals like aurochs (*Bos primigenius*: Evans 1975). These may have attracted hunters but there is no evidence for the purposeful maintenance of gaps by fire (e.g. Simmons 1996). Mesolithic communities continue to be shadowy and impressionistic in the data, seen indirectly, and only by what they triggered unintentionally, in promoting increases in runoff onto the valley floor from modest woodland disturbance (Section 2.3n, o). Only after c. 6500 cal. BP did the character of anthropogenic disturbance change when burning became widespread as a

tool (Section 2.2n). Why this change occurred is unknown because the scale of woodland clearance appears not to have increased.

Anthropogenic impacts after c. 6000 cal. BP were more marked. The pace of environmental modification quickened, mechanisms of alteration changed, responses and innovations in a changing world, but the purpose was not discernibly different (Section 2.3p). The use of fire in woodland clearance was abandoned, partly through a wetter climate reducing combustibility of organic matter, possibly through the focus of human activity now decisively turning away from the valley floor and towards the less flammable oak, elm and hazel woods of the slopes as paludification intensified. New techniques seem to have been introduced to clear this woodland: oak was abruptly removed, probably not by sustained grazing pressures but by the axe. The elm population was reduced more gradually, possibly through different techniques (Section 2.3n) or because the resource was more carefully managed, though ultimately elm almost disappeared from the landscape.

These losses may have been unintentional rather than purposeful reductions: much depends on how woodland resources were regarded. However, despite the novelty of some techniques after c. 6000 cal. BP, what is stressed is the continuity of landscape change through what is conventionally seen as the Mesolithic-Neolithic transition (Section 2.3p). Until after c. 5000 cal. BP resource use had the same pastoral focus that had driven Mesolithic change.

2.4c Economic intensification, diminishing resources and henge construction

By the early Bronze Age the Crooks Pow valley was a landscape familiar to human communities. This was no frontier, and the Pict's Knowe was not a monument located in a new setting. It was, as argued in Section 2.4a, a nodal point in the valley that divided or linked the extensive drier soils of the Upper Terrace, manipulated since the later Mesolithic (Section 2.4b) and the seeming wilderness of the moss covered valley floor north-west of Carruchan. We have few data pertaining to the resources available on these peats but it is reasonable to assume that hunted or gathered resources dominated.

This division between managed and wild landscapes was emphasised from c. 5000 cal. BP by the introduction to this part of the valley of cereal cultivation (Section 2.3q). At both Bauldie's Brae and the Pict's Knowe A, cereal pollen is recorded only after c. 4900 cal. BP and c. 4100 cal. BP respectively, at the end of the Neolithic period. This difference in age may not be real; both sites probably reflect the same source of cereal pollen, and this difference emphasises the difficulties of identifying this underrepresented and very poorly dispersed pollen type. These problems imply that the date of introduction of cereals to the valley cannot be confidently defined, but it is assumed here that cereals were not present earlier than the end of the Neolithic period. Introduction to the Crooks Pow at this date is not necessarily typical of the region: Neolithic macrofossil finds or grain impressions on pottery are known from Scottish contexts (Boyd 1987; Barclay 1997), but not from the Solway plain. Cereal pollen finds are known from the region in the earliest Neolithic (Tipping 1995b) but rarely and sporadically. In the Crooks Pow valley crop growing is argued to have been a new resource in the 3rd millennium cal. BC. Cereals may have been grown on the valley sides and not on the soils around the Pict's Knowe (Section 2.3q), but their appearance would have introduced a new contrast between the economic potentials of 'dryland' soils and moss.

There is an opposing trend in landscape change at the end of the Neolithic period that, rather than affirming the potential of agriculture, may have tended to remind communities of a diminishing resource. There is consistent evidence for increased waterlogging of all soils on the valley floor, whether on the Upper or Floodplain Terraces, after c. 6400 cal. BP (Sections 2.3m–q inclusive). This intermittently intensified following woodland disturbance and, increasingly, climatic instability. One result of this was the establishment of open pools more clearly demarcating barriers or borders on the valley floor (Section 2.4a). Another was the change from dry sandy soils to thin peats across the Upper Terrace surface within the early Bronze Age (Section 2.3q). This was probably more visually striking than physically demanding, but the combined impression may have been of an increasingly intractable and hostile valley floor.

Our reconstruction suggests the valley floor to have been an initial focus for woodland manipulation in the later Mesolithic period (Section 2.3l), but paludification may have forced a shift to utilising drier valley side soils (Section 2.3n–p inclusive). During the Bronze Age, farming communities would have observed the soil driven changes from woodland to birch heath around the Pict's Knowe (Section 2.3q), and perhaps wondered how much of this new landscape they controlled.

2.4d The 'daily round' and special elements at the Pict's Knowe

Agriculture was a new venture when the Pict's Knowe monument was constructed. But equally the valley floor where the monument was constructed was becoming a different, perhaps more hostile place. The Pict's Knowe was probably increasingly disconnected from day-to-day activities. Shortly before monument construction the site had been a dense alder and birch woodland, which might have occasionally attracted hunters and gatherers, although we have no evidence for this. Whilst the valley sides were being cleared and transformed, different changes occurred around what was to become the monument, with the loss of trees and expansion of heath (Section 2.3q), but changes disadvantageous to farming communities. The final clearance of trees at the Pict's Knowe was probably to clear the ground for construction or to make the monument visible, not to include the site into the agricultural activities of the community. It had become by this time a special place.

Its specialness may have been enhanced by increasing vulnerability to flooding. The peaty surface remained only seasonally waterlogged, but lower rates of organic matter decay and peat formation suggest a very high groundwater table across the Upper Terrace. People digging a ditch into this soil would, most probably, have met water at no great depth. At this site, we would support Richards (1996) in arguing for a link between henges and water. At the Pict's Knowe the significance of water may have been as a "metaphor for transition" (*ibid.*, p. 316), the spatial transition between a worked and a wild landscape, and of 'transformation' as the landscape moved from wild to worked, but at the Pict's Knowe this metaphor had an added urgency as water was the means by which this part of their landscape was being 'lost' to these communities.

3

Early historic land uses at the Pict's Knowe: palynological evidence from the West Cutting

Paula Milburn and Richard Tipping

Introduction

This short section discusses the interpretations of vegetation patterns and land uses in the immediate vicinity of the Pict's Knowe in the early historic period. The interpretations derive from a series of pollen analyses taken from peat accumulating within the ditch on the western side of the site, directly above the late Iron Age 'ard' described in Chapter 4. The pollen sequence is called the Pict's Knowe B (PKB). The analyses presented here span the period between c. 130–410 and 1220–1380 cal. AD.

Techniques and results

Within the cleaned vertical section provided by the West Ditch Cutting, excavated in 1994, a series of three overlapping metal 'monolith' tins (30.0 × 15.0 × 15.0cm) were placed to sample, from the base upwards, compact green clay (Context 0122), overlying poorly humified red peat (Context 0024) and more highly humified black peat (0004). Sealing these *in situ* organic deposits is a thick accumulation of mixed silts and fine sands, the lateral equivalent of Context 0697, derived from the interior of the site (Table 3.1).

Dating controls for this sequence were provided by ^{14}C assays on the humic acid fractions of two peat slices, from the boundary between green clay and peat at 80.0 to 82.0cm and immediately beneath the sand at 25.0 to 27.0cm (Table 3.2: see Section 2.2g for treatment of assays). Peat

accumulated at a mean rate of 19 to 20 years per centimetre, though the differing extent of peat decay (humification) suggests peat growth was not uniform. Within the green clay in this section, below 80.0cm depth (0122), the ard-like object has an AMS ^{14}C age of 1835 ± 65 BP (20 to 340 cal. AD at 2σ: AA–16250). Other assays on wooden finds (Chapter 28) confirm the late Iron Age date of this fill.

Twenty four subsamples were prepared and analysed for pollen and microscopic charcoal between 80.0 and 25.0cm depth using the methods outlined in Section 2.2l. These analyses lie above the single pollen count of leaves within the green clay presented by Ramsay and Miller (Chapter 13). The analyses from this small ditch fill have a restricted pollen source area (Section 2.2k), predominantly a few tens of metres around the site. The analyses have a temporal resolution of 55 to 60 cal. year intervals. The data are presented (see Section 2.2m) in Fig. 3.1 as a percentage based pollen stratigraphy (from counts of 500 land pollen grains per level), subdivided by visual inspection into three 'local pollen assemblage zones', lpaz PKBa to PKBc. Counts of microscopic charcoal are recorded in four size classes based on long axis length and calculated as % tlp+charcoal. Total pollen concentration data in Fig. 3.1 record the total numbers of pollen grains per cm^3. Pollen preservation data were obtained, but with 70 to 85% tlp of grains well preserved throughout, differential preservation does not distort interpretations and the data are not published.

Depth sampled	Description	Context
0–25cm	silts and fine sands; abrupt boundary to	0697
25–51cm	highly humified black peat; gradual boundary to	0004
51–65cm	less well humified black peat; gradual boundary to	0004
65–80cm	poorly humified reddish-black peat; abrupt boundary to	0024
80–125cm	green-grey laminated clay (base not sampled)	0122

Table 3.1

Lab. Code	Depth (cm)	Sediment	^{14}C Age	$\delta^{13}C$	Age Range Probability $(\pm\,1\sigma)$	Cal. BP $(\pm\,2\sigma)$ $(>95\%)$
GU-4205	82.0–80.0	poorly humified red peat	1760 ± 50	-29.0	1820–1540	1758–1545 (0.96)
GU-4206	27.0–25.0	humified black peat	730 ± 50	-28.5	730–570	<95%: not defined

Table 3.2 Details of ^{14}C assays and calibrations on the peat at the Pict's Knowe B.

Palaeoecological interpretations

In the basal lpaz (PKBa: c. 270 to 550 cal. AD) *Betula* (birch) and *Alnus* (alder) were common trees, and may have grown on the acid peat in the ditch itself, associated with, perhaps, *Myrica* (bog myrtle: *Corylus/Myrica* pollen). This was a species poor, secondary woodland. However, at least locally there were substantially more trees than had grown at the site in the early Bronze Age (Tipping *et al*. Chapter 2). *Salix* (willow) pollen is not recorded, although willow was present as a macrofossil in the basal layers of the ditch fill (Ramsay & Miller; Chapter 13). This wet woodland may have been dense and overgrown, because Cyperaceae (sedges) were apparently rare and possibly shaded out, although within the ditch grew herbs like marsh marigold (*Caltha* type) and buttercups (*Ranunculus*), scabious (*Succisa pratensis*), and *Sphagnum* (bog moss). The wood may also have contained spiky shrubs like roses (Rosaceae undiff.) and *Rubus* (brambles), and climbing plants like *Hedera* (ivy), possibly making the site unpleasant to move around in.

If the ditch supported a dense wet scrub, this may have screened out pollen derived from further afield (Tauber 1965), and the proportions of taxa away from the ditch might be underestimated. Nevertheless, *Calluna* (ling heather) communities and grasslands (Gramineae: wild grasses) were probably abundant on the acid sands of the terrace surface. It is difficult to know whether the peats that had developed on the terrace surface in the later Neolithic (Tipping *et al*. Chapter 2) had been lost. However, the grasslands supported many herbs that are inimical to waterlogging, and the terrace soils may have been largely minerogenic by Romano-British times.

The grassy heath was probably grazed, and *Plantago lanceolata* (ribwort plantain) was particularly common. Fires were not common, and the relative abundance of charcoal fragments <50μm suggests fires were generally small scale or distant from the site. The occurrence of grains of *Hordeum* type pollen (cf. barley) may indicate some crop growing, but this taxon includes wild grass species associated with ditches, and cereal cultivation is not assured on this evidence.

The boundary to lpaz PKBb at around 550 cal. AD represents a major change in the ditch sediments, the local vegetation and human activities at the site. Woodland reduction occurred very rapidly, and there is no reason to assume that trees grew near the Pict's Knowe between this time and the beginning of lpaz PKBc at c. 800 cal. AD. For a short time, perhaps one generation, *Salix* pollen was produced, and this is interpreted as an adventitious local response to woodland removal by a shrub previously outcompeted. If correct this would support the contention that this woodland was cleared from the ditch, given the very limited pollen dispersal of *Salix*. Scrub clearance at the ditch may have led to sharply reduced pollen influx to the peat, seen in lower pollen concentrations, and probably led to increasingly wet conditions in the ditch, seen in the deposition of a more poorly decayed peat. The lower and upper sediment boundaries of this less humified peat (40.0 and 27.0cm; Fig. 3.1) are undated, and because peat accumulation may have been accelerated in this phase, lpaz PKBb may span a shorter time than the c. 250 years suggested by the available ^{14}C dates. Wetter conditions are not supported by increasing proportions of corroded pollen (unpublished data), which represent pollen decayed under aerobic conditions (Havinga 1984), but this is more a reflection of the increasing abundance of highly susceptible Cyperaceae (sedge) pollen. Sedge growth was probably a response to both higher water tables in the ditch and the removal of trees, as was the occurrence or increased representation of herbs like *Galium* type (bedstraws), *Pinguicula* (butterworts) and *Primula* (primroses), and probably of *Saxifraga stellaris* (starry saxifrage), rare in lowland contexts and in this abundance (Fig. 3.1).

Woodland clearance was, in its abruptness, almost certainly human in origin. The reasons are not immediately apparent. Woodland may have been removed to satisfy local demands for wood rather than to increase land accessible to stock. Increases in indicator taxa are obscured by the expansion of Cyperaceae, but there is a gradual increase in proportions of grasses (Gramineae). The equally gradual decline in *Calluna* may represent a sustained intensification in grazing pressures, although this is not clear because *Plantago lanceolata*, a key grazing indicator, declines and was temporarily lost. As at many sites, a reduction in the abundance of microscopic charcoal accompanies losses in *Calluna*, and reductions in heath may have led to reductions in fire frequency or intensity.

By around 800 cal. AD (lpaz PKBc) local tree growth had resumed. A strikingly similar mosaic of plant communities to that seen in lpaz PKBa returned, and it is

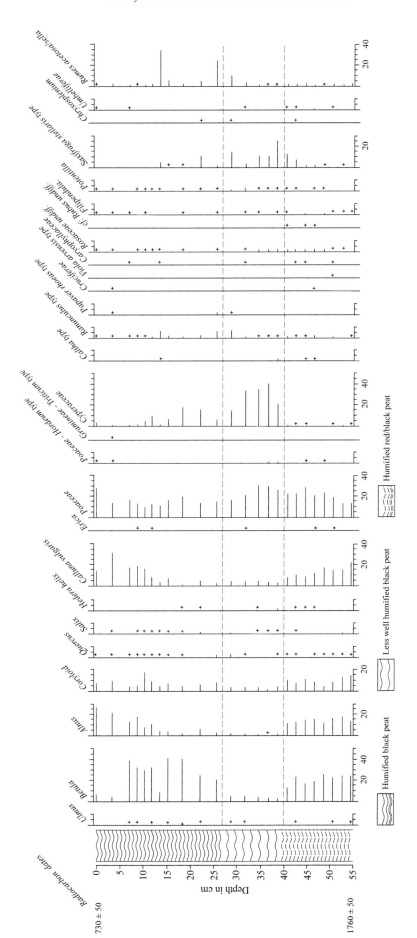

Fig. 3.1 ^{14}C dating controls, sediment stratigraphy and pollen taxa occurring more than once, calculated as percentages and plotted against depth below the sand of Context 0697 at the Pict's Knowe B and divided into local pollen assemblage zones. Also depicted are proportions of microscopic charcoal and total land pollen concentrations.

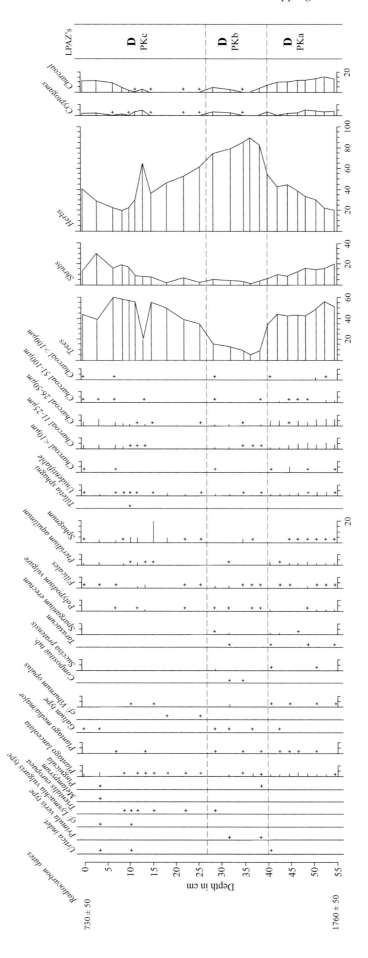

Fig. 3.1 continued.

assumed that the spatial patterning was also comparable. *Betula* (birch) was reestablished very rapidly, and in the sustained losses of Cyperaceae pollen it is assumed to have recolonised at least the ditch peats. Later, after c. 1100 cal. AD, birch was seemingly invaded in a more mixed scrub by *Alnus* (alder) and *Corylus/Myrica* (bog myrtle?): *Salix* (willow) was a consistently recorded and quite abundant shrub.

Few other indicators suggest anything other than a restoration of woodland specific to the site itself. The expansion at around 1100 cal. AD of *Calluna* (ling heather) communities including other heathers (Ericaceae undiff.), *Trientalis* (chickweed wintergreen) and *Melampyrum* (cow wheat), probably represents the colonisation as a dry heath of the sandy terrace soils once more, replacing in part the grassland and resulting in a decline in grazing quality. The reestablishment of *Calluna* and of a mixed scrubby woodland, rather than the former monodominant birch wood, may reflect a relaxation of grazing pressure and concern for woodland management.

However, in a final significant shift at around 1250 cal. AD, not defined in the pollen zonation because it spans only the uppermost two spectra, human impact on the scrub woodland was renewed by the complete removal of one taxon, *Betula* (birch). No other tree need have been affected, and the selectivity of clearance is a very strong indication of purposeful woodland utilisation. Perhaps less than a century later, part of the interior of the former henge was levelled as the sandy soils were pushed into the ditch on this side. This activity may be associated with modest but secure evidence for cereal cultivation, in the appearance of one pollen grain of *Avena-Triticum* (oats or wheat; Fig. 3.1), though whether the henge interior itself was ploughed is uncertain.

Discussion

The pollen analyses spanning the early to mid historic period at the Pict's Knowe depict activities that are highly site specific. They relate only to a small area in and around the archaeological site, and for this reason no attempt is made here to fit the land use changes to regional economic or political patterns. The pollen record is complex in that, spatially, a mosaic of different plant communities can be reconstructed. Such patchwork landscapes are emerging as characteristic both of pollen analyses which depict small scale variability, and of later prehistoric and historic settings (Tipping 1999).

The major reason for this heterogeneity is human activity, of course, and in particular the compartmentalisation of land uses. The division of the landscape into fenced or hedged compartments may be a later prehistoric trend (Fowler 1983; Dark & Dark 1997), and can be suggested from our analyses from at least the late Iron Age at the Pict's Knowe. The same patterns are not readily discernible at the Pict's Knowe in the early Bronze Age (Tipping *et al.* Chapter 2). We have no palynological

evidence for hedges at the Pict's Knowe (cf. Boyd 1984) although brambles and some shrub roses can be associated with these. Rather, we can discern these divisions because different land uses depicted from the pollen analyses appear to develop through time unrelated to each other.

There is evidence for two types of land use near the site from Romano-British times until the high Medieval period. The first is pastoral farming, and if interpretation of the balance between grasses and *Calluna* is correct (cf. Tipping 2000), then we can identify different grazing intensities over time, relaxed before the Anglo-Saxon period and again after c. 1100 cal. AD, but intense during the Anglo-Scandinavian (Higham 1986) phase. Such suggestions, however, assume that the mix of grazing animals, their habits and grazing efficiencies remained the same, which may not be reasonable.

This activity, though fluctuating in intensity, was at times seemingly independent of the second land use, woodland management. This is difficult to establish because there is an interdependency in pollen data, but as an example, reestablishment of birch trees in the 9th century AD occurred against a 'background' of sustained grazing pressures. Tree regeneration is best seen to have taken place protected from grazing animals, either within fences or hedges, implying some form of management. Careful manipulation of the woodland resource is also suggested by the selectivity with which certain types of wood (birch) were both established (planted?) and subsequently removed. It is probable that the woodland was managed as a resource independent of farmland, and for its own value. We have no direct evidence from our data for sustainable technologies like coppicing (Boyd 1988; Tipping 1997) though the trees grown (alder, birch) are readily coppiced.

Until c. 550 cal. AD the local birch and alder woodland may have been managed. The species composition is not that of natural woodland. Woodland management would accord with the abundant evidence for woodworking (Crone, Sands and Skinner, Chapter 6), and for metalworking (Heald and Hunter, Chapter 17), although there is a stratigraphic and temporal separation in these lines of evidence: the majority of the wood and metal objects are from below and earlier than the peat analysed here. Our analyses are also not contemporary with the ard, and the significance of this object for the local economy cannot be evaluated from our data. Some aspects of the inferred woodland structure suggest, however, that by the later 3rd century AD when our analyses commence, the wood was not well managed, with brambles, currants, roses and ivy possibly hindering access. The wood may have become overgrown and mismanaged after the industrial activities seen in the 1st and 2nd centuries AD. There is a sense of neglect until the 6th century AD, when the entire local woodland was abruptly cleared. At this time pastoral activities also intensified.

Later phases of woodland use suggest an invigorated local economy. In the 9th century AD the reestablishment of birch, and only birch, is seen as purposeful. Around 450 years later, after several generations, birch was then selectively clear-felled. For some 300 years only birch had been encouraged to grow locally, but eventually other trees were allowed to recolonise. The trees were still tended: there is no indication of the copse being overgrown, and alder was left when birch trees were drawn. Cereals were cultivated somewhere near, though not necessarily on the terrace surface, and at the site someone toppled sand from the interior into the ditch. These are small scale instances but indicative of economic vibrancy.

4

Fieldwork at the Pict's Knowe, 1994–7

Julian Thomas

with contributions by Maggie Ronayne, Matt Leivers and Chris Fowler

Introduction

The excavations at the Pict's Knowe took place over four seasons from 1994 to 1997. During the first season a detailed contour survey of the henge and its environs was carried out (Fig. 4.1), along with a pre-excavation survey of damage to the monument (Fig. 4.2). Excavations were then undertaken in the interior of the site, through the ditch and bank to the west, and over the north ditch terminal (Fig. 4.3).

During the second season a geophysical survey of the valley floor was undertaken (see Clark, Chapter 5 below); five ditch cuttings, Trenches A to E, were opened; together with a further cutting, Trench F, which was excavated outside the entrance.

Excavations in 1996 concentrated on the bank with a large area – Trench G – opened on the badly damaged south side of the monument. A cutting was also opened on the bank at the entrance, Trench H. Two cuttings, Trenches J and K, investigated the geophysical anomalies discovered outside the henge. In 1997 further, minor, excavations were carried out in an extension to Trench G (see Fig. 4.4 for location of trenches).

On-site recording was conducted using a modified form of the single context system (Museum of London 1980; Macleod, Monk and Williams 1988). Each distinct episode in the stratigraphic history of the site (cuts, fills, layers) was given a separate context number, and each context had a separate context sheet. As well as descriptive information, these sheets recorded the principal stratigraphic relationships between contexts, enabling the construction of a stratigraphic matrix (Harris 1979). This system has the virtue that individual excavators can undertake the recording of the features which they themselves work on, and this has an undoubted pedagogical value in a project which involves student labour. However, the concomitant disadvantage of single context recording is that it tends to atomise the elements of a site, and to privilege direct stratigraphic relations over

relationships of significance and sense (see Lucas 2001). For this reason, each supervisor (including the director) kept a site notebook throughout the excavation, while the majority of plans were executed on a multi-context basis. This latter policy accepts, as a philosophical point, that all recording is to some degree interpretive, and that interpretation does not begin at the post-excavation stage. All small finds were individually recorded in three dimensions using electronic distance measurement, and all of the finds of wooden objects in the ditch were planned. Sieving was conducted selectively rather than systematically, but large areas of the interior and ditch deposits were screened using a double-box swing sieve. Context sheets, site notebooks, field drawings and levels books, as well as lists of finds, context numbers, photographs and drawings now form the principal site archive.

The contour survey

Prior to excavation, a detailed survey of the earthwork enclosure was completed, using electronic distance measurement apparatus. This was later extended to provide a survey of a large segment of the valley bottom (Fig. 4.5). The morphology of the Pict's Knowe is largely characteristic of Class I henges, with a single entrance to the east and a bank external to a ditch with expanded terminals (Atkinson 1951, 82). However, the precise size of the enclosure, and its slightly 'flattened' aspect when viewed in plan can be attributed to the constraints imposed by the small sandy knoll on which it was constructed. For this reason it is best not to consider the structure as an exercise in abstract design, but as a modification of a very particular topography. The survey demonstrated that the domed interior of the site, which appeared to be rather higher than the surrounding landscape, was probably not an artificial mound or barrow, as had originally been conjectured. Once again, this was a consequence of the presence of the natural ridge of sand in the valley bottom.

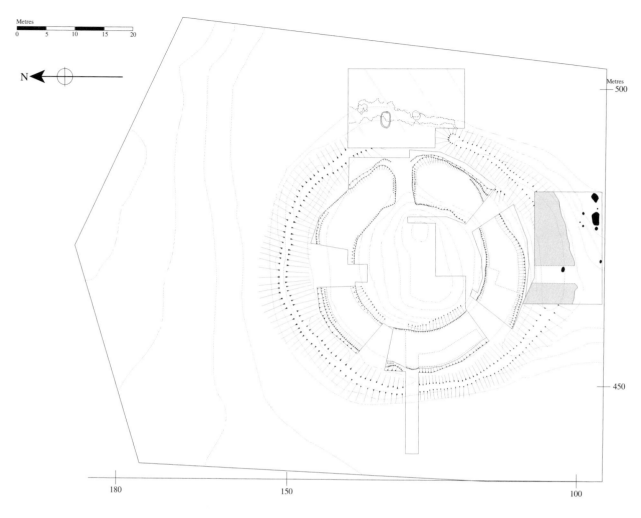

Fig. 4.1 Contour survey of the Pict's Knowe. Contours at 20cm intervals.

The damage survey

The survey of rabbit and cattle impact on the henge recorded all rabbit holes, places where the turf cover had been broken, and patches where subsoil had been exposed (Fig. 4.2). From this it was clear that rabbit burrow entrances occurred across the surface of the monument's interior and the external bank. Broadly speaking, any part of the monument in which the sand had not been cloaked by peat had received the attention of the rabbits. The interior was virtually devoid of turf, while the inner side of the bank was similarly denuded. Both terminals of the ditch contained standing water, and much of the ditch circuit was at least seasonally wet (see Plate 4.1). In consequence, cattle had been using the ditches as watering places, churning the soil as well as abrading the turf. The full extent of this damage to the ditch deposits did not become apparent until sections had been cut, revealing eroded and truncated layers capped with thick deposits of cattle dung.

The excavations

The interior

An initial decision was made to excavate the interior of the henge using the quadrant method. This was because it was at first considered possible that the interior consisted of an artificial burial mound or barrow, which would need to be recorded in section as well as plan. The dark brown humic topsoil (context 0001) proved to be exceptionally shallow, giving way to a very mixed, mottled loose sandy layer (0002). After each trowelling, it was possible to distinguish a complex pattern of rabbit runs, intersecting and running through what might have been the remaining traces of a subsoil surface. The trowelling was brought to a halt at the point where deposits of mottled peaty material (0004) lapping up out of the ditch were recognised in the western half of the site. These were removed to reveal the protected surface of the weathering cone of the ditch (cut 0019), where the

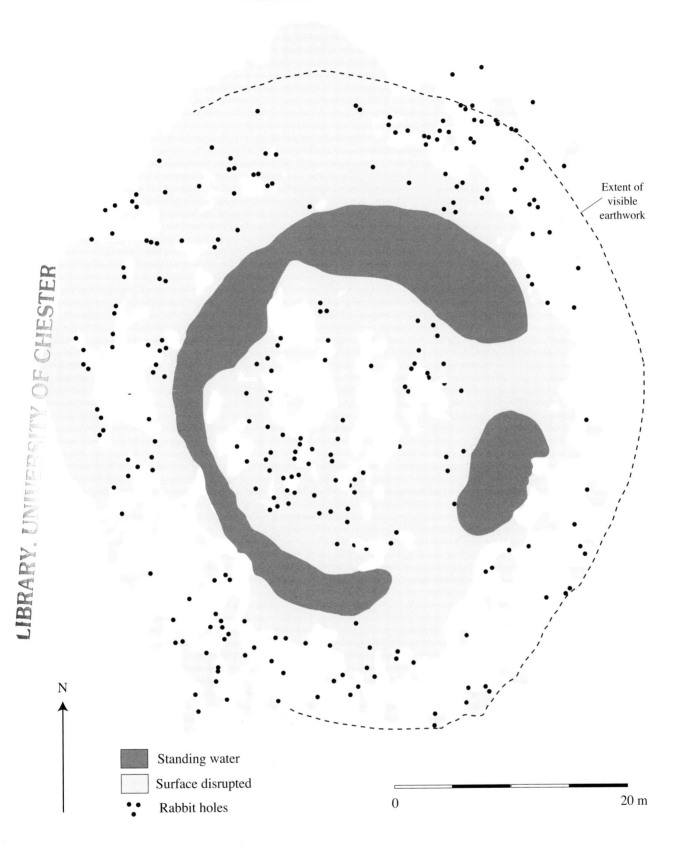

Fig. 4.2 The Pict's Knowe: damage survey.

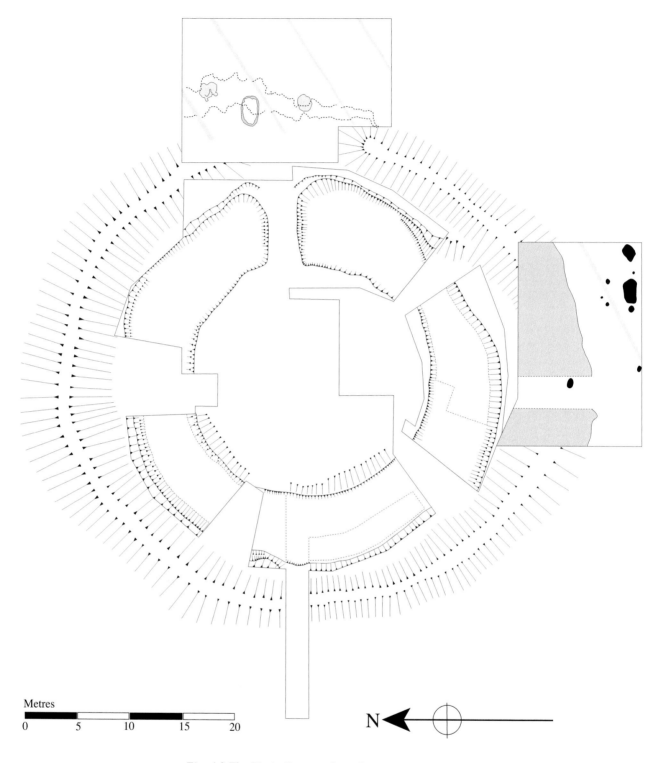

Metres

0   5   10   15   20

N

Fig. 4.3 The Pict's Knowe: plan of excavations, 1994–7.

subsoil material was rather harder, constituting some-thing akin to a degraded sandstone. The interior was then trowelled down to an arbitrary level, planned again, and allowed to weather. By this point approximately 1.4 m of overburden had been removed, and the standing sections showed that this material was virtually homogenous, mixed by rabbit activity (see Colour Plate 1). It seems

likely that any internal features had been completely destroyed by this agency. A potential feature which was identified after the surface had weathered for some days seemed to represent a tree throw, and indeed a group of trees had stood on the site in the inter-war years (A. Truckell, pers. comm.). One very shallow scoop (0015), which may have represented no more than an undulation

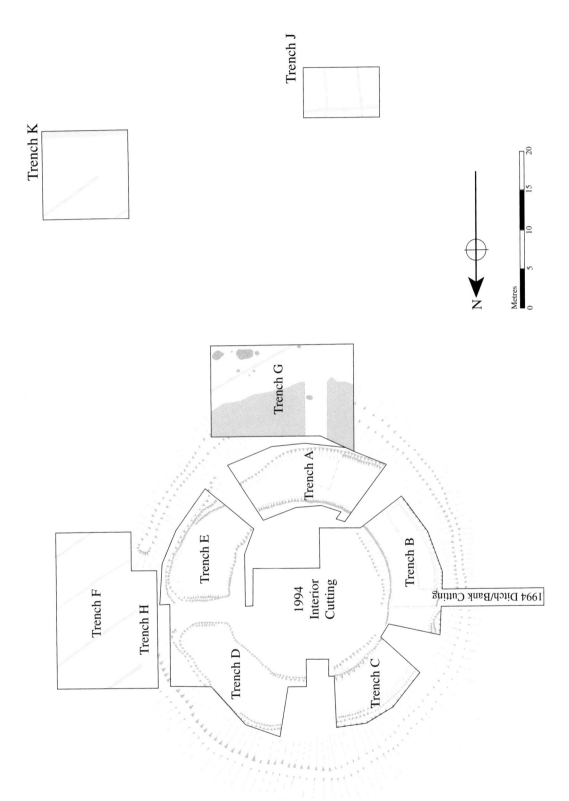

Fig. 4.4 The Pict's Knowe: layout of trenches on the monument.

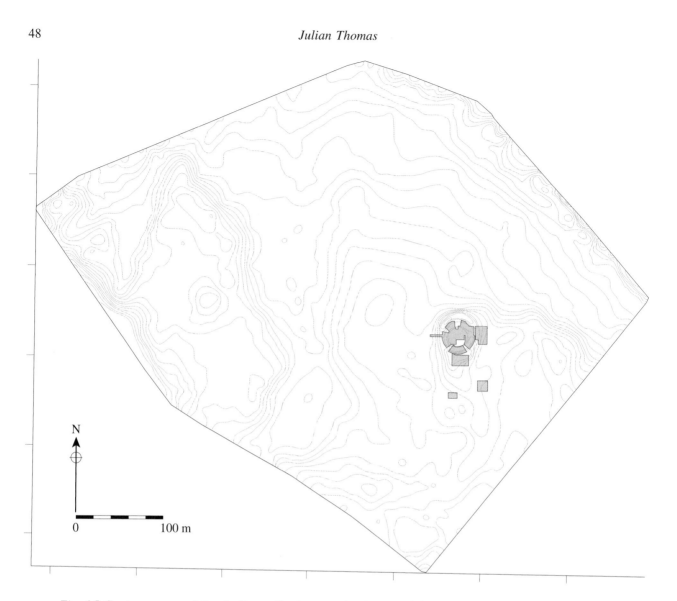

Fig. 4.5 Contour survey of Crooks Pow valley bottom, showing trench locations. Contours at 20cm intervals.

of the surface, was found within the ditch weathering cone in the south-west quadrant. This contained a fragment of pig jaw (FN 27). Other finds from the mixed sandy material included flint and chert blades and a large rim sherd of undecorated earlier Neolithic pottery (FN 44, Vessel 1: Fig. 15.1). This latter was probably associated with the pre-bank occupation identified in Trench G (see below).

Given that any cut features in the interior had been removed by rabbit action, it was suggested that finds from such features might now be distributed in the overburden. Consequently, a sampling exercise was undertaken in which a portion of the material in the remaining quadrant was removed in metre squares, and 50% of these squares totally screened using a swing-sieve. The results of this process were instructive. A concentration of highly abraded sherds of prehistoric pottery (Vessel 4) was found toward the centre of the monument (see Fig. 14.2), while sherds of a probable Collared Urn (Vessel 5) and some small fragments of cremated bone were found nearer to the entrance (see Fig. 14.3). This might suggest a focus of activity in the centre of the site, and a secondary cremation near the entrance causeway. However, the very fragmentary remains of the cremated bone were probably animal rather than human (John Robb pers. comm.).

The bank

The bank was sampled in three places: at the entrance (both in 1994 and in 1996 Trench H), in the western ditch cutting, and in Trench G (see below). In the former, the bank had been preserved by a shallow build-up of peat, and excavation in plan demonstrated the presence of a series of distinct layers (0377, 0391, 0454). These were all composed of soft silty sand, and there was little indication at this point that they represented anything other than different lenses within a unitary dump construction (Plate 4.2). In the western cutting (Fig. 4.6) the bank had been heavily disturbed and homogenised by rabbit activity (0023). However, on the top of the bank at this point there was a distinct capping or crust of fine,

Plate 4.1 (above) The Pict's Knowe before excavation, showing standing water in the ditch and damage to the surface.

Plate 4.2 Section through the bank, 1994 season.

silvery silty sand (0120). Here, as at other points around the circuit of the enclosure, a great many stakeholes could be detected penetrating the bank capping.

Of particular significance was the existence of a layer of tenacious black peat (0063) sealed beneath the bank in the western cutting, truncated by the cut of the ditch. Given that further peats existed within the ditch, this indicated that a number of separate phases of peat formation had taken place in the vicinity of the monument. Beneath this peat was a leached sand surface (0059), which contained no archaeological features in the western cutting. Both peat and sandy surface were also present in Trench G (Plate 4.3).

Trench G
by Maggie Ronayne and Julian Thomas

This cutting was opened in 1996, immediately to the south of Trench A (Fig. 4.7). A great deal of disturbance from roots, tree-throw, animal burrows and modern animal burials meant that the bank itself was in a very bad condition. However, enough of the bank deposits remained to establish the following sequence. A whitish leached sand (2404, equivalent to 0059) formed the pre-bank surface over the whole of the trench. This surface was sealed by a black peat, (2403, equivalent to 0063), outside the monument and also under its bank, thus pre-dating it. Above the black peat was an orange sand (3883),

Julian Thomas

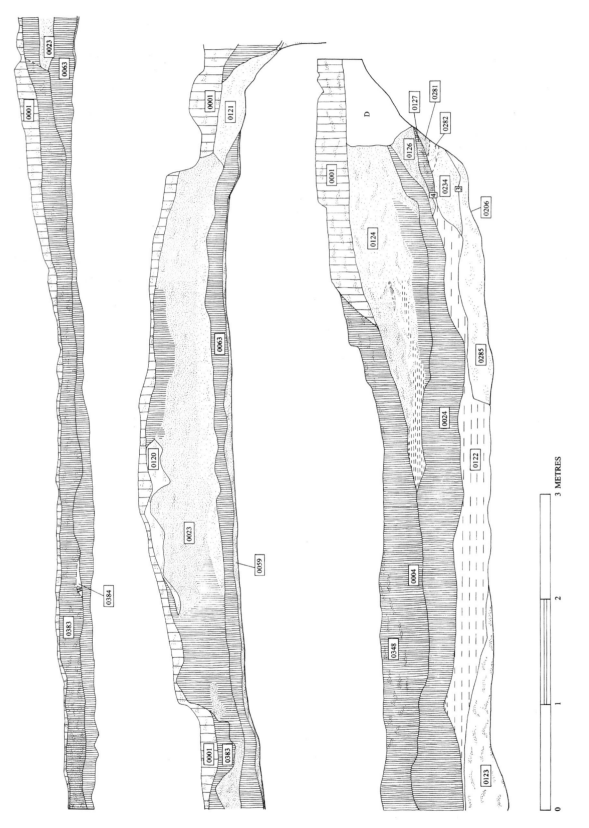

Fig. 4.6 Western bank and ditch cutting: section, south-facing.

Plate 4.3 Trench G bank section.

which formed the principal structural deposit of the bank, equivalent to 0023. Overlying the orange sand was a moist dark deposit with frequent inclusions of burnt material, identified at the time as slag, but which was more probably cinder produced by hearth fires, and which had no particular chronological significance (3882). This appeared to underlie the bank capping by a few centimetres, although this was quite possibly the result of a later slippage of those sediments. The capping material (2407, equivalent to 0120), was a leached grey/white sand deposit badly truncated by the disturbance mentioned above. Partially overlying the bank deposits and the earlier peats outside the monument was a grey sandy layer (2402), sealed by a dark peat (2401). This grey sandy layer may have been the remnant of an old soil horizon and it contained large quantities of post-medieval and modern potsherds, glass, and iron implements.

A land-drain (2405/2406) running from the north-east to the south-west across the old land surface was excavated, as were a great many stake-holes of varying depths, diameters and fills. One stake-hole (4292/4293) cut the land-drain, indicating that some of the stake-holes may have been modern. A number of the stake-holes had been disturbed by animal burrowing, making a judgement on their anthropogenic origin more difficult to achieve. Some others appeared to have peat at the tops of their fills, while several more had pieces of cinder in the fill. This evidence could suggest that the stake-holes were not all of one period, although the cinder was evidently not chronologically diagnostic. However, the earlier peat was patchy, and did not cover the whole of the white leached

sand (2404). It therefore cannot be said to have sealed all of the stake-holes and other features on this surface. It may have been eroded in the past, it might not have formed uniformly, or it may have been deliberately cut back to allow some activity to take place.

Trench G was eventually divided into two parts by a north-south running section, and the two parts worked at different rates in order to facilitate the cuttings through the bank without allowing the investigation of the bank surface and the area outside the monument to be compromised.

The eastern area

Throughout the whole of Trench G, stake-holes were very numerous (see Fig. 4.7), and appeared to be spread fairly uniformly over the trench, apart from in a slightly raised area just south of the base of the bank in the middle of the eastern area, where they thinned out considerably. The stake-holes continued up the sides and along the top of the bank, although not in such great quantities as on the old ground surface. Although tracing patterning in the stake holes was an highly speculative exercise, it did seem that there was a line of stake-holes following the base of the bank, at the edge of context 3880, and another line of stake-holes following the lower edge of the capping material (2407), on the slope of the bank. This appeared particularly convincing towards the eastern baulk. This potential patterning became less clear as new groups of stake-holes were revealed with each successive trowelling of the area. There was a thin scattering of stake-holes along the top of the bank in the capping material,

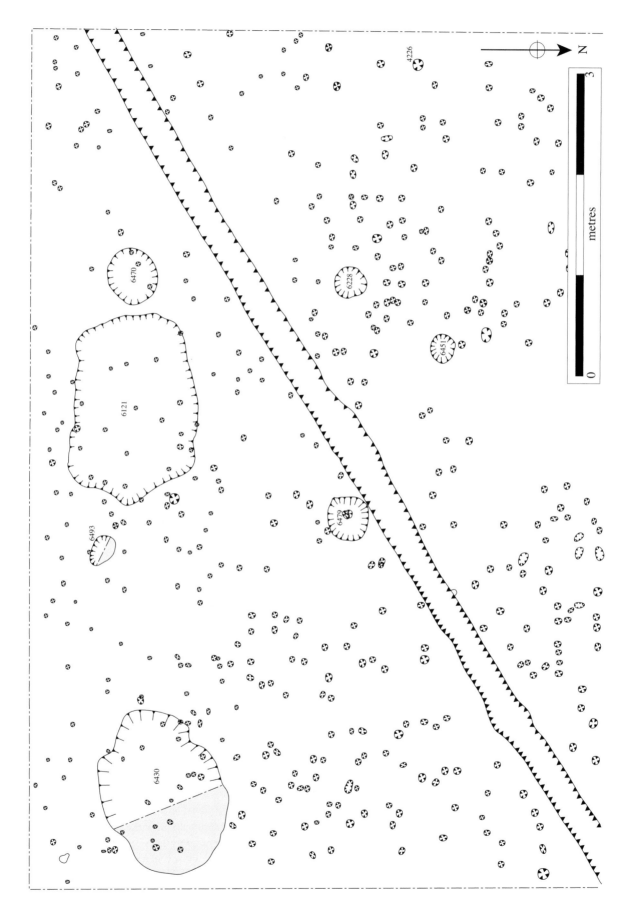

Fig. 4.7 Trench G: plan of south-east area.

although some of these were severely truncated, and their existence was in some cases questionable. Very few stake-holes could be seen in the orange/brown material (3883) on the top of the bank, possibly as a result of the various disturbances which had removed the overlying capping material, and which may have contained the entire depth of the stake-holes if they existed.

The majority of the stake-hole fills showed up as a dark grey peaty material, although some of the fills were a peaty brown, or as white as the old land surface (2404), distinguished only by a thin brown line around the edges of the fills. Those putative stake-holes which had a very black fill generally turned out to be animal burrows, diving off under the old land surface when excavated. The fills of some of the stake-holes in this portion of Trench G, especially towards the southern edge of the trench, occasionally contained modern pieces of glass, nineteenth or twentieth century pottery, or fragments of cinder. Some of the stake-holes in the southern portion of this trench apparently contained charred seed grains. The depth of stake-holes varied greatly, with deeper examples appearing to be concentrated in the south-east corner of the trench.

Initially no other features apart from stake-holes were identified in the white sandy material that comprised the old land surface (2404). On its surface, this layer contained a mixture of the occasional piece of modern material such as glass or pottery, as well as chips of flint and chert. The colour of the old land surface became increasingly darker towards the southern trench boundary, with darker patches in the south-east corner, and adjacent to the southern edge. This suggests that the subsoil surface took on its distinctive white colouration in precisely those areas where the earlier (pre-bank) peat was preserved.

One patch of darker material close to the southern edge of the trench did appear to have a firm edge cut into the old land surface. This feature (6121) seemed to be a large oval pit with straight, steeply sloping sides around the southern, northern and eastern edges. The western edge was much less clear, as it merged with an adjacent, shallow feature (6470). The top fill of 6121, (6120) was soft, dark and humic, and contained flecks of charcoal. This fill contained prehistoric pottery (Vessel 16, FN 2436, 2438, 2441, 2446, 2448, 2594, 2601) and worked chert (FN 2444). The fill below this (6270) contained a (possibly worked) fragment of shale (FN 2454), prehistoric pottery (Vessels 14 and 16; FN 2461, 2616, 2641) and a piece of cinder (FN 2639). This layer also produced a radiocarbon determination of 3790 – 3650 Cal. BC at the 95.4 % confidence level (SUERC-2093). The quantity of finds decreased with depth into the pit, with the lower layer, 6416 being a compact, dark reddish coloured mineral soil, containing no humus or charcoal, with only the occasional sieve find. The feature on the west side of the oval pit (6470) was not as clearly defined in its edges. It too showed up as a darker patch in the old ground

surface, possibly because it formed a collection point for moisture in the ground. Flecks of charcoal were found in the upper fill (6471) of the post-hole/pit, in addition to fragments of prehistoric pottery (Vessel 16). This fill gave a radiocarbon date of 3790–3650 Cal. BC at the 95.4 % confidence level (SUERC-2094). The lower fill (6485) also contained flecks of charcoal. It was not clear from the section which of these features, large oval pit (6121) or post-hole (6470), was the earliest. A further possible post-hole (6493) was found to the east of the large oval pit. The edges of this feature were far from clear. Like 6470, it first appeared as a slightly darker patch in the old ground surface, containing prehistoric pottery (Vessels 14 and 16), flakes of charcoal, and in this case burnt clay, in the upper part of the fill. It was unclear whether this feature was simply a variation in the colour of the old ground surface and containing finds typical of 2404 in general, or had definite cut edges carrying on into the material beneath the old ground surface.

A few metres to the north of these three features was a further collection of three post-holes/pits, this time with more clearly defined edges and fills (Plate 4.4). Two of these post-holes, 6228 and 6451, showed up as concentrations of charcoal flecks in the old surface although the actual edges of the features were very unclear on the surface. After trowelling through the charcoal flecked surface, the top fill (6229) of the post-hole 6228 appeared. This sealed the main fill (6230) which contained charcoal and a flint borer (FN 2456). Pit 6451 likewise had a thin upper fill (6452) covering the main dark-coloured fill (6453), and covered by material closely resembling the old land surface (2404). However, this feature did not contain any finds or charcoal. Both pits had steeply sloping straight sides, and were c. 0.4 m deep. It also seemed possible that both pits were surrounded by arc arrangements of stake-holes. The third post-hole/small pit in this area (6479) was shallower at 0.25 m. The dark fill (6480) contained a large fragment of prehistoric pottery (Vessel 14), and was cut by a stake-hole (6616) in its centre.

The other dark patch was in the south-east corner of the trench. At first sight, this feature (6430) looked as if it might be another large oval pit, but attempts to find a definite edge proved impossible other than on the south side, and it was concluded that the feature might represent a tree-throw hollow. However, large quantities of prehistoric pottery fragments (Vessel 16) were found in the upper levels of the fill of this feature (6431). It remains unclear as to whether or not this dark patch was the darker material (6486) beneath the old land surface (2404) showing through where the whiter material on top thinned out. The browner material removed as fill (6341) quickly came down onto extremely hard, compact, natural looking mineral soil with no evidence of artefacts or charcoal inclusions.

The removal of the old land surface over the entire trench showed that it was thinnest towards the southern

Plate 4.4 Early Neolithic features in the south-east corner of Trench G under excavation.

end of the trench. Towards the base of this layer, numerous finds of prehistoric pottery fragments (Vessels 14 and 16), flint, stone and chert chips, and flakes and the occasional flint/chert tools or blades were found (Fig. 4.8). Although digging ceased at this point, it was clear that further artefacts could be expected in the browner material (6486), which was beneath the old land surface, as large fragments of prehistoric pottery (Vessels 14 and 16) were wedged firmly in this layer in the section provided by the modern field drain. This was also suggested by the recovery of large numbers of fragments of prehistoric pottery (Vessels 14 and 16) in the browner material at the southern end of the trench. The mineral subsoil was not reached at any part of this trench, apart from in the sides and base of the large oval pit at the southern edge of the trench, and the hollow at the southeastern corner of the trench. This suggests that the old land surface and the browner material (6486) represented an ancient soil formation that had been protected by the bank and the peat layers, but which might not have survived in areas more remote from the monument.

The western area

On the western side of the running section a series of stake-holes were excavated along the bank capping (2407) on top and along the slopes of the bank material (3883). These did not appear to form as continuous a line as those excavated on the eastern side of the cutting. Stake-holes excavated at the base of the bank in the old land surface (2404) appeared to respect its edge and run in a line although they may be a part of a larger group found under

the bank in this area. In general, the number of stake-holes cut into the old land surface was not quite as great as that of the eastern side of the cutting.

Two darker areas with stake-holes cut into their fills, near the southern and eastern baulks, were also investigated. Although they appeared initially to be pits, with one fill (6469) producing earlier prehistoric pottery (Vessels 14 and 16) at the top, they had no clear edges and are more likely to be areas of puddling or the result of tree-throw. The fills may be taken to be disturbed versions of 6486, the layer under the land surface.

A three-metre section was taken through the bank on this side of the cutting (Fig. 4.10; Plate 4.5). The bank appeared quite homogenous in structure with the leached capping (2407) on top of a layer of sterile redeposited sand (3883), which seems to have been heaped up from the ditch. The capping was quite similar to the land surface (2404) and may have been a redeposited version of this, or material removed from the recutting of the ditch. Its leaching had caused variable effects in the bank material under it, with part of the redeposited sand appearing very iron-rich and compacted, and part remaining as softer yellow sand. In section the leached capping (2407) did appear to sit in a 'cut' into the bank material which might, with other evidence such as the position of the dark material with cinder (3882), lead to the conclusion that the leached capping was a later phase of bank construction than the redeposited sand (3883).

The bank had been built directly on top of the black peat (2403) with no intervening soil horizon. This would ostensibly suggest that no great duration of time separated

○	I vessel 14	●	IV vessel 6
★	XIV vessel 16	✩	XI vessel 13
◓	I vessel 2	⬡	I vessesl 1

0   4 metres

Fig. 4.8 Trench G: distribution of pottery sherds.

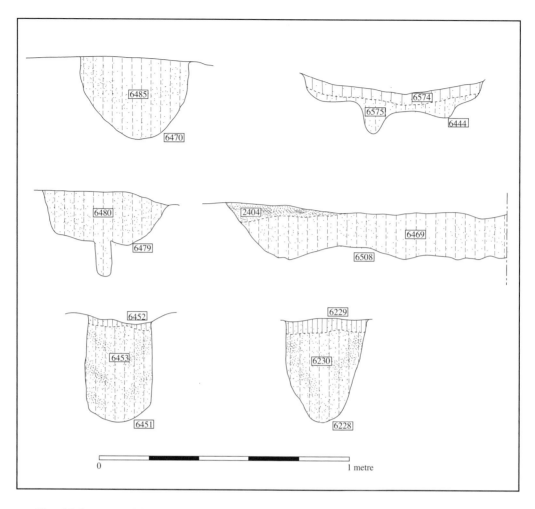

Fig. 4.9 Sections of features in Trench G, features 6740, 6444, 6479, 6508, 6451 and 6228.

the formation of the peat and the construction of bank and ditch. The peat overlay the old land surface (2404) as it did outside the monument. On its surface there were a number of areas of cinder concentration and a few pieces of worked flint; stake-holes were cut into it at the southern end of the section, with a single one at the northern end.

Beneath the old land surface was an undulating yellow-brown sand (6486), firmer than the old land surface, with charcoal flecking in places, this appeared to constitute a separate surface. Towards the interface between the old land surface and the yellow-brown sand (6486) and embedded in 6486 were concentrations of sherds (Vessels 14 and 16), flint and chert flakes, blades, debitage and retouched pieces. These concentrations were more frequent on the eastern side of the cutting and petered out towards the west. There was one particular concentration of such material, including worked quartz at the southern end of the section through the bank. This seemed to surround a small, roughly circular pit (6725/6724) which contained much charcoal, potsherds and worked stone. While the spread of pottery in the rest of the trench could be assigned to two fabric groups, and perhaps to as few as

two vessels, the sherds from the pit seemed to have been selected from the upper part of a number of carinated bowls (Vessels 1, 2, 11, 12, 13, 14, 15, 16) (see Fig. 4.8). 6725 produced two radiocarbon dates, 3770–3630 Cal. BC (SUERC-2095) and 3720–3630 Cal. BC (SUERC-2096) (at 95.4 % confidence level). These are remarkably consistent with the carbon dates contexts 6270 and 6471 in the two cut features further south in the cutting, and discussed above. Together, they suggest that the Earlier Neolithic activity on the site need not have been of long duration.

A number of stake-holes, many with dark fills, showed up in the yellow-brown sand (6486) but had not been visible in the old land surface (2404). The onset of peat formation, which provides a terminus post quem for the construction of the monument, would therefore seem to be dated to a time later than the earlier Neolithic, when pit 6724 was probably dug and the surrounding materials deposited. Radiocarbon determinations from the lower and upper surfaces of this peat gave dates of 2452–1900 Cal. BC (AA-21249) and 2454–2030 Cal. BC (AA-21250) respectively.

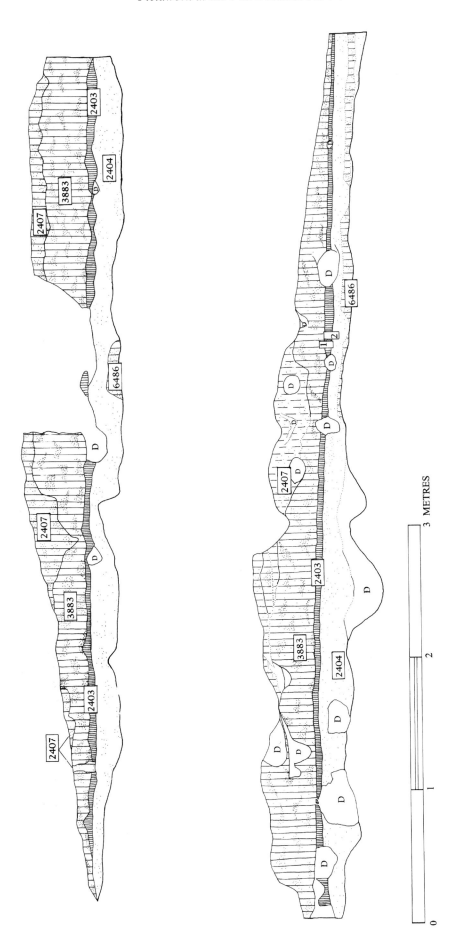

Fig. 4.10 Sections of the bank in trench G. Top: east-facing; bottom: west-facing.

Plate 4.5 (above) The bank cutting in Trench G, showing the surface below the pre-bank peat.

The ditches

Trench A

Trench A was a large cutting through the ditch on the southern side of the enclosure, excavated in 1995 (Fig. 4.3; Plate 4.6). Of all the work carried out in the ditch, this trench demonstrated most effectively how complex and varied were the processes of cutting and deposition involved in its history. The ditch (cut 2338) was broad and relatively shallow in profile (Fig. 4.11; Colour Plate 3). The primary silts which had filled this cut were extremely variable within themselves, and to some extent represented localised patches of deposit drawn from slightly different parent materials. Loose silty sands such as context 2374 were inter-mixed with friable sands like 2340 and 2375. Toward the west of the cutting, two quite distinct layers of very hard, compacted material (2337 and 2339) suggested brief episodes of radical change in the depositional regime. These were quite unlike the primary fills elsewhere on the site, except for the panning at the bottom of the ditch in Trench E (see below, 74–77), although it might be argued that they nonetheless resulted from damp conditions. On the west side of the cutting a series of friable sands and silty sands formed the primary deposits (2373, 2372, 2371, 2370). At the top of this sequence of silts and sands, a dark yellowish-brown silty sand (2089) appeared to represent a stabilisation horizon (not visible on Fig. 4.11). This layer was equivalent to 1901 on the south-western side of the recut. Within the

Plate 4.6 Trench A, with the ditch recut in the process of being removed.

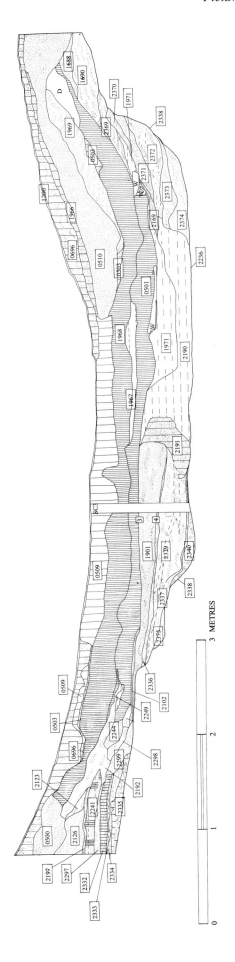

Fig. 4.11 Ditch section in Trench A, east-facing.

3 METRES

whole of this formation of primary deposits cultural material was extremely scarce, amounting to a very few worked flints and sherds of earlier prehistoric pottery.

At some time after the stabilisation of the primary fills, the ditch appears to have been recut (cut 2236). Within Trench A, the character of this recutting was quite different from that which had been observed in the extreme west of the enclosure and the north ditch terminal in 1994 (Fig. 4.12). In both of those locations, the recut was a broad, steep-sided feature which had removed the greater bulk of the original ditch fill. Yet in Trench A the recut was more irregular and slot-like. While both of the 1994 recuts had been filled with a relatively homogenous greenish-grey silty clay, which contained at most some thin runs of sandy material, in Trench A the filling was considerably more complex. Here, the green clay (1971) was a relatively late component of a series of fills. The earliest fill in the recut was a soft yellow/brown mottled sandy clay (2245; not visible in section). Other clays (2190 and 2130) then formed simultaneously with material slumping from the edges of the recut (2191). At the top of the slump material at the westerly end of Trench A was a thick deposit of extremely compact mottled sandy silt (2129/2169). In contrast to the layers of compaction in the primary silts, this may have gained its character from trampling rather than natural chemical processes. If so, it is possible that the sandy silt (2129) represented a deliberate deposit laid down in order to cover up the primary filling of the recut. A number of stake-holes cut through this compact layer, some seemingly cut directly into it, while others may have been dug from a slightly later horizon. The green clay (1971) lay above this, and it was only here that appreciable numbers of wood fragments were found. These included unworked roundwood (FN 624, FN 639); a possible offcut (FN 642); an irregular piece (FN 664); woodchips (FN 728, FN 730, FN 768a and b); and withies (FN 772). Generally, though, the density of worked wood was not as great as in some of the other ditch cuttings.

As elsewhere on the site, a red organic peat (0501) lay above the recut deposits. In areas of the ditch that had not been recut, this rested immediately on the stabilisation horizon (1901), or on a sandy slip from the interior (2102). Toward the bottom of the peat, a tangle of roots and wood lay in the western most part of the trench, which can be assumed to have been contiguous with the more extensive spread of wood in Trench B (Figs. 4.13 and 4.14).

Above the red peat lay a clean clay lens (1967), and a sequence of sandy silts (2369, 1690 and 1688), the latter probably derived from the interior of the site. Above these layers the black peat in the ditch (1968 and 1689) was overlain by a considerable body of sandy material which had slipped from the interior (0503, 0510 and 1969) and another mass of slip from the bank (0500). This latter contained artefacts of post-mediaeval date, although it was only one of a series of spreads and slumps of material derived from the bank which ran through the entire stratigraphic sequence, such as 2192 and 2249 beneath the black peat, and 2298 and 2102 between the red peat and the stabilisation horizon in the ditch. In the south-west of the trench it was possible to study the relationships between the bank material and the other ditch layers in considerable detail. In the course of this work the edges of the ditch and bank were cut back to reveal the pre-bank surface, a dark peaty clay (2241) above a leached sandy land surface (2297). However, in this case there was a

further peat layer (2332), and land surfaces (2333 and 2334) beneath this.

The 1994 west ditch cutting

Opposite the entrance, a cutting two metres wide was opened through the bank and ditch, and into the peat beyond, as part of the initial season of work at the site (Fig. 4.6). The ditch deposits here reached a maximum of 1.30 m in depth (Plate 4.7). The cut of the ditch itself proved to be relatively shallow, originally straight-sided,

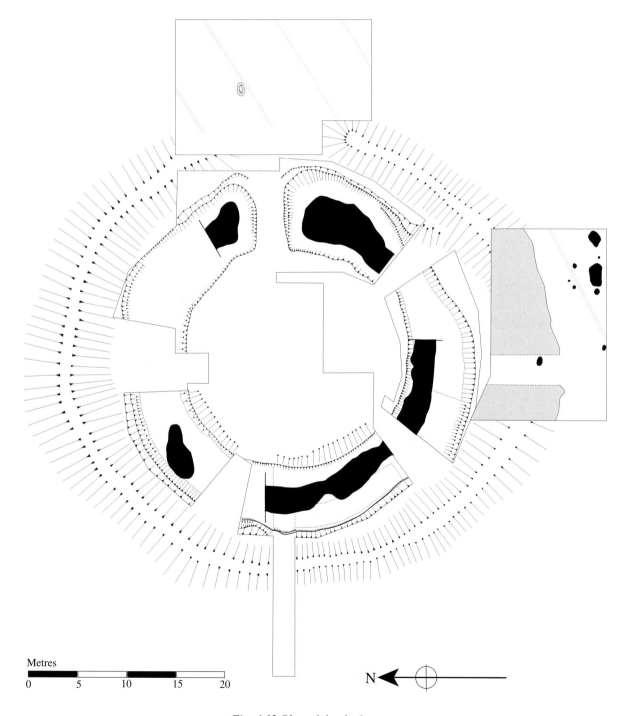

Metres

0   5   10   15   20

N

Fig. 4.12 Plan of the ditch recut.

and broad (cut 0206). It was this ditch morphology that had rendered the contents susceptible to damage.

The lowest ditch fills were yellow to brown sands (0123, 0207, 0285, 0282, 0281) and were noticeably laminated, being by turns more or less compacted. When trowelled clean, their surfaces revealed elaborate swirling patterns. These features seem to suggest that rather than simply representing a normal terrestrial silting pattern, these layers may have been laid down in wet conditions, and that standing water may have been present in the

ditch from its first use (see Tipping, Haggart and Milburn, Chapter 2 above). However, it is not absolutely clear that any organic materials had been preserved in the primary ditch silts, and this may mean that wet conditions had not prevailed through the entire history of the site. In the upper part of the primary fills, traces of what were initially identified as wickerwork or hurdling were discovered. These consisted of sharpened twigs and rods, seemingly of hazel and birch, often crossed over and intertwined. In two places these arrangements at first gave the impression

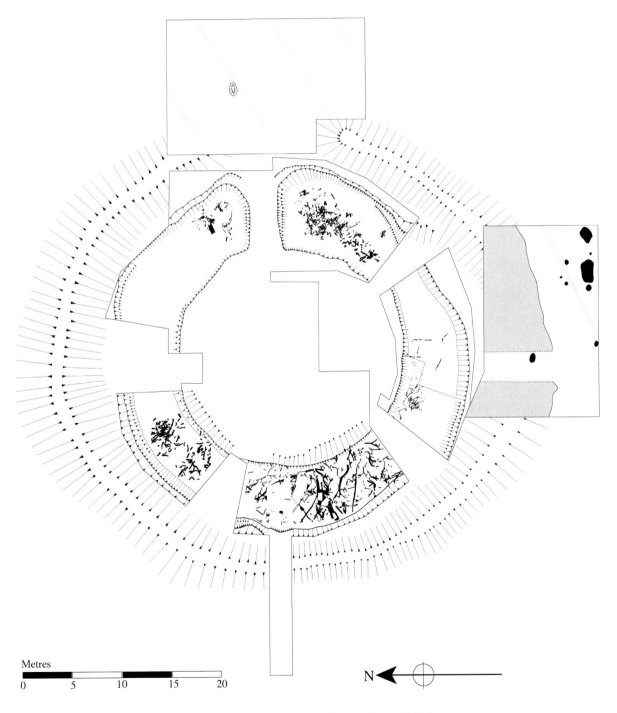

Metres
0 5 10 15 20

N

Fig. 4.13 The Pict's Knowe: plan of all wood finds.

Fig. 4.14 Trench A: wood deposits.

Plate 4.7 Section through the ditch at the back of the enclosure, 1994.

Plate 4.8 Keg fragment FN47, in the 1994 ditch cutting.

of representing wickerwork structures set up in the ditch silts, but given their fragmentary and disordered condition it seems more likely that these were pieces of hurdle which either collapsed or were cast down from the bank and the henge interior, or simply faggots thrown in to fill and drain the ditch (see Crone, Sands and Skinner, Chapter 6 below). In addition to these fragments, a number of small chips of wood which had evidently come from rather more substantial timbers were found in the primary fills. These are perhaps best interpreted as woodworking debris. While much of this material came from the upper surface of the sandy matrix of the primary ditch fill, the degree of slumping, trampling and reworking of the ditch deposits was such that they could not be said with any confidence to date to the primary use of the monument. Indeed, given that all of the radiocarbon determinations for wood from the site gave dates in the Iron Age/Roman period, it is probable that *none* of the wood recovered from the ditch relates to the primary use of the monument. The experience of the 1995 ditch cuttings suggests that all of the wood had entered the ditch fill from above.

These features were cut by a broad shallow recut (0233). This recut was filled with a compact green clay (0122), and a compact sandy peat layer (0127). Wooden objects were located in the upper part of the green clay. These included a fragment of a wooden keg, which had apparently been placed over a tightly-compacted ball of leaves (FN47; see Ramsay and Miller, Chapter 13 below) (Plate 4.8), and a composite wooden object, the so-called 'ard' (see Lerche, Chapter 7 below). Within the west ditch cutting these large objects appeared to contrast with the twigs, rods and chips found lower in the profile, but

it is open to question whether this distinction rests upon two discrete phases of deposition or the differential effects of taphonomic processes.

The inner edge of the green clay was covered by a layer of loose dark yellowish brown sandy silt (0126), which probably represented material that had slumped from the interior of the monument. Sealing these layers was an organic red peat (0024); this thick deposit was most remarkable for the quality of its organic preservation. In places it appeared to represent a densely matted carpet of plant matter, including leaves, reeds, turves and roots. Thick timbers extended out of the section a little way to the south of the ditch cutting, and were investigated by the opening of a 2 × 2 m area, which revealed an array of wood (see Crone, Sands and Skinner, Chapter 6 below). The organic peat visibly contained beetle cases, hazel-nut shells and fruit stones. Large amounts of this material were bagged as environmental samples.

A layer of friable dark yellowish brown silty sand with clay and peat (0124) partly overlay the red peat and was itself sealed by a thick layer of black organic peat (0004). At the top of the ditch, a mixture of cow dung and churned, trampled earth (0348) lay above and clearly truncated a series of other layers. This material was very damp, and was host to growing reeds.

Trench B
by Matt Leivers

Trench B was opened in 1995 across the backfill and to the south of the west ditch cutting of 1994 (Fig. 4.15; Plate 4.9). In general, the results obtained corroborated those from previous work in this part of the site. Within

Plate 4.9 The ditch in Trench B under excavation.

Trench B the cut of the primary ditch (2356) was broad (maximum 5.45m), straight-sided below the weathering cone, and shallow (maximum 0.60m). The bottom of the ditch was largely covered by an extremely hard layer (2349), which was interpreted as a mineral pan. It is possible, however, that this feature was a result of extreme compaction of the lowest fills. Below this hard layer was the natural yellow sand with gravel (2270).

Time did not allow for a complete excavation of the primary ditch silts in Trench B; only those on the eastern (inner) side of the trench were removed entirely, although on the western (outer) side the primary fills were completely removed at the southern end to facilitate the drawing of the section. It was possible to detect two main episodes of silting, but within these (2268 and 2348 to the east, 2269 and 2354 to the west) were very complex patterns of deposition typified by extremely mottled deposits of more or less sandy silts. It proved impossible to distinguish between individual lamina. Within these silts, a number of worked wooden pieces were found, mainly long, narrow branches sharpened into stakes or pegs (for instance, FN 853). While some of these were sampled, several were left in situ as a result of the

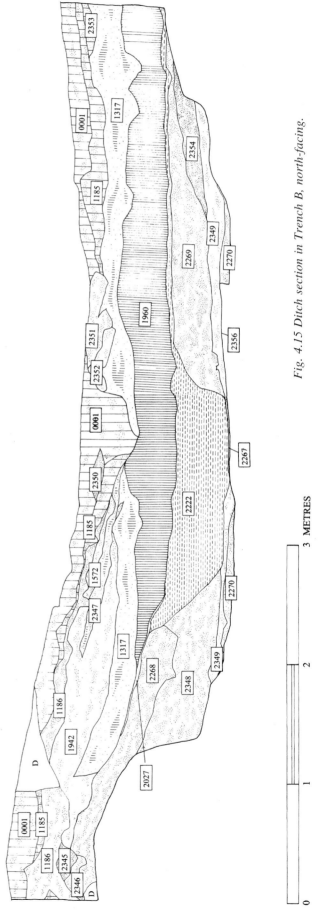

Fig. 4.15 Ditch section in Trench B, north-facing.

incomplete excavation of the ditch fills on the western (outer) side of the trench. As elsewhere on the site, too much confidence should not be placed in the primary character of these wood fragments, since some of these had clearly been trampled or pushed through from the recut.

The ditch recut in Trench B (2267) was shallow (at its maximum 0.45 m deep), originally straight-sided, and a maximum of 2.25 m wide. The extent of the feature was not altogether clear, this situation arising from the fact that there appeared to have been some collapse of the primary ditch deposits after the act of recutting and both before and during the filling of the recut with the green clay. As a result there was an area between the clean green clay and the primary silts which can best be described as a mixture of the two, although this did not show well in the section. In this area wooden objects were found which were distinctly different from those in the recut itself. These consisted mainly of small fragments of wood which, although obviously worked, were not finished objects. However, they differed from the woodchips and turning waste found in the ditch deposits on either side of the enclosure entrances (Trenches D and E) in that they were generally sharpened, chopped or whittled roundwood.

The ditch recut was filled and sealed by a tenacious green clay (2222) which contained a number of substantial wooden artefacts, as well as some smaller pieces and a large portion of a beehive quern (FN 855). Among the larger objects were a part of a keg (FN 835) and several less readily identifiable pieces (FN 809-814, 816, 836) (Plate 4.10).

Above the recut fill was a sandy layer (2027), which appeared to derive from the interior. Overlying all these layers was the red peat (here 1960) which again revealed a very high quality of organic preservation which would seem to indicate that, regardless of any periodic drying-out of the layers above, from this level down the ditch remained wet from an early date. The organic material preserved in this peat included bark, reeds, beetle cases, nut shells, seeds, fruit stones, and wooden objects (FN 402, 539, 578-81). Exceptionally, clumps of coarse hair were recovered from high up in this context, stained a coppery-red, and seemingly derived from cattle (FN 472, 473). Except for a single vertebrum (FN 471), no other faunal remains were recovered. Also present in the red peat were substantial quantities of large timbers (FN 692-703). As excavation proceeded it became apparent that these were a continuation of those pieces found in 1994 in the west ditch cutting and also in the 2 × 2 m area (see above), at the time interpreted as the root systems of trees which had been growing in the ditch. The apparent linear arrangement of these timbers together with the fact that they did not extend beyond a discrete area could suggest that they were in fact the remains of a structure – presumably a platform of some kind – which had at one point stood in or across the ditch (Fig. 4.16; Plate 4.11). Some of these timbers were very large and some were burnt and/or seemingly worked (some pieces seem to have been cut into half lap joints to facilitate their crossing of each other), and whilst some had the appearance of roots, many did not. It places, slots had been cut into the edge of the ditch to receive the larger timbers. Large quantities

Plate 4.10 Wooden object in situ *in Trench B, context 2222.*

Julian Thomas

Plate 4.11 The timber platform at the rear of the enclosure.

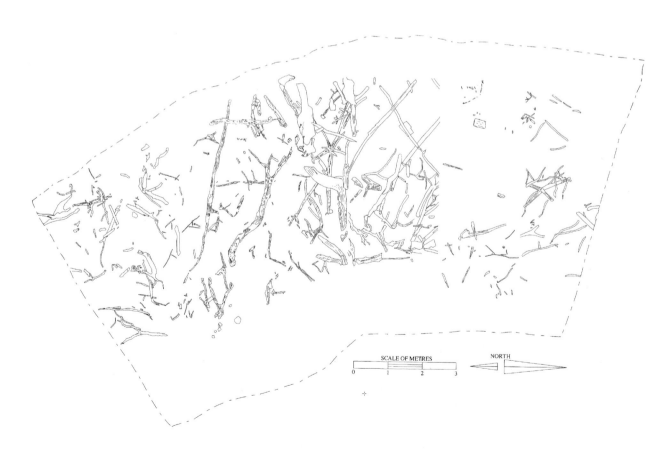

SCALE OF METRES
0 1 2 3

NORTH

Fig. 4.16 Trench B wood deposits.

of the organic material from 1960 were bagged as environmental samples (SN 042-4, 049). It should be noted that FN 703 was a piece of the same object as FN 835 from context 2222 (the green clay). Crone, Sands and Skinner argue that these two pieces were deposited within a short time of each other (see below, Chapter 6). If this is correct, then both the green clay (2222) and the red peat (1960) must have formed (or – in the case of 2222 – been deposited) in very rapid succession.

Above the red peat was a black peat which, unlike 0004, appeared to represent two separate episodes of deposition: the uppermost peat (2347) was present only on the eastern (interior) side of the trench and was interleaved with a relatively deep deposit of sandy material (1942) which was identified as slumped material associated with early mediaeval agricultural activity in the interior of the monument. This in turn overlay and interleaved with a second black peat (1317) which sealed the ditch deposits proper, and it is this second peat which is equivalent to 0004.

Above this black peat were a series of shallow sand and sandy loam layers (1186, 2353, 1185, 1572, 2352, 2351, 2350). Across the whole area of Trench B the topmost layers consisted of topsoil and cow dung, except in those areas on the eastern side of the cutting which overlapped with the 1994 season's excavation of the interior, and the south west corner where the bank and upper ditch deposits were found to have been destroyed by modern digging, presumably agricultural. As in 1994, these layers were found to be heavily disturbed by rabbit action and cattle trampling, and in the central portion of the trench other lower layers were truncated by this activity.

Trench C

This was the smallest of the ditch cuttings, located in the north-west part of the monument (Fig. 4.17). Here the primary ditch cut (2357) and the primary silts (1304, 2358, 2326, 2331 and 2255) were similar to those described in Trenches A and B, although a series of unusually large stake-holes were noticeable cut through the silts and ditch edge (Plate 4.12). However, it was the details of the recut and its filling which were more remarkable. In contrast with the broad crater-like recut in Trench B, Trench C contained a relatively narrow, boat-shaped feature (2227) (Fig. 4.18). The lowest fill of this cut was a grey-black silty clay containing patches of sand (2154), and above this were silty clays (2039 and 2038), which were extremely variable in colour ranging from red to grey, green and black. Although this material was rather different in character, it appears to be the stratigraphic equivalent of the green clay found elsewhere on the site, and as elsewhere it contained worked wooden objects (Fig. 4.19), and some fragments of leather (FN 754, 763, 765 and 766). As in Trench B, the clay was not entirely contained within the recut, but oozed outward in a thin film over the primary ditch deposits, often becoming mixed and interleaved with the layers above. Even the red organic peat (0823) was difficult to separate from this clay in some places. This peat contained more organic material, largely root matter, and some quern fragments (FN 355, 362). Above this was a black silty material (0505), which was interleaved with sandy material which had slipped from the interior (0508) and the bank (0507). As elsewhere it was quite difficult to distinguish the primary dump of the bank from the numerous individual

Plate 4.12 Trench C ditch layer 1304, showing cluster of stakeholes.

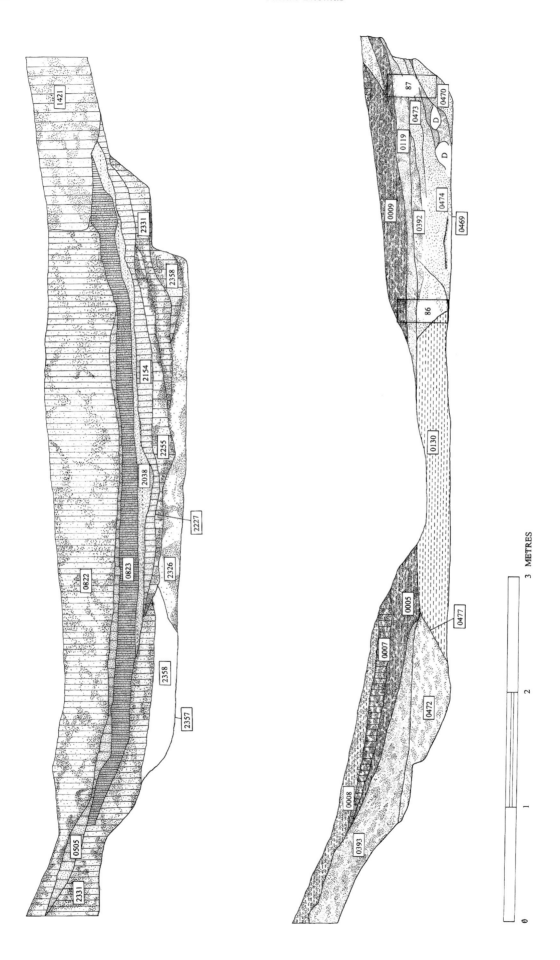

Fig. 4.17 Ditch sections in Trench C (above, west-facing) and the north ditch terminal (below, south-facing).

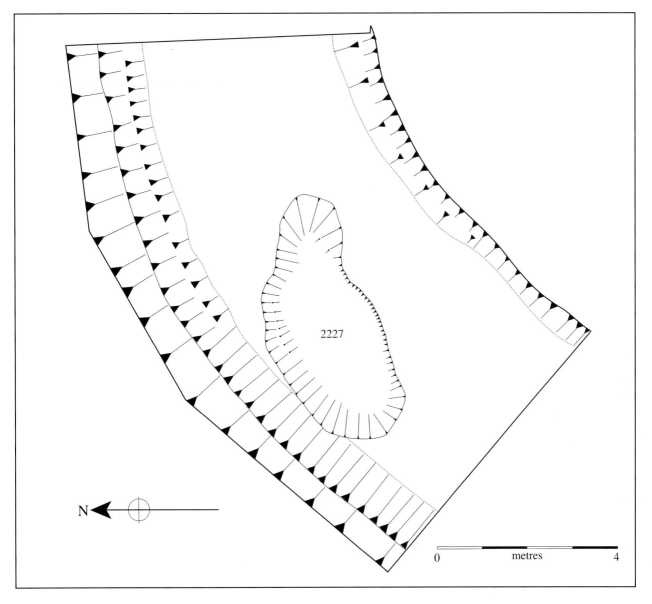

Fig. 4.18 The 'boat-shaped' recut in Trench C, 2227.

lenses of material slipping and slumping from it. These included dark, burnt lenses, from which came both recent glass fragments and a circular post-medieval cast-iron boss (FN 466). The problem was compounded by the fact that these layers had clearly been disturbed by a deep but recent feature cut through the bank (2240). Judging by much degraded fragments of bone from the bottom of this feature, it probably represented an animal burial (FN 828).

The north ditch terminal, 1994 cutting

At the entrance to the henge, the ditch terminal on the northern side of the causeway was investigated (Fig. 4.17). As elsewhere on the site, the pace of excavation was slowed by the need to uncover, record and lift large numbers of wooden objects. The terminal itself was not bottomed in 1994 (but see Trench D below), although a

two-metre cutting just north of the terminal ditch section (and separated from it by a one metre baulk) was completely excavated (Plate 4.13). This was particularly instructive, as it demonstrated the extent to which the disturbance caused by cattle had eroded the ditch deposits.

Above the broad, shallow primary cut (0469) were laminated wedges of sandy fill, which represented the primary filling of the ditch, (on the west side friable mid-brown sand 0472, and on the east sands and silty sands 0392, 0473, 0474 and 0470). These silting layers appeared to have been disturbed by the recutting of the ditch (cut 0477). However, the cut edge was by no means clear, and it seems likely that the sandy layers were eroding as the green clay (0130) gradually accumulated in the recut. It was in this green clay that the most substantial wooden artefacts were preserved. However, this clay, and the layers above, were so badly eroded by the cattle dis-

Fig. 4.19 Trench C wood deposits.

Plate 4.13 Section at the northern ditch terminal, 1994, demonstrating the extent of disturbance of the stratigraphy by animal trampling.

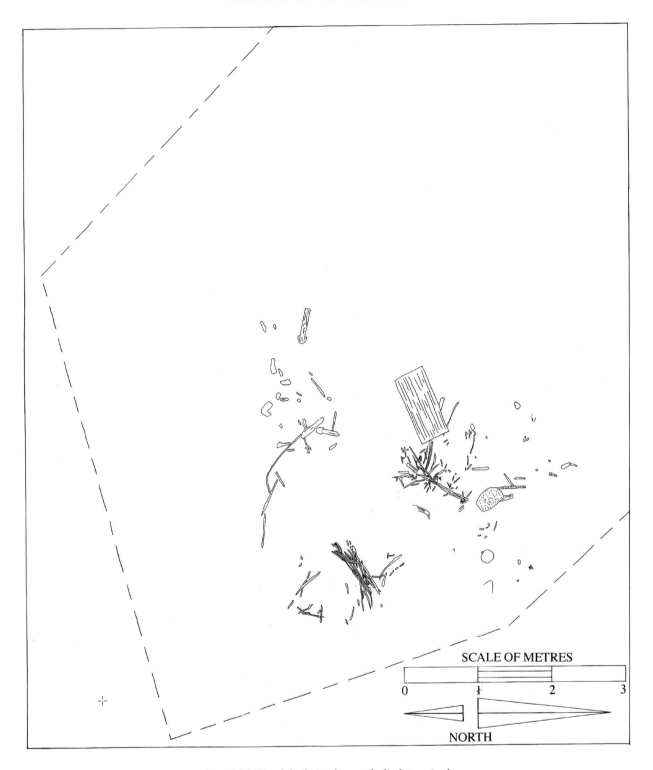

Fig. 4.20 Wood finds in the north ditch terminal.

turbance that many of the pieces showed signs of abrasion and drying. Lying over the green clay was a compact dark grey sandy silt (0119), which had probably slumped from the bank deposits. On the western side of the cutting a soft dark grey sandy silt deposit (0393) was probably a similar slumped material from the interior. These were sealed by a layer of black silty clay (0005/0009). In turn

this clay was overlain by a sandy black peat deposit (0007), and overlying the whole of the ditch was a layer of compacted cow dung and clayey sand (0008).

Wooden finds were particularly numerous in the ditch terminal (Fig. 4.19). As elsewhere on the site, a basic division can be made between fragments which may have been pushed into the primary fills from above, and the

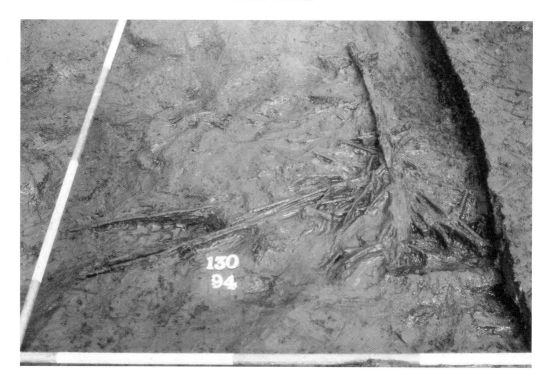

Plate 4.14 Hurdle or faggot (FN179) in situ, context 0130, 1994 north ditch terminal excavation.

more solid objects which seem to have been placed in the green clay. Amongst the fragments was a very substantial yet highly disturbed portion of a hurdle or faggot (FN 179) (Plate 4.14). Finds in the green clay included one indeterminate charred object, and a perforated peg (FN 169). In addition, there was a large, thick plank of wood with clear tooling marks on its surface, one end of which was cut at an oblique angle (Plate 4.15). The other extremity had rotted uniformly up to a line about 20 cm from the end of the plank, giving the impression that it might at one time have stood upright in the ground (FN 235).

Trench D

Trench D was opened in 1995 as a re-excavation of the 1994 trench, extended to cover the whole of the terminal. The sequence confirmed the impression which had been gained in 1994, of a highly mobile series of deposits. The primary ditch cut (2355) was much more rounded in plan than the southern terminal (see 74–77 below), and sloped down rather more gently along its southern edge. A series of silts were located in the extreme end of the terminal, although these had been badly disturbed by the cutting of the recut. Since the recut had taken out the whole of the base of the ditch, the remaining fragments of the silts had slumped forward and downward over the green clay as it formed, creating the most spectacular example of a stratigraphic reversal on the site (Plate 4.16). The lowest silts, separated from each other by green clay, were a loose yellowish-brown silty sand (2316) and a loose grey-

Plate 4.15 Plank in situ, context 0130, FN235.

Plate 4.16 Trench D Ditch section 2232.

Plate 4.17 Trench D Ditch section 2232: detail.

brown sand (2280). The latter ran right up the edge of the ditch cut, and was covered by a thin film of green clay which had somehow penetrated between two existing deposits. These silts, and the layer of dark grey-brown silty clay above them (2232), were extremely marbled, suggesting that they had been laid down in, or altered by, very damp conditions (Plate 4.17). At the top of the

primary layers were a reddish-brown sandy silt (1959) and a very dark brown silty sand (2176). This latter may equate with the stabilisation horizon found elsewhere on the site.

The extensive layer of green clay (1953) appeared to underlie all of these layers, and to interdigitate with them. At the extreme terminal the clay spread over a co-

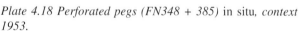

Plate 4.18 Perforated pegs (FN348 + 385) in situ, context 1953.

Plate 4.19 Bundle of twigs (FN544) in ditch context 1953.

nsiderably wider area at its base than above, giving the impression that the silts had collapsed or slid down onto it from its edges. Within the green clay, there was a high density of wooden objects. These included a pair of the same type of perforated pegs (FN 384, FN 385) as were recovered from the terminal in 1994 (Plate 4.18), and a bundle of sticks which appeared to have been tied together (FN 544) (Plate 4.19). Within the general scatter of wood were large numbers of worked roundwood fragments, woodchips and offcuts, and some pieces of turning waste. These different forms of waste were not spatially segregated in Trench D. However, in contrast with the other trenches, fragments of quernstone were relatively scarce here. Above the clay, traces remained of the organic red peat (1928) and a darker material above it (1954).

Trench E

Trench E provided an opportunity to excavate the extensive recut at the ditch terminal in plan, while at the same time investigating a substantial quantity of the primary fill (Fig. 4.21). At its southern terminal the ditch was especially broad, the northern edge being virtually straight in plan, so that the return of the inner edge was particularly acute (Colour Plate 4). The ditch (2266) was at its deepest here, and cut through a band of compact sandstone into a layer of loose irregular natural sand, which formed the bottom. On this base a thin layer of concretion had formed (2265), where panning had occurred at the abrupt change from ditch deposits to natural. Above this was a series of layers of primary fill, composed of yellow sandy silt (1687) (not visible in section) or coarser buff silt (2189). In the centre of the ditch terminal this material had all been removed by the recut, although at the far northern end a bank of sandy silt remained.

The remainder of the stratigraphy which pre-dated the recut (1686), was somewhat fragmentary since it constituted the truncated cones of layers dipping down from the outer edges of the ditch. Often these represented isolated patches of material which could, to a greater or lesser extent, be correlated with each other. Immediately above the coarse primary silts were the remains of a layer of creamy sand (2040 and 2087/88), which may have been the product of the erosion of the bank and interior. Above this were more localised patches of fine silt (2187,

2117), clay (2002) and marbled silty material (2080, 2001, 2127) which represented a complex pattern of secondary silting involving slumping from bank and interior, and the weathering of the sandstone in the edge of the ditch to produce fine, silty lenses. Some of these lenses were almost invisible in section, although they could readily be recorded in plan. A number of stake-holes cut into the sandstone edge appeared to date to this stage in the sequence. At the top of this whole formation lay a deposit of dark clay material (1985/1988), which is interpreted as a stabilisation horizon. These layers produced sparse fragments of earlier prehistoric pottery of indeterminate character (FN 548). If at this point a turf had formed in the ditch, it seems that later a renewed silting took place, resulting in the coarse sandy layer (0699), which predated the recutting of the ditch.

The recut (1686) was filled with the relatively homogenous green/grey clay (0888). This material was comparatively compact towards its base, suggesting that a certain amount of trampling (whether by humans or animals) had taken place while the deposit was forming. Moreover, the clay appeared in places to have become intermixed at its edges with the earlier deposits, perhaps as a result of this activity. The comparatively straight sides of the recut seemed to have collapsed over the green clay as it formed, creating a series of stratigraphic reversals. The consequence of this was that fragments of wood that were doubtless integral to this deposit appeared to have been recovered from earlier contexts. The recut was roughly oval in plan within the terminal, but narrowed to form a linear slot to the south-west, near to Trench A (Plate 4.20). Many fragments of wood were recovered from the green clay, but these were preferentially concentrated in the wider part of the recut (Fig. 4.22; Plate 4.21). They included some small objects which had evidently been turned on a pole lathe (for details of the wooden material see Crone, Sands and Skinner, Chapter 6 below, and appendices 2 and 2a). On the inner side of the ditch, a large number of flat wood fragments gave every impression of having tumbled into the ditch from the interior of the monument (Plate 4.22). This material was concentrated in the inner side of the ditch, in contrast with a small number of pointed roundwood rods, which were found on the outer (eastern) side of the wood scatter. Worked roundwood was, in general, quite scarce in this cutting. Amongst the dense scatter of wood in the centre of the terminal the sole of a Roman leather shoe was found (FN 486) (see van Driel-Murray, Chapter 12 below). Other finds included numerous quern stone fragments and a piece of crucible (Vessel 7). Toward the top of the clay deposit a hurdle was found together with unworked wood which included the trunk of a silver birch. Above this in turn was the familiar sequence of red organic peat (0698 and 1050), sandy slips, and dark peat (1049). On the inner side of the ditch the major sandy layer (0697), which might be associated with the ploughing of the interior, could be seen to overlie a clear turf-line (2290).

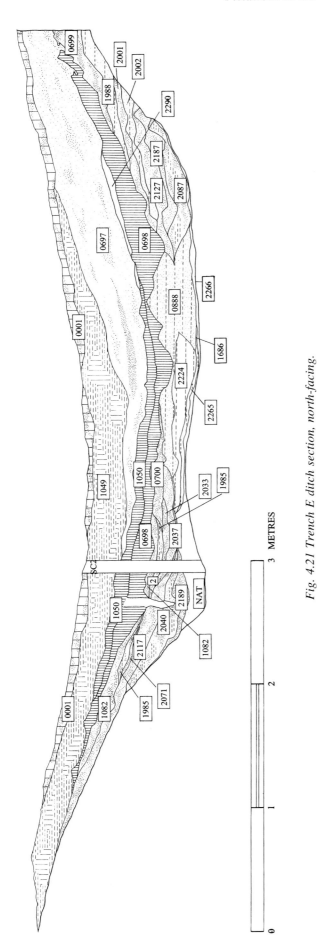

Fig. 4.21 Trench E ditch section, north-facing.

Plate 4.20 Trench E, after the removal of the ditch recut.

Plate 4.21 Spread of wood fragments in ditch context 0698.

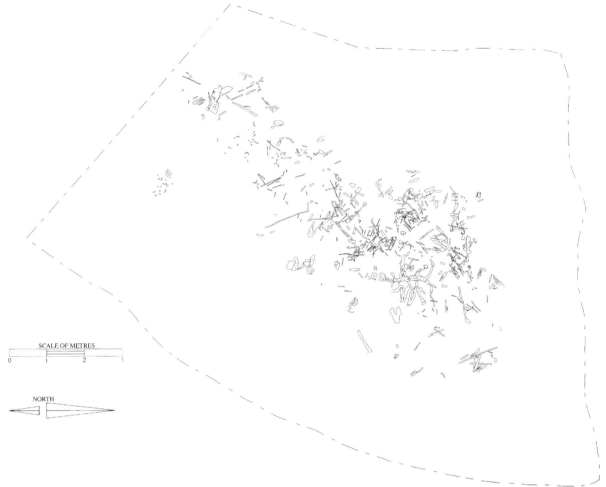

SCALE OF METRES

0   1   2   3

NORTH

Fig. 4.22 Wood finds in Trench E.

Plate 4.22 Tumble of small pieces of wood down the inner side of the ditch in Trench E.

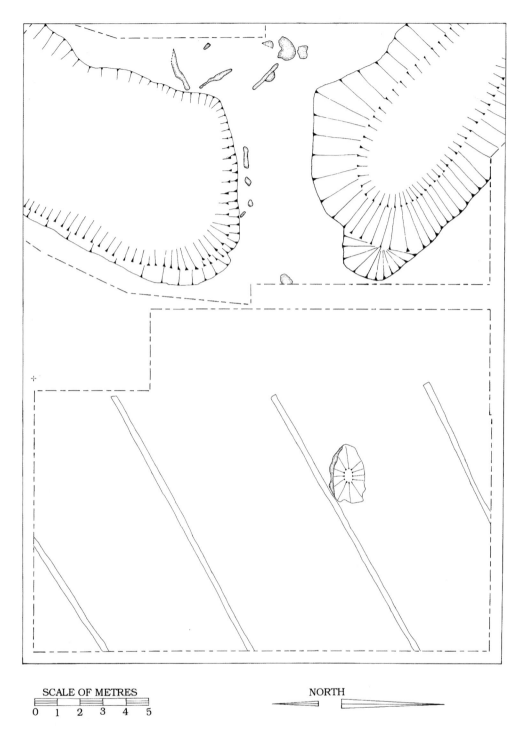

SCALE OF METRES   NORTH

0   1   2   3   4   5

Fig. 4.23 General plan of the area around the entrance of the henge.

The entrance causeway

Beneath the peat at the ditch edges a sand surface had been preserved from rabbit activity, particularly on the entrance causeway between the two ditch terminals (Fig. 4.23). Here, the sand was leached a silvery white, as opposed to the deep orange sand of the interior. In the preserved surface, a great many features were recognised, the most numerous of these being stake-holes, generally with a loose sandy fill (Plate 4.23). These were not evenly distributed, but formed a number of clusters. In general, they appeared to run around the edges of the ditches, and to avoid the centre of the causeway (Fig. 4.24). The stake-holes were particularly numerous immediately beyond the causeway in the interior of the monument. In addition to the stake-holes, there were a number of shallow slot features (Plate 4.24). These were initially dismissed as rabbit runs, but further investigation showed them to have

Plate 4.23 The Pict's Knowe entrance causeway.

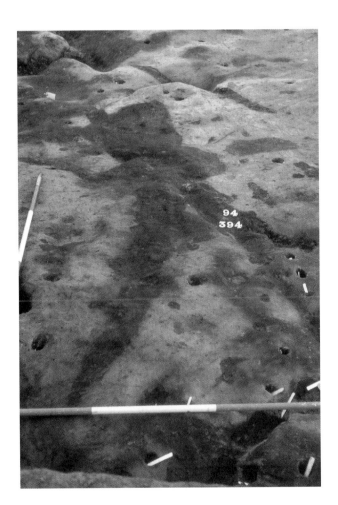

Plate 4.24 'Slots' on the entrance causeway.

a much more compact fill than the burrows, and to both contain and be cut by stake-holes. One slot, running along the southern side of the entrance causeway, resolved into a series of separate features in the course of excavation (0345, 0403 and 0475). A series of others were set in a rectilinear arrangement immediately inside the entrance causeway. Unfortunately, time constraints precluded complete excavation of all of these features.

It seems likely that these features relate to a series of light structural elements. Their clustered and intercutting nature suggests that these devices were renewed or replaced on a number of occasions. If they bear any relationship to the enclosure (that is, if they are not pre-henge features) these slots and stake-holes must have been cut through the thin peat that underlies the bank and spread across the entrance. It is consequentially difficult to be certain whether they relate to the later Neolithic/ Early Bronze Age or Iron Age/Roman phases of activity.

Trench F

In 1995 it was decided to open an area of 20 × 10 m immediately outside the entrance of the enclosure to determine the extent to which the cluster of stake-holes extended beyond the perimeter of the monument. This area was laid out in such a way as to investigate the outer skirt of the bank, and to determine whether another linear feature was butted onto the monument, closing off the entrance as had been suggested by the contour survey (Fig. 4.25; Plate 4.25). It was originally conjectured that such a feature might be a much later addition, such as a

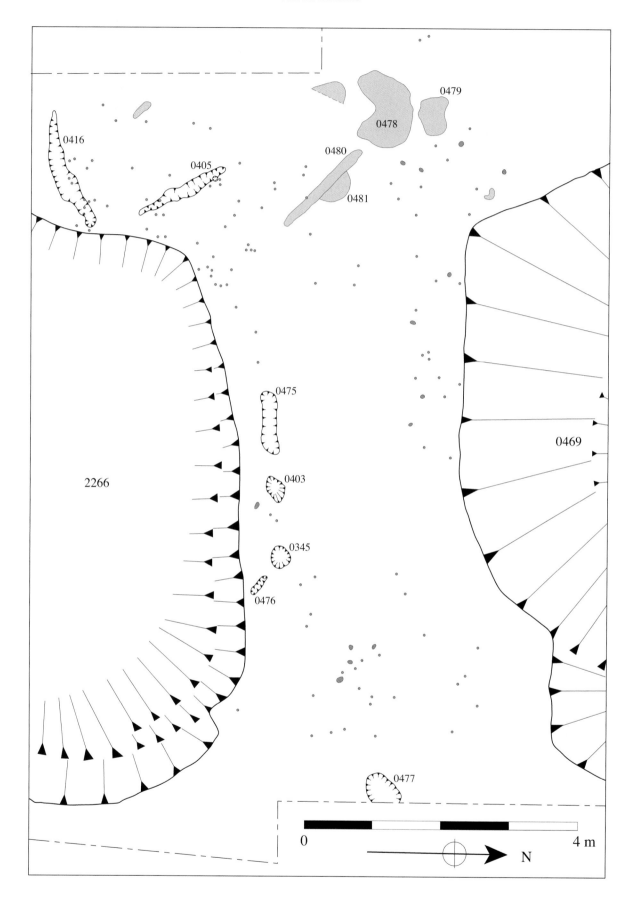

Fig. 4.24 Detailed plan of the entrance causeway.

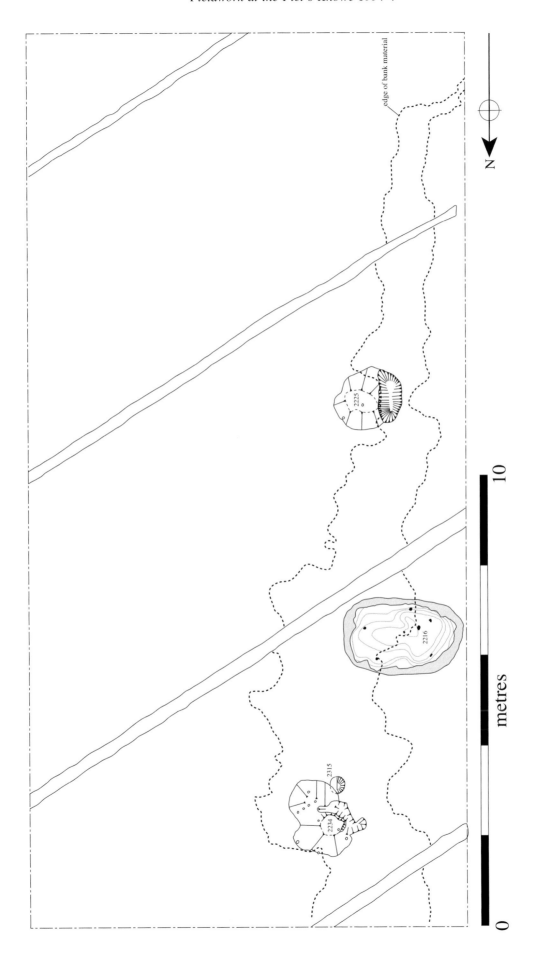

edge of bank material

N

metres

0 10

Fig. 4.25 Plan of Trench F.

Plate 4.25 Trenches E and F seen from above, 1995 season.

Plate 4.26 Trench F, showing the henge bank and levelling layer in the foreground.

field boundary. Beneath the turf (0519) and cutting through the topsoil (0518), a series of modern drainage ditches containing ceramic pipes were immediately visible (0527/0528, 0525/0526, 0511/0512, 0521/0522).

Beneath the topsoil, the surface or capping of the bank was composed of a firm sandy loam (2081). A great number of stake-holes were cut into it from above. Although the bank rose upward as an earthwork on either side of the entrance, this material also continued as an unbroken layer across the trench (Plate 4.26). So rather than another feature such as a ploughing headland having been added at a later date, material contiguous with the

Plate 4.27 View across Trench F following the removal of the bank and levelling layer, showing the oval mound in the middle of the frame.

bank itself formed the linear rise across the entrance noted in the survey. Beneath the bank capping was a friable dark reddish-brown sandy silt (1965), which represented the primary dump of the bank. Within both of these layers amorphous lenses and edges could be discerned. Few of these could be defined as separate contexts, and the effect appears to have been a consequence of the construction of the bank using a series of dumps of material. It was noticeable that the stone content of the bank increased toward the bottom.

As elsewhere on the site these layers rested on top of a dark peat (0520), which connected with the general layer of peat covering the valley bottom. Once this was removed from the whole surface of the trench, several hundred stake-holes were revealed cut into the leached white natural sand surface (0523), together with three amorphous deposits of clay (0515, 0516, 0517). The stake-holes were present over much of the trench, although they showed a clear clustering around the enclosure entrance.

Beneath the bank itself, a series of remarkable features was revealed (Plate 4.27). On either side of the entrance causeway, broadly in line with the two ditch terminals, were two small mounds of sand, each representing the upcast of a shallow cut feature (Fig. 4.26). In the case of feature 2225 a very clear sequence could be discerned in which this upcast covered a large post-hole (2258), the post from which had seemingly been withdrawn. Above the compact sandy fill of the post-hole (2259) was a layer of dark, burnt sandy material, which was bounded on the northern side by a dump of upcast, made up of reddish black silty sand (2314). This may have been derived from the post-hole itself, but it was surmounted by the dark grey sand of 2225, which had evidently been dug from a small depression immediately to the west of the post-hole. The other feature 2315/2234, was more disturbed but appeared similar in character. The obvious interpretation is that these two features had held free-standing posts which had stood at some time before the construction of the monument, and which had to some extent anticipated its layout (Plates 4.28 and 4.29). They had also been in place prior to the formation of the peat, and in a relation of stratigraphic equivalence with the Earlier Neolithic activity in Trench G. Seemingly, these two posts had been removed and their sockets 'hidden' by the piling up of small mounds of sand over them.

Between the posts on an east-west alignment was a small oval mound (Plate 4.30). The mound measured roughly 2.4 × 1.6 m, and its upper surface (2134) was cut by a series of stake-holes (Plate 4.31). Around the edge of the mound, the ground surface dipped down into what appeared to be a small ditch, filled with material (2218, 2327, 2220) which became more greasy and organic towards its base (Fig. 4.27). This impression was slightly misleading, since the material of the mound actually sat in a large pit, so that the accumulated soil deposits overall had a lenticular section (Plate 4.32). At some point in what appears to have been a rather complex filling before the deposition of the capping (2216), the darker material seems to have accumulated around what would then have been a lower mound. The pit beneath this small 'barrow' would have been of an appropriate size to receive a crouched burial, although no finds were recovered from the feature at all, and bone would not have survived in these soil conditions. Analysis demonstrated that there was no phosphate enrichment of these fills, which does not support the suggestion that the pit contained skeletal material (see Crowther, Chapter 9 below).

Trench H

by Chris Fowler and Julian Thomas

Following the excavation of Trench F it was decided in the 1996 season to explore the area between the entrance, bank terminals, and Trench F. Trench H covered an area 5m × 15m, taking in the backfilled edge of Trench F by 0.5 m (Plate 4.33). Two modern drainage ditches had cut

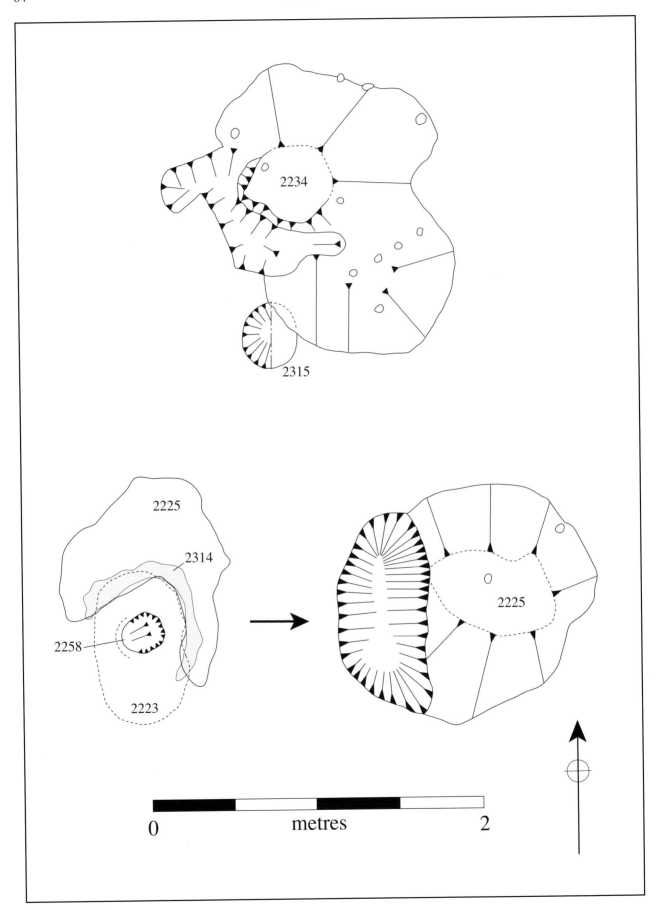

Fig. 4.26 Cut features in Trench F.

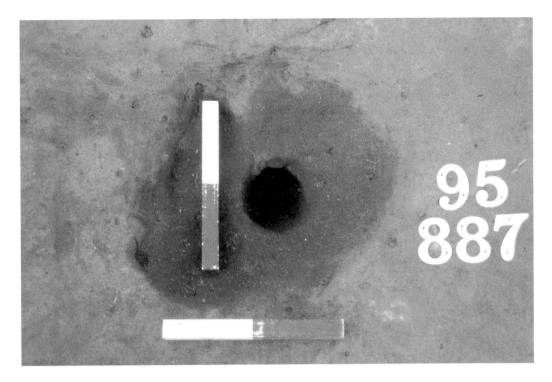

Plate 4.28 Post-hole 887.

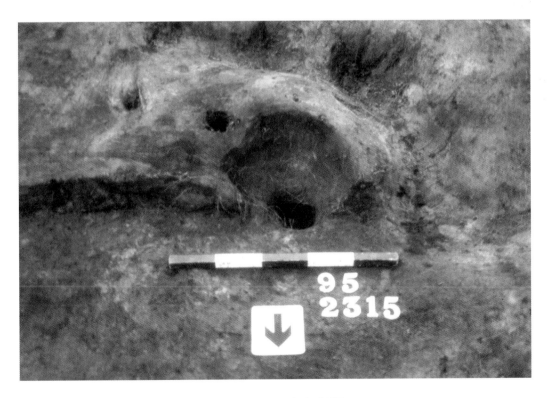

Plate 4.29 Post-hole 2315.

through the archaeological deposits at this point, forming features 2809 (fill 2808) and 2817 (fill 2816).

The old land surface in Trench H was a compact but friable grey-white leached sand (2822), cut by several clusters of stake-holes. The bank had been constructed on

a natural rise in the ground and the area of its northern terminal had previously been the focus for a high density of stake-holes.

Sealing the old land surface was a layer of puddled black peat 10 cm deep (2815), the equivalent of 0520

Plate 4.30 The oval mound, 2134.

Plate 4.31 The oval mound, section removed, seen from above.

Plate 4.32 Pit beneath oval mound.

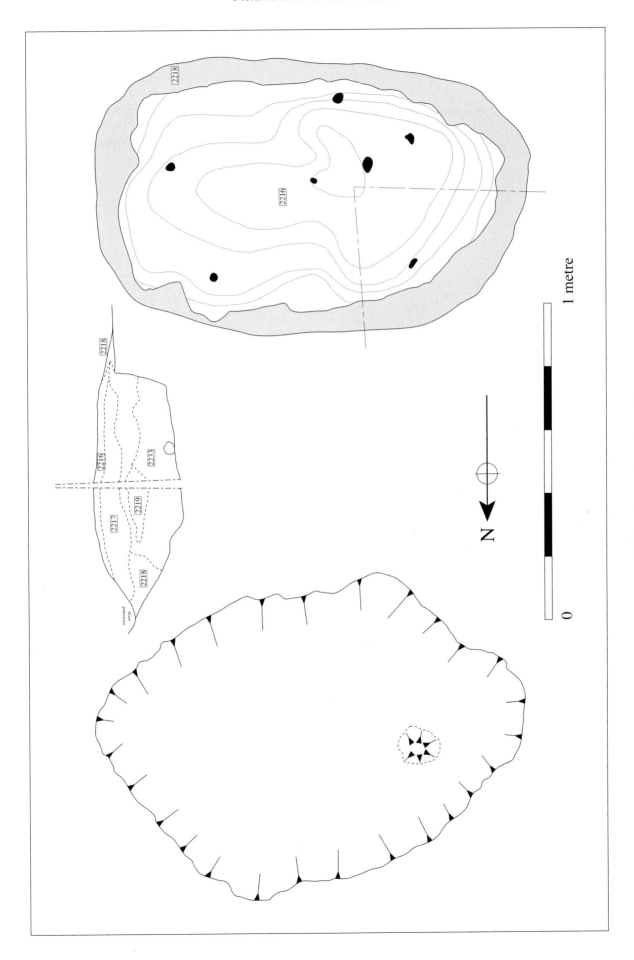

Fig. 4.27 The oval mound complex.

elsewhere. Above this was the lowest structural deposit of the bank (2813), a compacted layer of bright orange sandy loam containing many sandstone fragments (Plate 4.34). The base of a modern pit (fill 2819, cut 2821) cut into this layer from the surface, and contained sheep or goat bones. The series of dumps and capping deposits that made up the bank sequence was difficult to unravel in Trench H, where the layers thinned out toward the entrance. The compact dark brown sand of 2805 was stratigraphically equivalent to 2813, lying on top of the peat, 2815. Above this came a series of lenses of material of various degrees of softness and compaction, 2800, 2802, 2804 and 2814. 2802 appeared to be the latest in this series, sealing the other deposits. It was at this level that the full extent of the two modern field drains was revealed, along with a large amount of animal disturbance.

Overlying the main body of the bank was a series of interleaved compact dark sandy layers (2801, 2803, 2807, 2810, 2811, 2812). Only a few contexts could be discerned with any degree of certainty, none of which had definite edges since they appeared to be individual dumps of material. Differences in soil texture and consistency were slight. Towards the west section, where the bank sloped down towards the ditch, these deposits were more moist and consequently less hard than on top of the bank. In

Plate 4.33 (left) Trench H after excavation, looking southward. Note modern drainage ditches on the eastern side of the trench.

Plate 4.34 Section of the bank at the southern end of Trench H.

general these contexts were sterile although a flint arrowhead (FN 2017), broken laterally across the tip, was recovered from 2801.

It is not easy to relate the complex and highly disturbed stratigraphy in Trench H to the bank sequence elsewhere in the monument. Two radiocarbon determinations were taken on charcoal from the bank material, identified as having come from context 2813/4. They gave dates of 50 – 240 Cal. AD (SUERC-2097) and 120 Cal. BC – 170 Cal. AD (SUERC-2098) (both at 95.4 % probability). If these were clearly within the principal build of the bank, 2813, this would seem to confirm that the bank was Late Iron Age in date, and that the monument was not a henge. However, in other cuttings it was evident that the bank was a multi-phase stucture, and it is not obvious quite where the dividing line between primary build and capping fell in Trench H. Whether the hazel charcoal and oak twig that provided the two dates can be securely related to the construction of the primary bank is not clear.

Trench J
by Matt Leivers

Trench J (Fig. 4.28; Plate 4.35) was opened to investigate the 'terminal' portion of the larger sub-circular geophysical anomaly provisionally identified as a ring ditch (see Clark, Chapter 5 below). Unfortunately, no such features were revealed by excavation.

Beneath the topsoil (0001), three intersecting cuts were visible which, on the basis of previous seasons work, were identified as modern field drains. Consequently these features (2600/2601, 2602/2603, 2604/2605) were cleared of their fills, thus providing six sections through the deposits in the trench. From the junction of two of the drains came a small amorphous piece of polished chert (FN 2003) and two fragments of possibly cremated bone (FN 2004, 2005).

Cleaning of the subsoil surface (2606) revealed a very mottled loamy sand, overlaid in patches by a dark peaty loam (6353). At the western end of the trench however, this peaty material overlay an area where the natural subsoil had been leached white and dipped down slightly to form shallow depressions. The significance of this is not clear. The association of this feature with a small pit or post-hole also sealed beneath the peat layer (6353), may point to formation processes other than natural, for instance trampling by animals of the kind that occurs at a gateway or water source. However, the fact that the subsoil had every appearance of having been heavily affected by standing water – amorphous edges could be discerned within it which on investigation proved to be formed by lenses of sand lapping up over each other in a wave-like pattern – indicates that this could have been a natural phenomenon. A small sondage across this area showed that no cut was present and that the leached white colour of subsoil graded gently into the more usual dark reddish brown.

Once the peaty material had been removed it was seen that numerous stake-holes were cut into the whole subsoil surface across the trench (Plate 4.36). Ostensibly of random distribution, various patternings and clusters of

Plate 4.35 Trench J after excavation.

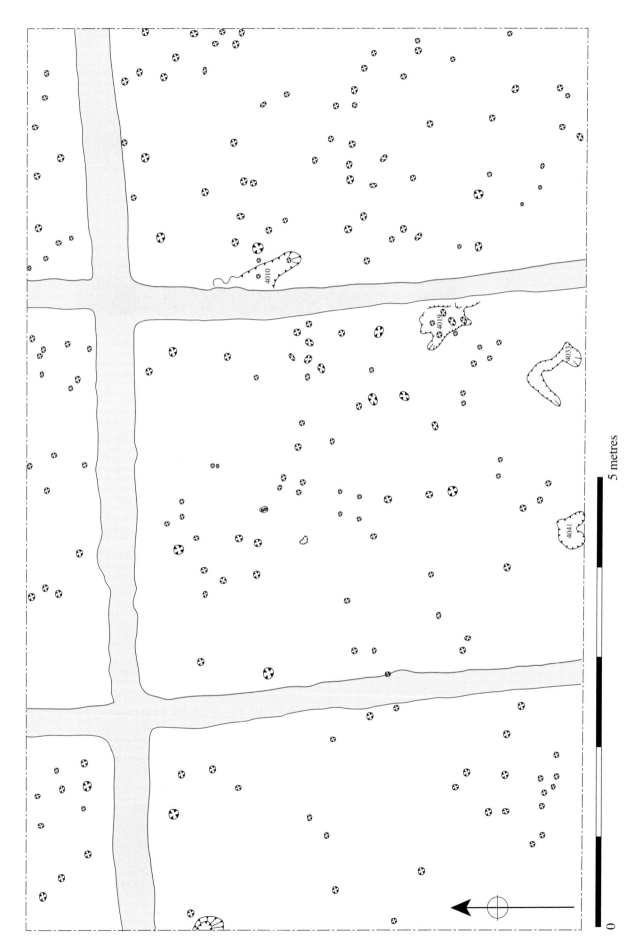

Fig. 4.28 Plan of Trench J.

5 metres

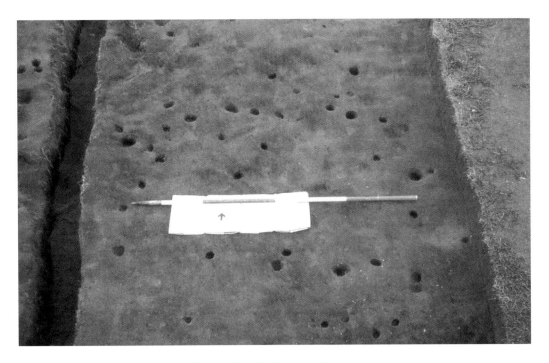

Plate 4.36 Stake-holes in Trench J.

these holes began to emerge with repeated trowelling. At the eastern end of the trench a group of around forty stake-holes seemed to form a sub-circular arrangement which may represent a small structure of approximately 3 m north-south by 2.5 m east-west maximum. Some of the stake-holes making up this possible feature contained small pieces of a slag or cinder-like material within their fills, as did other stake-holes elsewhere in the trench, and this highlights the possibility that all of the stake-holes may not be contemporary. Given this, rather than distinct and unified structures, any of the features identified may have been the result of fortuitous clusterings of unrelated stake-holes over long periods of time, or may have resulted from replacement of stake-holes through successive phases of use.

That there was more than one episode of the use of stakes on the site is made clear by a group of very amorphous 'slots' in the central portion of the trench where the subsoil was very compact and undulating. These 'slots' were nine in number and in some instances stake-holes were both sealed by and cut through their fills. In all cases, the fills of the 'slots' were identical to the fills of those stake-holes that they sealed, thus indicating that these stake-holes and 'slots' should be considered as a unit. Unfortunately, it was impossible to work out a stratigraphic relationship between the stake-holes in the 'slots' and those elsewhere in Trench J. Three 'slots' were cut by a drainage ditch.

Trench K

Trench K was located some 30 m to the south of the enclosure, yet still on the area of slightly raised ground

on which the monument had been built (Fig. 4.29). It was originally located in order to address the possibility of the presence of a ring-ditch in this area, which had been suggested by the geophysical survey (see Chapter 5 below), and to pursue any prehistoric features which might have existed in the immediate surroundings of the monument. Beneath soil and peat, the subsoil was sandy and grey, but not as brilliantly white as the surface beneath the peat in the immediate vicinity of the monument. Three modern pipe trenches crossed the cutting, two smaller ones on a north-east – south-west axis, and a very large one running across the extreme south of the excavated area. Initially, a number of oval features were recognised and investigated, but these proved to be attributable to differential drying and variations in the natural.

This left only a very large number of stake-holes, comparable in their density to those located in Trench F (Plate 4.37). Once these had been excavated and plotted onto a single plan, an attempt was made to search for structures amongst them. Scattergrams of the diameter and depth of stake-holes were constructed, and these demonstrated that the depths of holes had a bimodal distribution, with a minority of holes being greater than 9 cm deep. When plotted onto the plan, these deeper stake-holes clearly clustered along the northern side of the trench, with one tight grouping of holes to the south, which might represent some form of structure. Other aspects of stake-hole variability, including shape in plan, inclination, pointedness, colour of fill and texture of fill were also plotted, but did not demonstrate the same clarity of spatial patterning (Fig. 4.30).

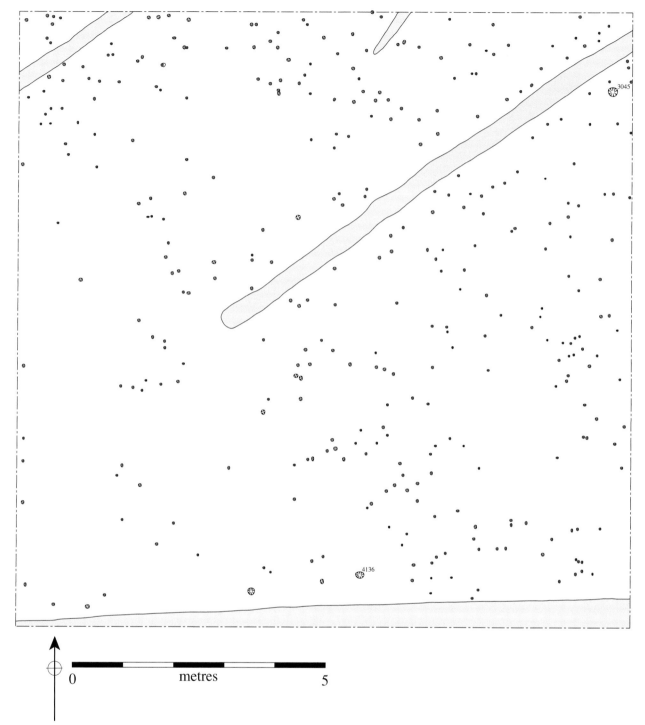

Fig. 4.29 Plan of Trench K.

Stake-holes

Some of the stake-holes contained finds that were of recent origin, such as fragments of clinker and glazed pottery, while more contained cinders or fire-ash. Yet it is important to compare these features with the stake-holes found in direct association with the enclosure, for while some of these were clearly late in the sequence, others evidently pre-dated the formation of the peat beneath the bank, indicating that they were Late Neolithic or Early Bronze Age at the latest. A possible explanation for this would be that stake-holes had been created in this area over a very long period, some being quite recent, others ancient. This might explain the distinction between deeper and shallower holes in Trench K, with the shallow holes being dug from a higher level, subsequent to the formation of the peat. The deeper holes, gravitating

Pict's Knowe 1996
Trench K: Deeper Stakeholes

0   3m

• Stakehole greater than 90mm deep

Modern disturbance

Fig. 4.30 Possible structures in Trench K.

toward the monument and apparently forming a small structure in the south of Trench K, would thus be the more ancient. There are, within the site as a whole, numerous examples of intercutting stake-holes, indicating that they do not represent a single coherent plan. This would accord with the smaller number of quite deep stake-holes in Trench J, and the deep stake-holes found cut into the ditch deposits in Trench C.

Plate 4.37 Trench K after excavation.

5

Geophysical survey

Kate Clark

Introduction

In August 1995 geophysical survey was undertaken over the immediate environs of the Pict's Knowe monument to investigate the possible extent of associated sub-surface features. The field in which the monument stands is in permanent pasture, but the region to the north of the earthwork has been colonised by dense rushes making it largely unsuitable for survey. In order to maximise data recovery within the time available it was decided to concentrate the investigation on the south, east and west of the earthwork.

A small resistivity survey of 20 m² close to the earthwork entrance had been undertaken in 1994, using a sample interval of 0.5 m. The results of this showed that, at that particular location at least, the interval could be increased to 1.0 m with negligible loss of resolution. The 1995 survey therefore employed a 1.0 m sample and traverse interval over 20 m × 20 m grids. The geophysics grid corresponded to the project site grid.

The site was assessed for suitability for magnetometer survey. 9600 m² were surveyed using a Geoscan FM36 gradiometer; the results produced a generally homogenous plot consistent with expectations on these types of sandy alluvial deposits. To optimise both time and available personnel it was therefore decided to continue the full survey using resistivity only (Geoscan RM15 unit).

Resistivity survey

August 1995 had been preceded by three months of very dry weather, and the lack of moisture in the soil is reflected in the range of readings. 90% of the data falls between 472 and 1411 ohms, with a median of 881, and this can be compared with the results from the 1994 survey where the range was 224 to 308 ohms. In the north-east of the 1995 survey area it proved impossible to obtain a contact at all.

In these conditions, and on an area where the near-surface geology results in sand 'islands' with interspersed alluvial soil, expectations should not be too high for the recovery of subtle archaeological features. The background resistance during the 1995 survey is very difficult to ascertain due to the noise induced by the variation in contact resistance brought about by the undulations in the sand substrata. As anomalies, both geological and archaeological, can only be identified by their contrast to the background resistance the 1995 Pict's Knowe survey has grave problems of interpretation. Furthermore, these are exacerbated by the extensive rabbit burrowing activity, which in places immediately to the south of the monument had resulted in subsurface cavities over which it was impossible to retrieve data.

The survey was completed on an area of 22000 m², and Figure 5.1 shows an image produced from unfiltered, normalised data. In this greyscale plot, dark corresponds to lower resistance and light to higher. The modern field drains show clearly running north-east to south-west. Also clear are the areas of very high resistance in the north-west and to the south of the centre section of the monument fence.

Figure 5.2 gives a basic interpretation overlaid on the grid plan. The feature marked 'probable line of old track' is poorly defined at the edges but conforms well to this feature type encountered on other sites.

The 'possible ring ditch' is a tentative interpretation of one of several sub-circular anomalies. Five of these are drawn on Figure 5.2 to demonstrate their variation in morphology and symmetry. It is highly likely that most of these sub-circular anomalies are products of sand intrusions close to the ground surface, but the smallest does exhibit greater symmetry than the others.

However, in Figure 5.3 none of these anomalies is really visible. Figure 5.3 has been subjected to Roberts cross filtering in order to identify real edges through estimation of the gradient of the data. While the field

PICT'S KNOWE RESISTIVITY SURVEY

UNFILTERED DATA

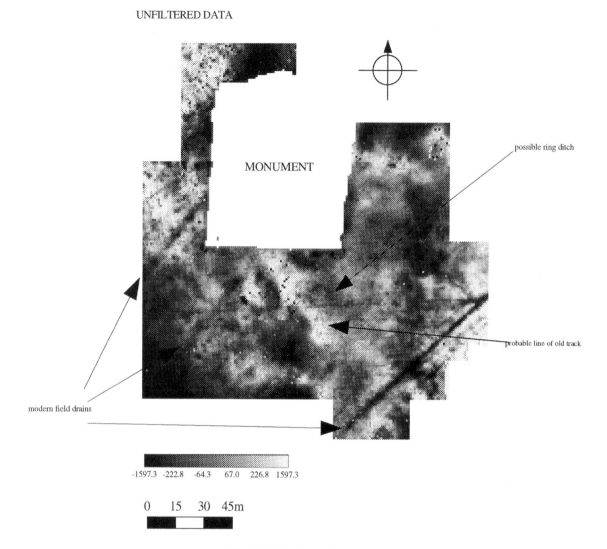

Fig. 5.1 Geophysical survey.

drains are still well defined, as are the broad areas of very high resistance and the 'possible old track', the image now appears more stable generally and the sub-circular anomalies would not be apparent without reference to the unfiltered plot.

Figure 5.4 explains much of the general trends of the resistivity data. Here the topographic survey undertaken in 1994 by Tim Sly has been overlaid onto the resistivity plot. The contour interval is 10 cms and, apart from the field drains, all the anomalies and variations in the geophysical data can be seen to correspond to the topographic plot.

The anomaly identified as 'possible ring ditch' can still be seen in the filtered image, albeit only through reference to the raw data of Figure 5.1. Figure 5.5 focuses on this feature and a general interpretation has been drawn onto the image. The image is the reverse of that

shown in Figure 5.1 – here low resistance is indicated by lighter shade and high resistance by darker areas. The straight line trending east to west can be seen on all the plots and resembles a modern cable or small pipe trench. It just intercepts the southern edge of the circular feature, and this may be causing some interference with the imaging, i.e. the modern feature may be contributing data which is being interpreted as a continuation of the 'ring ditch' on its southern edge. There is insufficient contrast in the raw data to assess this further.

Taking the circular feature alone, it is defined by a perimeter of low resistance indicating a diameter of between 10 and 15 m. The break in the perimeter on the western edge can be seen on Fig. 5.1 (1:1500). The impinging horseshoe-shaped anomaly on the east however is only really apparent at 1:500. Again, this smaller anomaly is defined as a partial circumferential band of

PICT'S KNOWE RESISTIVITY SURVEY

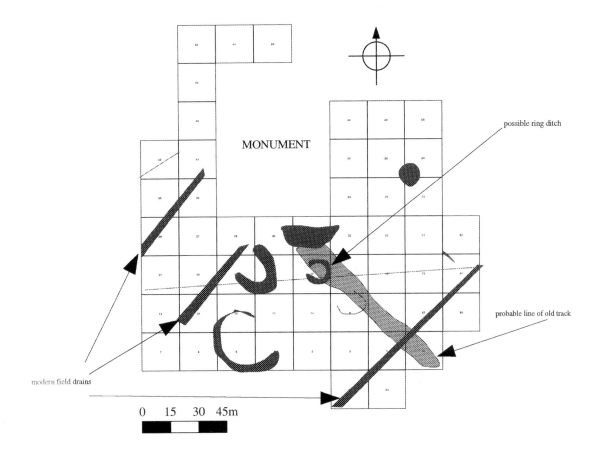

Fig. 5.2 Geophysical survey: interpretation.

lower resistance. If these are both archaeological features it is not possible to estimate their chronological order; the image in Figure 5.5 gives the impression that the smaller feature overlies the larger, but this is a reflection of signal strength only, not stratigraphy.

Kate Clark

PICT'S KNOWE RESISTIVITY SURVEY

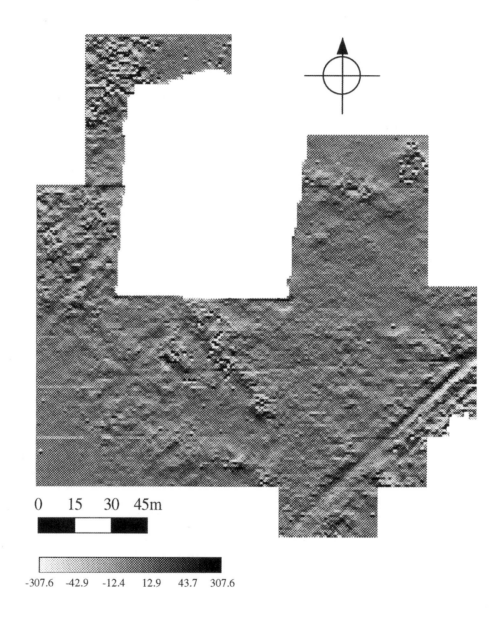

0   15   30   45m

-307.6   -42.9   -12.4   12.9   43.7   307.6

Fig. 5.3 Geophysical survey: Roberts cross filtering.

PICT'S KNOWE
COMBINED RESISTIVITY AND TOPOGRAPHIC PLOT

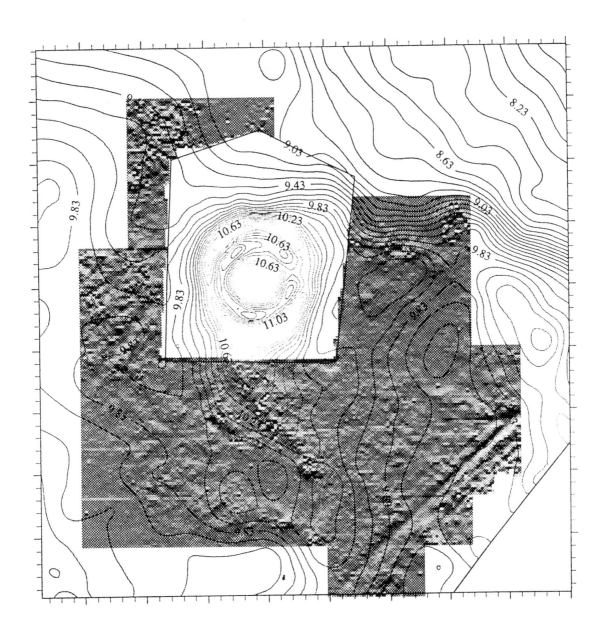

Fig. 5.4 Geophysical survey: trends in resistivity data.

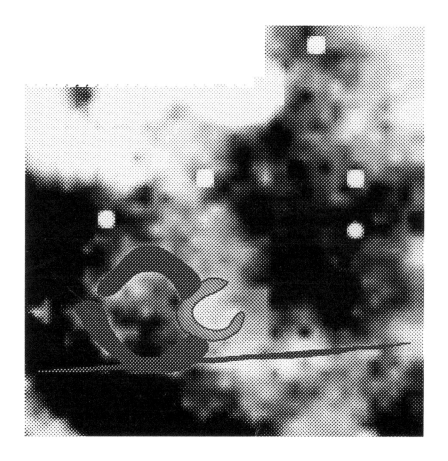

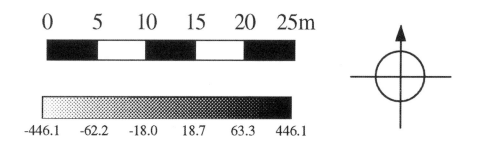

Fig. 5.5 Geophysical survey: possible ring ditch'.

6

The waterlogged wood assemblage from the Pict's Knowe

Anne Crone, Rob Sands and Theo Skinner

Introduction

Assemblages of waterlogged wood were retrieved from the re-cut Iron Age ditch during both the 1994 and 1995 seasons. The authors have examined various aspects of the assemblages at different times and independently of each other. Rob Sands examined artefactual material from the 1995 season in terms of woodworking techniques while Theo Skinner carried out the bulk of the wood species identifications from both assemblages. Anne Crone examined the 1994 assemblage and carried out additional species identifications where necessary. This report integrates these separate analyses and interrogates the whole wood assemblage from the Pict's Knowe in terms of species composition, wood use and artefact type. The nature of the activity on the site is discussed in the light of this evidence.

The assemblage; size, condition and content

Some 369 bags of wood, each with individual small find numbers were collected. The contents of each bag varied from a single fragment or artefact to, in some cases, a bulk sample of wood. The wood species of all artefactual material and the greater proportion of those samples showing signs of working were identified. In addition a representative sub-sample of the bulk samples, many of which displayed no signs of woodworking, were also identified as to species. Many of the small individual fragments, particularly from the 1994 season, were too degraded and too small to be successfully identified. The wood varied greatly in condition; much of the roundwood still retained the bark and was crisp when snapped in half while the structure of some of the larger items was so degraded that they could not support their own weight when out of water.

The assemblage falls broadly into three categories: artefacts, woodworking waste and roundwood debris. These divisions provide the structure for descriptive section of the report.

Artefacts

Despite the size of the assemblage it contains very few objects which could be described as artefactual, i.e. deliberately fashioned with a particular function in mind. There are twenty items in all that fall in this category and for most of them it is difficult to attribute a clear function.

The 'peg-like' objects
(Figs 6.1–6.3; Plates 6.1–6.3)

The assemblage has yielded a group of objects that while greatly varying in size are unified by a number of very distinctive attributes. Several of the smaller, complete examples were initially described as 'pegs' and, indeed they all have a peg-like morphology, with distinctive heads and shafts. Figure 6.1 depicts a generic example; the dimensions listed under a–j in Table 6.1 correspond to the attributes labelled a–j in Figure 6.1. What follows is a generic description of the objects.

All have bulbous, domed heads, the curved surface of which is charred. On the more complete examples the base of the head is flat and meets the shaft abruptly at a right angle. The shaft extends from the 'back' of the head and is rectangular in cross-section. Where sufficient length survives the shaft has been perforated by large holes. They have all been fashioned from branches of young, fast-grown oak (*Quercus* sp.) with the exception of FN808 which has been made from alder (*Alnus glutinosa*). They have been converted from the branch in such a way that the pith lies at the crown of the domed head and the growth-rings encircle it (Fig. 6.1). A large chord of wood, just under half its diameter, was cleft from the branch and this flat surface formed the 'back' of the object. The projecting head and rectangular shaft were probably formed by notching-and-chopping away the bulk of the wood from the remaining naturally curved surface. Although the surfaces of most of these objects were very degraded it was occasionally possible to distinguish toolmarks which indicate that they were fashioned using

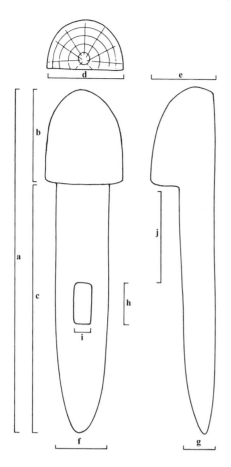

an axe. There are chopmarks in the junction between the shaft and head on FN169, and facets are visible on the underside of the head on FN385 indicating that axing has certainly produced the shoulder between the shaft and the head. Facets are also visible on one face near the tip on FN67 and on the sides of the shaft of FN169. Examination of the interiors of the holes did not reveal any clear toolmarks. However, the chord of the hole left in FN67 displays a ridge midway through the thickness, suggesting that the hole was formed by drilling or cutting, first from one face and then from the other.

The dimensions listed in Table 6.1 illustrate the large variation in size displayed by these objects. As three of the group survive only as very incomplete head fragments the length of the head is the only attribute available for comparison on most of the examples. This ranges from 85 mm to over 270 mm. Although FN48, the supposed 'ard' (see below) appears to be the largest of the group because more of it has survived there are other equally large examples. FN333 and FN808 are very incomplete head fragments and therefore their overall dimensions are unknown. However, the surviving lengths of their heads indicate that FN333 at least was larger than FN48.

Fig. 6.1 (left) Round headed peg FN169 (drawing by Marion O'Neil).

Plate 6.1 Perforated peg FN384.

Plate 6.2 Perforated peg FN384, side view.

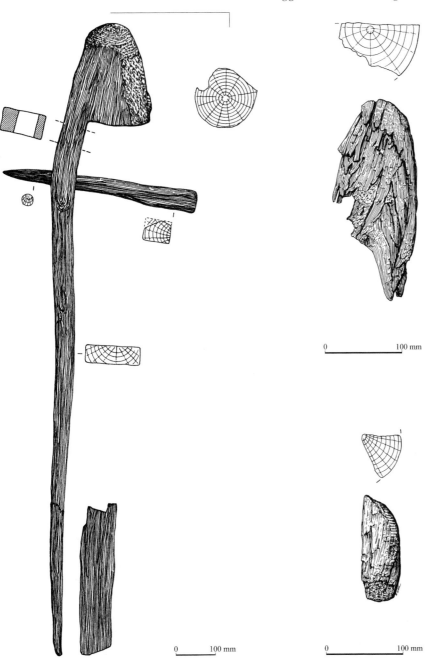

Fig. 6.2 Round headed pegs FN48 (left), FN333 (upper right) and FN833 (lower right) (drawing by Marion O'Neil).

Plate 6.3 Perforated peg FN385.

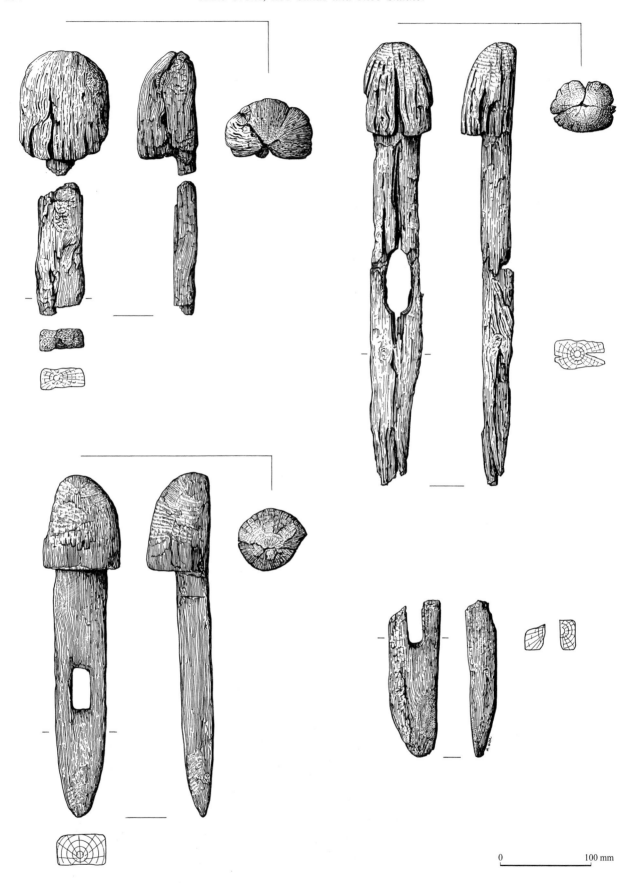

Fig. 6.3 Round headed pegs FN862 (upper left), FN169 (lower left), FN384 (upper right) and FN67 (lower right) (drawing by Marion O'Neil).

FN No.	a	b	c	d	e	f	g	h	I	j
48	1640+	250	1390	?	200	130	50	* see note below		?
67	/	/	175+	/	/	60	30	/	19	/
169	365	100	265	90	75	55	36	42	15	105
333	/	270+	/	110+	85+	/	/	/	/	/
384	455	100	355	80	56	52	27	58	25	120
385	350	85	265	90	70	54	34	39	20	110
808	/	210+	/	120+	110+	/	/	/	/	/
833	/	135	/	65+	50+	/	/	/	/	/
682	280+	120	160+	110+	70	65	28	/	/	/

Key
a - j; see diagram
+ measurement incomplete
/ no measurement available

* FN48 has 3 holes. A = 52 mm diam; B = 40 mm diam; C = unm

Table 6.1 Dimensions for peg-like objects.

Within the assemblage there are a number of large oak timbers with rectangular cross-sections, such as FN317, which may be the remains of shafts of these larger examples.

At the other end of the size spectrum are a group of three complete 'pegs', all of which are significantly smaller than the examples described above but which are roughly comparable with each other. On FN384, FN385 and FN169 the width of the shaft has been reduced at the end to a rounded, central tip and the thickness of the shaft has also been reduced at the tip. In all three cases the shaft has been perforated roughly midway along its length by an oval hole (Plates 6.1, 6.2, 6.3). FN67 is a shaft fragment of similar dimensions to this group. The remnant of the oval hole is visible at the broken upper end but in this case the tip lies to one edge of the shaft and not in the centre. The most complete of the large examples, FN48 differs from this group in that the shaft is perforated by three holes and the holes are round not oval. The uppermost lies just off-centre below the head, the second lies 120 mm below this and lies centrally along the shaft. Only a chord of the third hole survives and this lies some 0.83 m below the second hole.

A further two fragments indicate that the group cannot be polarised into distinct sub-groups of small and large examples. Although very fragmented the head of FN833 had survived from base to crown while the complete head and part of the shaft had survived on FN862. The lengths of these heads, at 135 mm and 120 mm span the size spectrum between the very large and very small 'pegs'.

As mentioned above the most complete of the large examples, FN48, was initially described in the field as an 'ard'. Grith Lerche, of the Danish *Commission for*

Research on the History of Agricultural Implements and Field Structures, examined the object and has laid out cogent reasons as to why this object cannot have functioned as an ard (see Lerche, Chapter 7 below) and the authors of this report are in full agreement with that conclusion. Its recognition as part of a group of morphologically similar objects which includes much smaller examples weakens the attribution still further.

Function?

As described above the heads of all these 'peg-like' objects are charred. The charring is restricted to and evenly distributed over the whole of the domical surface penetrating the wood evenly to a depth of c. 1 mm. There is no charring on any of the shafts or on the flat underside of the heads, nor does there appear to have been any on the flattened rear of the heads. Such restricted and even charring can only have been deliberate and appears to have been an essential element in their design and manufacture or their use. Indeed, three of the fragments, FN333, FN808 and FN833 were in such a spongy, degraded state that it is only the charred surface which had held the wood fibres together and made their domed heads identifiable.

i) Design and manufacture

In the absence of sandpapers or metal spokeshaves, it would have been difficult to produce the smooth domical surface of the head. It is possible that, after initial rough shaping with an axe, the head was repeatedly charred and the carbonised wood rubbed down (with or against a suitable stone, for example) until the smooth surface was achieved.

However, if the shaped 'peg' had been simply inserted into a fire it is difficult to explain why the base and rear of the head have suffered no charring. In reality, it seems necessary to conclude that the head was charred and shaped before the whole object was brought to its final shape. In their completed form, the rounded and blackened heads would have contrasted with the pale wood and the rectilinear outlines of the shafts. This, also, may have been an intended feature of their design. However it was achieved, the finished objects conform to a clearly conceived plan.

ii) Use: functional

The tips of all the complete examples have been shaped to a rounded point and their thickness tapered down at the tip. These characteristics are suggestive of their use for insertion into some larger structure. They display none of the compression damage at the tips that would be consistent with insertion into the ground, nor do the domical heads show any sign that they were hammered. It seems most likely, therefore, that they were intended for insertion into ready-made holes in other pieces of wood. The hole/s in the shaft may have been designed for the insertion of a peg or pin that would wedge the joint tightly shut and prevent any slippage. Unfortunately, the degraded surfaces of most of these objects means that wear marks have not survived and therefore there is no evidence to confirm or refute this suggestion. The surface of the shaft between the base of the head and the top of the hole on FN169, a distance of 110mm, appears to be a little less weathered than the rest of the shaft, suggesting that this part may have been protected, as it would have been had it been inserted into a thick plank, for example.

The length and size of FN48 rule out its simple use as a fastening in this way. However, it is conceivable that it was part of a large structure. Thus, as the footing for a bargeboard, it could have formed part of the wall plate, the additional holes being used to peg in the shaft as a capping-off of the wall head.

iii) Use: ritual

These objects have clearly been fashioned to a consistent design, albeit on different scales. It is this replication of attributes across a broad size range that brings ritual associations to mind. Ritual acts tend to be repeated acts that give rise to consistent sets of remains. For instance, the replication of attributes is suggestive of copying from a single, perhaps evocative image.

The manner in which FN48 was deposited, or 'placed' may have some bearing on the nature of the activity associated with these objects. FN48 was recovered with a stake *in situ* through the upper hole, apparently pinning it down within the re-cut ditch. The stake had been roughly fashioned from a radially cleft splinter of oak that had been trimmed to a point, the toolworking facets on which were still visible. In contrast, the upper end of the stake appears to have become weathered, either

because it was exposed for some time before burial or because it was drying out as the water table lowered. Of course, the position of FN48 in the ditch may have been fortuitous and the fact that the other examples were also found in the ditch cannot alone be adduced as proof of a ritual association with the ditch given that they could not have survived anywhere else on the site. The possibility remains that these objects form some kind of ritual structure, possibly an altar or a shrine. This could go some way to explaining the care and consistency with which they were designed and manufactured.

The keg (Fig. 6.4; Plate 6.4)

The keg is in three fragments, FN835, 703 and 47, all of which join together neatly but which were found separately in different contexts. FN47 was recorded in the field as a 'slightly curved small plank' which had a mass of leaves adhering to its underside; it was only after cleaning in the laboratory that it was recognised as another fragment of the keg. In all, the three fragments comprise approximately one-third of the original vessel.

The keg has been fashioned from a trunk of alder in such a way that the grain runs up and down the vessel and the outer surface of the vessel mirrors the bark surface of the original trunk. The vessel would have stood 370 mm high with a wall thickness of 20–25 mm. Burial has distorted the curvature of some of the keg fragments but it is estimated that it would have been approximately 360 mm in diameter.

The outer surface displays evidence of subtle adze work used to produce a smooth finish and it is bowed slightly from top to bottom. Close to the base of the vessel the wood has more knots, which would have made working more difficult and this is evidenced to some extent by slightly clearer facets.

On the interior the use of two tools is suggested, a larger (29 mm) and a smaller (19 mm) tool, possibly a chisel and a gouge respectively. On some of the surviving toolmarks on the interior the traces of tool signatures are evident. These are the product of damage to the blade edge and provide the possibility of tracing the work done by a particular tool (Sands 1997). However, the surface detail of the interior has been obscured somewhat by impressions from the underlying material and the signatures observed appear too ephemeral to provide clear associations.

The rim of the keg has a simple rounded profile. The remains of a flat, roughly rectangular handle project up above the rim, lying in the same alignment as the vessel walls. The top of the handle has broken off but it was at least 50 mm high (above the vessel rim) and 55 mm wide. The upper, broken end of the handle is pierced by a hole, 13 mm in diameter. In all probability there was a second pierced handle on the opposite side of the vessel, as is the case on other, more complete examples from Scotland and Ireland (Earwood 1993: 108–113). The holes could have been used to attach a rope handle for carrying;

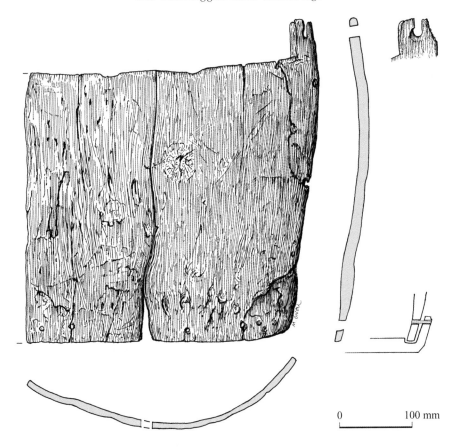

Fig. 6.4 Wooden keg (drawing by Marion O'Neil).

Plate 6.4 Segment of wooden keg FN835.

alternatively a stick passed through the two holes would secure the lid of the vessel in place, a mechanism seen on a number of Irish examples (*ibid*).

Just below the handle, in a line down the side of the keg is a series of three oval holes, between 10–11 mm in depth and 6–7 mm across. The upper lies just below the line of the rim, the second lies just above the belly, or midpoint of the vessel, and the third lies 100 mm above the base. A similar series of holes is visible down the side of the keg from Kilmaluag, Skye (Earwood 1993: 110); in this instance the holes had clearly been made to sew up a split in the wall of the vessel. Interestingly, the split on the Kilmaluag vessel occurs in exactly the same position as that on the Pict's Knowe vessel, just to one side of the handle, and may indicate a weak point on these types of keg. There is also a longitudinal split at this point on the keg from Morvern (Earwood 1991). The holes on the Pict's Knowe vessel are more widely spaced than those on the Kilmaluag vessel and it is possible that they acted as securing points for a series of hoops that fitted round the keg. Containers converted in this fashion are highly prone to splitting down the length of the vessel, i.e. along the grain and the presence of hoops would act to contain this problem. However, there are no marks on the walls of the keg to indicate the presence of hoops.

A series of small holes run in a line around the base of the vessel. The position of the holes in relation to the base and to each other is irregular and their size and shape varies. There are two large, oval holes (Fig. 6.4), 10 × 8 mm, which are angled upwards into the interior of the vessel, and which lie 20 mm and 23 mm respectively above the base. Two smaller holes (Fig. 6.4), 5 mm and 6 mm in diameter, both retain dowels *in situ* and both lie 17 mm above the base. There is a cluster of three holes (Fig. 6.4) in the knotty area of wood near the base. Two are 6 mm in diameter, contain *in situ* dowels and lie 24 mm above the base. Immediately below them is a very small hole, 3 mm in diameter, lying only 10 mm from the base. The interiors of some of the holes appear burnt and suggest the use of a heated rod in their production.

Running around the base of the vessel wall is a distinct band which lies below all the holes, where the original surface of the wood has survived, presumably because it was protected by something encircling the vessel. This feature, together with the holes described above, indicates the way in which the base was secured to the vessel walls. The base would have been larger in diameter than the hollowed-out trunk and would have had a prominent 'lip' around its edge within which the trunk fitted (Fig. 6.4). The upper edge of the lip would have been dowelled to the wall and the gap between lip and wall was probably caulked. The base of the keg from Morvern was secured in exactly this fashion and the caulking used was bark (Earwood 1991: 233). The variety in size, shape and position of the dowel holes on the Pict's Knowe keg may indicate that the base had to be re-secured to the walls on several occasions.

Earwood (1993) has summarised the available evidence for two-piece containers of this type from Scotland. Three complete examples have been recorded in detail, from Morvern, Kyleakin and Kilmaluag, all of which contained bog butter. The contents of the Morvern and Kyleakin kegs have been radiocarbon dated and produced dates of 1802 ± 35 BP (UB-3185) and 1730 ± 35 BP (UB-3186) respectively, making them broadly contemporary with the Pict's Knowe wooden artefacts. The Pict's Knowe keg is similar in size to the Kyleakin keg but differs markedly in terms of overall morphology, the latter having an everted rim and a shouldered, tapering profile. It is most similar to the Morvern keg which is relatively straight-sided, has handles projecting up from the rim and a lid-like base (see above) but which is much larger (725 mm in height and 420 mm in diameter). One notable feature of all three kegs is a pair of pierced lugs midway down the vessel. There is no evidence for similar lugs on the Pict's Knowe keg but it must be remembered that only a third of the circumference survives.

As noted above the Pict's Knowe keg was made of alder. This is the species most commonly used in the past to make containers of all kinds, from troughs, plates, bowls, etc. (e.g. Barber 1981; Barber 1982; Crone 1993; Crone 2000) mainly because it is easy to carve but also because it apparently does not impart any flavour to the foodstuffs contained within (Taylor 1981: 45). The keg could have been used to contain virtually anything. One fragment, FN47 was found with a mass of leaves adhering to it. The identification of this fragment as part of the keg raises the possibility that these leaves had been deliberately collected and stored in the keg.

At some point before burial in the waterlogged conditions of the ditch the keg was infested by woodworm. On the outer surface of the vessel there is a scatter of small holes, 1.4 to 1.9 mm in diameter. The hole size is consistent with the Common Furniture or Cabinet Beetle (*Anobium punctatum*) where the summer exit holes of the emerging beetle are never more than 2 mm in diameter (McGavin 1992: 94). The infestation is minor and must have occurred immediately prior to burial in the ditch while the keg was still in dry conditions.

The spatula (Fig. 6.5)

FN449 has been carved from a small branch of alder in such a way that the pith of the original branch lies along the middle of one face. The entire object is 275 mm long but is incomplete, the tip of the blade and the shaft of the handle being broken off. The blade is 47 mm wide and regular in width down its length. It is 11 mm thick in the middle of the blade, tapering to 4 mm at the edges which are angular in profile. Although the tip is broken off it is clear that it originally had a rounded shape. Traces of charring are observable toward the tip. The shoulders of the blade taper gently to the shaft which is very narrow, tapering from 14 mm to 10 mm along its length. It seems unlikely that a handle of this size could have supported

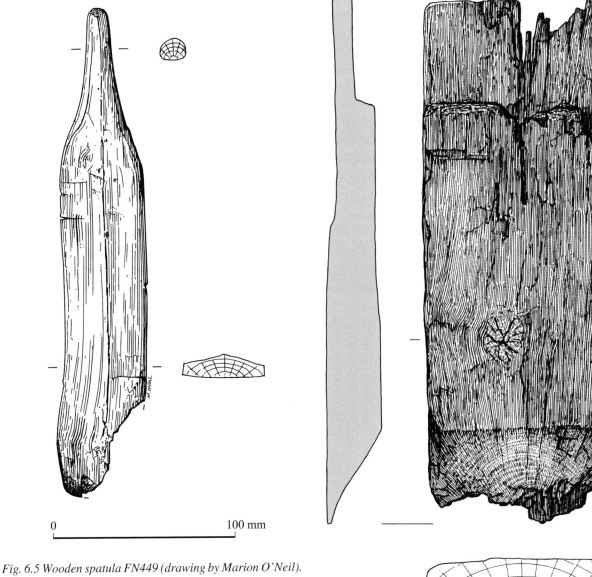

Fig. 6.5 Wooden spatula FN449 (drawing by Marion O'Neil).

0   100 mm

0   100 mm

Fig. 6.6 Wooden plank FN235 (drawing by Marion O'Neil).

the weight of the blade and it is suggested that this shaft may be a tang, for insertion into a separate handle.

The spatula could have had any number of functions. Objects of similar overall morphology, although of smaller dimensions, were retrieved from the early historic sites at Loch Glashan, Argyll (Earwood 1990; Crone 2005) and Iona (Barber 1981: 345). At Loch Glashan they were part of an assemblage which included a range of spatulate tools of varying shape and morphology, suggesting that each shape and size was fashioned with some specific function in mind.

The plank (Fig. 6.6)

FN235 is a large plank-like object which has been roughly cleft out of a half-trunk of very fast-grown oak. The object is 870 mm long, 350 mm wide and 100 mm thick at midpoint. Although eroded at both ends and along one

edge these appear to be its original dimensions. The thickness of the plank has been reduced at both ends. At one end a series of axe cuts starting some 160 mm from the end has tapered the thickness of the plank to a blunt (but eroded) edge. On two occasions the axe has bitten in more deeply, leaving clear impressions of a straight-sided blade, 45 mm wide. At the other end a step 40 mm deep and 175 mm long, has been cut out of the plank reducing its thickness by almost half. Faint incisions in the surface of the plank just behind the step suggest that the position of the step was carefully marked out. These modifications suggest that the plank had a specific purpose, but no obvious use springs to mind.

Miscellaneous

Simple pegs (Fig. 6.7)

Two incomplete pegs were found in the assemblage. FN453 and FN545 have both been fashioned from billets of radially-split ash (*Fraxinus excelsior*). FN545 is 21 mm in diameter and 75 mm long but both ends are missing. FN453 is 19 mm in diameter and 40 mm long. One end has been finely worked to a blunt point but the other end is broken. Both are heavily facetted along their length, resulting in a polygonal cross-section.

Pegs such as these are too small to have been used to secure major structural joints and were probably used in items of furniture, chests, etc.

Tent-pegs? (Fig. 6.8)

FN180 and FN664 are pieces of radially-split oak which are very similar in morphology although FN180 is somewhat larger that FN664 (250 mm long by 55 mm wide and 190 mm long by 36 mm wide respectively). One edge is straight whilst the other curves down the length of the object to meet the opposing edge at a sharp point. The curvature on both is deliberate; the ripples of axe facets can be seen on the curved edge. The pieces are trapezoid in cross-section, tapering in width from one edge to the other. Both objects are broken at their wider, upper ends. They are most reminiscent of the tips of Roman tent pegs, such as the examples found at Newstead (Curle 1911: 315).

Stakes (Fig. 6.7)

Most of the numerous small finds recorded as 'stake tips' are no more than pieces of obliquely chopped roundwood and show no evidence of having been used as stakes, i.e. buckled and compressed tips (see below). Stakes tend to have pencil-shaped tips fashioned by axe cuts encircling the tip. Only two objects in the assemblage meet this description. FN489 and FN801 are both oak but have been fashioned in different ways. FN801 has been simply fashioned by shaping the tip of a piece of roundwood to a sharp point with four or five facets, leaving the bark intact on the shaft of the stake. FN489 is more elaborate, having been fashioned by trimming a radially-split billet so that it is facetted along its entire length and sharpening the point with numerous small facets.

Walking stick/handles (Fig. 6.7)

FN491 is a very straight piece of ash roundwood, 660 mm in length although one end is missing. The bark has been stripped off and it tapers in diameter along its length from 25 mm at the top to 20 mm at the broken end, suggesting that it has been pared, although no toolmarks are visible. The edge around the top has been bevelled so that it is smooth. It looks most like a walking stick but could be a handle for some kind of implement. Ash was, and still is, the species most favoured for the manufacture of handles because it absorbs shock and for this reason, would have been equally suitable for walking sticks. Walking sticks fashioned from relatively unmodified lengths of ash roundwood have been found at the early historic sites of Buiston (Crone 2000: 124) and Iona (Barber 1981: 336).

FN525 is a short length of unconverted oak roundwood, 87 mm in length and 21 mm in diameter. One end has been shaped in the same was as FN491, i.e. the edge has been bevelled smooth while half way down the length of the object the surface has been finely pared and facets are still visible. It could be a trenail, although it has not been converted in the same manner as those described above. Alternatively it could have been prepared as a handle for a tanged blade.

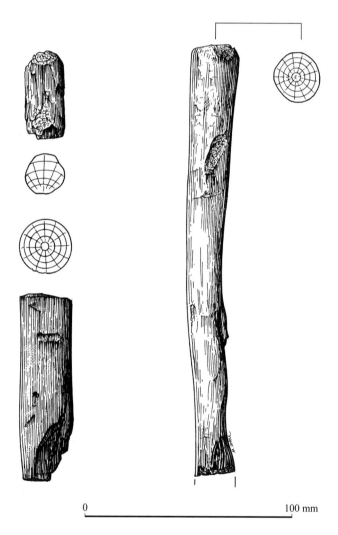

0   100 mm

Fig. 6.7 Simple wooden pegs, stakes and walking sticks/ handles, FN453 (upper left), FN525 (lower left) and FN491 (right) (drawing by Marion O'Neil).

Woodworking waste

Offcuts and woodchips

Just over 50% of the small finds identified consists of debris from woodworking. This debris is composed almost entirely of oak with a small amount of alder and a few pieces of ash.

In recording the woodworking waste a distinction was made between offcuts and woodchips. Offcuts tend to be larger and have facets that cut straight across the grain while woodchips tend to be smaller and have shallower faceted surfaces, running along rather than across the grain of the wood. Of seventy-five examples examined in detail only 30% were defined as offcuts. Most of the woodworking waste is the result of axe shaping although one offcut (FN695) does appear to show the use of a saw (Plate 6.5). It is a large piece of roundwood that has been cut at both ends. The cuts are straight across the grain and flat and no facets are visible. The surface is not well preserved so any characteristic ridges left by sawing would not be preserved.

Clearly the presence of woodworking debris in the ditches implies that woodworking was actually taking place on the site. This may seem like too obvious a conclusion but on sites such as Buiston crannog where there were extensive wooden structures still *in situ* and optimum conditions for organic preservation there was almost no woodworking debris, indicating that wood-working was taking place away from the crannog (Crone 2000: 98). Converting and dressing large timbers at source, i.e. in the woodland, makes ergonomic sense but the presence of the plank FN235 and the size of some of the offcuts at Pict's Knowe suggests that they were bringing some fairly sizeable logs to the site for preparation.

Woodchips can be used to consolidate ground, as at the Iron Age site of Goldcliff, near the Severn (Bell *et al.* 2000: 189). However, the quantity represented a Pict's Knowe is too limited to suggest that they were dumped in the ditches specifically to fulfil this role.

Lathe turning debris
(Fig. 6.9; Plates 6.6 and 6.7)

Within the assemblage there are four pieces which display evidence of having been turned on a lathe. FN521, 611, 679 and 823 are all short, cylindrical pieces, the first two of which are the most complete and measure 48 mm and 53 mm in length respectively. They are all similar in diameter, varying between 22 mm and 33 mm at the top and have been pared down their length so that they taper slightly from top to bottom. FN521 and FN611 were not identified prior to conservation but FN679 was made from birch (*Betula* sp) while FN823 was made from Pomoideae (cf. *Pirus / Malus/ Crataegus*). All appear to have been converted from quarter-logs in such a way that the grain runs along the length of the cylinder.

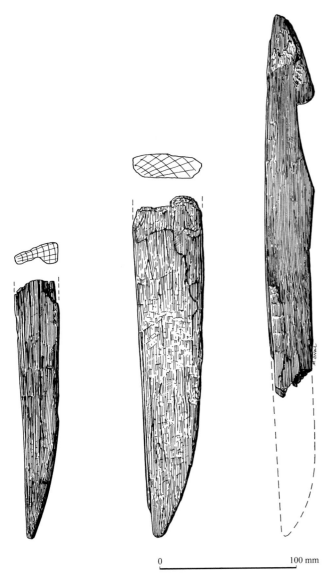

Fig. 6.8 Possible wooden tent pegs FN664 and FN180, with an example from Newstead on the right (drawing by Marion O'Neil).

Laths/panelling?

There are a few pieces in the assemblage that could be fragments of laths or panels on the basis of their relatively regular width and thickness. Most of them appear to have cleft surfaces and could be no more than woodworking offcuts (see below) although laths do not tend to have dressed surfaces. However, there are a number which appear to have been more deliberately shaped. For instance FN400, a fragment of radically-split oak 350 mm long, 75 mm wide and 16 mm thick has one neatly squared end and edges which appear to have been rounded.

Anne Crone, Rob Sands and Theo Skinner

Plate 6.5 Offcut with traces of saw cutting FN695.

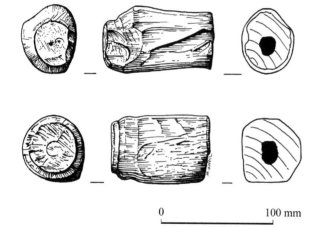

Fig. 6.9 (left) Lathe turning debris FN521 (top) and FN611 (below) (drawing by Marion O'Neil).

Plate 6.6 (below, left) Lathe turning debris FN 823.
Plate 6.7 (below, right) Lathe turning debris FN521.

The evidence for lathe turning consists of a series of two to three fine grooves, or chisel marks encircling one end of each piece. The two complete examples, FN521 and FN611, also have a characteristic cylindrical, or cone shaped hole at the other end. This is where the mandrel, usually an iron spike, was inserted into the roughout to position it on the lathe. The morphology of these pieces indicates that these were wasters, chopped off the base of the object being turned once it was completed. The shaping of the turned object would have resulted in the limited band of turning marks visible at the end of each waster. A single chisel mark visible on the surviving end of FN679 severed it from the turned object whereas on FN823 a series of chisel cuts were needed, leaving a raised 'nipple' in the centre of the surviving end.

The orientation of the grain on these pieces suggests that they were not the by-products of turning objects such as bowls or other large containers. To make a bowl that does not split or warp once seasoned the grain has to run across the piece, i.e. at right angles to the long axis of the waster (Morris 2000: 2123; and see Barber 1981 fig. 28). The grain runs parallel to the long axis of the Pict's Knowe wasters indicating that it was probably smaller billets of wood that were being spindle-turned. Small cups and boxes with lids as well as handles, chair legs, spindles, wheel axles, bobbins, etc. are examples of artefacts that could all have been made in this fashion.

Turning wasters of this type are most commonly found on later urban sites such as Coppergate (Morris 2000: 2141). The most common type from earlier sites is the classic cone-shaped form associated with the production of face-turned bowl interiors (e.g. Barber 1981). However, spindle-turned artefacts have been found on a number of Roman sites. The small lathe-turned boxes of willow found in the fort at Bar Hill, on the Antonine Wall (Macdonald & Park 1906) and at Newstead (Curle 1911) were almost certainly spindle-turned. The spokes of the chariot wheels discovered at both these sites were also spindle-turned. A large assemblage of spindle-turned artefacts and wasters has also been identified at the Roman site of Vindolanda and is currently being examined by one of the authors (RS).

Roundwood debris (Plates 6.8 and 6.9)

Some 40% of the small finds identified consists of lengths of roundwood. In contrast to the woodworking waste, only 7% of the roundwood was oak, the bulk of it being hazel, with some alder, birch and willow. Some of the roundwood displayed signs of working and this was usually a single, oblique chop across one end. In the field these chopped branches were frequently described as stakes but none of them display any indications that they were used as such. Forcing fairly slender green round-wood into hard ground results in compression damage to the tip and frequently in buckling above the tip (e.g. Bell *et al.* 2000, figs 12.16–17). The chopmarks displayed by the roundwood from the Pict's Knowe are simply the result of severing branches from the stool.

This material had clearly been deliberately brought onto the site and it has been suggested throughout the report that it may have been hurdling which collapsed into the ditches. However, there is no evidence that this material was ever used in the construction of hurdle screens. None of the roundwood displays the indentation marks that would arise from being woven. Furthermore, one of us (TS) 'excavated' several blocks of supposed

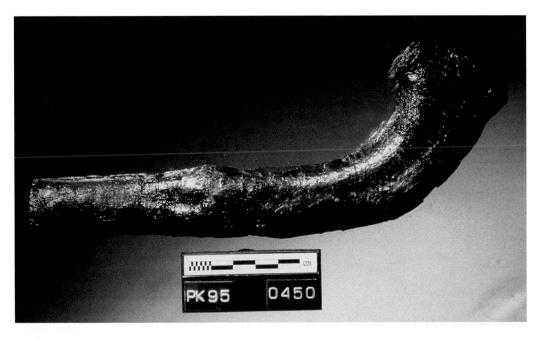

Plate 6.8 Roundwood debris FN450.

Plate 6.9 Roundwood debris FN722.

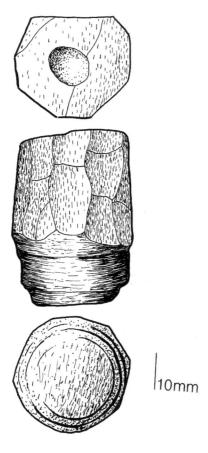

Fig. 6.10 Wood turning wasters.

10mm

Fig. 6.11 Twisted roundwood.

hurdling in the lab but found no signs of any structure. Finds such as FN179 and FN544 appear to be bundles of aligned hazel withies. It is possible that these are the remains of faggots, laid in the ditch to assist drainage. Two finds, FN772 and FN544.1 were lengths of hazel withy, twisted along their length and then, in the case of FN772, twisted back into a circle. These may have been used to bind the bundles of withies. In the *vallum* ditch on Iona, bundles of alder and willow withies, bound together with willow withies were found lying in a drain cut at the base of the ditch (Barber 1981: 295 & fig. 34). This was an early form of rumble drain which would maintain the free flow of water in ditch bottoms as sediments fell into the ditch, and it may been applied at the Pict's Knowe for the same purpose. It was a method certainly known to the Romans; it was first described by Columella in his *De Re Rustica* written early in the 1st century AD (White 1970: 150).

Species	No. of IDs	%
Quercus sp.	169	51.2
Corylus avellana	84	25.5
Alnus glutinosa	42	12.75
Salix sp.	12	3.63
Betula sp.	10	3.00
Fraxinus excelsior	8	2.42
Pomoideae	2	0.6
Prunus sp.	2	0.6
Taxus baccata	1	0.3
TOTAL	330	100

Table 6.2 Wood: species composition.

Species composition and wood use

The species composition of the wood assemblage is summarised in Table 6.2. Although nine species are present the assemblage is dominated by only two, oak and hazel. Apart from a small amount of roundwood the oak was found either as woodworking debris or as fashioned artefacts. Many of the oak offcuts could have come from the notching-and-chopping of the larger 'peg-like' objects and the shaping of structural pieces like the plank, FN235.

All the oak examined was young and fast-grown. For instance the largest piece of wood found, the plank FN235 had growth-rings which were up to 5mm wide so that, despite a diameter of roughly 400 mm the tree would probably have been only about 50–60 years old. This gives some indication of the type of woodland that was being exploited. It had probably been heavily cut over in the past, leaving large, open areas where young saplings could grow rapidly.

Some 99% the hazel identified was roundwood debris. There was no hazel woodworking debris, although one of the possible laths, FN821, was hazel. Although much of the roundwood debris was fragmented there were many long, straight lengths with few branch attachments suggestive of growth in a coppiced stool. One fragment, FN450 also displays the characteristic curvature of a coppiced heel. Hazel coppice may have been the understorey in the open oak woodland. All the birch and willow present in the assemblage was also roundwood debris.

It has been suggested that willow was growing on the site, hence the high percentages of *Salix* pollen in the leaf mass found on the keg fragment FN47 (see Ramsay & Miller, Chapter 13 below). However, the very small amount of willow identified in the wood assemblage would suggest otherwise and enhances the suggestion, made above that the willow leaves were deliberately collected. Willow leaves have no particular properties that would make them valuable, i.e. for dyestuffs or medicines, etc. so it is difficult to know why they should have been deliberately collected. Willow bark contains *salicin*, the active ingredient from which aspirin was originally made and which was used in folk medicines in the past. The leaves may have been the residue from stripping off bark for this purpose.

Conclusions

What does the assemblage represent in terms of the nature of the activity on the site? We are hindered in our ability to answer this question by the lack of wood assemblages of comparable provenance and date, not just from Scotland but the British Isles as a whole. Many of the Roman forts on Hadrian's Wall and the Antonine Wall have produced assemblages of wooden artefacts, i.e. Bar Hill (McDonald & Park 1906), Newstead (Curle 1911) and Vindolanda (Birley 1977) which are of comparable date but from a very different cultural background. Apart from a few isolated artefacts such as the bowl fragments from Torwoodlee broch, Borders (Piggott 1951) the only native site of this date which has produced an extensive assemblage of wooden artefacts is Glastonbury lake village in Somerset (Earwood 1988). This was a settlement site (Tratman 1970) and the wood assemblage reflects this, containing as it does a variety of utensils, tools and domestic equipment.

The only artefact from the Pict's Knowe with domestic associations is the keg; indeed, it is the only artefact in the assemblage with an unambiguous function (even if we can only guess at what it might have contained). This may, of course, reflect the orderliness of the community at the Pict's Knowe in that nothing of value was discarded, but it does leave an assemblage bereft of any evidence for domestic activities. The 'peg-like' objects dominate the artefact assemblage and it has been suggested that their consistency of form and repetitive patterning are indicative of ritual activity. They are certainly enigmatic objects for which no simple functional interpretation of all the observed attributes can be offered. Much of the woodworking debris, the oak offcuts and woodchips could be related directly to their manufacture on the site and it is tempting to suggest that the 'peg-like' objects formed the focus, or were an essential element of the activities taking place on the Pict's Knowe.

7

Wooden small find 48: the 'ard'

Grith Lerche

After a close examination of the c. 1.6 m long heavy wooden item (*Quercus* sp.; see Appendix 2a, Fig. 6.2) in its wet and untreated condition, my comments are as follows:

Concerning the heaviness of the Pict's Knowe find: The item is surprisingly heavy and large in size for a very early tilling tool. Finds of crook ards from the Bronze Age particularly in Denmark and Italy are more tiny, which also suits the general opinion on the early crook ards as suited for well tilled soils.

The long branch of the item (the beam) has surprisingly been worked into rectangular shape, in such a way that the upper and underside are broadest. Normally the beams of ards are close to the original shape of the branch in order to maintain strength. Where the beam is cut to shape, it will be the vertical edges which are affected. This is the case even with recent ards made in the third world.

On the Pict's Knowe beam there are still visible manufacturing marks on the underside, and no marks of any attachments, no marks from wear of ropes, and no holes, etc. The upperside seems to have been exposed to weathering, as the edges are a little rounded. The peg penetrating the beam near the thick end (which would be the ard head) ends in a point more like a pencil than as a

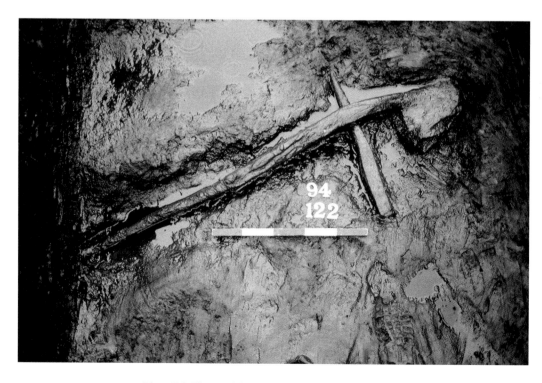

Plate 7.1 The 'ard' in situ in the 1994 ditch cutting.

point worn by being drawn through the soil. In the latter case I would have expected to see some obliqueness by wearing from a continuous draw. I therefore would rather attribute the pointed shape to the same weathering as that on the surface of the beam. This may have been the consequence of the action of water. Close to the end with the 'ard head', the beam has another manufactured hole, which is not directly in the centre. If the object is to be interpreted as an ard this hole is positioned where one would expect the stilt to be inserted. If this were the case, the pointed peg should have been positioned the opposite way round. After the holes comes the thick head which would have acted as the important part of the ard, the ardhead, which would have been the part that penetrated the soil during tillage. The forward-pointing part of the bifurcate should in that case have been well shaped as a sharepoint. This is not the case with the Pict's Knowe item. Its point could of course have been missing, but there is no sign of this. No pointing at all is observed here, and instead there are obvious manufacturing marks on another character: a vertical cut along the front of the head parallel to the pointed peg. The cut ends in a near-right angle to the beam, which also has a visible cut here. Thus at the angle where the beam and the head meet and where one would have expected some signs of more or less heavy wear from the constant contact with the soil the structure

signals for quite another interpretation. The missing evidence at the head of any sign that implies that this has been used as an implement for ploughing is the crucial argument for denying that the item is an ard of crook type.

Observations of the underside and end of the head show that it is manufactured but the general marks of wear from penetrating the soil, known from so many other finds, I did not identify.

The type of ard to which the Pict's Knowe find is most likely to be attributed is the crook type. The Danish Bronze Age find from Hvorslev is often used as a reference for this type. This is a simple ard plough with the beam and ardhead made from a single piece of wood, a bifurcate.

Prehistoric finds are often only known from small line-drawings in publications and thus it is first and foremost the outer shape's resemblance with other alike shapes which are the criteria for likeness, whereas the impression and comparison of the actual size and heaviness are seldom possible for readers. This means that the Pict's Knowe item interpreted as a crook ard should be depicted with the heavy head turned downwards and the inserted peg pointing upwards. Alternatively, the whole item might be turned with the point downward, so that the peg would penetrate the soil and draw a furrow. However, the point shows little trace of this use (see Chapter 8 below).

8

The 'ard' spike

Rob Sands

Introduction

Two questions formed the basis of the examination of the spike. Firstly, did the piece retain diagnostic tool marks and secondly, were there traces on the spike to indicate wear. The examination followed basic tool mark recording procedures (Sands, 1994).

Physical form

Examination of the spike was conducted at the Royal Museum of Scotland stores at Granton, Edinburgh, and displayed the following characteristics (Fig. 8.1).

The ard's spike or share is 52 cm long and can be divided into two worked areas. The first area is that which was seen projecting from the upper surfaces of the ard when the point was in place. This area consists of five surfaces, which have been formed by splitting the wood rather than cutting it. The first region terminates at a raised and somewhat irregular ring of wood, which also marks the beginning of the second area.

The second area is the point of the spike. The point has been neatly worked leaving a series of flattened surfaces running in vertical rows from its top to its bottom, with at least nine faceted surfaces evident. The inter-facet ridges – the point at which the edge of two faceted surfaces meet – are somewhat dulled but are still clearly visible (Plate 8.1).

The tip of the spike has been broken. Exactly when this occurred is difficult to say.

The nature of the tool marks

Although it is evident that some of the original faceted surfaces remain, it would be difficult to make reliable diagnostic statements about these. It seems reasonable to suggest that the tip has been axed to a point, probably using the axe in a shaving motion. However, there is too little evidence to make further firm assertions about the nature of the tool used. If a choice had to be made between

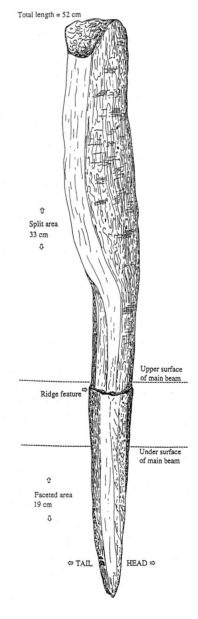

Fig. 8.1 The 'ard' spike.

Plate 8.1 The tip of the 'ard' spike.

metal and stone tools, metal would be the preferred option.

Comments on production

Two basic observations can be made about the fashioning of the spike. Firstly, it is clear, and not at all surprising, that the point was sharpened prior to insertion into the main object. The line of many of the faceted surfaces is continuous from the ridge feature, just below the upper beam surface, to the sharp end of the point. Secondly, the faceted point is slightly broader than the upper split area where the two areas meet. This suggests that the final splitting of the upper part was done after the point was produced. These two observations also tend to suggest that the point was not resharpened at any stage.

Surface wear

It would seem unlikely that the inter-facet ridges would survive any kind of heavy treatment, such as cultivation. Consequently if this is to be considered as an ard then it, or the spike at least, has had very little if any use at all. This observation alone would seem to confirm the statements made in the interim report.

In addition to the macro visual examination a small cast of part of the spike's surface was made to allow for closer examination in the laboratory. The purpose of this cast was to see whether any microscopic details of wear were present on the surface. The microscopic examination searched for scratches that might indicate movement of the spike past small stones, grit or other obstructions. A few horizontal scratches were observed but these were not sufficiently extensive to conclusively prove use.

Summary

The spike or share clearly retains the marks left from manufacture. The marks are particularly clear on the point of the spike, where a series of faceted surfaces are evident. Unfortunately, the marks are not sufficiently diagnostic to make any further positive comment. The fact that the faceted surfaces are still evident on the point would seem to suggest that, if the object is to be regarded as an ard, it had very limited, if any, use. Similarly, there is no conclusive microscopic evidence to suggest any extensive use.

Note

In Fig. 8.1 the term "Head" refers to the bulbous end of the ard.

9

Soil phosphate studies

John Crowther

Introduction

Phosphate analysis was undertaken in the hope of gaining additional insight into the nature and pattern of human activity at the Pict's Knowe. The samples (n = 162), selected by Julian Thomas as being potentially important in understanding individual contexts or particular stages in the development of the site, are taken from columns through the bank and ditch deposits, from a grid across the entrance causeway, and from a range of specific contexts.

Phosphates, which are present in all organic matter (e.g. plant material, excreta, urine and, especially, bone), are relatively insoluble and tend to become 'fixed' within the finer mineral fraction of soils as they are released by organic decomposition processes. Although widely used in archaeological prospection (see reviews by Hamond, 1983; Bethel and Máté, 1989), the results of phosphate surveys have to be interpreted with considerable caution (Crowther 1997). Unfortunately, the samples from the Pict's Knowe are either of very acidic sandy minerogenic soils/sediments or peats – both of which are problematic. Sandy soils naturally have a very limited capacity to fix phosphate, and under very acidic conditions even traces of bone can be lost within decades (Crowther, 2002). Moreover, variations in the proportion of finer mineral particles (silts and, especially, clays) and organic matter concentration from one sample to another within such sandy matrices can markedly affect the total phosphate (phosphate-P) concentration, thereby giving potentially spurious results. In peats, on the other hand, phosphate-P is partly dependent on the degree of humification (i.e. phosphate tends to become more concentrated as organic matter decomposes), and does not therefore necessarily closely reflect phosphate inputs. Caution must therefore be exercised in interpreting the results from such a site.

In addition, loss-on-ignition (LOI), which is used here as an estimate of organic matter, was measured for each sample, and pH and particle size were determined for representative samples. Low frequency mass-specific magnetic susceptibility (χ) was also investigated on many of the samples, but the values recorded were so low (<0–100 $\mu m^3 kg^{-1}$) as to preclude meaningful analysis and interpretation. The results of complementary work undertaken on five thin sections from the Pict's Knowe and on soil phosphate at the nearby Holywood Cursus sites are reported separately (see Chapters 10 and 26, respectively).

Methods

Phosphate-P (total phosphate) was determined by alkaline oxidation with NaOBr using the method described by Dick and Tabatabai (1977); LOI by ignition at 375°C for 16 hours (Ball, 1964); and magnetic susceptibility using a Bartington MS1 meter. Standard methods were used for pH (1:2.5, water) and particle size (Avery and Bascomb, 1974). In view of the high variability of organic matter content of the soils/sediments, with samples ranging from almost pure sands to peats, organic matter concentration clearly needs to be taken into account in identifying samples that show signs of phosphate enrichment (Crowther 1997). Here, samples with higher than expected phosphate concentrations have been identified from the relationship between phosphate-P and LOI, based either on simple scatter plots or, in the case of the grid across the entrance causeway, as positive residuals from the regression line.

Results and discussion

Full analytical data are presented in Appendix 3.

General character of the soils

The Pict's Knowe is located on fluvio-glacial drift deposits derived from Permian sandstones and conglomerates. These largely comprise well-sorted, medium and fine sands (Appendix 3.1), and include only small proportions of silt and clay (mostly <8% and <4%, respectively). The soils are very acidic (pH range, 3.4–5.0; Appendices 3.2, 3.4 and 3.5), and what organic matter is present in the samples is generally peaty in character, and poorly integrated with the mineral fraction. Many of the sand grains are 'bleached' – i.e. any iron that may originally have been present has been mobilised and leached by organic chelates. The capacity of these soils to fix phosphate is therefore limited by the small concentrations of clay and iron present (phosphates generally form insoluble compounds with iron in acid soils). Consequently, the phosphate-P concentrations are low (mostly <0.500 mg g^{-1}), and the few samples that have higher values (maximum, 1.25 mg g^{-1}) tend to be quite organic rich, including some that are peats.

Section (Column 1) through bank

Samples were taken in 2 cm slices down through the bank (including overlying peaty topsoil). The topsoil sample has one of the highest phosphate-P concentrations (1.22 mg g^{-1}) recorded on the site. While this might in part reflect the high organic matter concentration (LOI, 50.2%), it is interesting that the phosphate-P concentration is much higher than that of the underlying peat (range, 0.296 mg g^{-1}), which has a higher LOI (86.6%). Inputs of phosphate through grazing animals, and active uptake and cycling of phosphate by the vegetation, probably account for the higher concentrations within the modern topsoil. The figure from the underlying peat provides no evidence of significant phosphate enrichment, though it should be noted that peats generally have quite low phosphate-P concentrations.

It is evident from thin section analysis (see Chapter 10) that the bank comprises a dump of upcast material from the cutting of the adjacent ditch, which extended down through a thin layer of peat into unconsolidated sands. The bank thus largely comprises sands, with variable amounts of incorporated peat. The upper part of the bank is slightly less well sorted than the rest of the bank, with relatively high proportions of coarse sands (2.1%) and silts (11.7%). Organic matter concentrations within the main body of the bank are quite variable, but display a clear pattern, with LOI decreasing progressively down through the upper part from 3.98% (at 20–22 cm) to a minimum of 2.50% (26–28 cm), and then increasing through the lower part to 8.76% at the base (40–42 cm). The slightly higher values towards the top are probably simply attributable to the incorporation of organic matter from the topsoil by faunal mixing and/or as a result of down-washing of mobile organic acids. The increase recorded towards the base presumably reflects the incorporation of rather higher proportions of peat in this part of the bank, since the peats that covered the old ground surface would have been removed in the initial stage of

cutting the ditch. In thin section it is apparent that there has been relatively little disturbance of the bank/peat interface by faunal activity since bank construction.

Section (Column 3) through ditch fills of Neolithic age

Column 3 (Trench A) extends up through a complete sequence of Neolithic age deposits. The samples analysed are from every second 2 cm slice down the section (Appendix 3.3). The lowermost context (at ≥86 cm depth) is identified as being 'natural' on archive section drawing 138. It is therefore somewhat surprising that the three samples analysed between 86 and 96 cm contain higher concentrations of organic matter (LOI, 3.63–4.05%) and phosphate-P (0.162–0.215 mg g^{-1}) than the immediately overlying contexts (2189, 2040, 2117 and 2037). On this evidence it seems likely that the upper 10 cm of this context is also a ditch fill – possibly an initial layer of primary fill that happens to contain a significant proportion of peat fragments from the cutting of the ditch (see Chapter 10). The four overlying contexts, which extend from 86–68 cm, are each very similar in character and have properties that are typical of minerogenic primary fills (LOI, 1.81–2.45%; phosphate-P, 0.052–0.100 mg g^{-1}). Further up the sequence, through contexts 1985, 1082 and 698, LOI and phosphate-P both show an irregular upward trend, though the sediments remain largely minerogenic (maximum LOI, 7.34%). The remainder of the sequence comprises peats of Roman Iron Age date. The lower peats (context 1050) are distinguished by their very high LOI (mostly >90%) and relatively high phosphate-P concentrations (range, 0.962–1.13 mg g^{-1}). These characteristics are somewhat difficult to explain in that the high LOI would indicate an environment in which peat was accumulating with only limited input of minerogenic material (e.g. from the centre of the monument), whereas the elevated phosphate concentrations might be linked with higher levels of human activity. The upper peats (context 1049) contain increasing proportions of mineral material (LOI at 0–2 cm, 52.7%) and, apart from two samples (12–14 and 0–2 cm), show less evidence of phosphate enrichment. However, the 0–2 cm sample was taken from the surface of the ditch fill which was of recent date and therefore affected by the considerable animal grazing and consequent faecal inputs.

Phosphate survey of entrance causeway

There is clear archaeological evidence for a concentration of activity in the area of the entrance causeway, and it was hoped that further insight into this part of the site might be gained through phosphate analysis. Apart from the general problem of poor phosphate retention on the site discussed above, this specific area poses further significant difficulties, for two reasons. First, the old

Plate 9.1 Pict's Knowe: phosphate survey across the entrance causeway.

ground surface, wholly or partly on peat, may well have been eroding during the time the site was occupied, and the critical surface layers may well have been lost. Secondly, even if that were not the case, then the surface may well have been a patchwork of sands, sandy peats and peats, that would have had variable phosphate retention capacities, thus leading to spurious patterns in the phosphate data. A full discussion of the difficulties that arise in these circumstances is presented in Crowther (1997). In an attempt to achieve some degree of consistency, samples (n = 65) were taken on a 0.5 m grid from the very top of basal sands exposed in the excavation. Despite this, the organic matter content of the samples taken is quite variable, with lower LOI values (<4.00%) being recorded along the central axis of the causeway and the highest values (6.00–9.99%) confined to the outermost northern and southern edges. This variability seems likely to reflect an inconsistency in sampling the top of the sand (e.g. incorporating some material from the base of the overlying peat in some samples), rather than inherent variations in the character of the sands themselves. Phosphate-P concentrations are generally very low (mean, 0.163 mg g^{-1}), with a maximum value of only 0.472 mg g^{-1}. Unfortunately, there is a very strong correlation (r_s = 0.888, p<0.001) between the phosphate-P and LOI, and this overwhelmingly dominates the results of the phosphate-P survey. While this might simply be attributable to the phosphates present within the organic matter itself, it could also reflect a greater retention of phosphates where there is a higher organic matter concentration present in these sandy soils.

In order to 'filter out' the influence of organic matter, the residuals from the regression between phosphate-P and LOI were determined. Overall, four of the 65 samples (grid ref: 480/128, 480/129, 488/131 and 484/133) had residual phosphate-P concentrations of ≥0.100 mg g^{-1}. These are identified as being potential locations where enrichment has occurred (Appendix 3.4), but display no obvious pattern.

Specific contexts

A further 57 samples were analysed from a range of different contexts across the site, including various ditch and stake-hole fills (details in Appendix 3.5). Of these, eight samples show signs of possible phosphate enrichment: three from stake-hole fills (Contexts 0194, 0227 and 0324); two from burnt ashy material from the top of the bank (1731 and 1732); one from a pre-bank pit (6725); and two from post-recut fills of the ditch – the red organic peat (0501) and a less organic fill (2130). The fact that these ditch fills have elevated values could be indicative of human activity, though the possibility of enrichment from recent animal grazing may need to be taken into account, depending on the depth at which the samples were taken. Of the remaining samples, two merit comment. First, the basal sample (context 2134) from the large oval pit at the entrance to the henge, which it is thought might have contained a burial, displays no sign of phosphate enrichment. Secondly, one of the stake-hole fills (0441) has a higher pH (5.0) than the others (maximum, 4.4), and therefore perhaps merits further attention.

10

Soil thin sections

John Crowther

Introduction

The following five thin sections were examined in the hope that they might provide additional insight into environmental conditions and human activities at various stages in the evolution of the site:

MM1 Top of the peat layer [Context 0063] and base of the henge bank [0023] – **Section 37**

MM2 Henge bank material [0023] – **Section 37**

MM3 Natural sands [0285] and henge ditch silts [0234] – **Section 38**

MM4 Henge ditch silts [0234, 0127 and 0126] – **Section 38**

MM5 Natural sands and base of peat [0036] on entrance causeway – **Section 39**

In relation to the thin sections, please note:
MM1 extends into the top of the underlying peat. Context 0285 (MM3) appears to comprise natural sands rather than being the fill of the primary ditch cut.

Methods

The samples were taken in Kubiena boxes, approximately 75 × 50 × 40 mm in size. They were acetone-dried, prior to impregnation with resin and thin section manufacture (Guilloré, 1985; Murphy 1986) – the work being undertaken at the University of Stirling. The thin sections have been described according to Bullock *et al.* (1985). A coarse/fine limit of 10 μm is used for both the mineral and organic components.

Results and interpretation

In order to facilitate discussion the results are presented in a chronological sequence, starting with the underlying 'natural' and working through to the most recent of the ditch deposits. In the case of certain contexts evidence is presented from more than one thin section. Where colours are stated these refer to the colour under plane polarised light (PPL).

Natural sands (MM3 and MM5)

The natural deposits underlying the site largely comprise fine to medium sands. These are smooth and angular to subangular in shape, and are mostly (95%) quartz. The microfabric has an enaulic related distribution (i.e. the sands form a self-supporting matrix, with the finer fraction only partially filling the spaces between them). Finer materials between the sands appear largely to have been either washed down into the matrix or incorporated as a result of faunal activity. In MM3 the fines mostly comprise coatings of clay-humus complexes which have washed down from the overlying ditch fills, whereas in MM5 fine, yellowish brown amorphous organic matter, burnt peat, charcoal and silts have been incorporated as a result of disturbance by burrowing. In MM5 there is no clear evidence of weathering and soil development at the surface of the sands prior to peat formation.

Base of peat (MM5)

MM5 includes a section through the bottom 20 mm of the peat that directly overlies the sands. Radiocarbon samples AA-21249 and AA-21250 have given dates of 1765 ± 80 BC and 1810 ± 60 BC for this peat layer. The peat is largely amorphous, though occasional to many horizontally-lain plant tissues are present. As a whole the peat contains abundant to very abundant charcoal, including the fine stems (up to 1 mm diameter) of what appear to be ericaceous plants, probably *Calluna vulgaris*. More significantly, there is clear evidence of periods of *in situ* burning of the peat, notably in the lowermost 2–3 mm and from c. 7 and 10 mm, and more generally above about 13 mm. The burnt peats are dark reddish brown to black in colour, whereas the intervening peats are typically light brown to reddish brown. Despite having developed on loose unconsolidated sands, these basal peats contain only occasional (3%) sand and silt grains, which suggests that the surface was not heavily disturbed during the early phases of peat development.

Top of the peat (MM1)

Although only the top 10 mm of the peat is included in MM1, significant variation in the character of the peat is evident up through the section. Three principal micro-fabrics are present (the depth shown indicates distance up from bottom of the thin section):

> 0–6 mm: The lowermost 6 mm comprises a mostly quite amorphous, dark reddish brown peat with only few to frequent (15% overall) strands of horizontally-lain plant tissue. Despite being relatively well humi-fied and having a generally pellety form, with very abundant coarse micro to fine meso excrements in places, clear horizontal lamination is still evident. A 1 mm thick horizontal band of charcoal extends across two-thirds of the thin section, and rare to occasional coarse and fine charcoal is present throughout this part of the peat. In contrast to the basal peats (MM5), the charcoal in this case is clearly not the product of *in situ* burning, and has pre-sumably been blown or washed onto the accumu-lating peats from adjacent areas. Occasional grains of fine to medium sand are present, which suggests that some exposed sands and/or sandy topsoils were present in the vicinity of the site – i.e. the peat cover was not ubiquitous.

> 6–9 mm: Horizontally-layered, strong brown to brownish yellow monocotyledon plant fragments are very dominant, with occasional to very abundant coarse micro to fine meso excrements. Besides being much less decomposed than the underlying peat, this layer is also distinguished by the absence of both charcoal and sand grains. Whilst these latter con-trasts might suggest a change environmental con-ditions and/or human activity in the local vicinity, it should be noted that this particular layer may have accumulated very quickly, possibly over only 2 or 3 years. The absence of charcoal and sand may there-fore simply be due to chance, and certainly needs to be interpreted with caution. The fact the horizontal laminations are strongly preserved in this layer and the top of the underlying peat suggests that the ground surface was not significantly disturbed by trampling as the peats accumulated.

> 9–10 mm: This layer in turn is overlain by a very thin band of more heavily decomposed dark reddish brown peat. This is distinctly pellety, with very abundant excrements. In places this organic-rich excremental fabric extends up into the void spaces of the overlying bank material, which suggests that

some post-burial disturbance and decomposition has occurred at the peat/bank interface. Recent investiga-tions at the Wareham Experimental Earthwork have demonstrated the effectiveness of post-burial dis-turbance processes beneath a bank of acidic sand deposits (Macphail *et al.*, 2003)

Henge bank material (MM1 and MM2)

It is clear from the thin sections studied that the sand bank lacks any form of structure – e.g. there is no evidence in MMl that peat or turf material from the area of the ditch cut was laid down at the base of the bank. Instead, the bank simply comprises a complex and random mixture of materials derived from the pre-existing sands and peats (as detailed above). Indeed, disturbance during bank construction, which is inevitable in such a loose sandy matrix, and subsequent mixing by mesofaunal activity has led to a blurring of the edges of the individual units. MM1, for example, includes part of a lump of peat that is virtually identical to the *in situ* peat at 0–6 mm, and this merges over a distance of 4 mm into the surrounding sands. Similarly, in MM2 there are pieces of what appears to be material from the burnt peat layers. Also in MM2 there is a microfabric in which amorphous organic matter, with very abundant charcoal, is much more closely admixed within the sand matrix. Although this appears as though it may be derived from a former Ah horizon (which would be indicative of locally drier conditions), some caution must clearly be exercised in view of the degree of disturbance and intermixing that is evident within the bank.

Fills of first ditch cut (inner side)

The fills investigated are all from the inner side of the ditch, and are therefore derived from the central part of the monument rather than the bank.

Primary fill [0234] (MM3 and MM4)

The primary fill occurs as a cone of material, some 20 cm deep, in the angle between the flat floor and wall of the ditch. The bottom 30–40 mm of the fill (MM3) comprises a complex mixture of material from the ditch sides, some of which has clearly washed or fallen into the bottom of the ditch in intact pieces. This includes, for example, a relatively large (20 mm) flat piece of peat, similar to that described at 0–6 mm in MM1, and small (1–2 mm) fragments of burnt peat. These peats are presumably derived from the upper part of the ditch cut, and thus demonstrate that the sequence of peats identified beneath the bank extended upslope onto the monument, at least as far as the line of the inside of the ditch. The majority of the fill, however, comprises much more disaggregated material. This is dominated by fine to medium sands, but these are set within a matrix of finer sediments (i.e. a porphyric related distribution). The finer fraction mostly comprises a mixture of peats and silts. Charcoal is present in varying proportions: rare to occasional in the disaggregated fine fraction, but locally abundant within the burnt peats. This basal fill as a whole lacks any clear layering and would appear to have accumulated very quickly, probably within a year or so of ditch/bank construction.

At the top of this fill (MM4) the overall composition is very similar to that at the base in that it comprises a mixture of sands and fragments of different peats. However, three differences are apparent. First, the sands that form the bulk of the fill have an enaulic related distribution. Secondly, about 50% of the finer fraction comprises yellow to strong brown amorphous organic gels, which may well have washed down into the sediments at a later stage. Thirdly, the peat fragments that are present are concentrated in two thin (2–4 mm) bands. These characteristics suggest that as the primary fill accumulated there was a general reduction in the erosion of the exposed peats. The upper fill is therefore predominantly sand, though periodically some peat has fallen/washed in to produce the peaty bands. A puzzling feature of the bands is the fact that they are horizontal, and slightly concave, in the cross section, whereas the apparent angle of repose of the cone of primary fill (and of the overlying fill) is about 30°. One possibility is that rotational slumping has occurred, though there is no clear evidence of this. Alternatively, it may be that this fill was originally much more extensive with a much lower gradient, and that the steep surface of the fill has been artificially cut. Certainly this is something that needs to be given serious consideration. In this respect it is interesting to note that the section drawing also shows some horizontal layering in the primary fill upslope of MM4.

Later ditch fills (MM4)

The immediately overlying fills dip at about 30°, which probably corresponds with the angle of repose. The lower context [0127] is about 35 mm thick. In its lower half there is a 20 × 10 mm block of sandy fill, with an enaulic

related distribution, that appears to have been washed in as an intact block. Otherwise, the context largely comprises fragments of peat that have been washed in, presumably from exposures at the edge of the ditch. As would be anticipated, these vary markedly in character, ranging from generally smaller (typically <1 mm) dark reddish brown fragments of burnt peat with abundant charcoal, to larger pieces of strong brown peat with rare to occasional charcoal. These peaty fills display clear banding, particularly in the uppermost 15 mm of the context, with intervening layers being a mixture of sands and peats. Such banding might reflect annual cycles of sedimentation. There is no evidence of *in situ* peat development within the ditch at this time. However, compared with underlying fills, context 0127 includes greater numbers (occasional to many) of *in situ* roots, some of which run parallel with the banding. It is also distinguished by the presence yellow amorphous organic gel. Some is contained within roots, but there is one large unit, 8 × 10 mm in cross-section. The gel appears to be a decomposition product of plant tissues from vegetation that was growing in the ditch.

The upper context [0128] comprises fine to medium quartz sands with an enaulic related distribution. It does, however, include occasional (3%) fragments of peat, which are again extremely variable in character, and occasional *in situ* roots. The boundary between contexts 0127 and 0128 is sharp, and reflects a significant change in the nature of the material being supplied to this particular section of the ditch. This might reflect, for example, the fact that by this stage the exposed peats at the edge of the ditch were quite stable and/or largely covered by accumulating sands that might have been eroded from the ground surface at the centre of the monument. Detailed section drawings should provide clear insight into the relationship between this fill and the adjacent land surface.

Acknowledgments

The author gratefully acknowledges the assistance given by Dr Richard Macphail in the interpretation of the thin sections.

11

Charred plant remains

Penny Johnson

Introduction

This report examines the charred plant remains extracted from samples taken during the 1995 season of excavation.

The excavator's interpretation of this henge site has emphasised the use of the site as focus for ritual activity, rather than for habitation (see Chapter 18 below). Archaeobotany is primarily used as a means to explore the economic endeavour of past human populations. On ritual sites, however, economics can sometimes be a secondary consideration. At the Pict's Knowe the absence of any evidence for large scale economic or domestic activity is reflected in a dearth of archaeobotanical remains.

None of the samples from the Pict's Knowe meet criteria for statistical analysis (>50 cereal items and/or >30 weed seeds). Cereal remains are few, but some deposits affirm the presence of certain crop types on the site or available in the area. Weed seeds are even less abundant than cereal items.

The small amount of charred plant remains restricts archaeobotanical interpretation of the site. The following account reports on the methodology used in this study, some of the problems encountered, and describes the charred seed remains that were recovered. Interpretation on the basis of these discoveries is, however, limited.

Methodology

Methods of sampling and processing plant remains from the Pict's Knowe have been in the hands of a variety of people, from sampling on the site, to the eventual identification in the laboratory.

Sampling strategy targeted the deposits especially relevant and of interest to the excavators, and limited itself to those that seemed to be from prehistoric contexts.

The samples were processed in Edinburgh, by water flotation, using a Cambridge flotation system. A uniform size of 3 litres was taken for each sample, apart from sample no. 72, which was 1.5 litres in volume (Ciara Clarke, pers. comm.).

The >1 mm flots of each sample were sorted for preliminary assessment in Edinburgh. All those samples that seemed likely to contain plant remains were then sent on for further examination, including the sorting of all or fractions of the <1 mm flots and the heavy residues, and the identification of the plant remains.

Heavy residues and <1 mm flots of small volume were sorted in their entirety. However, some flots were much larger, and sorting their entire volume would have been unnecessarily time consuming. Instead each flot was scanned thoroughly for one hour. Results of the scan were recorded, noting the frequencies of modern seeds, fungal material and charred seeds, using the DAFOR system (which stands for, respectively, dominant, abundant, frequent, occasional and rare).

Similar records were made for the samples that were sorted in their entirety. The results of this are tabulated in Appendix 4.1. While this system may be somewhat subjective, it allows for a description of the main components of each sample, and it facilitates the selection of relevant samples for further archaeobotanical analysis.

After this assessment, the fine flots of relevant samples, if not already sorted, were completely sorted for charred seeds. There was one exception; only half of sample 45 (context 1731), being very large, was sorted.

The plant remains were subsequently identified using a ×20 microscope. A table of summary information, including contextual description and broad categories of plant remains found, was recorded for relevant samples in Appendix 4.2. The detailed contents of the samples that contained relevant plant material were recorded in Appendix 4.3.

Problems

While carrying out preliminary assessments of samples, it emerged that many of the seeds were of a very similar nature; spherical, with few diagnostic features, and present in a large variety of sizes, in flots both larger and smaller than 1 mm. These seeds were then identified as *Cenococcum geophylum*, a fungal sclerotia that likes certain soil conditions. These seeds are not necessarily antique, and despite appearances, are not charred. After this was recognised, it became apparent that, in fact, very few of the 44 samples examined contained relevant charred material. Fungal material was much more common than relevant archaeobotanical material (see Appendix 4.1).

Another problem is the content of sample from context 0528. Only one seed was found but it is charred and therefore could be considered as archaeobotanical material. However, 0528 was later recognised as a modem drainage feature. This raises questions about the disturbed nature of deposits on the site. At the Pict's Knowe many areas of the site had evidently suffered many years of damage and erosion.

Analysis of sample contents

Samples are impoverished in plant remains and therefore statistical analysis is unthinkable. Analysis of the plant remains is therefore limited to numerical description. This information is provided in Appendix 4.3.

The following is a general account of the main plant remains found.

Cereals are few, but the following are present:

Hordeum sativum was the most common cereal item present among the samples from the Pict's Knowe. *Hordeum* grain remains were found in five of the prehistoric samples. Two of these are from the same context (0524), from upper bank material. One was from 1731, a deposit of burnt ashy material, from 1943, a layer within the bank (0524), and from 2232, a sample which appears to represent fill of the recut ditch, and seems to be redeposited primary silts.

Triticum grains were not well represented on the site. Bad preservation has led them to be classified in undetermined, or uncertain categories. However, the samples that contain wheat remains mostly correspond to those that had barley remains. For example, the two samples from 0524 bank material that contained barley also have wheats. 2232 also seems to have wheat remains, as does another redeposited primary fill, 1954. There is also wheat chaff present in 1953.

Weed seeds

Few weed seeds have been found. Those that have emerged are, in some instances, not well preserved and difficult to identify. These have been typed. There are also two examples of different Cyperaceae types.

Interpretation of samples

Appendix 4.2 presents samples containing archaeobotanical remains, along with some limited contextual information.

For some contexts, multiple samples were taken. However, the archaeobotanical remains from samples of the same context are not uniform. For example, context number 0524, (upper bank fill), was sampled four times, but only two of these provided interesting archaeobotanical material. The contents of these two samples included cereal remains. Sample 41 was taken from a layer (1943) within the bank material (0524). This sample also contained some cereal material.

Other possible bank material was also sampled. For example, material interpreted as slump from the bank was also examined, but it contained no archaeobotanical material.

Most of the other samples taken from various contexts within the ditch were also barren (for example samples from 2316 and 2033). Some contexts interpreted as redeposited ditch silts were slightly richer; 1954 has cereals and unidentified weed seeds, as does 2232.

Similarly, of the later material, taken from the fills of the recut ditch, few contain any plant mater, but 1963 and 2130 contain one weed seed each.

Most of the material compared here is from samples associated with the bank and ditch; the sampling strategy focused on these features. However, these remains are so impoverished it is not proper to compare or contrast the results from each individual context; basing interpretation on such a small quantity of plant remains would lead to unsound conclusions.

Conclusion

Sadly, the archaeobotanical material from the Pict's Knowe samples is of an impoverished nature. This has made interpretation of the samples difficult, and analysis was limited to numerical description and a short discussion of the contents of the samples containing archaeobotanical remains. Crop remains were slightly more common than weeds. Of the crops, *Hordeum* remains dominated, but these were present in such small numbers that frequencies cannot be interpreted as a reflection of economic practise during the period of site occupation. The poor and undiagnostic nature of the plant remains has meant that the charred plant material from the Pict's Knowe is of an inconclusive and unsatisfactory nature.

12

The Roman shoe sole

Carol van Driel-Murray

The remains of a Roman shoe were recovered from the recut fill of the ditch in Trench E (context 0888). It is a left sole, made of cowhide and composed of an inner sole with complete middle sole attached with a leather thong passing through four pairs of thong slits down the length of the sole. The outer sole and all traces of the upper are missing, though nail punctures provide evidence of the original, typically Roman hobnailed construction. The edges of the two soles are chamfered to allow the upper a smooth fit. The sole is worn, with the foot imprint visible, the tip of the toe is damaged, but the foot size can be reconstructed as 25.5 cm, size 38, a fairly normal adult male size in any Roman context. The nail punctures indicate fairly dense nailing, with peripheral nailing doubled along the outside foot, and straight infill lines.

The mere fact of a nailed construction means that the shoe was made by a professional shoemaker working within the Roman cultural tradition. Shoes with uppers cut separately from the sole are unknown outside the influence sphere of the Roman Empire in the North, and hobnails are so specifically Roman that there can be no question that this shoe is as much a Roman 'import' as would be a samian bowl or a bronze patera (van Driel-Murray 2003). In contrast to metalwork, footwear is unlikely to circulate for long, so the dating of the object is of some interest. Unfortunately, neither the nailing pattern nor the shape of the sole are particularly specific, but the presence of a complete middle (rather than a packing of several smaller pieces of leather) could support a narrowing of the range to the first half or middle of the

Plate 12.1 The Roman shoe-sole, as excavated.

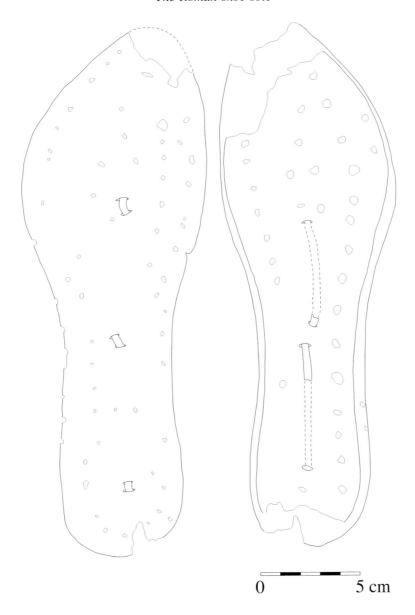

Fig. 12.1 The Roman shoe sole.

second century AD. It is noticeable that at Vindolanda complete middle soles are most popular in the early second century, but have disappeared by the later second century. The nailing pattern and the sole shape are not inconsistent with such dating, but it is still no more than an indication.

Such a shoe could have been obtained from a nearby Roman settlement as a 'prestige item', but could equally have been discarded by some passer-by. If actually used in a native context, the shoes would make the wearer quite distinctive, as besides leaving obvious and telling nail patterns in unmetalled roads, the rigid, foot enclosing Roman footwear affects the gait and carriage of the wearer. That someone was wearing Roman, as opposed to soft, native, footwear would have been visible from afar (van Driel-Murray 1999). Though there is some evidence

for a preference for left shoes in ritual depositions both inside and outside the Roman empire, it would be difficult to substantiate such a conclusion from this isolated find.

The shoe was recovered from the south terminal of the enclosure, amongst a quantity of wood, including stakes and small pole-lathe turned items and woodworking debris. The lathe dates this firmly to the Roman period, probably the first half of the second century AD. Above this deposit was the red organic peat which occurs across the whole ditch, and is presumably later in date. This peat may account for the absence of the hobnailed outer sole, since iron tends to disintegrate in peat, destroying the surrounding leather in the process. The thick, cow hide inner pierced only by nail shafts could however withstand the corrosion.

13

Botanical investigation of the Pict's Knowe leaf sample PK94 FN47

Susan Ramsay and Jennifer Miller

The site

The excavation of the west ditch cutting opposite the entrance revealed a disturbed surface overlying layers of black organic material interlaced with sand lenses, below which was highly organic red 'peat'. The bottom of the ditch contained compact green clay in which was found a slightly curved small plank (see Crone, Sands and Skinner, Chapter 6 above) with a mass of leaves adherent to its underside, interpreted as a fragment of a wooden keg.

Sample description

The depth of leaf material on the plank varied between 1–3 cm and was enclosed in a sandy/silty matrix. Preservation was good, although the sample was compacted and difficult to disaggregate. Small twigs were visible, but few in number.

Methods

Samples for pollen analysis were removed from the matrix directly below the plank and from amongst the leaves before further investigations were undertaken. These samples were approximately 2 cm^3 in volume and the pollen preparation techniques followed Moore, Webb and Collinson (1991). Samples for macrobotanical investigation were taken from various locations in the matrix and disaggregated in distilled water to separate individual leaves for identification. Recognisable whole leaves and fragments were isolated and identified. Some of these were then dried for future ^{14}C accelerator dating. The remainder were mounted on slides for reference or stored in 2/3 ethanol, 1/3 glycerine and 20 cc formalin. The remaining fractions, which had a total volume of approximately 500 ml (displaced) after leaf removal, were sieved for further botanical investigation, using 500μ and 150μ sieves. Nomenclature follows Stace (1991) and Smith (1978).

Results (see Appendix 5)

There was no significant difference in the macrofossil content of the various samples obtained. Consequently they were treated as one combined unit. The matrix description was as follows:

leaf detritus	abundant
seeds	occasional
insect	rare
moss	rare
buds	sparse
twigs	sparse
epidermis detritus	frequent
sand	common

Terminology follows Hubbard and Clapham (1992).

Conclusions

All identifiable leaves were of *Salix cinerea* (grey willow) and, as *Salix* is an insect pollinated species, the high percentages of *Salix* pollen found in the samples indicate on-site growth. Twigs and buds found within the matrix were also identifiable as *Salix* species and being few in number, imply leaf litter origin rather than manual gathering for a specific purpose. The mono-specific nature of the leaf litter and paucity of macroscopic evidence for other tree species suggests a pure stand of willow shrubs on site. However pollen evidence for alder, birch and hazel/bog-myrtle indicates a more varied woodland cover in the vicinity of the site.

Strong evidence for fen woodland is found in both the pollen and macrofossil record, with an indication of standing water in the vicinity, as suggested by the *Lemna c.f. minor* (common duck weed) seeds and pollen. Finds of *Calluna vulgaris* (heather) stems, leaves, capsules, seeds and pollen imply a heathland component to the vegetation.

Arable/grassland species are also evident and it may be that the elements of these habitat types are present due to the occurrence of turf on the hillock of the Pict's Knowe. It is also possible that the macrofossils have come into contact with standing water prior to deposition either by floating onto the site or, if the sandy/silt matrix was deposited in situ manually, then the macrofossils found within it could have had a variety of origins.

In summary, the archaeobotanical evidence shows a varied landscape with both wet and dry land vegetation types. There is clear evidence for *Salix* species shrubs growing on site.

14

Prehistoric ceramics

Rick Peterson and Julia Roberts

Introduction

The excavations recovered 544 separate finds of pottery, 356 of which were recovered as part of the dry sieving undertaken during 1994 of contexts 0001 and 0002 in the south-eastern quadrant of the site.

The material was examined using a hand lens of ×10 magnification and placed in fabric groups on this basis. The classification of the fabric is based the categories suggested by Orton, Tyers and Vince (1993, 231–241), but slightly modified to take into account the more variable nature of prehistoric pottery. While Orton, Tyers and Vince use 'feel' as a category of classification we felt that the surface damage to much of the pottery precluded such a division. We also added a classification of fabric thickness on a three point scale of thin (10 mm or less), moderate (10–15 mm) and thick (15 mm or more). Thin section analysis of six representative vessels (vessels 3, 4, 5, 7, 14 and 16) was used as a control on these macroscopic identifications.

Summary

The pottery is all in an extremely fragmentary condition, making detailed vessel description difficult. Enough evidence survives to show that the site was in use over a long period of time. Vessels 1, 2, 3, 11, 14, 15 and 16 all date to the early Neolithic period. All these vessels are of a broad Scottish tradition of early Neolithic carinated and S-profiled bowls, which Kinnes sees as dating from 3100–2700 bc (c. 3900–3300 BC) (Kinnes 1985, 23). Most of this material comes from beneath the henge bank and points to a pre-monument use of the site stretching over a long period of time. Vessel 4 probably dates to the early part of the late Neolithic, together with Vessels 9 and 12 (cf. Cowie 1993, 16–17 and 31).

The next phase of activity at the site represented by pottery is the remains of a possible cremation burial within the destroyed Collared Urn (Vessel 5) inside the entrance to the henge, around grid point 475/128. All stratigraphic relationships in this area have been destroyed by rabbit burrows. The late prehistoric activity on the site is represented by the remains of a crucible used for Copper-alloy working (Vessel 7), and possibly by the lamp (Vessel 6, Fig. 14.1, 6).

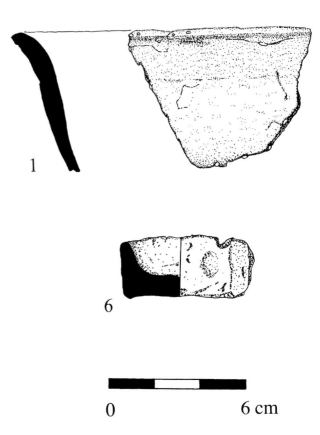

Fig. 14.1 The Pict's Knowe: pottery.

Carinated and S-profile bowls

Fabric group 1

A hard granular fabric, gritty to the touch. Around 20% of the matrix is very coarse very angular granitic particles, a further 5% of the matrix is coarse angular quartz pieces.

> Vessel 1 (Fig. 14.1, 1): Open S-profiled bowl, in a thin fabric, with a simple, slightly everted rim. The vessel is around 150 mm in diameter at the rim and has been burnished externally. Vessel 1 is part of a general Scottish tradition of S-profiled and carinated bowls which have a broad distribution (Kinnes 1985, 21–24: Cowie 1993, 15–16).

> Vessel 2: is within the same fabric group and presumably the same style but only two sherds were recovered.

> Vessel 3: Single plain body sherd of around 8 mm in thickness.

> Vessel 14: Carinated bowl, in a thin fabric, with a simple upright rim. Due to the acidity of the soil the surfaces of the sherds have been badly abraded.

Fabric group 9

A hard laminated fabric. Around 5% of the matrix is coarse sub-angular granitic fragments.

> Vessel 11 is probably also a thin carinated bowl. The three sherds recovered indicate it is in the same tradition as fabric group 1.

Fabric group 11

A very hard laminated fabric. Around 10% of the matrix is medium to very coarse angular limestone fragments with a further 5% being very coarse sub-rounded quartz pieces.

> Vessel 13 is a single sherd of a pot of moderate thickness.

Fabric group 13

A hard hackly/laminated fabric. Around 10% of the matrix is medium to coarse angular granitic fragments, a further 10% is coarse very angular grog or metasediment particles.

> Vessel 15 is represented by a single sherd which probably belongs in the same thin carinated bowl style.

Fabric group 14

A very soft irregular fabric. Around 10% of the matrix is very coarse sub-rounded granitic fragments.

> Vessel 16 is an open carinated bowl, of moderate thickness, with a simple rim. These sherds were seriously affected by the acidity of the soil, leading to the breakdown in the sherds in many cases.

Later Neolithic pottery

Fabric group 2

A soft granular fabric, often highly abraded. Around 5% of the matrix is very coarse, very angular grog particles.

> Vessel 4, many very badly abraded thick plain sherds of what was probably one vessel, one sherd (FN 221) could be reconstructed as part of a necked bowl, perhaps similar to the Ebbsfleet style of Peterborough Ware. Most of the sherds were recovered during the sieving in the SE quadrant and appear to cluster around grid point 471/123 (see Fig. 14.2).

Fabric group 7

A soft slightly granular fabric, smooth and slightly slippery to the touch. There are no visible particles in the clay matrix at ×10 magnification.

> Vessel 9: Badly abraded plain rim sherds, of moderate thickness, from a vessel with a simple, pointed, upright rim. The sherds may be part of a Grooved Ware vessel, although no decoration survives.

Fabric group 10

A soft fine fabric. Around 10% of the matrix is very fine sub-angular quartz particles, 5% of the matrix is fine sub-angular metasediment pieces and a further 5% is fine sub-angular ?granitic fragments.

> Vessel 12: Two rim and one body fragments. While it is impossible to be definite on such scanty evidence the fabric indicates that these could be part of the early Neolithic heavy bowl tradition identified by Cowie (1993: 16–17 and 31).

Collared urns

Fabric group 3

A soft granular fabric. Around 5% of the matrix is coarse rounded red and black iron ore particles, a further 5% is voids left by the leaching out of coarse angular limestone particles.

> Vessel 5, many very badly abraded thick plain sherds of what was probably one vessel. In view of the presence of parts of a collar (FN 216), and the distribution of fabric group 3 sherds and cremated bone, it seems likely that they represent a destroyed Collared Urn, which had contained a cremation burial, located around grid point 475/128 (see Figs. 14.3 and 14.4). None the less, the cremated bone, while too fragmentary for positive identification, may have been animal rather than human.

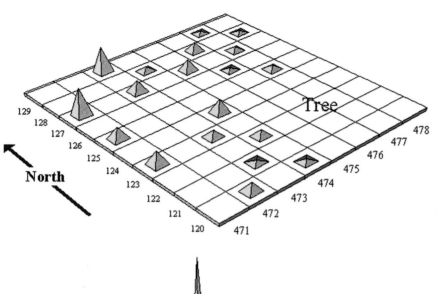

Fig. 14.2 Distribution of sherds of Vessel 4, Fabric Group 2.

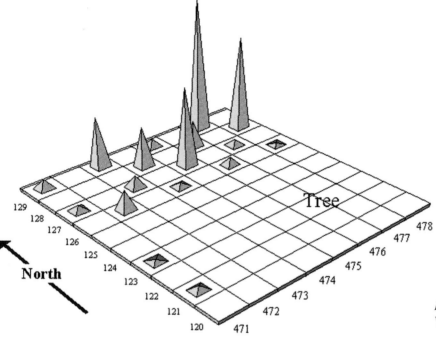

Fig. 14.3 Distribution of sherds of Vessel 5, Fabric Group 3.

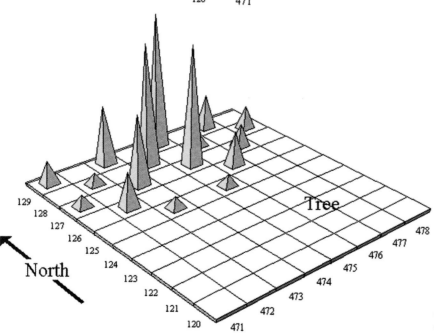

Fig. 14.4 Distribution of fragments of cremated bone.

Later prehistoric pottery

Fabric group 4

A hard compact slightly laminated fabric, fine and smooth to the touch. Around 5% of the matrix is very coarse very angular grog particles.

> Vessel 6 (Fig 14.1, 6): Part of a small, square, pinch formed vessel. The vessel is 8 mm thick, 25 mm tall and 58 mm along the surviving side. The vessel is probably a simple, floating-wick fat lamp.

Fabric group 5

A hard, very laminar and extremely friable fabric, all the sherds present are vitrified to a greater or lesser extent. Around 20% of the matrix is very coarse rounded quartzite particles. A further 5% of the matrix is very coarse rounded metasediment particles.

> Vessel 7: A badly distorted crucible with a simple upright rim. Around 8–10 mm in thickness. In all the sherds present it is only a deposit of Copper-alloy slag which is holding the fabric together, other sherds may well have broken down completely.

Fabric group 6

A hard granular fabric. Around 20% of the matrix is coarse angular quartz particles. A further 5% is very coarse very angular feldspar particles.

> Vessel 8: Two small plain moderately thick body sherds from a vessel of unidentified form.

Wheel thrown pottery

Fabric group 8

An extremely soft laminar fabric. There are no visible particles in the clay matrix at ×10 magnification.

> Vessel 10: A single fine very abraded sherd. This sherd has possible traces of a dark slip colour coat on one surface and may be part of a Romano-British fineware vessel.

A full sherd by sherd catalogue appears as Appendix 1.

Summary of petrological analysis carried out by Helen Joyner and Kerry Tyler

Neolithic vessels

Vessels 3, 14 and 16 all appear to be made of the same fabric. The clay matrix and inclusions are typically identifiable to granite. The granoblastic properties of the pottery sherds suggest they are naturally occuring in the clay. This would suggest the vessels were made in the same vicinity as one another. The occurrence of sandstone in vessel 16 could be interpreted as a deliberate inclusion. However, because of the homogeneity of the other sherds it is likely that the sandstone occurred naturally as sedimentary rock particles in the clay. During the last glaciation of south-west Scotland the area was scoured by part of the Southern Uplands ice-sheet. As the ice-sheets ablated, large quantities of sand and gravel were deposited by the outwash streams. Extensive spreads accumulated in the Nith and Cairn Water valleys, forming a complex accumulation of different fabrics from different geological time periods.

Bronze Age and Iron Age vessels

Vessels 4 and 5 are undoubtedly of the same fabric. The lamination of the clay and the presence of a clay pellet both suggest that the clay received little preparation. It is unlikely that any of the inclusions were deliberately added, all show signs of being naturally occurring in the clay. The long thin voids observed may be from the addition of some kind of organic temper, but may also simply be another result of the clay receiving little preparation. Unfortunately the commonness of quartz and mica inclusions makes it impossible to tie down a source for the materials from petrological analysis alone.

Vessel 7 is of a very different fabric to vessels 4 and 5. The natural clay has a very high quartz content, but the variety in size of the quartz grains suggest it is also likely that much of the quartz has been deliberately added. This fact could support the suggestion that this is part of a crucible. Such a vessel would benefit from a high quartz content as it would need to withstand the constant expansion and shrinkage of being heated and cooled. The friability of the sherd, and the voids where quartz may have been lost, could also be explained by this kind of usage. Once again the question of source is difficult to answer with such common inclusions. The source of the quartz that was added is impossible to tie down.

15

Worked stone artefacts

Graeme Brown, Mike Roy and Diane Dixon

Eighty-seven pieces of worked stone were collected during the 1994–1997 excavations at the Pict's Knowe. Several kinds of raw material were used to produce the modified pieces, chert being the most common, accounting for more than half of the assemblage. Of the other types the most notable is a devitrified pitchstone, a stone which cannot have been procured in the immediate locality of the site, in contrast to all the other materials.

Despite the small size of the assemblage it contains evidence for both simple and complex debitage practices carried out using several different reduction techniques. Simple edge modification of flakes and blades is present; more accomplished, and extensive, retouch is also evidenced on the bifacially flaked projectile points.

Materials

The bulk of the lithic material is made up of chert (fifty-six pieces) and pitchstone (twenty pieces). Seventy-nine percent of the total comes from three main contexts: 2404, 6486 and 6725. Chert is the most prevalent material in all three contexts with small numbers of pitchstone represented in 2404 and 6486 (ten and nine pieces respectively). The chert exhibits some variability in its colour and texture: grey or brown being most common, but with green and honey coloured varieties also represented. Both translucent and opaque kinds of chert are present in this assemblage.

By contrast the twenty pieces of devitrified pitchstone show less variability in colour and texture. The pitchstone is commonly of a grey opaque type, although the grey colour ranges from light through to a very dark, almost black, shade.

Small numbers of other raw materials were worked including two types of fine grained volcanic stone, quartz and silicified siltstone. Four pieces of this volcanic stone have become very degraded in the soil, a post-depositional process which had rendered the original material almost unrecognisable.

Chert and pitchstone also sustained varying degrees of post-discard/post-depositional alteration. Several pieces were subject to weathering, while the changes in colour and texture usually associated with burning are particularly apparent on the chert from context 6486.

Thirty-three pieces (37%) of the assemblage are damaged, missing either the proximal or distal ends or both. Breakage can be caused unintentionally during the knapping process or as a result of post-depositional conditions.

Twenty-two of the damaged pieces were excavated from contexts identified as old land surface deposits (2404 and 6486); therefore it seems more likely that the damage was post-discard, perhaps caused by trample while the objects were lying on this surface.

The majority of artefacts in this assemblage are small with maximum dimensions (length and width) under twenty millimetres, a generalisation which holds good for the most common types: regular flakes, irregular flakes and bladelets. No cores were discovered but the presence of a small core rejuvenation flake and a small overshot bladelet also suggest the production of small lithic debitage. The small overall size of the assemblage perhaps points to a problem in procuring large sized raw material in the local area. The chert and volcanic rock could have been procured in the local area, probably in pebble form from a gravel or beach source. The pitchstone could not have been found locally, with a likely source being one hundred kilometres away on the island of Arran.

Sixty-nine percent of the assemblage retains some cortex, and of this total most of the chert and pitchstone are the products of tertiary stages of reduction with only one piece (chert) categorised as primary. This bias is particularly strong for the pitchstone component with seventeen out of twenty pieces belonging to the tertiary stage. This absence of cortical material implies that we are not seeing the traces of *in situ* knapping at this site, the primary working taking place elsewhere.

Technology

Twenty-five flakes or blades of chert and ten of pitchstone retain their proximal ends – the part necessary to glean information on reduction techniques. Six pieces of chert have the diffuse bulbs of force and elongated platforms associated with direct percussion using a soft hammer. No evidence of this technique is present in the pitchstone sample although, as noted above, the pitchstone has proportionally more damage and more pieces missing proximal ends.

Seven pieces of chert and two of pitchstone have attributes associated with both hard and soft percussion: poorly developed bulbs of force and small platform remnants but clearly visible ripples. This probably indicates the use of a percussor of medium hardness. This explanation is offered with the caveat that bulbar type can be affected by a number of different factors of which type of percussor is only one.

Nine pieces of chert and nine of pitchstone show the characteristics of hard percussion. For the chert component no single reduction technique dominates, however for the pitchstone we see a greater emphasis on reduction by hard percussion. It is possible that the predominance of hard percussion in the pitchstone component is the result of the fracture mechanics of pitchstone rather than an accurate representation of reduction technique. Fine grained rocks like obsidian or good quality pitchstone require less force to fracture than coarse grained varieties like chert and therefore use of a medium or soft percussor on pitchstone may have produced traces similar to hard percussion.

If we look at the two main contexts of discovery, 2404 and 6486, which together account for seventy six out of eighty seven pieces, we can examine the issue of reduction technique in greater detail. In the material from context 2404, traces of both hard and soft percussion are represented in almost equal numbers. Evidence of hard percussion is seen mainly on pitchstone with chert showing predominantly soft or medium soft percussion. This divide along raw material lines is not witnessed in context 6486, here both chert and pitchstone exhibit the traces of hard percussion. Only one piece in 6486 and two in 2404 display the evidence of a more complex reduction technique accomplished by means of indirect percussion.

Table 15.1 illustrates that the assemblage is composed mainly of debitage: irregular flakes, chips and chunks. Traces of both hard and soft percussion are seen on irregular flakes although it should be pointed out that soft percussion appears mainly on chert flakes from context 2404. Regular flakes and bladelets form a significant portion of this assemblage. The blade/flake ratio for the whole assemblage (45%) highlights that the number of bladelets is significant. While this pattern is certainly worth highlighting, the small size of this assemblage cautions us against placing too much emphasis on this figure. Some of the regular flakes and bladelets are missing their proximal ends. Of the eleven with this part remaining seven show evidence of hard/medium hammer reduction, and only two bladelets seem to have been produced by indirect percussion.

Although no cores are present in the Pict's Knowe lithics, a core rejuvenation flake (FN 2577) can shed some light on the type and size of cores being used. This chert flake was struck from the base of a small conical shaped platform core to remove some cortex and aid the striking of small bladelets, the scars of which remain on the side of this piece. Two core trimming flakes (FN 2012, FN 2483) also add to the impression that only small cores were worked.

Other information on core size can be gleaned from a small chert overshot bladelet. Overshot bladelets are pieces which remove the base of the core from which they have been struck. They can result either from knapping errors or from a predetermined attempt to remove the base of the core to correct previous knapping mistakes. By virtue of the fact that this type of bladelet removes the bottom of the core it gives information on core length.

These observations plus the absence of many large pieces in the assemblage argue that only small cores were worked. It may be that this pattern was a function of the availability of raw material.

Type	Chert	Pitchstone	Total
Irregular flake	22	6	28
Regular flake	4	3	7
Chip	7	2	9
Chunk	6	2	8
Bladelet	5	4	9
Segment	-	1	1
Retouched bladelet	3	-	3
Core trimming / rejuvenation flake	1	2	3
Complex retouched piece	5	-	5

Table 15.1 Lithic assemblage composition.

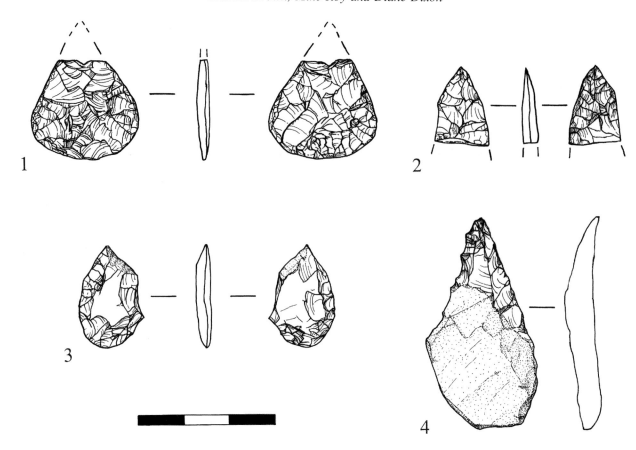

Fig. 15.1 The Pict's Knowe: lithics.

Only nine retouched pieces exist in the Pict's Knowe assemblage: all are of chert. The level of retouch ranges from simple edge modification of bladelets (e.g. FN 10 and FN 2424) to the more complex bifacial flaking seen on the fragmentary pieces 19 and 2017 (Fig. 15.1, 1–2). All but two of these chert objects are in fragmentary or damaged condition, only FN 2456, (Fig. 15.1, 4), a borer, and FN 2618 (Fig. 15.1, 3) an invasively flaked (leaf shaped) projectile point, are complete. The complete leaf shaped point is unfortunately rather a poor example of its type, quite unbalanced in overall shape and without the accomplished shaping and covering retouch seen on damaged point FN 2017.

Culture and chronology

The assemblage is composed mainly of debitage, lacking many of the formal types of artefact which have been conventionally used as chronological or cultural indicators. As such it is difficult to draw a firm conclusion as regards date and cultural significance from these lithics.

This is a particular problem as the vast majority of the assemblage, the material from the pre-monument contexts 2404 and 6486, contains only one conventionally recognised type-leaf shaped point FN 2618. The existence of a leaf shaped point in 6486 can provide some indication of that deposit's chronology: although the type persists into the later period they are much more common in the earlier Neolithic.

No complex retouched pieces were recovered from pit fill 6725, a feature which was cut through the aforementioned pre-monument contexts.

In spite of these difficulties several aspects of the material can be used to draw some tentative conclusions. The material from 2404 and 6486 includes a significant proportion of bladelets as well as undiagnostic debitage. Blade assemblages are normally thought of as being of Mesolithic date, although these are normally found in association with microliths. The absence of microliths coupled with the diminutive size of many of the pieces probably indicates an earlier Neolithic date, an attribution which agrees with pottery finds from the same contexts (see Chapter 14 above).

16

Iron objects from the Pict's Knowe

Fraser Hunter

Catalogue

All nail fragments are from hand-forged square-sectioned nails with approximately square heads.

208 Nail tip. L 30 mm, shank 8 × 8 mm. PKN 94, context 001: topsoil.

305 Nail, lacking tip. L 32 mm, shank 6 × 4.5 mm, head 9.5 × 9 mm. Trench F, context 1021: stake-hole fill.

442 Nail, lacking tip. Heavily corroded. L 36.5 mm, shank 6 × 5 mm, head 12 × 11 mm. Trench C, context 823: red organic peat in ditch.

466 Cast iron circular boss. The whole piece is slightly conical, and ornamented with a central dome 53 mm D surrounded by two raised concentric ridges. The edge is fragmentary. There are no clear signs of an attachment mechanism, but the edge is slightly concave rather than flat, as if to fit over something. The very regular thickness seen on the broken fragments implies this was cast rather than wrought, and it is therefore post-Medieval. It is likely to derive from an agricultural implement, perhaps as a wheel fitting. D 135 mm; H 50 mm, T 5 mm. Trench C, context 507: bank slip.

503 Tool fragment. Rectangular-sectioned bar, broken at one end; the intact end terminates in a blunt tip. Corrosion at the broken end preserves organic remains of grass and wood; one side has clear wood grain running perpendicular to the bar's axis, extending for 15 mm from the broken end. This may represent the remains of a handle, suggesting this was a small hand-held punch or embossing tool. With a wooden handle it is unlikely to be a metalworking tool, and was most likely for an organic material such as leather. Two joining fragments. L 33.5 mm, W 5.5 mm, T 2.5 mm. Trench C, context 1732: disturbed layer of burnt material in ditch.

582 Disintegrated remains of a nail shank. L 42 mm, other dimensions unrecoverable. Trench F, context 524: modern drain fill.

2434 Unidentified fragment – possibly nail shank fragment. 9.5 × 9 × 6.5 mm. Trench G, context 6111: stake-hole fill.

Discussion

With such a small assemblage, mostly poorly contexted or post-medieval, little can be made of it. The nails are all hand-forged and thus of any date between the Iron Age and the 18th century; only one (FN 442) comes from a secure Iron Age context, with two others from undated stake-holes. This reinforces the general picture of a scarcity of nails on Iron Age sites (Hunter 1998a, 366–7). As the structural wood from the Pict's Knowe illustrates, nails were largely superfluous in Iron Age woodworking traditions, with joints and pegs entirely of wood.

Only one other item, the ? punch fragment FN 503 is from a fairly secure Iron Age context. It is worthy of note as Iron Age tools are still rare in Scotland, and each new example, while a minor incidence in the site picture, is valuable in the larger scheme of things.

In general there is nothing to mark this sparse assemblage out from the run-of-the-mill Scottish Iron Age site, which is characterised by the poverty of its metal remains.

17

Fired clay, vitrified material and slag from the Pict's Knowe

Andrew Heald and Fraser Hunter

Five ceramic objects from the Pict's Knowe were associated with pyrotechnic processes. Only one can be attributed to a specific industrial process, the crucible fragment (FN 230) associated with non-ferrous metalworking. All of the ceramic objects were analysed non-destructively by X-ray fluorescence (XRF) to ascertain if they were indicative of specific activities, such as non-ferrous metalworking, and to give broad characterisation of any metals used.

Crucible

FN 230 is a sherd comprising the corner, rim and body of a triangular crucible. This form was used from the first millennium BC to the mid- to late-first millennium AD and is the most common type recovered from Scottish Iron Age sites (Tylecote 1986, 98–9; Lane 1987, 55–6). XRF analysis of deposits on the rim and interior detected very high levels of zinc and copper; lead and tin were not detected. Further interpretation is hindered because different elements fluoresce more or less strongly and their relative abundance may therefore not be an accurate reflection of the original alloy. For example, tin and silver fluoresce weakly while the volatility of zinc encourages its vapour to penetrate into the crucible more readily (see Barnes 1983; Dungworth 2000). That said, the very high levels of zinc suggest that it was a significant component of the alloy melted, indicative of a gunmetal or brass.

Copper alloys containing zinc are common in Roman and post-Roman times but are almost entirely absent from the pre-Roman period (Dungworth 1996). Thus the alloy content of the Pict's Knowe crucible gives a fairly secure *terminus post quem* for the metalworking activity. It also illustrates that the smith used metal ultimately of Roman origin (Dungworth 1996; Bayley 1990, 21). Such re-use and re-cycling activity is recognised on other native sites (Dungworth 1996; 1998) and in other imported Roman materials such as pottery (Hunter 1998b, 400) and lead (MacKie 1982, 71).

230 Fragment of rim, corner and body of triangular crucible. Fine orange-sandy fabric with limited inclusions (less than 0.7mm) typically of quartz and mica. Vitrified on rim and reduced grey on the exterior and interior. Metallic deposits on rim, exterior and interior. H 17mm, W 24mm, B 7mm. PKN 94, context 002, sieving: mixed layer under topsoil in interior.

Other fired clay

The remaining ceramic objects all lack diagnostic features and only two have surviving original faces. All have been exposed to high temperatures resulting in extensive vitrification or in grey reduced surfaces to varying degrees. These features can be formed during any high temperature pyrotechnic process and are not necessarily indicative of deliberate industrial activity (McDonnell 1986). This is confirmed by XRF analysis – no metal traces were detected on any of the objects. They can not, therefore, be associated with metal-working activity.

One example (FN 303) has two surviving faces and is a fragment of daub. The remaining four pieces (FN 223, 430 & 577) are more fragmentary and heavily vitrified to a glassy state. All are vitrified slags, perhaps the remnants of hearth lining. These form when the non-combustible components (earth, clay, stone or ceramic which contain silicates) of clay structures, for example furnaces or hearths, are heated. During heating, these materials react, melt or fuse with the alkali in the ash, producing glassy (vitreous) materials (Bayley 1985). Thus, the slag formed is essentially clay vitrified by intense heat (McDonnell 1995).

223 Vitrified material / hearth lining. One surviving face, heavily vitrified to a glassy state. Fabric pale orange and coarse with limited inclusions. Grey buffing within matrix. L 38mm, H 9mm, W 29mm. 13g. PKN 1994, context 002, spit 1, sieving: very mixed layer under topsoil in interior.

303 Daub. Miscellaneous fragment with two surviving faces, broken at both ends with no diagnostic features. Fabric pale orange with gritty gneiss and quartz inclusions. Grey buffing on exterior and one side. L 48mm, H 17mm, W 18mm. 16g. Trench F, context 977: stake-hole fill.

430 Vitrified material / hearth lining. Two fragments, no surviving faces. Vitrified to a glassy state. Fabric pale orange and coarse with inclusions of quartz. Grey buffing throughout matrix. Combined L 48mm, H 18mm, W 21mm. 18g. Trench E, context 888: green clay infill of recut.

577 Vitrified material / hearth lining. One fragment, no surviving faces. Mostly vitrified to a glassy state. Fabric pale orange and coarse with inclusions of quartz and stones (>2mm). Grey buffing throughout matrix of one piece. L 9mm, H 4mm, W 7mm. 2g. Trench F, context 524: modern drain fill.

Fuel and fuel ash slag

Small fragments of fuel and fuel ash slag were recovered from many deposits on the site, primarily from stake-holes in trenches G and J or from late (post-Iron Age) deposits. A full catalogue is held in archive. The fuel is all coal, and thus is almost certainly Medieval or later: although coal was used in the Iron Age where there were local deposits (e.g. Haselgrove & McCullagh 1996, 7), there are no immediately local sources for the Pict's Knowe (Greig 1971, fig. 13) and it should be seen as later material. All were from late deposits or stake-holes of dubious antiquity.

Fuel ash slag is a non-diagnostic byproduct of heating activities, from domestic hearths to industrial activities. It is not functionally or chronologically distinctive. The great majority came from stake-hole fills in areas G and J, with only two fragments from stratified deposits: FN 2639 from a lower fill of pit 6121 in trench G, and FN 537 from the red peat in the ditch in trench B. However there were no marked concentrations to indicate primary rubbish disposal. Along with its small size (average mass 0.59 g) and general occurrence in single pieces, this indicates we are dealing with highly comminuted and widely dispersed fragments. Given their small size, they would be highly mobile when deposits were disturbed.

Iron smithing debris

Only one piece of slag indicative of ferrous metalworking was recovered from the Pict's Knowe. The piece (FN 559) is a hearth bottom created during smithing. These are accumulations of slag that developed in the hearth during the forging or welding of iron objects. When the slags became too large and interfered with the efficiency of the hearth they were discarded (McDonnell 1991).

The identification was based on morphology (weight, density, colour, streak, texture, porosity and inclusions: after Bachmann 1982; McDonnell 1983; 1986). The object's plano-convex shape, size and weight, the nodular texture of the outer surface, charcoal impressions (<10mm) and silica grains throughout are typical of a smithing hearth bottom. The areas of red oxide powder throughout, indicating active corrosion of an iron-rich zone, further support this identification.

This visual identification is supported by XRF analysis. Although many plano-convex slags cannot be ascribed to smelting or smithing on the basis of external characteristics alone significant levels of manganese are likely to be indicative of smelting rather than smithing (McDonnell 1986, 1988). The slag from the Pict's Knowe does not have any manganese present, supporting the identification as a smithing hearth bottom. However its discovery in a modern context, and the lack of any other slag from the site, means it cannot be treated as evidence for iron smithing on-site during the Iron Age.

559 Smithing hearth bottom. Large fragment of a plano-convex slag lump and attached hearth lining. Outer surface nodular in texture with evidence of charcoal impressions (<10mm) throughout. Silica grains common throughout. Dark grey in colour and section. Much of the slag is fairly dense although there are zones of porosity with an abundance of red oxide powder indicating active corrosion of an iron rich zone. Trench 4, grid 4b, context 524: modern drain fill. L 89mm, H 28mm, W 65mm, m 171g.

Discussion

The evidence of heat-related processes from the Pict's Knowe is small and unimpressive: only the single crucible fragment indicates Iron Age metalworking activity. The context of the solitary smithing hearth bottom makes it unreliable evidence in the absence of any other ferrous metalworking slag. The fuel ash slag is as likely to be domestic as industrial, and it cannot be closely dated: the coal fragments are Medieval or later. Unlike the wood-working debris in the ditch, there are no comparable dumps of metalworking debris or even significant hearth material (based on the limited occurrence of fuel ash slag and vitrified clay). On this evidence metal-working was a very minor component of site activities. There are very few local sites which have produced metal-working evidence, due no doubt to the lack of excavation, but comparison with slightly later sites such as the Mote of Mark (Curle 1914) reinforces the sparsity of the metal-working debris at the Pict's Knowe.

18

The Pict's Knowe: discussion

Julian Thomas

Landscape and location

The position of the Pict's Knowe in its landscape is one that invites discussion. When the initial contour survey of the site was undertaken, it was apparent that the monument could be compared to a relatively characteristic Class I henge, although with certain unusual features. The enclosure had a single entrance to the east, external bank, and expanded ditch terminals. But the plan of the henge was somewhat flattened, being a little broader on the north/south axis, while the interior appeared to be rather domed. This latter feature was initially conjectured to have been a result of the ground surface's having been artificially built up, or even representing a denuded round barrow, placed in the centre of the henge. However, closer attention to the surrounding topography made it clear that this was not the case, and that the enclosure had been constructed about the highest point on a low ridge of compacted fine sand, which probably represents a survival of late Devensian marine deposits (Fig. 4.5). This sandy ridge emerges from the peat that presently cloaks the floor of the Crooks Pow valley, which itself was inundated by the post-glacial marine transgression (see Tipping, Haggart and Milburn, Chapter 2 above) and appears to have remained damp throughout much of later prehistory. The complex sequence of local sea-level changes, climatic developments and human interference with vegetation resulted in a series of fluctuations in the groundwater table, to the extent that on at least one occasion the sandy knoll was itself subject to peat growth. While the ridge on which the monument stands would generally have been easily accessed from the south, to the north-east the sub-peat surface drops away from just beyond the enclosure entrance. Given that areas of the valley floor would have been either boggy or covered by standing water for much of the prehistoric period, the enclosure would often have stood at the juncture between wet and relatively dry land. An indication of this is given by the finding in the last century of 'an oak boat and other lacustrine relics' in the

deeper peat immediately to the north-east of the site (Coles 1893, 123). The flattened circular plan of the monument could also be attributed to the immediate topography, and the practicalities of surrounding the highest part of the sand ridge with a bank and ditch.

While the position of a henge in a valley bottom location is entirely consistent with expectations for this class of monument, the use of the sandy ridge is rather less usual. However, henge monuments were often constructed with their banks and ditches surrounding the summit of a low hill. This was the case for both very large henges like Mount Pleasant (Wainwright 1979) and smaller examples like Milfield South (Harding 1981, 93) and Cairnpapple (Barclay 1999, 24). Richards (1996, 320) has pointed out that henge monuments were frequently located in close proximity to water, particularly in river valleys, and that an intimate relationship often obtains between these structures and the local landscape. In the Milfield basin, for instance, the orientation of the entrances of a number of small henges appears to follow the direction of flow of the major watercourses. Richards suggests that the henge architecture serves to establish a connection between the movement of water through the landscape and the movement of people, both within and between the henges. The henge becomes a kind of microcosm of the landscape, embodying various experiential characteristics of the surrounding topography. In the case of the Pict's Knowe, the henge ditch itself would probably have been wet for much of the time after its construction. The interior of the enclosure would have been comparatively dry, contrasting with the damp, marshy ground which was immediately outside of the entrance. Entering the monument by crossing the standing water of the ditch might consequentially have given access to a small enclosed area which contrasted with the landscape that one was leaving. We have seen that the entrance of the enclosure faces eastward, in which direction the ground drops abruptly toward both the present course of the Crooks Pow and the palaeochannel, rather than toward the upper terrace to the south and west. There are thus compelling reasons to suggest that the intention was for people to approach the monument from out of an area of wet or boggy ground. At the time that the monument was constructed, the upper terrace would have been covered by a thin peat, with sparse alder and birch vegetation, but the lower ground would have been bog and moss, probably with expanses of standing water located centrally within the valley bottom. Visiting the site would have involved exposure to a variety of contrasting aspects of landscape, which were actually embodied in the enclosure itself. Performances or ceremonies held within the henge might therefore have involved a heightened awareness of the surrounding landscape, for which the monument formed a focus and a microcosm. While we often consider prehistoric monuments to be dominating cultural forms imposed on the land, it may be that the Pict's Knowe was quite the opposite. It was a physical modification of landscape which afforded a more intense and focused experience of place through its critical location, through the materials and substances that it was composed of, and through the physical sensations to which one would be subjected in travelling toward it.

This is not to suggest that the contrast between wet and dry was the sole reason for the selection of the Pict's Knowe as a location for the construction of a henge monument (if such it was: see below). From at least the early Neolithic onward the sandy ridge had been frequented by groups of people for a variety of purposes, and my intention is to argue that it retained a certain significance over comparatively long periods of time. This is not to suggest that the precise meaning of the place, or the character of the activities that took place there remained unchanged between the Neolithic and the Iron Age. In this sense we should avoid relying on a notion of 'continuity' which implies that the status of a location was unaltered through the millennia. But I will hope to argue that the Pict's Knowe was recognised as a place of importance, which was periodically reinvented, in accordance with changing historical conditions.

Damage and preservation

The 1994–7 fieldwork at the Pict's Knowe was a rescue project, and yet the extent of damage to the site could only be fully appreciated once excavation had begun. The damage survey that was conducted before digging demonstrated that virtually the whole of the exposed sand surface (enclosure interior and bank) had been burrowed by rabbits. The opening of areas in the interior of the monument showed that the entire soil profile had been homogenised by rabbit action, which had resulted in the destruction of any archaeological features in the interior. When areas of the interior were exposed and trowel-cleaned the only features that could be discerned were densely cross-cutting burrows. The bank had fared rather

better, and while it was extensively burrowed it had retained much of its former structure. However, it was the damage to the ditch deposits by cattle trampling that was only revealed when sections began to be cut. Particularly at the two ditch terminals, the action of beasts using the ditch as a watering place had disturbed the upper part of the profile, almost to the level at which the wood deposits lay. The impact of this activity had been exacerbated by the draining of the valley bottom in the 1960s, manifested in the linear slots containing ceramic pipes which encroached into the henge bank in places, and which were plainly visible in Trenches F, J and K. As a consequence the ditch deposits were gradually drying out. David Dungworth (pers. comm.), who undertook soil moisture readings of the ditch sediments, was of the opinion that they were already in a terminal state of decline. A quite unexpected development was the discovery of waterlogged wood in the ditches, and it seems likely that this material would not have survived for more than another decade, even though it had been preserved for many centuries. Already, an appreciable portion of the wood was too fragile to lift. Where this was the case, wooden objects were given finds numbers, photographed and planned *in situ*, but they obviously do not appear in the analysis of the wood assemblage (Crone, Sands and Skinner, Chapter 6 above). The same applies to a small number of very large wooden objects that could not be accommodated in the tanks that were helpfully set up on site by Historic Scotland. The wood assemblage should therefore be recognised as a sample of what would at one time have been present in the ditch.

In all of these respects, then, the Pict's Knowe can be said to have been in a damaged condition that was rapidly worsening by the time that fieldwork took place. The excavation was in the full sense a rescue exercise.

The pre-henge occupation

Pollen analysis gives some indication that there may already have been some human interference with the vegetation in the vicinity of the Pict's Knowe during the Mesolithic (Tipping, Haggart and Milburn, Chapter 2 above). However, the first direct evidence of a human presence on site dates to the Earlier Neolithic, and can confidently be assigned to the second quarter of the fourth millennium BC on the basis of four radiocarbon determinations (SUERC-2093 to 2096 inclusive). Peat humification values indicate that while the surrounding landscape had been very wet through most of the Mesolithic, these conditions had ameliorated somewhat by the late Mesolithic and early Neolithic (Tipping, Haggart and Milburn, Chapter 2 above). As we have noted already, these changes in groundwater can be attributed to localised variations in sea-level. The ground immediately surrounding the sand island may have been marshy at this time, but there was woodland dominated by birch, alder and hazel nearby.

Early Neolithic activity was most clearly manifested in the scatter of pottery sherds and worked stone located beneath the southern enclosure bank, underlying the thin black peat layer. This material occurred within a leached white sandy matrix which evidently represented an ancient soil formed on the compacted sand, and which survived to its greatest depth where it had been protected by the enclosure bank. The cultural debris gave some indication of the character of this early occupation. Only a small number of carinated or s-curved plain pottery vessels were represented, while the chert and pitchstone had been carefully curated and worked down to objects of small size. Evidently, the earlier stages of the lithic reduction sequence had taken place elsewhere. Accordingly, it seems likely that the site was not a permanent settlement, but had been visited, perhaps on more than one occasion, by a relatively mobile early Neolithic community with contacts as far afield as the Isle of Arran. This presence could be explained in terms of the seasonal movement of herders with cattle, or of a community periodically gaining access to specific local resources, such as wildfowl or particular kinds of wood.

Associated with this activity were a number of cut features. Some of the largest of these may have been pits, but might equally have represented tree-throw holes, as they generally had one edge that was more clearly defined than the other. However, while these holes did contain sherds and fragments of chipped stone, these were not densely concentrated in the manner that has been reported for some tree-throws in southern Britain (Evans, Pollard and Knight 1999). A small number of clear, deep post-holes were found in the same area, and these are very likely to relate to temporary dwelling structures or platforms of some kind. Most striking of all was the small pit 6724 (fill 6725, Fig. 18.1), which appeared to be literally crammed with cultural material, and which was situated a little apart from the main concentration of early

Neolithic artefacts, beneath the southern henge bank. What principally distinguishes the contents of the pit, apart from the sheer density of the material, is the range of different fabrics represented amongst the ceramics. 6725 contained fourteen sherds, from eight vessels in six different fabrics. These contrast with only two fabrics found amongst the sherds scattered across the ancient soil surface. Evidently, the sherds in the pit had been carefully selected, and this indicates that the event of deposition constituted a definite statement of some kind, distinct from the more casual pattern of discard represented by the artefact scatter. Yet interestingly enough, only two of the sherds in 6725 came from vessels that were not represented elsewhere on the site. Fragments of the other six vessels were found in the ancient soil and subsoil, in the secondary fill of the ditch, in the ditch stabilisation horizon, in the bank make-up, and in the pre-bank cut features. The lithic assemblage from 6724/6725 also appeared to be somewhat selective in its character, including no complex retouched pieces and no pitchstone, and being dominated by chert. Radiocarbon dates were acquired from three of the cut features, including 6724/5, and all fit into the period 3790 to 3630 Cal. BC, which probably indicates that they belong to a relatively constrained period of time. Whether this means that there was just one episode of habitation, or whether the sand island was frequented periodically over a century or more during the Earlier Neolithic is quite impossible to say.

In the various areas where the bank was sectioned, stake-holes were located in the old land surface. This was particularly the case in the eastern part of the monument, beneath the levelling material that lay across the henge entrance, contiguous with the bank itself. Stake-holes were also identified within the sandy subsoil that underlay the ancient soil horizon, although it is not clear whether these were simply not recognised at a higher level. This

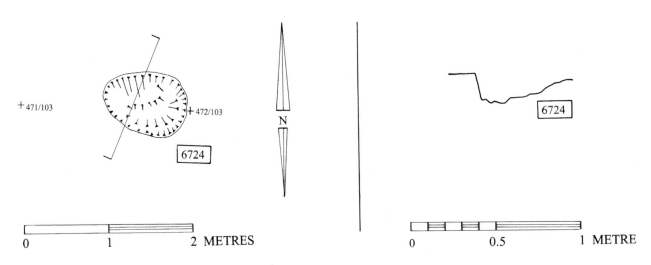

Fig. 18.1 The Pict's Knowe small pre-bank pit 6724: plan and profile.

raises the acute problem of the very large number of stake-holes investigated at the Pict's Knowe, and their relative dating. There were astonishing numbers of stake-holes in the immediate vicinity of the enclosure, to the east and to the south, as well as stake-holes on the top of the bank. Those that clearly pre-dated the monument were very much fewer in number, but at the very least they demonstrate that the practice of erecting wooden stakes had a very long history on the site. In Trench C, a group of very deep and clear stake-holes was found cut into the primary silts of the enclosure ditch. Trenches J and K demonstrated that the stake-holes tended to be more densely concentrated around the enclosure, and also that different phases of stake-hole activity could perhaps be distinguished, some of them possibly very recent. There are verbal accounts of the site having been used for gatherings of travelling people in historic times (A. Truckell, pers. comm.). It would therefore be unwise to assume that all of the stake-holes at the Pict's Knowe relate to a single kind of activity, still more so to imagine that they were all in any way connected with the enclosure and its use.

The most remarkable of the pre-monument features were found beneath the levelling layer that spanned the enclosure entrance. These produced no artefacts, but were stratigraphically equivalent to the cut features and artefacts scatter beneath the southern bank, being sealed by the same thick black peat layer. They consisted of two large post-holes, which flanked a small oval mound, itself sealing a large oval pit. The posts had been withdrawn, and their sockets had seemingly been hidden by small mounds of sand scraped up from the adjacent surface. Posts and mound were located on the axis of the henge entrance, and shared its orientation to the east. So although the posts had been quite deliberately removed and the whole complex was sealed by the black peat, it is hard to avoid the conclusion that they anticipated (or were commemorated by) the later monument in some fashion. The relationship between a henge monument and an earlier oval structure set within its entrance recalls the mortuary enclosure associated with the Maxey henge (Pryor and French 1985). The oval pit which underlay the mound was entirely empty. While it was similar to pits containing crouched burials (as beneath the bank at Windmill Hill: Whittle, Pollard & Grigson 1999, 79), phosphate samples do not support the view that it held any organic material (see Crowther, Chapter 9 above).

The precise date of the mound and post-holes is entirely unknown, and may fall anywhere between 4000 BC and the inception of peat growth, no earlier than c. 2400 BC. Obviously, the earlier within this range we choose to place them the more difficult it becomes to argue for an explicit relationship between the oval mound and the enclosure. However, the peat is sufficiently thin and the mound enough of a positive feature that its presence could probably have been identified once the sandy knoll began to dry out at the end of the Neolithic. It is an open question how far the levelling layer across the henge entrance represents a deliberate attempt to hide the mound, and how far it simply served to enable unencumbered access into the enclosure.

Evidence for middle Neolithic activity at the Pict's Knowe is limited to two sherds that may have come from a necked Ebbsfleet vessel, found in the sieving of the henge interior and the stabilisation horizon in the ditch. The black peat which covered the entrance causeway and lay beneath the bank formed swiftly at the end of the Neolithic, over at most 325 years and quite possibly much less. Indeed, the radiocarbon dates for the top and bottom of the sequence are statistically indistinguishable. This peat presumably accumulated during a short phase of waterlogging, and in the course of its growth certain changes in the immediate landscape can be identified. The peat contained pollen indicative of wet and densely wooded conditions: alder, hazel and birch, with sphagnum moss and sedge. At the very top of the peat there were extensive traces of burning, and an increase of ling heather. A number of episodes of burning took place, presumably anthropogenic in character, and there is some indication of cultivation having taken place nearby toward the end of the sequence. Shortly after the final burning of the heather, the enclosure bank was probably constructed, to judge from the soil micromorphological evidence.

The henge monument – or Iron Age enclosure?

The two radiocarbon dates for the pre-bank peat, 2452–1900 Cal. BC (AA-21249) and 2454–2030 Cal. BC (AA-21250), provide a *terminus post quem* for the construction of the henge monument. Ostensibly, this seems rather late, given that many of the larger and better-known henges have construction dates that fall between 3000 and 2500 BC. However, there are a number of predominantly small, late henges which have produced dates in roughly the same bracket as the Pict's Knowe. Woodhenge (Wiltshire), for instance, is dated to 2480–2039 Cal. BC (BM-677) and 2350–2030 Cal. BC (BM-678) (Richards 1990, 260). Condicote (Gloucestershire) has dates of 2400–1770 Cal. BC (HAR-3067) and 2210–1750 Cal. BC (HAR-3064) (Saville 1983, 33). An internal pit at Milfield South gave a date of 2622–2034 Cal. BC (HAR-3071), while the ditch fills at Milfield North gave 2314–2110 Cal. BC (BM-1149) and 2407–2100 Cal. BC (BM-1150) (Harding 1981). Finally, at Gorsey Bigbury (Somerset) the ditch yielded primary dates of 2461–2018 Cal. BC (BM-1088) and 2452–1983 Cal. BC (BM-1089) (ApSimon *et al.* 1976, 158). These determinations technically place all of these structures into the Early Bronze Age, and certainly into the period of currency of Beaker pottery, demonstrating the longevity of the henge tradition.

Whether the construction of the Pict's Knowe monument took place soon after the formation of the peat, and was therefore contemporary with these late henges, is a vexed question. The evidence can be read in two entirely different ways. On the one hand, there was no distinct soil horizon between the peat and the lower build of the bank. This would suggest that the bank was built soon after the cessation of peat formation, or even that it was the throwing up of the bank that brought the peat growth to an end in the immediate area. On the other hand, we have much later radiocarbon dates from the bank in Trench H, in the immediate area of the enclosure entrance. In this area the bank is thin and heavily disturbed by animal activity and modern drainage ditches. It is thus plausible that the dates relate to the capping of the bank in the Late Iron Age, using material removed from the ditch recut. However, just as there was no soil horizon between the peat and the bank, so there was no clear soil formation in the bank profile, between the primary build and the later capping, even if the latter did represent a distinct stratigraphic entity. It is therefore extremely difficult to construct a conclusive argument that the Pict's Knowe was *either* a later Neolithic henge *or* a Late Iron Age enclosure. We will proceed on the basis that each is potentially possible (see Ashmore, Chapter 28 below).

Bradley (1998: 101) has argued that the construction of henge monuments provided a relatively public enclosed arena, in contrast with the enclosed chambers of passage tombs, which preceded them in some areas. Henges were often built in locations which epitomised a circular conception of space, shading off and receding from a central point, and frequently encapsulated the distinctive qualities of the surrounding terrain (*ibid.*, 122). We have seen already that the Pict's Knowe henge was positioned in such a way as to overlook an expanse of marshy, low-lying ground between the two valley sides. The enclosure of the sandy knoll served to distinguish the domed eminence from its wet surroundings. The broad, flat-bottomed ditch was presumably cut by opening circular pits which became the two bulbous terminals, and then working around the circuit digging to a face, as Barclay (1983, 181) suggested for North Mains. The bank was composed of dumps of upcast derived from the digging of the ditch. Some peaty material was incorporated into the bank, particularly toward its base, and this reflects the way in which the ditch-digging would have begun by cutting through the layer of black peat on the surface. Two main layers of dump could be identified in the bank, composed of numerous lenses of sand and more stony material. As we will see below, the bipartite structure of the bank has considerable bearing on the question of the dating of the monument.

The primary ditch fills were clearly striated, being by turns more or less compacted. When carefully trowelled clean their surfaces revealed elaborate swirling patterns. This presumably indicates that rather than simply representing a normal silting pattern, these layers must have been laid down in wet conditions, and that standing water might have been present in the ditch from its first use.

According to the results of the micromorphological work (Crowther, Chapter 10 above) the earliest fills in the ditch accumulated very swiftly. The silts of the henge ditch in general contained very few artefacts, and few charred plant remains. Quantities of worked wood were found in the silts, but in no case could one say with confidence that wooden objects were Neolithic in date. The ditch deposits appear to have been highly mobile, slumping forward over recut fills in some cases, while extensive trampling seems to have pushed wood down into the top of the silts; much of the wood from the silts was composed of the tips of stakes and pegs, which may have been stuck in from above. Furthermore, all of the facet marks identified on the worked wood derive from metal tools. The upper part of the silting had generally been disturbed by the later recut and activities associated with it, but in Trench E a fragment of a stabilisation horizon was identified, demonstrating that the ditch deposits had come to rest and that some form of vegetation had become established before the recut was made into the ditch.

Finds from the primary phase of activity at the henge are somewhat sparse, in contrast with the pre-monument occupation. There are a few chipped stone fragments, and there is one probable Grooved Ware vessel. However, this is not unexpected, and is virtually the norm for henges on the Scottish mainland. At Balfarg, for instance, almost all of the ceramic assemblage was deposited before the construction of the henge. There were no artefacts whatever in the primary silting of the ditch, and there was little charcoal prior to the formation of the turf-line (Mercer 1981, 66). Similarly, at North Mains only four sherds could be attributed to the primary phase of activity at the henge, as opposed to the later burials, and only 74 pieces of chipped stone were recovered from the entire site (Barclay 1983, 155; 167).

Little can be said concerning the internal organisation of the Pict's Knowe henge, since the subsoil of the central area had been entirely disrupted by rabbits. However, on the entrance causeway the later layers of peat lapped up out of the ditch, preserving a leached sandy surface from rabbit activity. Here, a great many features could be identified. These included numerous stake-holes, and also a series of slots. One of these ran parallel with the entrance on the southern side, and contained a series of distinct post-holes, while others crossed the entrance on the inner side of the ditch. Presumably these represented some form of entrance structure, or rather a series of structures, renewed on a number of occasions. The difficulty in interpreting these structures lies in attaching them to a specific phase in the site's history. The causeway features were sealed by a layer of peat, but this was the post-Iron Age dark peat that filled the top of the ditch, rather than the thin dark peat which underlay the henge bank. Stratigraphically, then, the entrance features could be attributed to any period from the pre-henge occupation to the Iron Age re-use of the site. The former seems quite unlikely, but it remains possible that the slots and stake-holes in the henge entrance are either late Neolithic/Early Bronze Age or Iron Age. Indeed, given the density of features within this part of the site it is entirely plausible that they relate to both periods of activity.

This returns us to the problem of dating the stake-holes at the Pict's Knowe. We have seen that the overall stake-hole distribution on the sandy knoll is skewed toward the henge; the stakes are most densely concentrated immediately outside of the bank and the entrance. This implies that a majority of the stake-holes were created at a time when the monument was in active use. The stake-holes in the entrance and on top of the bank suggest some form of fence or screen, perhaps of hurdle-work, presumably renewed or replaced on numerous occasions. There are indeed pieces of hurdling securely stratified in the Iron Age ditch recuts and radiocarbon dated to the second century AD. But on the other hand, there are also stake-holes beneath the bank and cut into the primary ditch fills. This is not the first time that stake-holes have been reported in the context of a henge monument. At King Arthur's Round Table, Penrith, R. G. Collingwood (1938) identified numerous stake-holes. Their presence was famously disputed by Gerhard Bersu, who claimed that they had been inadvertently been fabricated by excavators pushing their trowels point-first into suspicious dark patches in the gravel, and twisting them (Bradley 1994; Helgeby & Simpson 1995; Simpson 1996). However, in more recent years stake-holes have been located at a number of sites. At Mount Pleasant, a cluster of stakes was found cut into the ditch fills at the east terminal of the north entrance, bracketed between two infant burials (Wainwright 1979, 42). At Moncrieffe, stakes were identified in the primary ditch fill, on the outer side of the ditch (Stewart 1985, 129). Groups of stake-holes were also present in the interior of the monument at Coneybury (Richards 1990, 138–49).

These occurrences indicate that in addition to the massive timber and stone uprights there may in some cases also have been a more ephemeral component of henge architecture. Indeed, Mercer (1981) suggested that there may have been some kind of fencing between the posts of the timber circle at Balfarg. If as well as free-standing or lintelled uprights, henge interiors were surrounded and subdivided by fences and screens, even if these were only temporary additions, the extent to which the activities conducted inside would have been hidden and secluded would have been greatly enhanced. Henge architecture was not intended to restrain an aggressor from entering the site forcibly. Instead, it constrained the movements and restricted the experience of people who are abiding by social convention (Barrett 1994, 50). It is arguable that secrecy was of cardinal importance to these monuments: not a total exclusion from specific places at all times, but a restriction on who might witness particular performances at particular times. In the case of the Pict's Knowe, screens which imposed a zig-zag pattern of movement through the entrance, and fences surrounding the monument would have served to further mystify the practices undertaken in the interior. The stake-holes in the ditch might conceivably have marked the location of some significant deposit, on the basis of the comparison with Mount Pleasant. However, as we have noted, only the features in the ditch are demonstrably identified with the primary use of the henge.

As we have seen, the build of the bank continued unbroken across the entrance as a much thinner levelling layer. In the top of the bank numerous stake-holes were detected, and these were particularly evident in the cutting opened on the southern side of the enclosure (Trench G). Here, distinct lines of stakes ran along the line of the bank, seemingly forming a kind of revetment. However, in this cutting it was observed that the bank capping seemed to be set in a cut feature of some kind within the primary sand dump of the bank. The presence of this cut feature might provide a partial explanation for the absence of a turf line or other sign of soil formation between the dump bank and the capping. During excavation the discovery of slag-like material in a layer overlain by the capping caused much concern, and as a result much attention was paid to the stratigraphic relations between bank dump and capping. However, the post-excavation study of the fuel and fuel-ash slag from the site (see Heald and Hunter, Chapter 17 above) clarified that only material from clearly post-Iron Age contexts derived from industrial activities and the burning of coal. The presence of this material consequentially has no bearing on the date of the enclosure.

More perplexing are two radiocarbon determinations acquired on charcoal from the bank in Trench H in 1996. These were 50–240 Cal. AD (SUERC-2097) and 120 BC – 70 Cal. AD (SUERC-2098). As mentioned above, at this point the bank was quite thin, was disturbed by animal activity and modern drainage ditches, and was sloping down from the north and south toward the entrance. However, the dates appear to have come from hazel and oak twig charcoal which was securely stratified in the bank. Two possibilities present themselves at this point: either the bank capping is of Iron Age date, while the primary bank is Neolithic, or the entire bank and ditch monument was constructed in the Iron Age. If the former were the case it is possible that the bank capping material was derived from the recutting of the ditch, and that both recut and capping represented a general refurbishment of the monument in or around the first century AD. As we have seen, this interpretation fits better with the evidence from the dark peat beneath the bank, which formed in the Late Neolithic/Early Bronze Age, while the bank was built directly onto the peat without the formation of an intervening soil horizon. It is also difficult to account for the 'levelling layer' across the entrance, sealing whatever traces of the oval mound and its attendant posts could be discerned through the thin peat, in a scenario in which construction post-dated the formation of the peat by more than two millennia. Furthermore, an Iron Age construction would require that the position and orientation of the mound and post-holes was entirely coincidental, and in no way anticipated the layout of the enclosure. On the other hand, we have seen that there was no soil formation between the primary dump bank and the bank capping, although the evidence that the surface of the former was (in some places at least) prepared by the cutting of some kind of feature before the dumping of the latter provides at least a partial explanation.

There are four radiocarbon determinations from the ditch which might support an Iron Age date for the Pict's Knowe (see Ashmore, Chapter 28 below). Two of these (AA-17473 and AA-17474) are from ditch layer 0119 in the north ditch terminal (see Fig. 4.17). This sandy layer of ditch fill spread across the surface of 0130, the green clay filling of the major ditch recut, suggesting that its deposition was of later date. Moreover, 0119 ran across the surface of silting layers 0392 and 0473, which appeared to have been truncated, indicating an episode of erosion between the formation of the primary ditch silts and the deposition of 0119. Two further dates, AA-17475 (350 Cal. BC – 50 Cal. AD) and AA-17476 (350 Cal. BC – 60 Cal. AD) came from wood fragments from the sandy layers in the ditch bottom in the west ditch cutting of 1994 (contexts 0123 and 0285). These fragments were retrieved from the marbled surface immediately below the green clay recut fill (context 0122) (see Fig. 4.6). It was recognised at the time of excavation that these small pieces of wood might have been deposited in the recut itself, and have been pressed into the underlying sand by trampling. The status of the two dates is therefore equivocal.

However, it is worth considering the possibility that even the primary bank and ditch were of Iron Age date. What parallels could be cited for a penanular ditch-and-bank enclosure in the Iron Age? While penanular enclosures are common in the Iron Age of England, Scotland and Wales, examples with an external bank are rather scarce (Cunliffe 1991, Chapters 12–13). In Ireland, some of the so-called 'royal sites' have internal ditches and external banks. These include the Ráith na Rí at Tara, Navan Fort and Knockaulin (Waddell 1998, 325–54). However, all are considerably larger than the Pict's Knowe, and none demonstrate the architectural emphasis on the entrance that distinguishes henge monuments. On the other hand, some of the enigmatic 'ring barrows' of the Irish Iron Age are distinctly hengelike in form, although these are rarely more than 30 metres in diameter (*ibid.*, 365–9). In any case, these were funerary structures rather than settlement or ceremonial enclosures. Perhaps more pertinent to the discussion of the Pict's Knowe is the little-known site of Shiels Farm, near Glasgow, which is discussed by Ashmore in Chapter 28 below. This site had both a morphological similarity with the Pict's Knowe, and a series of waterlogged deposits within its ditch. However, the character of the evidence from Shiels

was such that its nature and history remain ambiguous (see below).

Later prehistory

If the Pict's Knowe enclosure really was a Neolithic henge monument it is quite unclear for how long it may have been in use. The entrance causeway features, if they date to the primary phase, suggest structures that were renovated on a number of occasions. A concentration of sherds of Collared Urn was identified immediately inside the entrance, associated with some fragments of burnt bone. The latter are very small and poorly preserved, and are not even certain to have been human. However, the most likely explanation is that this material represents a cremation introduced into the henge interior, at some time after the site had ceased to be used for ritual or ceremonial activities. Such an act might be construed as a means by which the significance of the enclosure was transformed, effectively connecting it with the presence of the dead. Of course, the currency of Collared Urns was such that this deposition need not have taken place more than a century or so after the construction of the henge (Burgess 1986). The consequence of this is that there remains a very great period of time between the Early Bronze Age and Iron Age activity at the Pict's Knowe, during which there is little or no archaeological evidence for any human presence.

The Iron Age occupation

The principal structural evidence for Iron Age activity at the Pict's Knowe took the form of a series of major recuts in the ditch, and the timber platform erected over the recut at the rear of the enclosure. On balance, it is likely that the capping of the bank also dates to the Iron Age. The resulting structure is one that is difficult to parallel amongst the hillforts, enclosures and hut-circles of Iron Age south-west Scotland (Banks 2002, 32). By this time it is suggested that the immediate surroundings of the enclosure where characterised by standing water, woodland, heather and some grassland, possibly on the sandy hillock itself (see Ramsay and Miller, Chapter 13 above). There was possibly a stand of willow shrub nearby, perhaps in the ditch. The presence of three fragments of a wooden keg in the green clay that filled the recut and the red peat which lay above it suggests that there was little interval between the formation of these two layers, and that the peat at least was laid down very quickly. Much the same is indicated by the large quantity of organic material that the latter contained. Moreover, it can be assumed that the red peat formed in very wet conditions. Conceivably, the inwash of the green clay might have been a consequence of the onset of damper conditions, but given that there was no sign of a silting on the base of the recuts it is equally likely that they were dug into a ditch that was already wet. This would mean, in effect, that from their inception the recuts would have amounted to a series of small pools or ponds. In places, the green clay was not entirely contained within the recuts, and lapped up over the primary ditch fills, suggesting that the water level may have been higher than the stabilised level of the ditch deposits.

These conditions explain some of the difficulty encountered in excavating these features. Particularly at the two ditch terminals, the sandy primary fill of the ditch had repeatedly collapsed forward from a standing edge, onto the green clay fill of the recut beneath. The consequence of this would be a stratigraphic reversal, which proved difficult to comprehend when digging in plan. Only when complete sections could be consulted was the character of the stratigraphy fully appreciated. An argument could be constructed that the water-worn surfaces of the recuts were natural features of some kind, perhaps a product of erosion. However, this was clearly not the case with the peculiar 'boat-shaped' recut in Trench C, or the linear extension westward from the craterous recut in the southern ditch terminal in Trench E. On balance, it is most likely that all of the recutting was a product of human action, the resulting features merely being weathered back by water action.

While the 1994 ditch sections, at the north terminal and opposite the entrance, had given the impression that the recut was broad and regular, the more extensive excavation of the ditch in 1995 demonstrated that the character of the recutting varied considerably around the circuit (Fig. 4.12). This suggests that particular areas of the ditch had been dug out preferentially. On the southern side of the enclosure (Trench A) the recut was a mere slot, which disappeared entirely in the centre of the trench. At this point, the recut was relatively difficult to isolate within the complex interleaving of bank slip, lenses of sandy material derived from the interior of the monument and ditch silts which underlay the red peat. Further to the west the recut became much more extensive, occupying a large area at the back of the enclosure. Yet in the northern sector of the ditch, only the 'boat-shaped' feature was present. At both ditch terminals the recuts formed massive craters, the southern one extending westward as a slot. We have noted already the possibility that the capping of fine white sand on the top of the bank may date to the Iron Age. If this were the case, it is possible that it represents the upcast from the recutting activity, which would have dug into the fine-grained silts of the primary ditch fill.

Immediately above the large recut at the back of the enclosure a timber platform was discovered, composed of roughly-worked tree boughs laid in a criss-cross fashion (Fig. 4.15). In places, the edge of the ditch had been cut back to receive these members. Stratigraphically this structure rested within the red peat that overlay the recut fills. This renders it distinct from the other finds of wood, which were encountered within the green clay, although we should remember that the temporal interval between these two horizons may not have been very great. Indeed, some of the numerous roundwood fragments (worked and unworked) in Trench B might have been stripped from the platform timbers in the course of their preparation. It is also possible that some of the unworked roots and branches that formed the upper part of the wood deposit in Trench E represent an equivalent to this feature. Two explanations for these phenomena suggest themselves: either material was introduced into the ditch in order to soak up the moisture and provide a hard-standing, effectively increasing the usable area within the enclosure, or a deliberate effort was made to hide the artefacts deposited in the recuts. Of course, these two arguments are not mutually exclusive. In Trench A, the patch of sand and clay that was apparently laid over the surface of the recut may be thematically related to the platform, although it was *below* the main wood deposit in this area. What is significant is that the platform-building demonstrates that the site had not ceased to be of importance once the wood deposits had found their way into the recuts. This has considerable implications for the way in which we choose to understand these deposits.

Looked at in general terms the wood deposits appear to represent a dense and undifferentiated scatter of material. However, it is possible that they include a series of different components, which may be spatially and chronologically distinct. The assemblage was composed of fragments of hurdle, turning waste and wood chips, the remains of presumably discarded artefacts, several planks, and a small number of large and complete objects. The collection as a whole is dominated by discard from manufacturing activity, and Crone, Sands and Skinner (Chapter 6 above) argue that it does not represent a characteristic domestic assemblage. It is notable that both turning waste and woodchips have a distribution which is concentrated toward the ditch terminals on either side of the entrance (Fig. 18.2). In Trench E this material could be observed tumbling down the inner edge of the ditch from the interior of the monument. This may indicate that particular kinds of woodworking activity were quite localised within the site, and that the other wood deposits were not so closely related to this activity. Worked roundwood fragments were not exclusively concentrated at the ditch terminals (Fig. 18.3), and in Trench E they had a distribution which was complementary to that of wood chips.

Other elements of the wood assemblage may have been structural in character. It is possible that some of the hurdling derived from light structures which may have stood in some of the stake-holes that may date to this phase, or from a building of some sort. In addition, there was the large, thick plank in the northern ditch terminal with very clear tooling marks on its surface, one end of which had been cut to an oblique angle (FN235). The other end had rotted uniformly up to a line about 20 cm from the end of the plank, giving the impression that it might at one time have stood upright in the ground. This

Julian Thomas

○ Perforated Pegs
□ Oblong Pieces
△ Wedge Shaped Pieces

0   20 metres

Fig. 18.2 The Pict's Knowe: distribution of woodchips and turning waste.

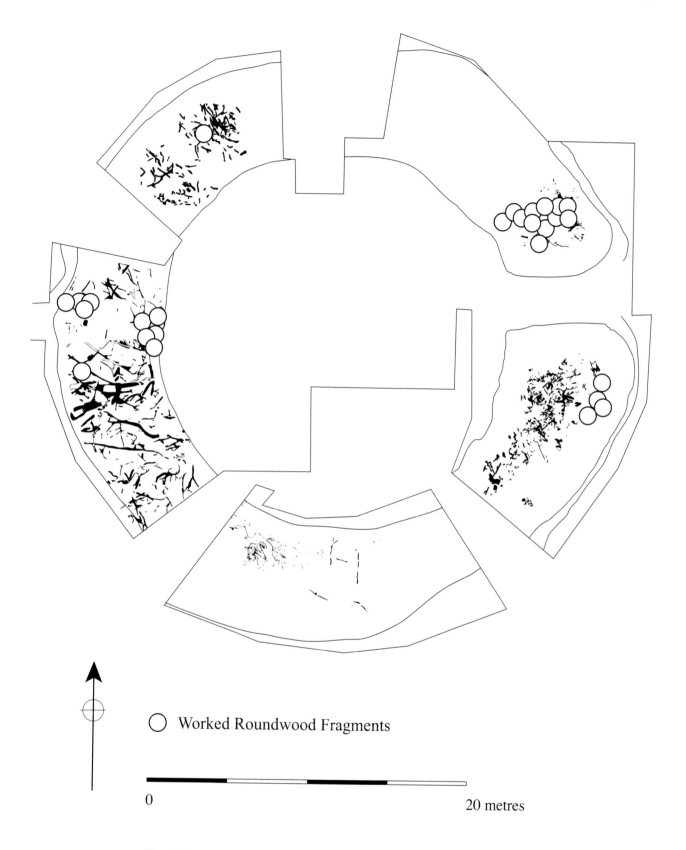

Fig. 18.3 The Pict's Knowe: distribution of worked roundwood fragments.

○ Worked Roundwood Fragments

0

20 metres

might suggest part of a structure, or an isolated upright of some kind. Further very large timbers, in too advanced a state of decomposition to have been lifted, were found in Trench B. Finally, there are the perforated pegs, which were particularly concentrated in the north ditch terminal. Sands originally suggested that these might have formed parts of an adjustable pole lathe frame, and this argument is perhaps supported by the spatial coincidence of the pegs with fragments of turning waste. An alternative view, that they may represent a group of artefacts with a symbolic or ritual significance, has also been discussed (Crone, Sands and Skinner, Chapter 6 above). Equally, they may have represented elements of a more substantial timber structure, perhaps being slotted into prepared holes in larger pieces of wood in order to bind them together. Taken together, the hurdles, planks and perforated pegs might have formed parts of a building, which was either decommissioned, destroyed, or simply collapsed. If, as Crone, Sands and Skinner suggest, the structure was some form of altar or shrine, the parts may have been deposited in the ditch with a degree of formality.

There were a number of other wooden objects whose presence in the ditch may be a result of deliberate deposition. Alongside these we might wish to consider the numerous fragments of broken quernstone located in the ditch. How much can be said about these objects is limited, as the entire assemblage was unfortunately mislaid by the specialist to whom they were entrusted. None the less, it is interesting to note that the quernstones represent what is ostensibly a quintessentially domestic artefact, and this conflicts with the non-domestic character of the wood assemblage. However, we might compare the Pict's Knowe quern fragments with the smashed querns deposited in a wet, ceremonial context (of later Bronze Age date) at Flag Fen, Cambridgeshire (Pryor 1992). Moreover, the sole of a Roman shoe was recovered from the terminal of the recut ditch at the Pict's Knowe, also apparently dating to the second century AD. This object might date to the brief Roman occupation of southern Scotland. None the less the shoe was presumably quite remote from its context of production, and would have been exotic amongst the indigenous communities of south-west Scotland. And as van Driel-Murray notes (Chapter 12 above), the left shoe is more commonly found in Roman votive deposits. The possibly placed wooden deposits include a keg fragment (FN47), apparently positioned over a tightly-compacted ball of grey willow leaves. These leaves gave the impression, in the field, of having been rolled up by hand and inserted under the plank. Also potentially 'placed' was the so-called 'ard' discovered at the back of the enclosure in 1994, FN48 (and another similar object, in a terminal state of disrepair, identified nearby in 1995: Plate 4.10). The 'ard' does not fit with any of the established typologies of tillage tools. Its spike or share showed little or no evidence of wear. Indeed, it could not have functioned as a plough (Lerche, Chapter 12 above),

although it may be that a prosaic use for the object could be found as a seed-drill or the like. However, given that the precise reason that we have a good knowledge of the technology of prehistoric ploughs is because they represent one of the principal types of artefacts that were deliberately deposited in bogs in northern Germany, Poland and Scandinavia (Aberg and Bowen 1960; Sherratt 1981), it is possible that this object was not so much a real plough as a representation of a plough constructed with deposition in mind. During much of prehistory, the Pict's Knowe was in any case somewhat remote from locations where ploughing could have taken place. On the other hand, Crone, Sands and Skinner (Chapter 6 above) have noted the similarity of FN48 to the perforated wooden pegs, and it may be more likely that it too formed a part of a larger structure.

So the wood assemblage from the Pict's Knowe ditch can arguably be characterised as a composite of several kinds of material: the debris from working large timbers and pole-lathe work, roundwood worked with smaller tools, faggots thrown in to drain or fill up the ditch, the remains of a collapsed or dismantled structure, and a small minority of what may be 'placed' objects. The latter two categories shade into one another: as we have already noted, parts of a structure may have been deposited with some care after its dismantling. However, not all of the wood finds need have been precisely contemporary. We have suggested that any structure may have dated to the second century AD, but there are other radiocarbon dates for wood that are both earlier and later than this. Moreover, the construction of the timber platform *over* the remains of the structure demonstrates that even if the latter were a dwelling of some sort, its destruction did not terminate the use of the enclosure.

How can we best explain the character of the Iron Age activity at the Pict's Knowe? In general, the re-use of Neolithic monuments in later prehistory or protohistory has been discussed in terms of 'squatting': the opportunistic use of existing structures for shelter or raw materials (Hingley 1996, 232). Recently, Richard Hingley (*ibid.*) has drawn attention to recurrent patterns in the re-occupation of chambered tombs in the Western and Northern Isles, which demonstrate a conscious appropriation of ancient sites whose general significance was appreciated. Of course, this need not imply that Iron Age people had a precise understanding of the original uses and meanings of Neolithic monuments. Conceptions of the past in later prehistory may have been mythic, or entirely fabricated, or may have involved the maintenance of some kind of history in oral tradition. Moreover, different kinds of understanding of the past may have prevailed at different points in British prehistory (Gosden and Lock 1998, 4). Hingley's suggestion is that the re-use of Neolithic monuments involved little in the way of continuity of function or significance: these sites were 'reinvented' in terms that were appropriate to Iron Age communities (1996, 241). Very often, in both Scotland

and Ireland, domestic sites were built into or onto the ruins of chambered cairns, often in such a way as to control access to the chambers and the bones that they contained (Hingley 1999). Re-use thereby acted to establish claims of lineage back to very ancient ancestors. In a similar way, we could suggest that whatever structure was built on the Pict's Knowe served as a means of controlling the past, monopolising access to a place whose antiquity and importance was understood in only the most general of terms.

The re-occupation of the Pict's Knowe in the Roman Iron Age is of particular interest because as well as being in keeping with practice in Iron Age Scotland, it also foreshadows developments in the early Medieval period. Stephen Driscoll (1998) points to the way in which the process of Scottish state formation was grounded in the establishment of locations where royalty could meet with their subjects, or conduct public ceremonies such as investitures. These places were often provided with legitimacy by locating them in or nearby to ancient monuments, as at Forteviot and Dunadd (*ibid.*, 151). While most of these royal centres were stopping-off places for peripatetic monarchies, in some cases the lesser nobility made use of ancient monuments as the locations of their permanent residences (*ibid.*, 147). Henge monuments in particular appear to have represented a focus of interest in the early medieval period in both Scotland and northern England. Early Christian cemeteries have been found within or close by the henges of Cairnpapple, North Mains, Milfield South and Milfield North (Barclay 1983, 145; Harding 1981, 93). Moreover, the Yeavering henge and stone circle were juxtaposed with the early Medieval palace site (Harding 1981, 129). Bradley (1993, 115) was rightly critical of Hope-Taylor's (1977) suggestion that this indicated continuity of ritual use from Neolithic to Northumbrian times. Driscoll, similarly, argues that the interest that was shown in ancient sites in the early medieval times was a very specific one, which depended upon the development of notions of linear time which were associated with Christianity. However, it is

legitimate to ask whether in some cases particular places can be identified as being, in a broad sense, important, and whether this importance can be maintained in memory and tradition for generations, even if their specific meanings and uses are radically transformed.

This general significance of ancient monuments is also demonstrated in the way in which they were so often chosen as places where metalworking was undertaken in later prehistory. Hingley (1999) has argued that the production of metal and its fashioning into artefacts 'may have been considered a magical and marginal process', and that this resulted in its being restricted to various special places. Amongst these places were henges and stone circles. Examples include the bowl furnace at Moncrieffe (Stewart 1985, 124), the pit containing iron-working residue at Loanhead of Daviot (Kilbride-Jones 1936), and the extensive bronze working evidence at Thwing (Manby 1988). At the Pict's Knowe, there is limited evidence that metalworking took place in the Iron Age/Roman period. Two interpretations of this are possible. Firstly, it may have been that the substantial timber building that we have hypothesised represented a permanent or temporary residence, or a ceremonial centre or shrine used by a locally powerful group. Such a group may have been maintaining their authority through control over a series of productive processes (metalwork, certain wooden objects) as well as monopolising an ancient site of mythic significance and the depositional activities that were conducted within it. Alternatively, the use of the site might have shifted abruptly at the point when the timber platform was constructed in the ditch, and small-scale metalworking might have been conducted in a marginal location that was no longer permanently occupied. That the importance of the Pict's Knowe may have continued to be acknowledged into medieval times is suggested by the presence of a holy well some 200 metres to the north-east of the henge. It is presently known as St. Quernan's Well, but its connection with the monument is suggested by the older name of 'the Pict's Well' (A. Truckell, pers. comm.).

PART TWO
HOLYWOOD AND HOLM FARM

19

Introduction

Julian Thomas

The second group of monuments discussed in this volume are all located in the immediate environs of Holywood, a village north of Dumfries, and form part of a broader distribution of cursus and cursus-related monuments in and around the Nith valley. Most of these have only been revealed by aerial photography in the past few decades, and are represented by little or nothing in the way of a standing earthwork. Consequentially, the recognition of such a group of large earth-and-timber monuments amounts to a realignment of the Neolithic archaeology of the Scottish south-west, which has hitherto been concerned primarily with megalithic structures. The cursus monuments at Holywood, Holm, Fourmerkland and Gallaberry are all grouped together, while the cursus at Curriestanes lies a little to the south, on the outskirts of Dumfries (Fig. 1.1). All are low-lying, and all related to a greater or lesser extent to the River Nith or the Cluden Water (Gregory 2000, 13). The two cursuses at Holywood are rather shorter and more clearly rectilinear than others elsewhere in Scotland (Brophy 1999, 122), and consequentially find closer parallels to the south. Holywood South is a classic ditch-defined cursus with squared terminals, while Holywood North is a fraction longer at c. 350 metres, and has rounded terminals. Holywood North is further distinguished by the presence of one or more lines of large post-holes (as they were demonstrated to be by excavation), running parallel with and inside the ditch. The post-holes are clearly visible on aerial photographs of the northern part of the cursus, but not in the southern portion, where definition is poorer. It is consequentially not certain that the post-structure continued for the full length of the ditched cursus, and it may have been shorter. The presence of the post-holes aligns Holywood North with the post- and pit-defined cursuses, which are an almost exclusively Scottish phenomenon (Maxwell 1979). To the south of the two cursus monuments lies the stone circle of the Twelve Apostles, so positioned that the southern portion of the northern cursus is aligned upon it. Interestingly, two of the 'causeways' that interrupt the ditch of the southern cursus are so positioned as to allow unhindered movement between the stone circle and the northern cursus (Brophy 2000, 61).

Only one kilometre away from the Holywood sites is another group of features recognised from the air at Holm Farm, which appear to have some affinities with the post-defined cursuses. At first sight, the aerial photographs of Holm suggest an undifferentiated scatter of features, but these contain a number of broadly parallel lines of postholes and pits, as well as transverse lines and arcs indicating the presence of an enclosure rather than simply a series of alignments. It is possible to argue that Holywood and Holm together amount to a single, integrated monumental complex (see Fig. 19.1). Fieldwork conducted in the summers of 1997 and 1998 thus provided the opportunity to investigate a variety of the different sites which are collectively referred to as 'cursus monuments', in a context where comparisons could realistically be made between the different structures concerned. All of these monuments are located on the coarse-grained fluvio-glacial terraces and outwash gravel sediments which fill the ancient and deeply-incised valley of the Nith (Tipping 1999a, 13).

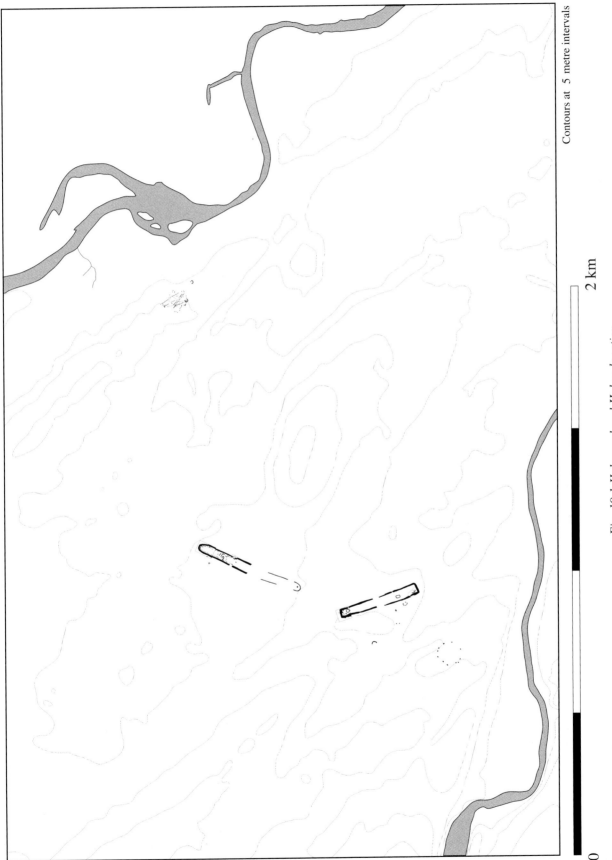

Contours at 5 metre intervals

0   2 km

Fig. 19.1 Holywood and Holm: location.

20

The cursus monuments of south-west Scotland

Kenneth Brophy

Introduction

Although this chapter is ostensibly about cursus monuments, the sheer variety of monuments with this label attached in south-west Scotland has tested the value of the term; in fact, what links them really only is that they are all in one form or another rectilinear enclosures that may be of Neolithic date. That all but one are known only as cropmarks suggests further caution. While the term cursus monument is used frequently here, it is done so with a degree of caution as I will elaborate on.

There are two main 'concentrations' of cursus monuments in Scotland, one in the eastern lowlands of Angus and Perthshire, the other in south-western Scotland (Brophy 1999, Brophy & RCAHMS in press). The three excavated cursus sites discussed in this volume are part of a series of sites along the Nith valley, from upstream at Thornhill, to as far south as the estuary where the Nith meets the Solway Firth (Fig. 20.1). This chapter is intended to place the Holywood / Holm sites (centrally placed in the Nith group) within this wider context. Through a discussion of the known sites – their form, location, and the limited previous work undertaken on them – and a review of the aerial photographic evidence, I hope to begin to develop a few themes that connect these monuments, themes taken up and further developed throughout this volume.

Before looking at the sites more closely, I will briefly discuss two histories. Firstly, that of the recognition and discovery of cursus sites in Scotland through the Aerial Survey Programme of the Royal Commission on the Ancient and Historical Monuments of Scotland (RCAHMS), first established in 1976. Secondly, I will briefly recount the development of cursus monument typology. Scotland's cursus monuments are drawn together by their similar ground plans, sometimes because they cannot be labelled with any other preconceived nomenclature. However it is also becoming increasingly apparent that we can characterise Neolithic monuments in different ways that may help us break free from traditional typological schemes, and some of these characteristics will also be touched on below.

Cursus monuments in Scotland

Although cursus monuments have been known of in England for several centuries, only one site in Scotland, Gallaberry, Dumfries and Galloway, had been positively identified before 1976. Like a handful of other sites across lowland Scotland, Gallaberry had been photographed from the air during occasional sorties north by the Cambridge Committee for Aerial Photography (CUCAP) from the 1940s–1970s, that largely focussed on Roman material (Jones 2005). With no real tradition of the monuments within Neolithic studies in Scotland, these sites remained unidentified until later excavations or re-interpretation of the cropmarks; notable examples include Douglasmuir, Angus (Kendrick 1995), Inchbare 1, Angus (St. Joseph 1976) and Bennybeg, Perth and Kinross (Darvill 1996). Furthermore, the Cleaven Dyke, an earthwork monument in Perth and Kinross, was until the 1980s thought to be Roman (Maxwell 1983a) despite having been recorded first in the 18th century and subsequently excavated three times (Barclay & Maxwell 1998, 14–22).

Indeed, it was not until RCAHMS embarked on their concentrated aerial reconnaissance programme in 1976 that a range of cursus monuments were recorded across Scotland. Gordon Maxwell pioneered this work, and noted the existence of a potentially previously un-recorded 'type' of cursus monument, one bounded by pits or post-holes rather than ditches (Maxwell 1983b, 28). Such so-called pit-defined cursus monuments are rectangular in plan, with length often exceeding 100 m. Internal divisions are common, sometimes more than one along the length of the monument. In effect, they were morphologically cursus monuments, although only excavation would show that they were actually Neolithic (e.g. Kendrick 1995; Rideout 1997; Ellis in prep.).

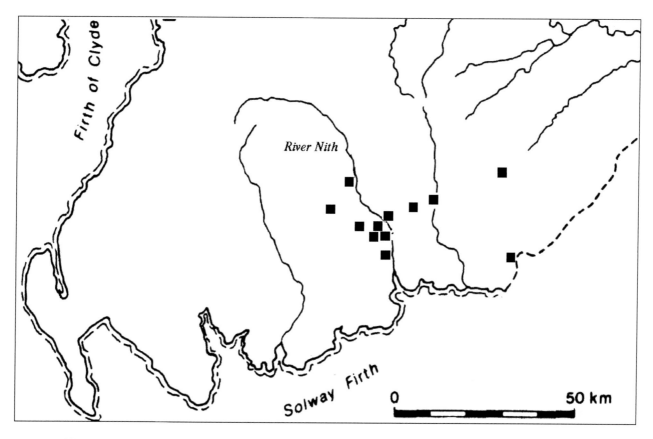

Fig. 20.1 Location map of the 12 possible and probable cursus monuments in Dumfries and Galloway, Scotland.

Roy Loveday's (1985) exhaustive thesis on cursus monuments included the first real list of cursus sites in Scotland. (None had been included in an earlier 'gazetteer' (Hedges & Buckley 1981).) Loveday included nine Scottish sites, six of which were pit-defined. A list collated by Gordon Barclay in the mid-1990s (and later published as a distribution map (Barclay 2003, 136)) included fifteen sites, and undergraduate research produced a gazetteer of twenty-one cursus monuments (Brophy 1995).

The establishment of a cursus tradition in Scotland drove a rash of new discoveries in the 1990s (Brophy & Cowley 2005, 15–8). The re-interpretation of aerial photographs (see for instance Armit 1993; RCAHMS 1997) revealed possible new sites, missed amidst other cropmark sites or previously mis-interpreted. Aerial reconnaissance sponsored by RCAHMS has also helped discover new sites, particularly in Aberdeenshire and Moray (Shepherd & Greig 1996). New sites have been identified through developer-funded excavations (e.g. Upper Largie, Argyll (Ellis in prep.) and Castle Menzies, Perth and Kinross (Halliday 2002)), and RCAHMS aerial survey itself has continued to identify more sites (such as Reedielies in Fife (Cowley & Gilmour 2003). The number of possible cursus monuments in Scotland now numbers over fifty (Brophy & RCAHMS in press).

The distribution of these sites of course reflects in great part the arable areas of the country most commonly flown (Angus, Perthshire and Dumfries and Galloway), although interestingly the Lothians and Berwickshire, where some of the most concentrated aerial reconnaissance has occurred, have produced only a handful of possible cursus sites, and only two of these were actually recorded on oblique aerial photographs.

A few words about typology

This chapter reflects a group of monuments that have been called 'cursus monument' or 'cursus monument (possible)' in south-west Scotland. Before recent standardisation in the National Monuments Record of Scotland, many of these sites had been classified as 'linear cropmarks', 'enclosure: rectilinear', 'ritual enclosure', 'pitted enclosure' or 'enclosure: pit-defined'. These rather more vague terms may yet hide further examples.

Why should we concern ourselves with the labelling of a superficially connected group of sites? It is of fundamental importance when entering into a dialogue with the reader to establish common ground, to know what one means by a certain terminology. In this case, 'cursus monument' is a rather antiquated label describing a group of Neolithic monuments, based on the initial erroneous presumption that they were Roman chariot racing arenas. It is an established *type*, which has become, rather like 'henge' or 'hillfort', an increasingly generalised catchall classification in recent decades (Brophy 2005).

As more cursus sites have been discovered in Scotland, it has become a terminology that has looked increasingly insufficient to capture what is essentially an eclectic group of archaeological sites. The morphological definition of cursus has been stretched, and stretched again. Furthermore, the nature of the record (all but one of the sites are now known only as cropmarks) has meant that the study of these sites (most of which have not been excavated) has concentrated on the plans and exterior boundaries of the cursus monument. This has been the sole basis for the inclusion or exclusion of sites.

We must also reflect on the preconceptions that we bring to studying these monuments. The very fact that the site is included in the list of possible cursus monuments is a judgement that must be questioned and reflected upon. The label 'cursus' has baggage attached, regarding the nature of form, construction, dating, function, meaning and place in the world. This cannot be taken for granted, but rather we must question the status of our sub-divisions of the past.

Cursus monuments have proved less easy to sub-divide than other monuments (such as barrows and henges), although it has been attempted. Divisions based on size (relative width and length) have differentiated Major cursus sites, Minor cursus and smaller Oblong Ditch enclosures (Loveday & Petchey 1982), while Loveday (1985) constructed typological sequences based on terminal shape, from A (rounded) to B (squared) and i–iii subgroups of these. Pryor (in Pryor & French 1985, 301) suggested a more helpful three-way division of cursus sites, based on the sequence of construction and the longevity of usage. In the case of the sites discussed here, they are almost impossible to order chronologically and a more pragmatic descriptive approach has been adopted instead.

Yet the label is still a hindrance – as so many typological labels become – with too many implications, grouping sites together on a general morphological basis, emphasising similarities over differences, so that differences no longer matter, except to subdivide and refine the typology. These ideas are difficult to shake off. Tilley (1999, 97) suggests that 'difference is....the unthinkable'. The sites may be better served when studied from the site up, and not the typology down. Yet ironically, the sites here would not even be discussed if they were not initially classified as cursus monuments.

Loveday's (1985, 33) definition of 'cursus monument' is fairly wide:

> Elongated parallel sides sites normally totally enclosed by their defining ditch or pits, but on very rare occasions having one open end...they may possess either internal banks or more rarely an axial mound.

This vague definition is stretched to its limits in areas like Dumfries and Galloway, where cursus sites vary greatly in size and shape and begin to blur between one of our monument types and another. A discussion of the suspected inter-changeability of bank barrow and cursus monuments, for instance, is continued elsewhere (Bradley 1983; Barclay & Maxwell 1998), and this is perfectly illustrated by the so-called bank barrow at Eskdalemuir.

The sites

The cursus sites in south-west Scotland, as earlier mentioned, are mostly found in the Nith valley (Fig. 20.1). The others tend to be on the coastal fringes or inland river valleys, a distribution probably reflecting areas of more concentrated aerial reconnaissance and the higher cropmark potential of this low-lying arable land (Hanson & MacKinnes 1991; Brophy 1999). Indeed, the sites are all known only as cropmarks, with the exception of the anomalous Eskdalemuir. Some show as only intermittently visible cropmarks, with only a few known to their full extent, terminal to terminal (such as Holywood South).

The sites as presented here are sub-divided on a simplistic morphological basis, between those that were probably defined by standing timbers, and those that were earthworks. As stated previously, this does not mean that they served different purposes; nor does their shared rectilinearity mean that they all had similar roles or even that they are contemporary. A third category, that of bank barrow, includes only one site, Eskdalemuir, a remarkable earthwork in eastern Dumfriesshire. It is included due to its probable Neolithic date, and the noted similarity between this type of site and certain cursus monuments with single axial mounds such as the Cleaven Dyke and Scorton, Yorkshire (Topping 1982).

Pit-defined cursus monuments / rectilinear enclosures

During the 1990s, a small number of pit-defined rectilinear enclosures were discovered in Scotland, mostly through the re-assessment of older aerial photographs for the RCAHMS *East Dumfries-shire* volume (1997). Previously, save for Holm and Lochbrow, only a relatively small rectilinear enclosure within Fourmerkland Roman temporary camp had been recorded, and its shape and size (at least 54 m east to west by 28 m, with only the west end visible) led Loveday (1985) to include it at the very minimum limit of his Minor cursus class. One side intersects the cropmark of a ring-ditch, dividing it cleanly in two, although it is unclear which was the earlier. Fourmerkland lies 3.2 km west of Holywood village, in a location over-looking the Cluden Water.

More recent reconnaissance has identified a number of similar sites (Fig. 20.2). A slightly larger pit-defined enclosure lies within a different Roman temporary camp, at Trailflat. The 'pits' are widely spaced and describe a

Fig. 20.2 Trailflat pit-defined cursus visible as a cropmark within the central area of the Roman camp (© Crown Copyright RCAHMS, SC 981213).

rectilinear shape of at least 60 m by 17 m. Yet another one of these small sites in the Nith valley, Tibbers, sits in a large field immediately to the west of the Nith, amidst a series of cropmarks of pit-alignments and possible pitted enclosures, a circular palisaded enclosure, and old river channels. Visible cropmarks of groups of pits suggest a rectilinear enclosure of some 100 m length and at least 16 m width (Fig. 20.3). The cropmarks of similarly inter-mittent pit-alignments have been recorded within a meander just north of Kirkland Station on the valley floor of the Cairn Water. These suggest a pit-defined rectilinear enclosure with a curved terminal; only one side of the possible rectilinear enclosure can be traced, but for at least 100 m. Other pits within the same field do not appear to be part of the enclosure. This site has only ever been photographed once, in the dry summer of 1992.

In eastern Dumfries-shire, and to the east of the Nith valley, in a field beside Lochbrow farm, runs a sinuous parallel pit-alignment, at least 195 m long and about 20 m apart. It runs downhill, and terminates literally overlooking the River Annan, less than 30 m away. Reminiscent of the Angus pit-defined cursus sites (Brophy 2000a), it has an internal pitted sub-division. Further away from the river in the same field, cropmarks of ring-ditches, pit-alignments, and square and round

barrows have been recorded, placing the 'cursus' within a long-lived cluster of ritual and burial monuments (RCAHMS 1997, 110).

Earthwork cursus monuments

Sites more traditionally regarded as cursus monuments, that is, defined by a near continuous earthwork are found only in the Nith valley in Dumfries and Galloway, with one exception. The aforementioned site of Gallaberry is situated 3 km to the north-north-east of Holywood North cursus, with which it shares its orientation. Located on the opposite side of the Nith from Holywood, Gallaberry is visible for at least 480 m and presumably terminates at the terrace edge looking over the valley floor at the southern end. The parallel ditches are intermittent and sinuous, and vary in distance apart from 29 m to 42 m. The cursus passes through the edge of a small Roman temporary camp, which runs parallel to the cursus, perhaps suggesting the latter was still visible when the former was constructed. This site was proposed as a putative cursus monument by JK St Joseph, at least privately, in 1959, recorded in one of his aerial survey notebooks (held in the NMRS, Edinburgh).

On the southern side of Dumfries, and the western side of the Nith, is a large cursus enclosure beside a farm

Fig. 20.3 One terminal of the Tibbers pit-defined cursus is visible in this aerial photograph (A), adjacent to a presumably later prehistoric palisaded enclosure (B) (© Crown Copyright RCAHMS, SC 981224).

called Curriestanes. It runs for at least 300 m in an east-west direction, towards a rounded terminal (the only recorded terminal) with a distinct causeway in its centre. It is unusually wide for a cursus – narrowing from 98 m to about 75 m at the terminal – giving an enclosure with a known area of at least 3 hectares (Cowley & Brophy 2001, 54–6). The ditch, as a cropmark, appears to be both very wide (at least 7 m), and very irregular, having the appearance of being composed of series of short segments of ditch (Figs. 20.4 and 20.5a). A trench cut through the ditch as part of a pre-development evaluation revealed both lateral ditches to be heavily truncated, surviving to no more than 0.6m deep. A pit containing a beaker burial was recovered from within the cursus (Brann 2003). Curriestanes runs across a rather flat low-lying un-inspiring piece of land, built over in parts by roads, houses and a golf course. A solitary cropmark ring-ditch lies about 200 m to the south of the terminal.

Further south, on a hillside overlooking the Nith estuary and Solway Firth at Cavens, a large possible cursus monument has been identified from only two aerial photographs (Truckell 1984, 203). This site rather unusually runs uphill on the lower slopes of Criffel, the highest point in the area, visible on the horizon when walking south along Holywood South cursus. The domi-

nant location surveys the Nith estuary and Solway to the south and east, and aligns towards Criffel inland. Its hillside location lead to it being dismissed as a cursus by the RCAHMS (Brophy & RCAHMS in press).

Cadgill, a small rectilinear enclosure just north of the English border, was initially identified as the cropmark of a plantation bank. At least 180 m long, and 17 m wide (see Fig. 20.5b), it has been re-interpreted as a possible cursus monument with a distinctive angled terminal at the east-south-east end (RCAHMS 1997, 107–10).

Bank barrow

Just north of Eskdalemuir lie two linear banks, one on either side of the river White Esk and each running up the valley side. Initially recorded individually, but subsequently thought to represent two halves of the same monument (RCAHMS 1997, 107), they represent potentially the best surviving traces of such a monument in Scotland alongside the Cleaven Dyke. Previously classified in the NMRS as a 'cursiform earthwork', this site is now known as a bank barrow.

The south-western terminal, Tom's Knowe, was initially interpreted as burial cairn built on top of a natural knoll, and in fact where the topography stopped and the monument started was the subject of much ambiguity (see

Fig. 20.4 Kirkland Station pit-defined cursus. Often the cropmarks of cursus monuments have to be traced across several fields making their identification and characterisation more difficult (© Crown Copyright RCAHMS, SC 981225).

for instance Yates 1984, 91–2). However, re-evaluation and survey undertaken by the RCAHMS (1997, 107–9) recorded a long mound running from this 'cairn' into forestry and sharply downhill towards the valley floor. This mound, visible as a combination of earthwork and cropmark for at least 255 m, survives to a height of only 0.5 m in the forestry. A flanking ditch on either side, giving the monument a width of 20 m, runs around the terminal.

A matching mound was subsequently discovered on the opposite side of the valley running along a spur near Raeburnfoot Roman fort. Terminating with a slightly oval mound (which appears to mimic a series of long natural mounds on this hillside), it runs downhill over undulating ground, visible as an earthwork for 650 m, and again with a width of about 20 m including central mound and flanking ditches (Fig. 20.6). Using aerial photographs, it is possible to extend the monument by a further 150 m from snow-marks and cropmarks, right down to the current valley floor. If initially one unitary site (and this is impossible to prove or discount because of large alluvial deposits on the valley floor post-dating the Neolithic), it would have had a length of about 2.1 km, and been bisected by the White Esk.

Discussion

All of these sites have been described at one time or another as possible cursus monuments, or even cursiform. As with any group of sites that are known largely as cropmarks with only a few excavated analogies, we cannot be sure of the date or function of most of the sites. Their inclusion on a morphological basis alone is problematic, but at this stage, unless more sites are given the intensive treatment afforded Holywood and Holm, this is the best that we can hope for. Sites such as Kirkland Station, Tibbers and Cadgill may be on the very fringes of what we call cursus monuments, but at least their inclusion in this discussion saves them from the fate of forever hiding within the National Monuments Record of Scotland as pit-alignments and linear cropmarks.

Stripped down, these sites are a collection of rectangular enclosures. To be more brutal, they are a collection of difficult cropmarks, intermittent pit-alignments and parallel wobbly ditches. Such disorder in the archaeological record is rarely tolerated, and so we tend to assume that things that are similar (shapes of monuments, the form of flint tools, the decoration on a pottery vessel) mean that conceptually they were linked in some way, forming a pattern or shared idea. In the same way, things

Fig. 20.5 Aerial view of the cropmark of Curriestanes cursus, looking from the east. The irregularity of the ditch is especially clear in this image (© Crown Copyright RCAHMS, SC 587116).

which are vastly different (henge versus cursus, Grooved ware versus Unstan ware) are kept apart, the products of different social groups, or different functions and needs. These ideas are difficult to escape:

> The unthinkable of the archaeological discourse which controls us is to suggest that all megaliths, or different typological groups of megaliths, have nothing whatsoever to do with each other.
> (Tilley 1999, 97)

Similarity is celebrated, difference is superficial and immaterial.

We should not fall into the traditional trap of thinking that all things which look alike are the same, or that things which are dissimilar have nothing in common. Superficially the enclosures discussed above share little other than their rectilinearity. They range in length from about 50 m to almost 500 m (excluding Eskdalemuir), and have boundaries of pits or posts, ditches or even a

combination of posts and ditches (Holywood North). It is difficult to discuss, say, Kirkland Station and Curriestanes as the same thing.

Yet a closer look at the cropmarks (and the excavated sites) suggests other similarities. Irregular boundaries suggest segmented construction at sites like Curriestanes and Gallaberry, and potentially a few of the pit-defined sites. Re-use and reconstruction of monuments is also suggested by the re-cuts of the ditches at the Holywood sites and the continual re-use of the post-holes at Holm. Extensions and embellishments could be postulated for the third post line at Holm, the boundaries at Holywood North, the terminal mounds at Eskdalemuir, the division within Lochbrow and so on.

Another feature of some of these sites that should be noted is an association with Roman sites, including Gallaberry, Fourmerkland, Trailflat and Eskdalemuir. There is a possibility that remnants of earthwork sites, or knowledge of the location of sacred indigenous sites, were

Fig. 20.6 The Raeburnfoot section of the Eskdalemuir bank barrow, running from a cairn down the valley side. The parallel ditches are indicated by gorse and vegetation. Raeburnfoot Roman fort, and the valley floor, are visible at the top of the photograph (© Crown Copyright RCAHMS, SC 505280).

met with a specific colonial response by the Romans (for a similar argument see Loveday 1998). It is equally probable that this unusual relationship is due to cursus builders and the Romans preferring similar landscape settings on flat river terraces. The location of most of these sites very close to rivers, even terminating overlooking rivers (Lochbrow, Gallaberry, and to a lesser extent Holywood North) may also have had some significance in the Neolithic (Brophy 2000b).

Yet these things do not reinforce our classification of cursus monuments. These are not defining properties of cursus sites, but rather aspects of Neolithic life in this area, themes of returning to special places, of embellishing them, and of close links between land and monument. These are themes common to the excavated sites discussed in this volume.

Little is known about the rectangular enclosures in this discussion, and yet they do form part of a seemingly wide-ranging tradition of linear monuments in Scotland's

Neolithic (Brophy & RCAHMS in press). As Tilley suggests, perhaps we should not overplay the similarities to group them together, but rather risk chaos and see them as individual monuments and special places where people took a basic model (a rectangle, not a circle in these cases) and did their own thing with it, building big or small as they saw fit, to address various social concerns.

These concerns, on whatever geographic or social level they operated, transcend our monument typologies so that these places do not reflect merely another ritualistic cursus, but very personal and localised projects, carried on through unknown time, where the differences between monuments do matter because they mattered in the past, and have always mattered. We should see more than the ground plan, the pre-conception, and look to the individual wobbles in the ditch line or the misplaced posthole at Holm. In the Neolithic, nobody set out to build a cursus monument.

21

Holywood cursus complex, excavations

Julian Thomas
with contributions by Matt Leivers, Chris Fowler and Maggie Ronayne

Background

The Holywood cursus complex lies to the north-west of Dumfries (c. NX 9581), and represents an important concentration of Neolithic field monuments. It is composed of two cursus monuments and a stone circle, the Twelve Apostles. There are also a number of minor features, which may represent ring-ditches, small enclosures, or ploughed-out mounds. Of the two cursus, the southern example (hereafter Holywood South) has squared terminals, while the northern has rounded terminals (Fig. 21.1). This difference in morphology may have chronological implications, as monuments with rounded ends are sometimes considered to be earlier in date (Barclay *et al.* 2003, 95). Holywood North has a slight change of alignment about halfway along its length, and the orientation of the more southerly part on the stone circle is an unusual feature of the complex. This presents the opportunity to investigate the relationship between what are conventionally taken as lowland and upland traditions of monument-building. Moreover, Holywood South runs along a small promontory, while Holywood North terminates at its northern end on a small hillock with extensive views, suggesting a close relationship with the details of local topography: a theme which has informed much recent research on prehistoric linear monuments (e.g. Barrett, Bradley and Green 1991; Tilley 1994). The argument that the linear monuments might influence movement across the local landscape is given some force by the way in which two of the entrances in the sides of the southern cursus are so positioned as to allow unimpeded passage from the north cursus to the stone circle, or vice-versa (Brophy 1995).

The monuments are located on a sand and gravel subsoil, and ground cover today varies between arable, pasture, and patches of woodland. Aside from the stones of the circle, there was little upstanding evidence of the structures prior to excavation, the only evidence of their existence having come from aerial photography. In places, particularly in the wooded areas, there was evidence of severe rabbit damage. The excavation was intended to test the preservation of the monuments in the face of animal and agricultural damage over a very long period. As such, it was conceived as a sampling exercise. Large areas were opened to provide an extensive plan view of the monuments, but the total excavation of all the features revealed was not contemplated. Rather, a number of features were selected, with the aim of acquiring representative sections, and samples for radiocarbon and environmental analysis. A principal objective of the project was the investigation of the chronological sequence of the construction and use of the monuments.

Holywood North

At the northern cursus, a large cutting (Trench 1) was opened, over the northern terminal (Colour Plate 5), while a smaller area was excavated to the south, in order to investigate an entrance in the side of the monuments (Trench 2).

Trench 1

This cutting was 60 by 40 metres in extent, and was located over the northern terminal of the cursus (Fig. 21.2; Colour Plate 6). The topsoil was removed by machine (a large JCB with 4.5 tonne bucket, plus a smaller machine with a ditching bucket for finer cleaning of the surface), and the surface was shovel-scraped before trowelling. The revealed subsoil was quite heterogeneous, ranging from coarse gravel to loose silty sand. The cursus ditch immediately showed as a dark feature, contrasting with the orange and buff colours of the natural subsoil. To the east, several large post-holes were readily apparent, while there was some indication of the presence of surviving bank material where the sand seemed densely packed and mottled in colour. In the middle of the terminal was a large dark feature.

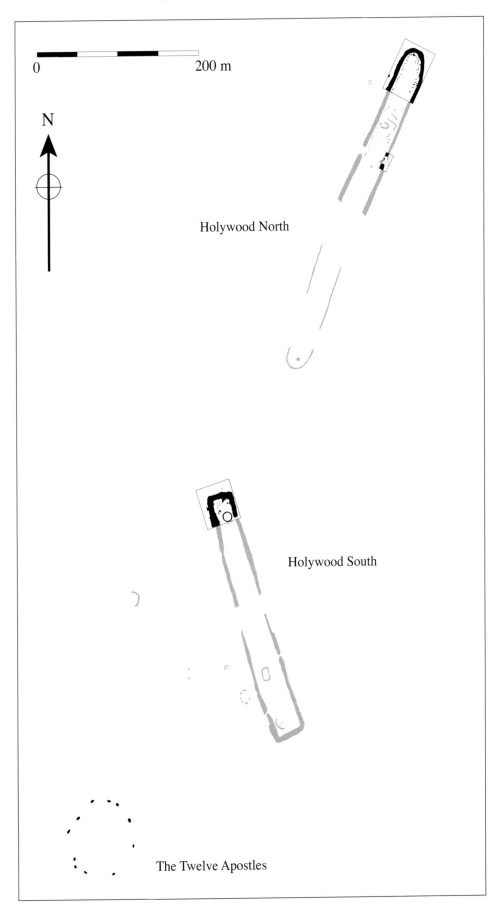

Holywood North

Holywood South

The Twelve Apostles

Fig. 21.1 The Holywood cursus complex.

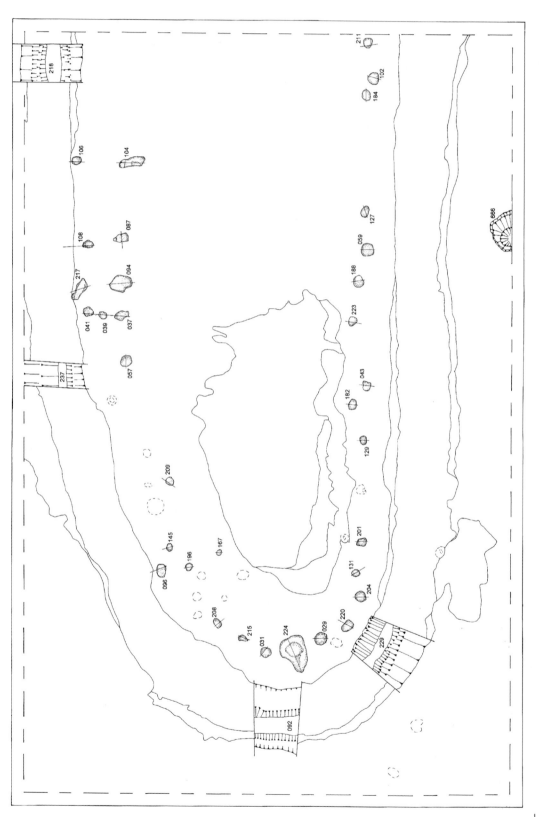

Fig. 21.2 Holywood North: Trench 1 plan.

The ditch

The cursus ditch was sectioned in four places within Trench 1, and proved to vary in depth between 1.20 and 1.45 metres (Figs. 21.3 and 21.4; Plates 21.1 and 21.2). The precise details of the filling of the ditch varied between the four cuttings, but it appeared that the principal cause of difference was the parent material into which it had been cut. In broad terms, the ditch sequence was similar throughout. The ditch had originally had a flat bottom and slanting sides, but these were heavily eroded. In particular, a substantial weathering profile could be noted at the top edge of the ditch, while the sides

Plate 21.1 Ditch section 218, on the eastern side of the cursus.

Plate 21.2 Ditch section 092, at the north terminal of the cursus.

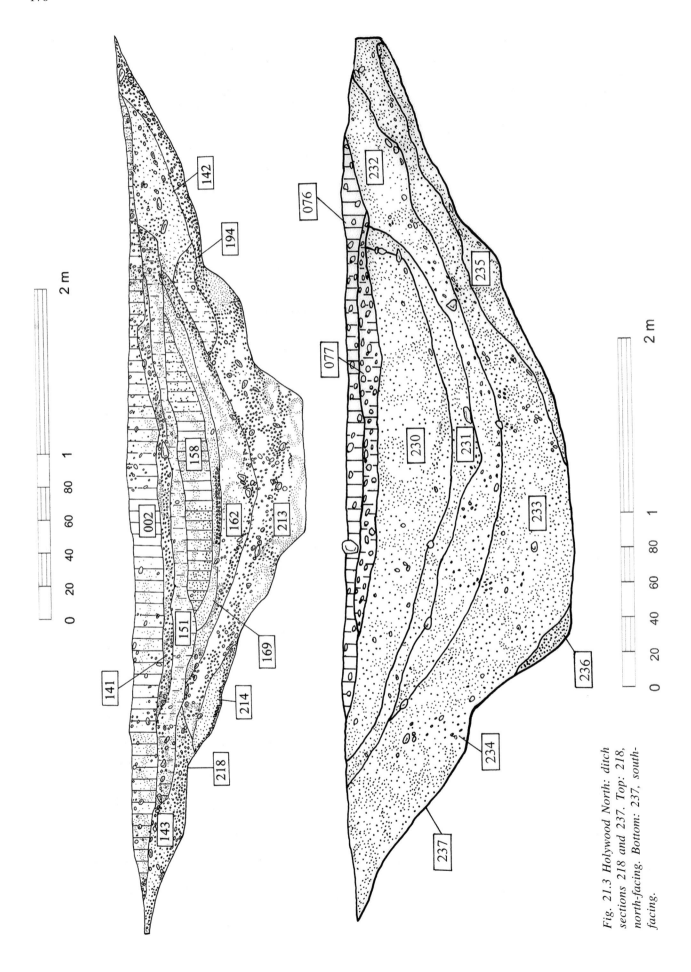

Fig. 21.3 Holywood North: ditch sections 218 and 237. Top: 218, north-facing. Bottom: 237, south-facing.

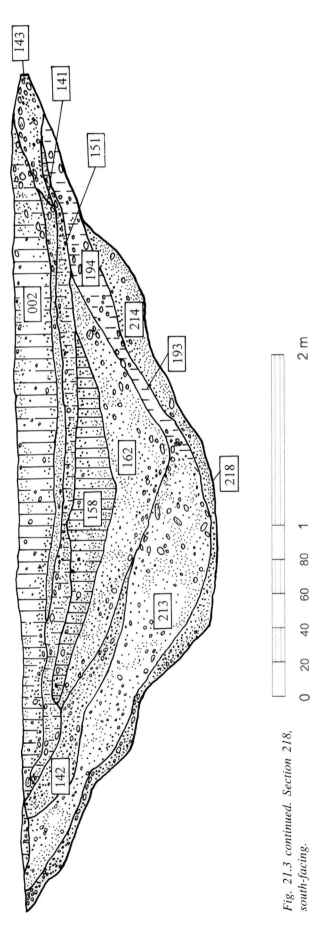

Fig. 21.3 continued. Section 218, south-facing.

were sometimes 'stepped' as a result of the differential weathering of the bedded layers of sand and gravel in the natural. The earliest deposit in the ditch was generally a small amount of coarse, gritty sand and gravel, the product of the initial weathering of the ditch edges (091, 090, 214, 236). This was generally yellow to strong brown in colour. In places, the clean sand layers of the natural had slumped forward into the ditch. These layers and lenses of eroded material were more substantial in the two cuttings in the extreme terminal of the ditch.

Above this primary material, a massive wedge of reddish-brown sand and gravel could be recognised, sometimes containing tip-lines and lenses of clayey sand (070, 213, 197, 233, 234). This was often surmounted by a deposit of dirtier, mottled gravel (026). Both of these layers were heavily skewed toward the inner side of the ditch, and for this reason they are interpreted as having derived from the collapse (or quite likely the deliberate dismantling) of an inner bank. The material which lay above this deposit appeared to rest upon it unconformably, and there was some indication that a degree of truncation had taken place before silting had commenced. In places, and particularly at the extreme terminal of the ditch, this truncation gave the impression of a cut feature, although it is within the bounds of possibility that the fans of collapsing (or backfilled) bank material had simply come to rest at a relatively oblique angle. In any case, the truncation was recorded as a deliberate recut (060, 193, 239, 191), which was present at all points in the ditch that were investigated. This feature was somewhat irregular, varying in width and sometimes being v-shaped while in other cases it had more of a u-profile. In some sections there was a hint of some redeposited gravel and stones in the bottom of the feature, but in all cases the major primary fill was a coarse, bright orange sandy silt (079, 162, 231). This was the only layer in the cursus ditch from which artefacts were recovered, including a re-touched flint knife from the south-eastern cutting (FN3). Above this orange silt was another, darker coarse silt (055, 158, etc.). These fills which succeed the putative recutting of the ditch contrast with the primary ditch fill, and indicate that the history of the monument which followed any reinstantiation was quite different from its first phase of use. Oak charcoal from the ditch recut produced a radiocarbon date of 2310–2120 BC at the 95.4 % probability level (SUERC-2117). This would seem to indicate that the recutting took place a considerable time after the original digging of the ditch. However, the recovery of earlier Neolithic pottery from the recut in Trench 2 conflicts with this result (see below).

In the two cuttings on the eastern side of the cursus (Plate 21.1), the recut fills were sealed beneath a thin layer of iron pan, and this and the layer of degraded sandstone fragments above it (151) rested on an un-conformity with the earlier layers. Seemingly a horizon of erosion preceded the renewed filling of the ditch, which may have been associated with ploughing of the site. A

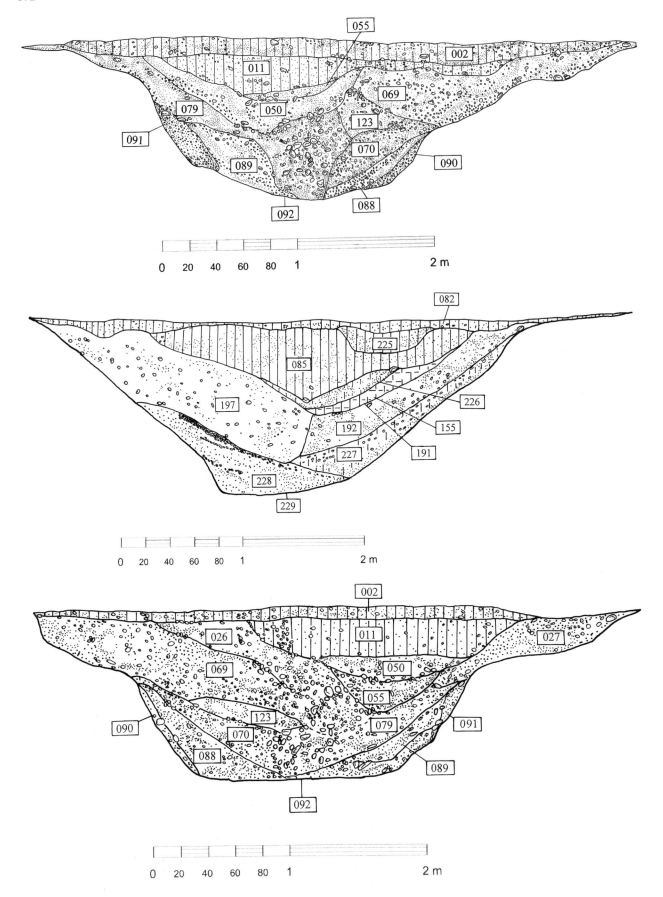

Fig. 21.4 Holywood North: ditch sections 092 and 229. Top: 092, west-facing; middle: 229, north-facing; bottom: 092, east-facing.

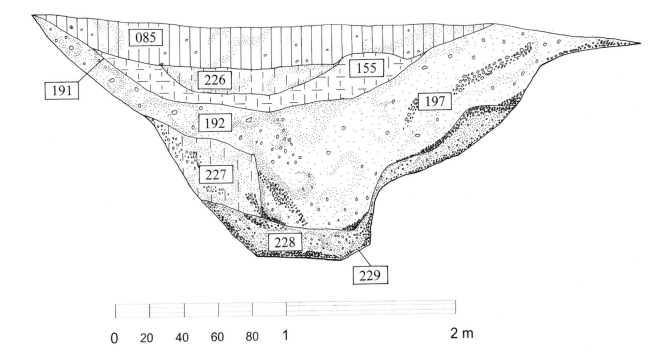

0 20 40 60 80 1 2 m

Fig. 21.4 continued. Section 229, south-facing.

thin, creamy-grey layer of silt (141) lay above this, and some quantity of humic plough-soil had slumped into the top of the ditch (002).

Internal features
by Matt Leivers and Julian Thomas

Numerous internal features could be observed on aerial photographs of the site prior to excavation. Once the topsoil had been stripped from the trench it was apparent that some of these features were easily discernible on the subsoil surface, and investigating a large sample of them became a priority. However, it was only over the course of the excavation, as the weather conditions changed and periods of wetting and drying alternated, that further features became visible. The character of the subsoil and the pit and post-hole fills were such that some features were only temporarily visible, while others gradually revealed themselves through the process of weathering. Consequentially, it is possible that some cut features remained undetected. It is also apparent that some of the putative features that were initially identified were not products of human action. Nevertheless, fifty-three possible features were located in the cursus interior (and three outside the cursus ditch) of which some forty were excavated. Excavation showed that all of these features had been severely truncated by post-Neolithic agricultural practices.

Of these features, five were found to be natural subsoil variations, whilst a sixth – a very large expanse of dark soil positioned in the centre of the interior of the cursus at its northern terminal – was an area of plough soil caught in a shallow depression in the natural. This contained glazed sherds and clay pipe stems, demonstrating its recent origin.

The remaining features were of several different types. At the extreme northern end of the area enclosed by the cursus ditch was the very large pit complex 224. A series of post-holes (some demonstrated by the presence of a post-pipe, others presumed) ran parallel with the inner edge of the ditch. While from the air a single circuit of post-holes had been suggested, it was evident that on the eastern side of the cursus at least there were two or three parallel lines of cut features. Finally, a large pit or ditch terminal lay outside and to the west of the enclosure.

The large post-pit
(Figs. 21.5 and 21.7; Plate 21.11)

Cut 224 revealed a rather complex sequence of events of cutting and filling (Plate 21.11). The principal cut (224 itself) was almost three metres long and relatively shallow, but the various fills and cuts within it demonstrated an involved stratigraphic history. Its principal fill was layer 154, a fill of large stones in a matrix of loose yellowish-red sandy silt. Some of these stones (about twenty percent) appeared to have been deliberately broken; the edges of some were still sharp. This was cut by 238, a deep, round-based and straight-sided post socket, filled by 152, a firm reddish-brown silty clay with large stones arranged around its edge (perhaps as pack-

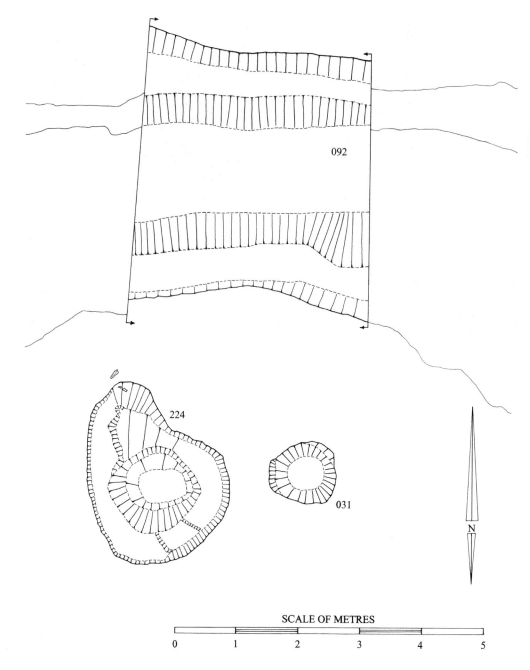

Fig. 21.5 Holywood North: location of large post-pit 224 in relation to cursus ditch 092.

ing), and containing numerous lumps of wood charcoal. At the time of excavation, it was implied that cut 224 had been left open for some while, and that at a later point 238 had been cut through it and had held a substantial timber upright, which had burned and collapsed to the south. This episode was represented by the considerable quantity of charcoal (fill 053), 2.60 metres long, running away to the north of the post-hole. The pattern of visible wood in this charcoal suggested that it did not represent a coherent entity, but was characterised by plant fibres running in different directions. This might indicate that the charcoal deposit was composed of successive dumps of material. A lens of sand (fill 054) within charcoal 053

might indicate that more than one episode of burning took place. It is more likely, though, that the charred post lost its coherence as it toppled over. Context 053 produced a radiocarbon date of 3640–3490 Cal. BC at 95.4% probability (SUERC-2116).

However, on the drawn section it appears that the burnt material 053 was itself truncated by cut 238 (see Fig. 21.7), and it is perhaps significant that fill 154, composed largely of stones, had the character of a packing deposit rather than the silting of an otherwise empty pit. It is therefore likely that the sequence was rather more complicated than originally imagined. The large post that collapsed to form deposit 053 was probably replaced by

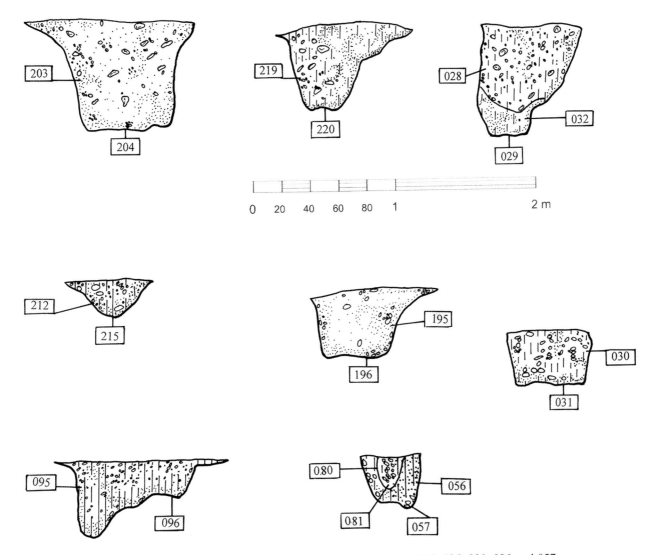

Fig. 21.6 Holywood North: sections, features 204, 220, 029, 215, 196, 031, 096 and 057.

another post held in feature 238 and packed by deposit 152. The charcoal content, texture and colouration of 152 would seem to suggest that this second post was also burnt, although it is also possible that the charcoal was derived from 053. It is conceivable that fill 154 was the packing for post 053, which collapsed forward over it. But equally, it is possible that 154 represent an earlier event than 053, and that the burned timber was actually the second in a series of posts. This has some significance for the interpretation of the radiocarbon dates from the site (see below).

A series of fills sealed the upper portions of cuts 224 and 238: fill 168 (a dark reddish brown loamy sand) lay beneath a layer of granular pebbly sand (fill 052), in turn sealed by a layer of sand mixed with gravel and large stones (051). It is notable that the northern boundary of 168 rose to a near-vertical angle (see Fig. 21.7). This implies that it might possibly have been the fill of a cut feature, which may potentially have truncated contexts 154, 152 and 053. Fills 168 and 052 were subsequently

cut by post-hole 015. This was filled by 014, a friable, dark yellowish brown sandy loam containing numerous pebbles and some charcoal. 014 contained a clear post-pipe, 012, a loose strong brown sand. It is possible that this post-pipe represented the foot of a post that was burned at a higher level, resulting in a change of the colour and consistency of the deposit. Context 014 produced the radiocarbon date SUERC-2113, which calibrates to 3640–3370 Cal. BC at 95.4% probability. As discussed below, it is perplexing that this date is little different from SUERC-2116.

Feature 224 formed the apex of the post structure at Holywood North, and was arguably the feature around which the cursus ditch was constructed, as well as being the largest pit or post-hole in the interior. The precise sequence of its cutting and filling is not entirely clear, but it is possible that a series of as many as five separate uprights stood at this point (represented by fills 154, 053, 152, 168 and 014/012, in that order). While none of the other post-holes exhibited such a complex stratigraphic

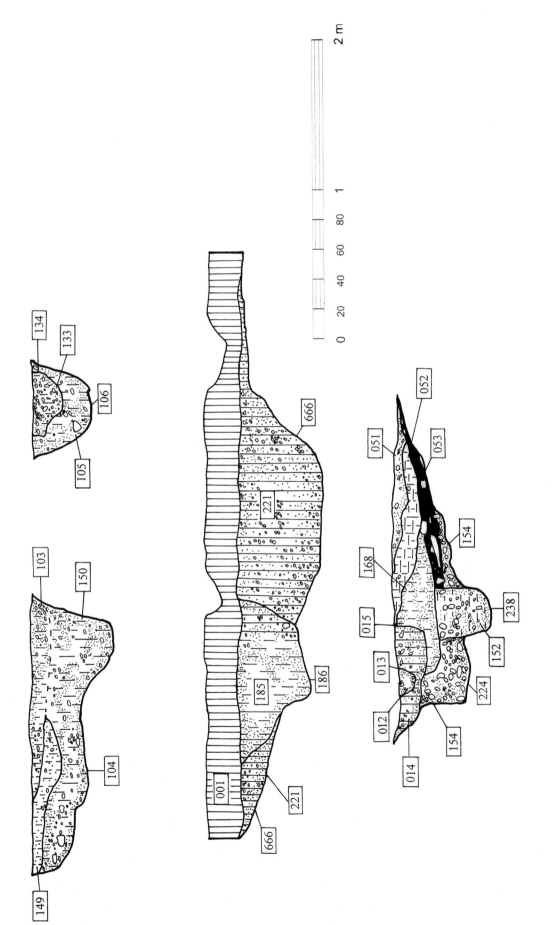

Fig. 21.7 Holywood North: sections, features 104, 106, 666 and 224.

sequence, it is worth considering that as the axial element in the timber architecture, 224 may have been renewed on a series of occasions, and that on each it would have been complemented by a slightly different array of other uprights. This would suggest that the somewhat untidy scatter of cut features that was particularly evident on the eastern side of the cursus actually represented a palimpsest, composed of as many as five separate phases of post architecture. The implication of this is that the timber monument may have had a lengthy history.

The post-holes
(Figs. 21.6–21.9; Plates 21.3–21.10)

By far the most numerous of the excavated features were post-holes. From the aerial photographs it was evident that the cursus ditch was ringed within its terminal section by a line of internal features. On excavation, however, it was apparent that these post-holes were both more numerous and more diverse than had been expected on this evidence.

Feature 015
The post-hole which cut large pit 224 (see above).

Feature 029
Revealed through differential drying, the edges of this feature were difficult to define, and it may have been slightly over-cut as a result. The cut (029) was broadly circular and flat-based, and contained two layers of fill. The upper of these was 028, a loose/friable yellowish-red loamy sand with small pebbles, and the lower was 032, a loose, slightly loamy yellowish-red sand. The junction between 028 and 032 was clear and curved, and suggests that 028 was the fill of a recut. There was no clear post-pipe preserved, but it is possible that none would survive in this loose sandy material.

Feature 031
Cut 031 was oval in plan, flat-bottomed and step-sided, suggesting either the base of a post-socket within a larger cut, or two separate events of cutting. The homogeneous fill of the feature was 030, a friable, dark reddish brown loamy sand with numerous small pebbles.

Feature 037
Cut 037 was an amorphous, kidney-shaped feature, which contained a deeper, near-circular, flat-based portion which probably held the base of a post. The fill was context 036, a friable dark brown sandy loam with numerous small pebbles.

Feature 039
A deep, circular, flat-based cut (039) contained 038, a loose, reddish-brown sandy loam with many small pebbles.

Feature 041
Oval post-hole cut 041 appeared slightly ramped on the eastern side. Single fill 040 was a loose, reddish brown sandy loam with many small pebbles.

Feature 043
The circular, flat-bottomed and straight-sided cut 043 contained a packing of 042, a loose dark brown sandy loam, which surrounded 067, a clear post-pipe of loose, strong brown sandy loam. The context number 068 was assigned to the interface between post-pipe and packing.

Feature 057
The oval, flat-based, vertical-sided cut 057 contained packing deposit 056, a loose, strong brown sandy loam with many small pebbles, within which a clear post-pipe of loose, strong brown loamy sand, 080, was evident. This material contained extensive charcoal staining, suggesting that the post had been burnt out. Context number 081 was assigned to the interface between post-pipe and packing.

Feature 059
059 was a shallow, gradual-sided circular cut, filled with packing 058, a friable, reddish-brown loamy sand with numerous small pebbles. Within this, context 083, a slightly darker loamy sand, appeared to represent a post-pipe, but descended into a deeper, narrower cut (084). It is likely that 084 represented a second cut, for a replacement post, although it may have been that the post-hole was simply stepped, with a distinct socket receiving the post in the base of a larger feature.

Feature 087
087 was a large post-hole with a distinct post-ramp on the western side, descending to the base of the cut feature. It was filled by context 086, a loose to friable dark brown loamy sand with many small pebbles, and no obvious post-pipe could be discerned.

Feature 094
Large oval ramped cut 094 with three vertical sides, had three distinct fills, the lowest being loose yellowish red sand 140, followed by a deposit of large stones in a matrix of similar sand (139), and finally loose yellowish-red sand 093. These fills did not give the impression of representing packing, but were bedded from west to east, and there was a slight lip on the western side of the feature. This might indicate a deliberate backfill, or more likely the collapse of packing following the removal of a post, pulled down from the westward side.

Feature 096
Cut 096 was oval in plan with an uneven base which sloped toward a potential post-socket, potentially amounting to a post-ramp. It contained 095, a loose to friable dark brown sandy loam with moderate numbers of small to medium-sized pebbles. A post-pipe was not evident, and this might be a consequence of the collapse of the packing into the post-void, or of post-withdrawal. Such a withdrawal might explain the sloping edge of the cut, which would then not constitute a ramp.

Feature 102
Feature 102 was a cut measuring 0.78 by 0.83 metres at the top, and 0.36 metres deep, which contained two fills.

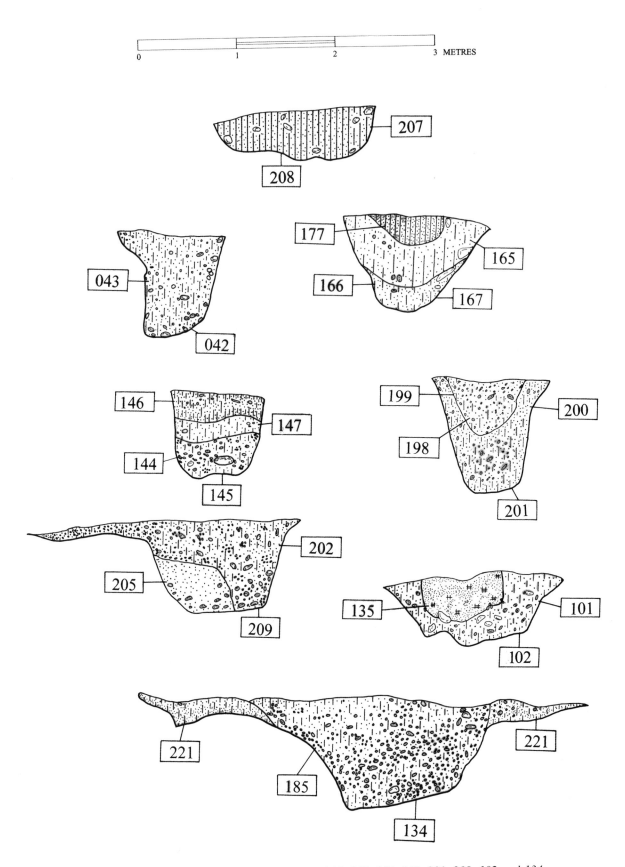

Fig. 21.8 Holywood North: sections, features 208, 042, 167, 145, 201, 209, 102 and 134.

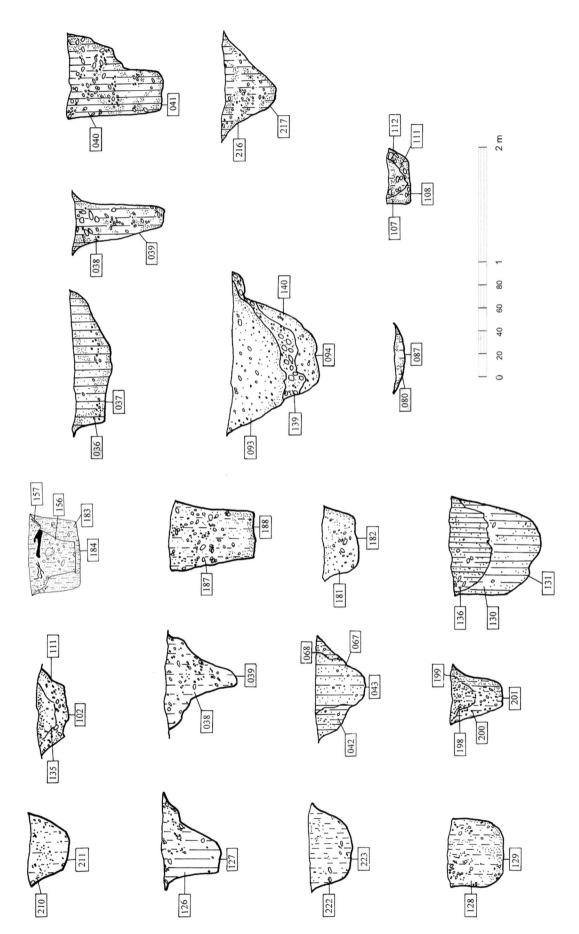

Fig. 21.9 Holywood North: sections, features 211, 102, 184, 037, 039, 041, 127, 039, 188, 094, 217, 223, 043, 182, 087, 108, 129, 201 and 131.

Plate 21.3 Post-hole 129.

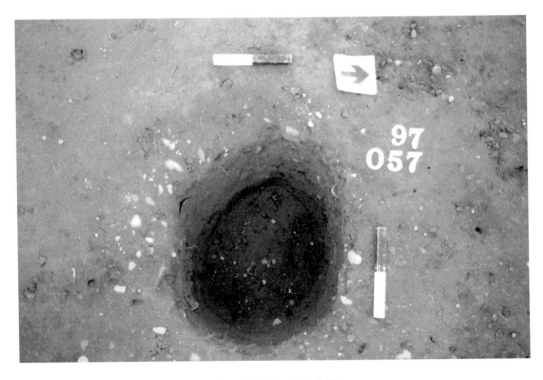

Plate 21.4 Post-hole 057.

In stratigraphic terms 135 was the later, and was composed of compact black silt containing fragments of
charcoal. It is possible that it represented the filling of the
lower part of a post-pipe, in which case the feature could
have been single-phase. However, it seems more likely

that 135 represented an intrusive feature, cut into an earlier
post-hole. This would suggest that two distinct posts stood
on this spot in succession, and that the later of the two was
probably burned *in situ*. The lower fill (101) was a compact
dark red silt, which contained large quantities of charcoal,

Plate 21.5 Post-hole 059 (fill 058).

Plate 21.6 Post-hole 031 (fill 028).

as well as numerous fragments of carinated bowl (FN 8, FN 17, Vessel 4), a single piece of burnt bone (FN 10), and some fragments of burnt nut-shell (FN 12). Stones in the fill also appeared to have been exposed to fire, but there was little direct indication that burning had taken place in

the pit itself, in the form of reddening of the subsoil surface. Given that the feature lay within the main line of post-holes, it is probable that it originally contained a post. Fill 135 (the potentially intrusive feature) produced a radiocarbon date of 3800–3650 Cal. BC at 95.4 %

Plate 21.7 Post-hole 037 (fill 056).

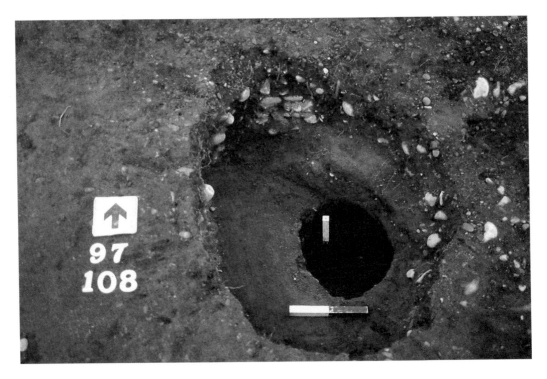

Plate 21.8 Post-hole 108.

confidence (SUERC-2115). If context 135 was a second post, the hazel nut-shell from which SUERC-2115 was derived might date the insertion of the post, or its burning, as it might have been part of the fuel used to fire the upright. This radiocarbon date is stratigraphically later than context 101, so that the initial construction of the monument and the deposition of the carinated bowl pottery might potentially have been appreciably earlier than SUERC-2115. Alternatively, it is possible that the nut-shell originated in the matrix of 101, and was redeposited

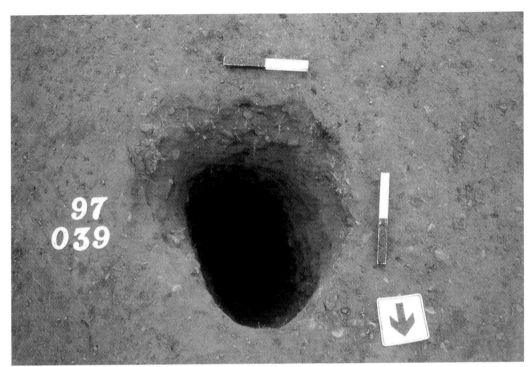

Plate 21.9 Post-hole 039.

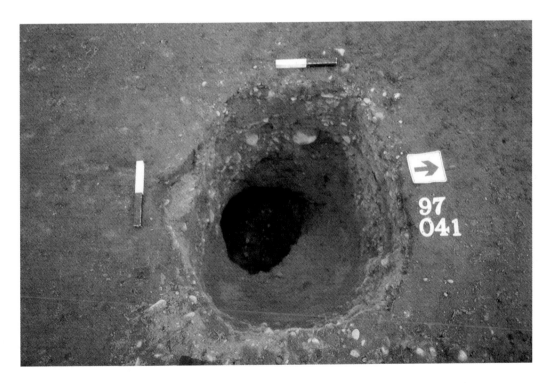

Plate 21.10 Post-hole 041.

in 135 in the course of the recutting of the post-hole, so that SUERC-2115 dates its initial digging. This being the case, the recut containing 135 might have been contemporary with the events dated by SUERC-2113 and SUERC-2116 (see feature 224 above).

Feature 104

An irregularly-shaped elongated cut with steep sides and an undulating base (104) suggested a post-hole with a ramp, or one that had been expanded by the toppling of a post. The primary filling was context 150, a loose, strong

Plate 21.11 Large pit/post-hole 224 after excavation.

brown loamy sand with many small pebbles, above which was the sandier silt loam 149, and the uppermost fill, 103, a friable dark brown sandy loam. These layers dipped gently into the feature, and gave little impression of the presence of a post-pipe, possibly indicating that the post had been withdrawn.

Feature 106
Irregular oval cut 106 was shallow and flat-based. It contained fill 105, a friable brown loamy sand containing a number of rounded stones. This was cut by a recut, 134, which contained 133, a dark brown loamy sand more pebbly than 105.

Feature 108
An oval cut with abruptly stepped sides and a flat base, 108, contained loose, dark brown loamy sand 107. Although the fill was uniform, the stepped base suggests the possibility that a sequence of two distinct cuts existed here.

Feature 127
Oval post-hole cut 127 was deep, with slanting sides and a flat base. It contained loose yellowish-red sandy loam with small and large pebbles 126. It is notable that a pronounced 'shelf' existed on the western side of the cut, and that the larger pebbles were concentrated within this shelf and in the upper part of the feature. It is possible, then, that a shallower feature with a stonier fill cut into the top of an earlier, deeper post-hole, and that this was not recognised during excavation.

Feature 129
Oval post-hole with flat base 129, contained friable dark reddish-brown loamy sand with many small and large pebbles 128.

Feature 131
Deep, oval, flat-based cut 131 contained loose-to-friable yellowish-red sandy loam with many small pebbles 130. The layer that sealed this, 136, was a compact dark reddish brown sandy loam with many rather larger pebbles, and this was probably the fill of a recut, rather than a post-pipe.

Feature 145
Flat-based oval cut 145 contained a series of three fills: compact brown loamy sand with numerous pebbles 144, friable strong brown loamy sand with few stones 147, and friable very dark brown loamy sand with numbers of medium-sized stones 148. The filling is curious, and suggests neither post-pipe nor recut, but perhaps backfilling.

Feature 167
Primary cut 167 had a slightly bowled base, and contained fill 166, a friable yellowish-red loamy sand with many small stones. This had apparently been cut across by a broader and shallower feature, which contained fill 165, a friable reddish-brown sandy loam with a lesser stone content. Within and above this was 177, a compact very dark brown loamy sand containing a great deal of charcoal. This probably represented the burnt-out post of a second post-hole at this location.

Feature 182
Relatively shallow, flat-based oval post-hole 182 contained friable yellowish-red loamy sand 181, which had a moderate stone content.

Feature 184/157

Shallow, flat-based oval cut with vertical sides 184, contained loose brown coarse sand 183, which had a moderate stone content. This was cut by the narrower, flat-based feature 157, which was filled by 156, a loose brown loamy sand containing a great deal of charcoal. This material possessed a coherent structure, rather than simply representing flecks of fragments, and appeared to be the remains of a burnt-out post. One sherd and one fragment of Neolithic pottery were found in context 156 (FN 31), both from Vessel 4 of Fabric Group III, the same burnished and probably carinated vessel represented in contexts 101 and 135 (see above and Appendix 8).

Feature 188

Deep, flat-bottomed cut with slightly slanting sides 188 was oval in plan but more circular at the base, with a more gently sloping side on the north, which may have amounted to a post-ramp, or even distortion caused by the withdrawal of the post. The fill, 188, was a friable yellowish-red loamy sand with moderate numbers of medium-sized pebbles. In section, this material gave little clue as to whether a post had rotted in situ or had been withdrawn.

Feature 196

Oval, flat-bottomed cut with irregular edges 196 contained loose dark red fine sand with moderate stone content 195.

Feature 201

Deep, irregularly-shaped cut with slightly bowled base and near-vertical sides weathered back at the top 201 contained friable dark red sandy loam with low stone content 200. This was cut by 199, a round, more shallow feature with a shallow base which was evidently a recut of the post-hole. The fill of 199 was 198, a friable strong brown loamy sand with numerous small stones.

Feature 204

Deep, near-circular flat-bottomed cut with a distinct lip on one side 204. Filled by 203, a friable dark reddish-brown loamy sand with occasional medium to large pebbles. No clear evidence for a post-pipe, the 'lip' on the edge of the cut may possibly suggest post-withdrawal.

Feature 209

Oval, flat-based and steep-sided cut 209 was filled by loose yellowish-red sand with sparse small stones 205. Much of this had been cut away by a later feature with steep sides and a flat base, and with a potential post-ramp. This was filled by context 202, a loose, strong brown loamy sand with numerous small pebbles.

Feature 211

Near-circular cut 211 had steep sides and a slightly bowled base. It contained 210, a compact dark reddish-brown loamy sand with numerous small pebbles.

Feature 217

Feature 217 had an elongated oval plan, a bowled base

and sloping sides. It was filled by 216, a loose, yellowish-red loamy sand. At its eastern end, this feature junctioned with the cursus ditch. The relationship was unclear, but on balance it was thought that 217 was earlier than the ditch. During excavation it was conjectured that the elongated shape of 217 was a consequence of the feature representing both a post-hole and a post-ramp. On reflection, this seems unlikely, as the putative post socket was not very much deeper than the rest of the cut: the slope was probably too gradual for a ramp. An alternative view is that the cut had been elongated by the act of removing the post, which would have been pulled down against one side of the pit, dislodging the parent gravel in the process. This situation is comparable with feature 096 (see above).

Feature 220

Cut 220 was oval in plan, with a flat base and slightly sloping sides. The gentle slope on one side may have represented a ramp, or perhaps evidence for a post-withdrawal. The fill was 219, a friable, dark reddish-brown loamy sand with numerous medium-sized and large pebbles.

Feature 223

Cut 223 was near-circular in plan, with a gently bowled base and slightly slanted sides. The fill was 222, a friable dark reddish-brown loamy sand with appreciable numbers of small to medium-sized pebbles. No post-pipe was visible in the section, but the excavator noted the presence of a dark stain in removing the second half of the fill.

Some observations on the post-holes

The complex variety of the post-holes observed during the 1997 excavation indicates that they were probably not all precisely similar or contemporary. Indeed, we have suggested already that they may have represented a palimpsest, composed of a series of post-structures. Some simple observations may help to clarify the issue. Firstly, several of the features appeared to have been recut. Post-holes 029, 059, 102, 106, 127, 131, 167, 184/157, 201, 209 and 224/015 all contained multiple cuts and fills, while features 031, 037 and 108 had cuts which had stepped profiles, and with less confidence suggested more than one episode of digging at a single location. In these cases, the existence of a sequence of posts seems assured.

In five cases, 057, 102, 167, 184/157 and the large post-socket 224, there was strong evidence (in the form of substantial quantities of charcoal) that the post had been burned out. A majority of these were recut posts, and in most of these cases the evidence for burning was in the recut rather than the primary post-hole. Thus, if the post structure within the cursus had a number of distinct phases of construction, it is probable that if a distinct episode of building and use ended with a burning event, this was not the earliest one.

Where the fill of a post-hole contained distinct traces of burning, such as large fragments of carbonised wood, it was notable that the soil matrix had often taken on a distinctive dark reddish-brown colour, presumably a direct effect of extreme heat. This same colour was sometimes seen in the fills of other features, and it was recognised that relatively compact dark reddish-brown fills were often found in the tops of features, as recut fills, but much less often as the primary fills of post-holes. This suggests that rather more than five posts were actually burned, and that in the severely truncated cut features it was sometimes only the effects of fire on the soil that could be identified, rather than the trace of the burnt timber itself, which may have only existed above ground level or higher in the eroded profile.

At the time of excavation a series of post-holes were identified as having ramps cut into their sides, on the analogy with the ramps well known from a series of later Neolithic henge monuments in various parts of Britain (for example, Wainwright and Longworth 1971: 30). Such features facilitate the erection of a post, by allowing the base of the upright to be toppled into its socket. However, in the case of the Holywood post-holes the putative 'ramps' were often too gentle to help in this way, and they were often combined with fills which suggested disturbed packing deposits. It is now considered more likely that the elongated plans of some of the post-holes were a consequence of the posts having been withdrawn from their sockets, which would involve their being rocked back and forth on an axis until they came free of the earth. This operation may have disturbed the relatively fragile subsoil surrounding the post-hole, with the effect that a 'ramp' was produced.

It is significant that there was no overlap whatever between those post-holes that were 'ramped' and those that contained traces of a burnt post. In other words, burning and withdrawal were alternative ways of removing a post, and were unlikely to have been combined. Furthermore, all of those post-holes that were 'ramped' were single-phase features: none of them was subsequently recut. It may be that where a post had been physically removed and no rotted stump remained it was more difficult to establish the original location of the upright and reinstate it. Potentially withdrawn posts of this kind were more common on the eastern side of the cursus, where multiple parallel lines of cut features were identified, while recut features were much more prevalent on the western side. Here, the cut features appeared to represent a single line, but it seems that this was a partial illusion in that a series of separate posts had sometimes been inserted into a single location.

The external pit/ditch terminal (Fig. 21.7)

Beyond the area enclosed by the cursus ditches, a small feature was found, entering the cutting from the western section (cut 666, with fill 221, a friable dark reddish brown sandy loam). This had been cut through by cut 186, with fill 185, a loose, strong brown loamy sand. It is not clear whether the latter represented a formal recut of the original feature, or whether it was an unrelated feature which cut through it fortuitously. The precise character of both features is unclear: no sign of any feature was visible on the aerial photograph, but it seems most likely that either might represent the terminal of a small ditch or part of a large pit. The only finds from the fill of the later feature (185) were some fragments of charcoal, pieces of burnt nut shell (FN56), and some seed cases (FN55) which may be intrusive. These produced a radiocarbon date of 2580–2340 Cal BC at 95.4 % confidence (SUERC-2118), a date sufficiently similar to that from the recut of the cursus ditch (although the two do not overlap) to hint that these two events may have been related.

Trench 2 (Fig. 21.10)
by Chris Fowler

This 20 by 10 m trench was laid out to incorporate an entrance/exit to the cursus between two ditch terminals (cuts 117, 120) (Plate 21.12). The fills of the ditch terminals were extremely distinct prior to excavation, while to the east (i.e. on the external side of the cursus), a number of post-holes were visible. These formed a row of posts abutting the northern ditch terminal and extended across the entrance causeway at an oblique angle (cuts 170, 115, 020, 005, 009, 003, 006, 018, 113, 111). These features generally had brown silty fills. Two further post-holes were situated by the extreme eastern edge of the cutting (cuts 024 and 022). A semi-circular feature referred to as a ring-ditch was identified between the terminals and extending beyond the western edge of the trench (cuts 118 and 172).

Each of the post-holes was excavated, with cut 006 producing a set of large packing stones rammed down the sides of the cut. There were no finds from these post-holes, which were some 0.20–0.30 m deep. While the innermost eight post-holes were clear features with hard edges, cuts 018, 113 and 111 were much less distinct and are, at best, putative features. None the less, the line of posts can be interpreted as a façade or screen, running at an angle to the line of the ditch, and partially closing off the entrance.

The terminal ditch cuts 117 and 120 were 1.05 m and 1.10 m deep respectively, and truncated since the Neolithic. These terminals were both filled with gravelly and sandy material (fills 075 and 122/132), which probably derived from a bank. The northern ditch terminal was noticeably square at its base, while the southern terminal was somewhat shallower and not so clearly defined at its sandy base. The shape of the cuts indicates a severe weathering cone, into which the bank material had slipped or been pushed quite uniformly. The weathering cone of the north terminal (120) intersected with post-hole 170. Despite careful excavation, it was not possible to ascertain the stratigraphic relationship between these two features. Three scenarios can be imagined to account for the relationship:

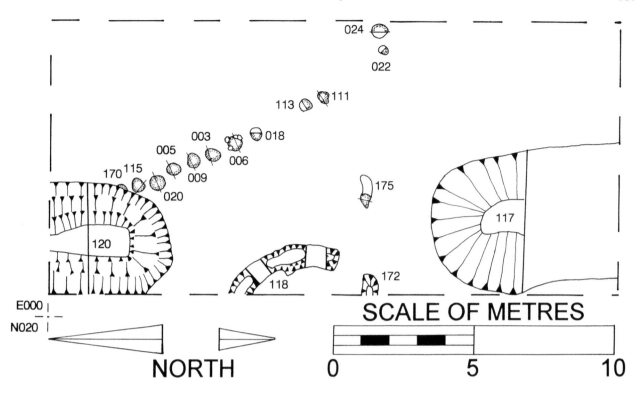

Fig. 21.10 Holywood North: Trench 2 plan.

Plate 21.12 Ditch section 120, to the north of the entrance causeway, south-facing.

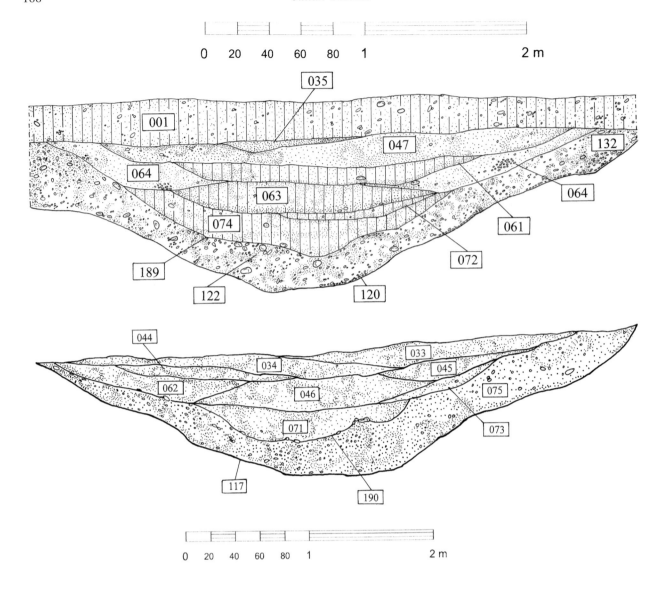

Fig. 21.11 Holywood North: ditch sections 120 and 117.

1. the post line was earlier than the ditch, and thus the cursus, and cut by it; it represented one aspect of pre-cursus activity on the site;

2. the post line was contemporary with the ditch, and was an integral element of the construction of the cursus; it was cut by the weathering back of the ditch edge;

3. the post line was later than the cutting of the ditch, and cut into the primary filling. The structure made up by the post-holes might then be contemporary with the recutting of the ditch. This would indicate that in the second phase of its existence, the conditions of access to the cursus had changed, by screening the entrance.

Following the initial cut and filling, the ditches appear to have been recut (cuts 189 and 190). Unlike the recuts at the northern end of the cursus in Trench 1, these cuts

were placed centrally within the original ditches. Given that the bank material that filled the ditches is likely to have had an asymmetrical surface profile, this location is a further indication that the feature is a recut. These recuts filled with orange sandy layers containing numerous large pebbles. The northern terminal had a somewhat different history of use from the southern at this point. At the bottom of the orange sandy fill (074), fragments of early neolithic pottery were deposited (FN 21, FN 44, FN 46, FN 50, FN 51, FN 53: Vessel 5), both as small sherds near the end of the terminal, and also as a compacted matrix some 3 m further north. It is notable that this pottery was quite distinct from that found elsewhere on the site, in that it represented a heavy, round-based bowl. Such a vessel might arguably be later in date than the carinated bowl pottery associated with the timber structure (Cowie 1993, 15–17). The more fragmented pottery was one element in a series of depositional events

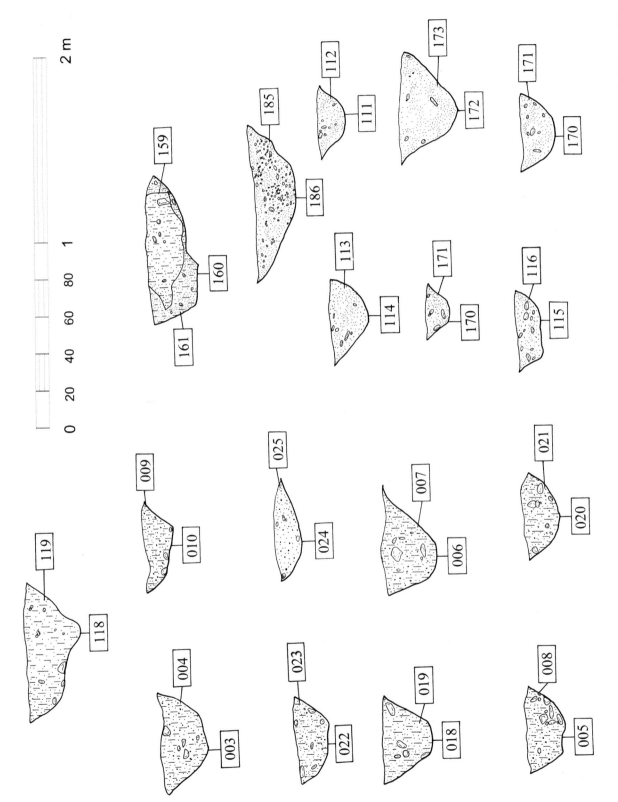

Fig. 21.12 Holywood North: Trench 2 sections, features 118, 003, 010, 160, 022, 024, 186, 114, 111, 018, 006, 170, 172, 005, 020, 115 and 170.

involving a group of distinct fills consisting of large pebbles averaging 0.10 m by 0.05 m by 0.05 m, and some flint chips (FN 47). These stones, the compacted pottery, flint waste and possibly other substances now decayed appear to have been thrown into the ditch at the same time as the re-filling of the recut began. Above this fill, at a later date, burnt material, perhaps timber, was deposited at the very end of the terminus (charcoal inclusions of large mass in layers 063 and 061). Considering the proximity of the post-holes to this terminal, this may represent the destruction of the postulated screen after the ditch recut was partially refilled. It may either be that the refilling episode incorporated this burning during its course, or that the burning took place as the final act of refilling the recut. The southern terminal followed a similar stratigraphic sequence, but had none of the depositional events of the north terminal.

The excavation of the ring-ditch did not produce any material culture. The ditch bottomed some 0.20 m below the subsoil surface. Situated within the cursus exit/ entrance, the ring ditch may have either provided an obstacle to access through the monument, or been a later addition to a partially decrepit monument, drawing upon its particular connotations of power and significance.

Holywood South
by Maggie Ronayne, Matt Leivers and Julian Thomas

The southern cursus in the Holywood monument complex is visible only as a crop mark originally identified by aerial photography. It is located between 20–30 m OD, adjacent to the A76 and to the west and south of Holywood village, on arable land, cut by a minor road, the B729. The monument is situated on the sands and gravels of a low fluvial terrace with glacial outwash between two rivers, the Nith and the Cluden Water (Fig. 21.1).

The cropmark shows two ditches which run for approx. 300m NW/SE at 30 to 40m apart at the northern and southern ends respectively. There are a number of gaps in the ditches, and several internal and associated features show on the aerial photographs. These interior features consist of a half-circular ditch with two pit-like features at the southern end; a rectangular enclosure also towards the southern end; with a ring-ditch and two pit-like features towards the northern end (Plate 21.13).

A trench 40m E–W by 45m N–S was opened at the northern terminal in order to provide sections of the cursus ditch and the ring-ditch; to allow investigation of a gap in the cursus ditch to the east of the ring-ditch; and to excavate a sample of any other internal features (Fig. 21.13; Colour Plate 7). The subsoil was rather more homogeneous than at Holywood North, being a soft coarse sand with gravelly patches.

The topsoil (001) was removed to a depth of 0.30 m by machines. It consisted of a sandy silt loam with a high gravel content in places. It did not produce any stray prehistoric finds. 001 lay directly on top of the natural subsoil (002) into which the prehistoric features were cut, apart from at the south-west corner and northern end

Plate 21.13 Holywood South: the ring-ditch under excavation.

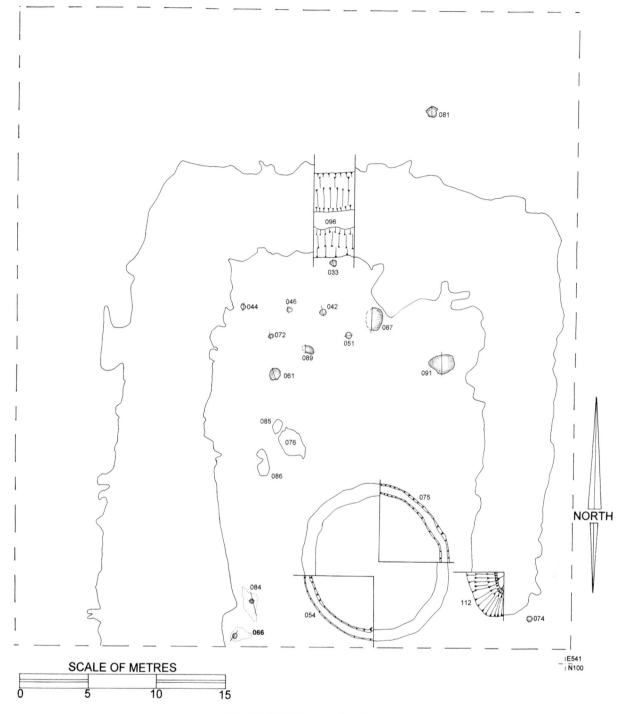

Fig. 21.13 Holywood South: plan.

(outside the terminal) of the trench where there appeared to be traces of the base of a mineral soil. These were not investigated owing to time constraints. In general the features were heavily truncated resulting in only the very bases of some features surviving. The subsoil was very variable in texture and colour, ranging from fine and coarse sand to gravel and sandy gravel and so on, although the consistency generally tended to be loose. The character of this material made those contexts with gravely/sandy fills difficult to identify and excavate.

The cursus ditch

Two cuttings were opened across the ditch: one at the cursus terminal at the north end of the trench; and a second at the break in the ditch on the south-east (Fig. 22.12). Upon excavation, the terminal ditch was found to be 1.15 m deep at maximum, with a broad low 'U'-shaped profile (Fig. 21.14). The cut as found (096) did not represent the original form of the ditch, but rather the weathered-back profile (Plate 21.14).

Within this cut was a complex series of fills, the lowest of which was context 109. Occuring only on the northern (outer) side of the ditch, this was a 50 mm deep by 600 mm long area of very compacted grey gravel which most probably represented the first episode of weathering of the original ditch profile. Above this lay fill 108, a loose dull orange sandy gravel, and above this was fill 105, a friable dark brown silt. The silting patterns evidenced by both of these fills indicated that they had been formed by the silting of an internal bank: both extended across the base of the ditch, but were more substantial on the southern (inner) side. None of these layers formed the kind of dense wedge of material that had been found in the ditch of Holywood North, implying that a more gradual collapse of the bank had taken place at Holywood South.

Above fill 105 lay fill 104: a fairly compact mottled orange/brown silty clay, which in turn lay beneath fills 106 and 107, which were friable orange/brown sandy loams. These last two fills were barely distinct from each other, and probably represented an undifferentiated depositional regime. They were possibly cut by feature 113, which may have been a recut of the ditch. Alternatively, 106 and 107 may have represented episodes of weathering of the upper edge of the ditch cut. At this point in the stratigraphy, a series of contexts merged into one another, and it was almost impossible to determine whether they represented a recut or not. Potential recut 113 contained fairly compact silty clay loams 103 and 102 on the northern and southern sides respectively, and friable silty clay loams 101 and 065 on the northern and

southern sides. These last four contexts appeared to have been cut in turn by 110 – a narrow, steep-sided cut feature with a rounded base in the centre of the ditch – filled in turn by 111, a fairly compact dark brown clay loam which was very similar to the dark reddish brown clay loam 077 immediately above it. Fill 077 sealed all of the earlier contexts in the ditch and was in turn sealed by fills 058 and 037, which appeared to be more recent deposits and the base of the topsoil.

The cutting opened across the 'entrance' to the cursus on the south-east of the trench demonstrated a somewhat different pattern (Fig. 21.15). Here, the ditch was a maximum of 1.20 m deep. A section was cut north-south along the ditch (rather than across it), and the profile of the terminal at this point showed a gradual slope to a depth of 0.80 m, followed by a much steeper slope to a flat base.

The original cut of the ditch (cut 119) was considerably more substantial than that at the northern terminal. Its primary fill (117) was a loose to friable yellow/orange sand and gravel matrix representing the early erosion of an internal bank. The sequence of siltings throughout this ditch was complex: at the base of the ditch, fill 117 was interleaved with fills 116 (a friable light brown sandy matrix), 114 (a friable dark brown gravel), and 115 (a very loose and friable mid-brown sandy silt with large pebbles). On balance, these contexts seem to have represented the relatively swift erosion of an unconsolidated dump bank, together with the weathering of the ditch edge (in the case of fill 116). Above these fills were a series of more humic silty clays (fills 010, 011, 012), and

Plates 21.14 Holywood South: Ditch section.

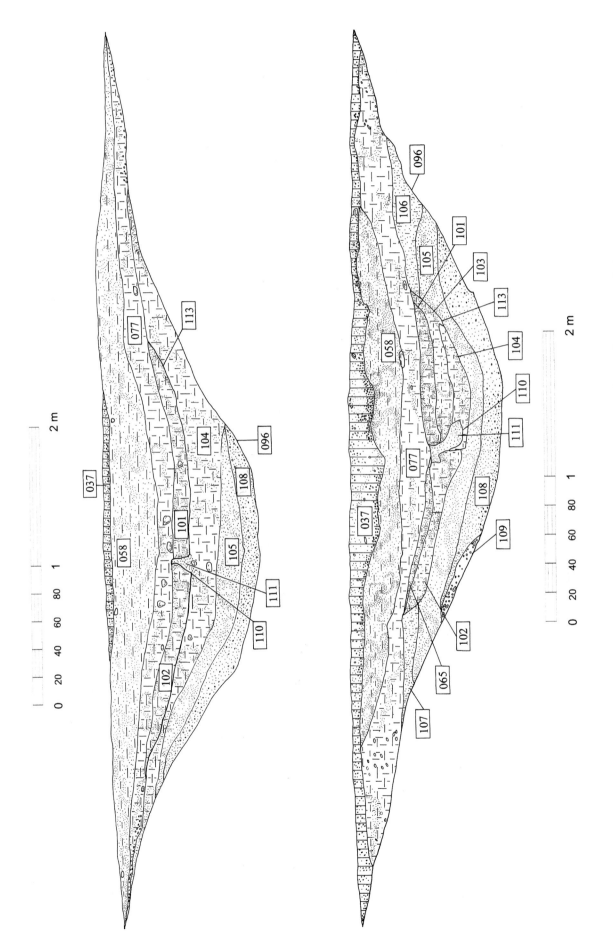

Fig. 21.14 Holywood South: ditch section 096. Top: east-facing; bottom: west-facing.

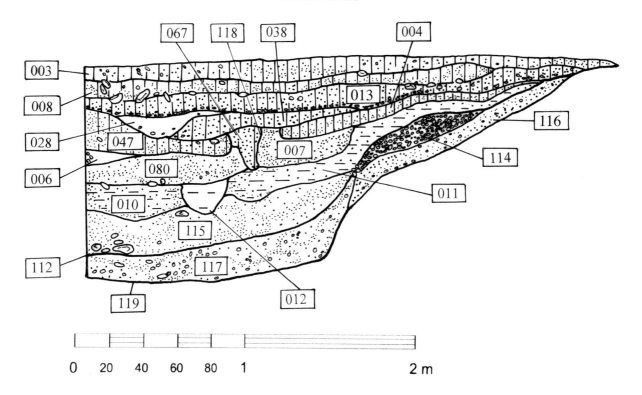

Fig. 21.15 Holywood South: ditch section 112.

silty sands (fills 006, 007, 080). Over this latter series were a pair of contexts (fills 047, 004) which were friable silt loams, cut by 118, which may have been a small pit or post-hole, filled by a firm silt loam (fill 067). This was sealed by fills 038/028 – friable silt loams – the latter of which had a high proportion of stone in the matrix. Three silt loam contexts filled the ditch above this point (fills 013 with charcoal flecking; 008 with a notable sand content and charcoal flecking; and 003 – residual plough layer).

Although numerous samples of charcoal were taken from the southern cursus ditch and other cut features, all proved to be from oak heartwood, and unsuitable for radiocarbon dating.

The post-holes (Fig. 21.16)

A series of small cut features were identified in the interior of the cursus enclosure. The majority of both the pits and post-holes were located in the area that would have been occupied by the internal bank that is suggested by the ditch deposits. While some of these might have been cut through the bank, it is considered more likely that the cut features as a whole relate to an episode of pre-cursus occupation. It is conceivable that this activity had some influence on the location of the monument. However, post-hole 066 lay close to the cursus ditch in the interior to the south end of the trench, and it appeared to cut the ditch fills at this point. Most of the features identified as post-holes had single, sterile, homogeneous

fills. This might mean that the posts had been withdrawn, or that the features were small pits rather than post-holes, or simply that the sand/gravel matrix was a poor medium for preserving a post-pipe that was distinct from the packing. The post-holes were on average 0.31 m deep, and it is arguable that the group within the north-west part of the cursus terminal represented some form of structure (features 033, 042, 044, 046, 051, 061, 072 and 089).

Feature 033

Irregular, steep-sided oval cut with rounded base 033, filled by 032, a soft brown sand. The fill was overlain by context 037, the upper fill of the cursus ditch terminal, but since this was residual plough zone material which had spread beyond the ditch cut itself the post-hole and the ditch cannot be related stratigraphically.

Feature 042

Steep-sided near-circular cut with flat base 042, filled by orange/brown gravelly sand 041.

Feature 044

Irregular oval cut with steep sides 044, filled by friable dark reddish brown silty loam 043, which contained numerous small stones.

Feature 046

Steep-sided round cut with rounded base 046, containing loose dark reddish brown sand with numerous small pebbles 045.

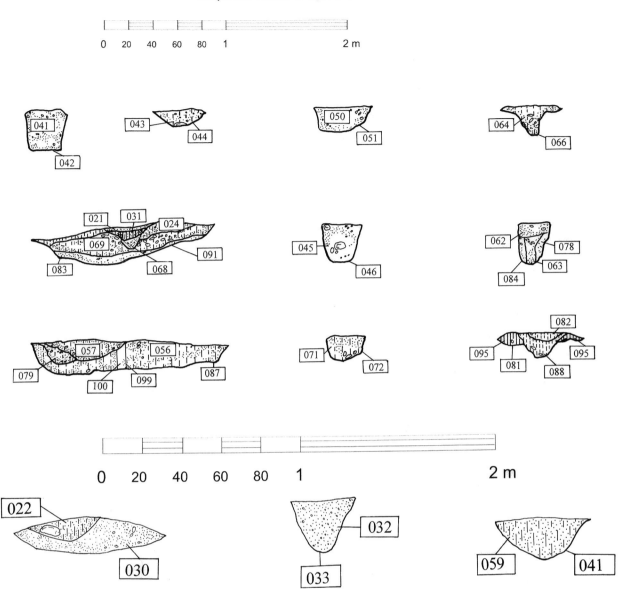

Fig. 21.16 Holywood South: sections, features 042, 044, 051, 066, 091, 046, 184, 087, 072, 081, 030, 033 and 041.

Feature 051

Near-circular cut with sloping sides 051, containing friable dark reddish brown silty gravel 050.

Feature 061

Large sub-circular post-hole, which may have been overcut during excavation, with near-vertical sides and gently rounded base, 061. Filled by loose dark brown loamy sand with numerous pebbles 060.

Feature 066

The relationship between this post-hole and the cursus ditch was unclear, but it is possible that it cut into the ditch fills. A flat-based oval cut, steeper on the northern than the southern side, 066. Filled by friable dark reddish brown silty loam 064.

Feature 072

Steep, oval cut 072, filled by loose dark brown sandy gravel 071.

Feature 074

Cut 074 was identified immediately outside of the entrance to the cursus in the south-east corner of the trench. An irregular, sub-circular cut with a pointed base. This had one fill of loose dark brown sand (073) and was 0.25 m deep.

Feature 081

Cut 081 was a post-hole to the north of the cursus, outside the terminal. There were two fills: a burnt black post-pipe (082) surrounded by a friable very dark brown silt loam (088). A smear of compact dark reddish brown silt loam

(095) surrounded this material, suggesting that the post had cut through another, almost entirely eroded feature, which was given the cut number 120, although little of the character of such a cut could be discerned.

Feature 084

Cut 084 was a steep-sided oval post-hole 0.36 m deep cut into an area of charcoal-rich material (layer 092) inside the cursus ditch to the south of the trench. This feature contained three fills: a weathered dark reddish brown charcoal-rich silt at the top (062) representing the collapse of the top of the burnt post; the post-pipe fill of firm very dark brown silt (063); and the post packing, 078, a friable dark brown silt.

Feature 089

A shallow oval cut 089, with a basal fill of loose dark brown loamy sand (059) and a possible post-pipe of compact dark red loamy sand (049).

The pits (Fig. 21.16)

Within the same general area as the post-holes, there were a number of larger pits. Amongst these features, the extent of their truncation was more immediately obvious. One such feature had been reduced to a charcoally deposit of sandy loam (022) on top of a lump of dark reddish brown silt (030). There was no cut remaining to be recorded as the materials stood above the gravel surface. Their widest extent was 0.41 by 0.33 m by 0.11 m deep. Two potsherds (FN 13 and FN 14: Vessel 1) came from the charcoal deposit (022). This feature may have been the remains of a post-pit but given the nature of the adjacent pit (cut 091) this is uncertain.

In the area immediately to the south of the group of pits and post-holes in the terminal of the cursus, but north-west of the ring-ditch, three further features were identified, 076, 085 and 086. Any of these might conceivably have been further prehistoric pits, but they were not excavated owing to a lack of time, and their date is unknown. In all three cases, it seemed probable that the features were very shallow, and were the bases of pits which had been substantially abraded.

Feature 091

The larger pit (091) measured 1.55 m in maximum extent but was also quite shallow at 0.30 m deep. This pit was the site of a complex sequence of activity and deposition. The primary fill was a rough dark brown sand, 083, above which was a similar material (039/069) that was rather redder in colour. 039/069 contained angular gritstone pebbles, which were unlike any of the pebbles occurring naturally in the subsoil. Above this was a more compact dusky red sand, 024. From this level a slot (048) had been cut down to the base of the pit, and this had filled up to a depth of 0.9m with a sterile orange sand (fill 068). A stake-hole (cut 097) was cut into this fill, the stake from which may have been removed again quite quickly as its fill of loose dark reddish brown sand (098) had been

covered over by the upper fill of the slot (031), a compact very dark brown sandy loam, with a greater humic content than the lower layers, and much evidence of burning. The charcoal flecking within 031 was especially concentrated around the numerous potsherds found in this context (FN 16 – FN 30, FN 33, FN 50, FN 51: Vessels 1, 2 and 3). This upper fill of the slot was overlain by 021, a compact black silty material which formed the uppermost fill of the entire pit. This layer again contained traces of charcoal. While it is possible that the various spreads of burnt material in this feature relate to posts or stakes that were burned out, the presence of numerous sherds of pottery within this feature suggest that some of the deposits were redeposited, and had been brought to the pit from elsewhere. Pottery was present in all the upper, more humic fills of the feature, but was less common in the lower, more sandy layers. This supports an interpretation in which the pit was dug and partially silted before burnt organic material with pottery was deliberately deposited, following the episodes of slot- and stakehole-cutting.

Feature 087

Pit 087 was slightly smaller than 091. The initial cut of the feature was shallow and oval, and the principal filling was context 056, a firm dark reddish brown loamy sand with numerous small stones. At some point in the filling of the feature, a stakehole had been inserted into it (cut 100), filled with friable reddish brown loamy sand (099). Layer 079, above this, was a compact dark reddish brown loamy sand, while the uppermost fill of the feature was 057, a mottled dark reddish brown loamy sand. Both matrices contained many pebbles and other small stones. It is possible that by contrast with 091, feature 087 had originally held a post, and that 057 represented the bottom of an eroded post-pipe. Both 079 and 056 would then amount to packing deposits. If so, then the post in 087, within the area enclosed by the cursus yet potentially predating the construction of the monument, could be compared with the very large post which initiated the sequence at Holywood North.

The ring-ditch (Figs. 21.13 and 21.16)

A small ring ditch was visible on aerial photographs, set inside the cursus, just within the eastern entrance/exit area. Like the pits and post-holes, it extended into the area which must have been occupied by the cursus bank, suggesting that it was not contemporary with the initial use of that monument. Two quadrants were investigated: the south-west and the north-east. The cut of the ring ditch proved to be quite shallow, which may have been an effect of the truncation of the remaining bank deposits through which it may have been dug. In general the deposits in both quadrants were similar with coarse sand and gravelly fills (fills 014sw and 027ne) along the base and silting from the sides above (fills 015 and 023sw, 035 and 040ne). A charred hazelnut shell was found in the outer silts (fill 040) of the northeast quadrant but otherwise all fills were sterile. However, the early silting (014) in the southwest quadrant only extended half-way along the ditch, and coupled with the truncated appearance of the silting from the side, suggested a possible recut of the ditch. Another recut (cut 055) had been made into fill 014 and all the side silting in the southwest quadrant and filled with a compacted, pebbly material (fill 037), across the width of the ditch and stretching 1.30 m north-south. Towards the northern end of the southwest quadrant, fills 020 and 019 seem to represent later slumping of materials into the ditch in this area. The latest fills on both the quadrants (fills 016 and 009) were slumping of residual ploughzone material into the ditch. The ditches seemed to show a tendency to narrow and widen at random points rather than being evenly dug.

A stake-hole (cut 018) in the southwest quadrant, immediately outside the ditch itself, was the only indication of any possible associated activity. This was close to the area of the recut (cut 055) and deposit of compacted material and may be related to it.

Other features

A number of other features occurred inside the area defined by the cursus ditches which are highly ambiguous and do not allow any definite interpretation. Context 092 consisted of a compact loamy sand with a high proportion of rounded stones of all sizes. Two connected oval features made up this context, and a tenuous interpretation sees it as a post setting (context 084 which cut 092 appears to be a post-hole).

The sequence of activity

Generally, there were no direct stratigraphic relationships between the interior features and the cursus ditch which could establish the sequence of activity. One post-hole (cut 066) appeared to be cut into the inner part of the cursus ditch where it widened at the south-western end of the trench, but this post-hole cannot be related to any other features in the area.

Charcoal finds were infrequent. The ditch contexts showed no substantial evidence for burning, although some fills had more charcoal flecking than others. A burnt hazelnut shell came from the ring-ditch silts but again there was no evidence for burning. The burnt material at the tops of the pits proved to be quite shallow but was sampled.

The bulk of the artefactual assemblage was composed of 35 potsherds which appear to be of earlier Neolithic date, with some definite early rim sherds and carinated pieces (see Peterson and Roberts, Chapter 23 below). The entire assemblage came from two pit features in the north-

eastern part of the interior: 33 pieces from pit 091; the remaining 2 from the adjacent possible pit 022/030. There is one possible piece of struck quartz (FN 43) from the cursus ditch at the entrance terminal. There are no other artefacts from the cursus ditches or the ring-ditch.

The ring-ditch is problematic. Traditional interpretation suggests that it is a later addition, adding to the significance of the entrance/exit. However, the monument may have incorporated an already existing pathway between several places now marked by the Twelve Apostles and Holywood North. The excavation of Holywood South provided no clear indication of its relationship with Holywood North.

The Twelve Apostles stone circle
by Chris Fowler and Julian Thomas

As part of the fieldwork at the Holywood complex, it was decided to investigate the Twelve Apostles stone circle by carrying out a resistivity survey over the whole monument, with the aim in mind of locating subsoil features. In particular, it was hoped that it might be possible to isolate a stonehole, which could provide a closed context containing material suitable for dating, or timber features denoting an earlier phase of use of the site. Recent work at sites like Machrie Moor (Haggarty 1991) and Torhouskie (Stell 1996, 168) has demonstrated that stone settings sometimes replaced timber circles of earlier date. Given that the two cursus monuments at Holywood were earth and timber structures of earlier Neolithic date, it was a plausible hypothesis that a non-lithic structure of some form had preceded the stone circle. However, the results of the survey were entirely negative, showing no more than undulations in the subsoil (Fig. 21.17). In order to test this outcome, a trench 20 by 10 m was opened on the southern side of the circle, cutting across the circuit of the stones, but not including any of the stones themselves (Fig. 21.18). Here, the topsoil (context 001) came down onto an earlier, more mineralised ploughsoil (002). Beneath this, the natural sandy gravel (003) was found to be utterly featureless. This suggests that no earlier features exist on the same circumference as the stone circle, and certainly that a large concentric timber setting comparable with that at Stanton Drew was not present (David *et al.* 2004). This none the less leaves it open to question whether some structure existed in the centre of the existing monument, or indeed whether each stone had been preceded by a timber post of exactly the same location. On the whole, though, the evidence as it stands does not support the view that any structure existed on the site before the Twelve Apostles.

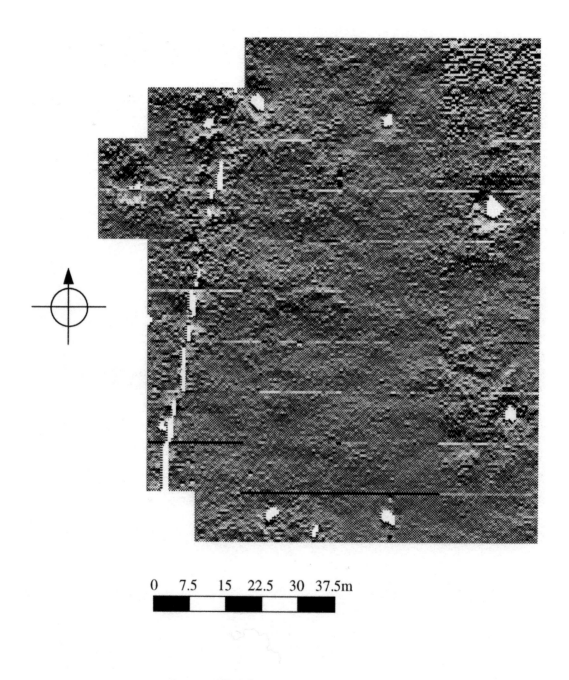

0   7.5   15   22.5   30   37.5m

1292.9 1369.6 1381.1 1457.7

Fig. 21.17 The Twelve Apostles: resistivity survey.

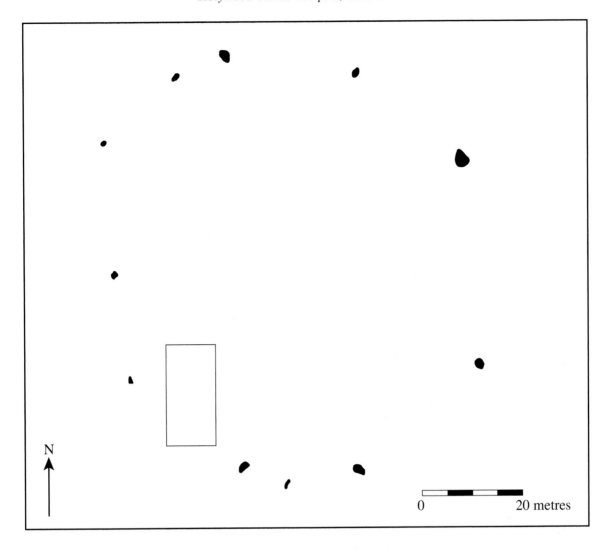

Fig. 21.18 The Twelve Apostles: location of excavation trench.

22

Holm Farm, excavations

Julian Thomas and Matt Leivers

Background

The complex of crop-mark features at Holm, three miles north of Dumfries (NX 9596 8038), was originally identified from the air by the Royal Commission on the Ancient and Historical Monuments of Scotland in 1992 (RCAHMS 1992). The group consists of a number of distinct elements: three parallel lines of posts or pits running NNW-SSE; an avenue of paired posts or pits running across these NW-SE; two apparent ring ditches, and a scatter of other posts or pits (Fig. 22.1). The two northernmost lines of the former post/pit alignment appear to be linked by further pits at either end, forming a closed rectilinear enclosure. On these grounds, the feature was tentatively identified as a pit-defined cursus, one of a number of such sites found in Scotland (e.g. Halliday 2002; Kendrik 1995; Taverner 1987). This complex of features is arguably related to the two cursus monuments and stone circle at Holywood/Twelve Apostles, c. 1 km to the west. The Holywood monuments were investigated in the summer of 1997 (see above), and work at Holm was intended to complement the results of those excavations. A further group of crop-marks, suggesting linear avenues of posts or pits, lies less than a kilometre to the south of Holm.

The features at Holm are located on a low, flat gravel terrace on the southern side of the flood plain of the river Nith, and the alignment of the linear arrangements is roughly parallel with that of the river (Plate 22.1). Excavation took place for three weeks in July 1998, with the aim of characterising the various features, and identifying any relationships between them. A trench 35 × 20 metres was laid out at the point where the two linear alignments overlap, and a smaller cutting 10 × 3 metres was opened over the westernmost of the two ring ditches.

The 'cursus' and related features (Fig. 22.2)

From the air, the cursus appeared as an enclosure roughly 70 metres long, bounded on either side by lines of post-holes or pits, broader at its south-east end. The north-west end appeared to be closed by a line of pits running NNE/SSW, while the complicated series of features at the south-east end might suggest a curved terminal. However, another line of pit/post-hole features runs roughly parallel with the southern side of the cursus, with a pronounced kink which leads its south-east end further to the south, directly toward the westernmost of the two ring ditches (Plate 22.2).

All three of these lines of features were sampled in Trench A, and all proved to represent sets of post-holes (Colour Plate 8). These post-holes varied in size, and the majority of them had been recut on at least one occasion. Most contained traces of burning, presumably derived from burnt posts which had been washed down into the voids left by the rotting out of the unburnt portion of the post, below ground level. However, in some cases a portion of the burnt post was found in situ. The post-holes of the southern alignment, although generally among the smaller of the post-holes, appeared generally similar to those of the cursus proper, suggesting that for at least a part of its history the structure might have been composed of three rather than two lines of posts. This southerly alignment of posts appeared to be composite rather than a single-phase structure. The western-most triad in the excavated area were on a slightly different alignment to those further east (in the southern extension of Trench A and in Trench B) as well as being smaller in size and recut less often, if at all. It is possible that these smaller post-holes were dug at the same time as the later recuts in the larger post-holes of the southern alignment and the post-holes of the cursus proper (see below). What

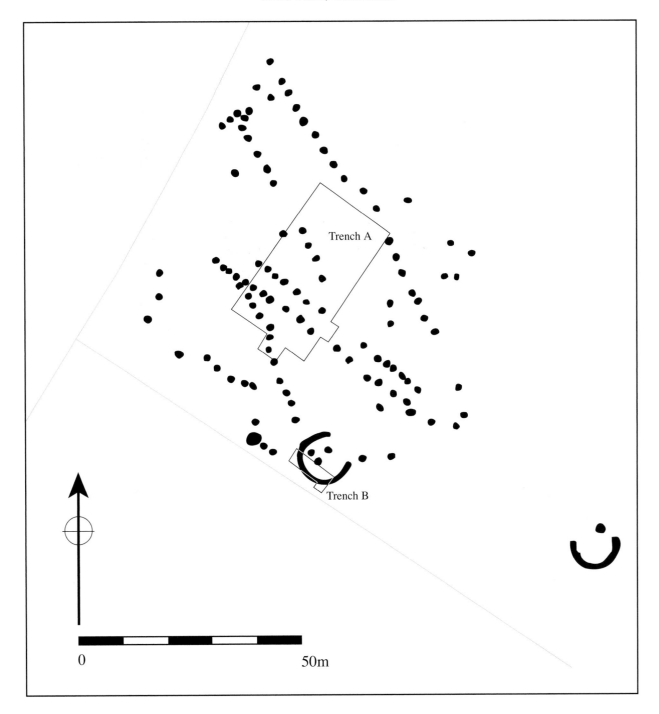

Fig. 22.1 Holm: location of trenches.

is unclear is whether the monument consisted of three lines of posts throughout its history, or whether at some stages the two northernmost or the two southernmost lines of posts formed a true enclosure.

The cursus (Figs. 22.3–22.6)

Post-hole 088

Post-hole 088 was the most westerly feature in the northern post-alignment of the cursus within the excavated area. After excavation the feature was apparently 0.85 metres in diameter (approximately one

third of the feature lay outside the limits of the excavation) and was a maximum of 0.40 metres in depth. In plan the cut seemed circular, with near vertical sides descending to a shallow saucer-shaped base.

The basal fill of this post-hole took the form of a loose dark reddish brown silt loam of 0.05 metres depth (context 098) containing a large proportion of a very dark material. This context is most probably a mixture of soil and charcoal deriving from the burning of the first post to stand in the post-hole. There was no evidence of any packing for this post. Above 098 were contexts 214 (on

Plate 22.1 Holm Trench A from the south, with the river Nith in the background.

Plate 22.2 Holm Trench A from the north, with the 'cursus' post-holes in the foreground and the pit avenue in the background.

the west) and 215 (on the east), both apparently natural fills resulting from either the weathering of the sides of the pit once the unburnt (below-ground) portion of the post had either rotted out or been withdrawn, or alter- natively material washed in from above. Both contexts were loose dark reddish brown silty sands.

Both of these layers were then truncated by a recut (context 216) which destroyed the upper portions of 088

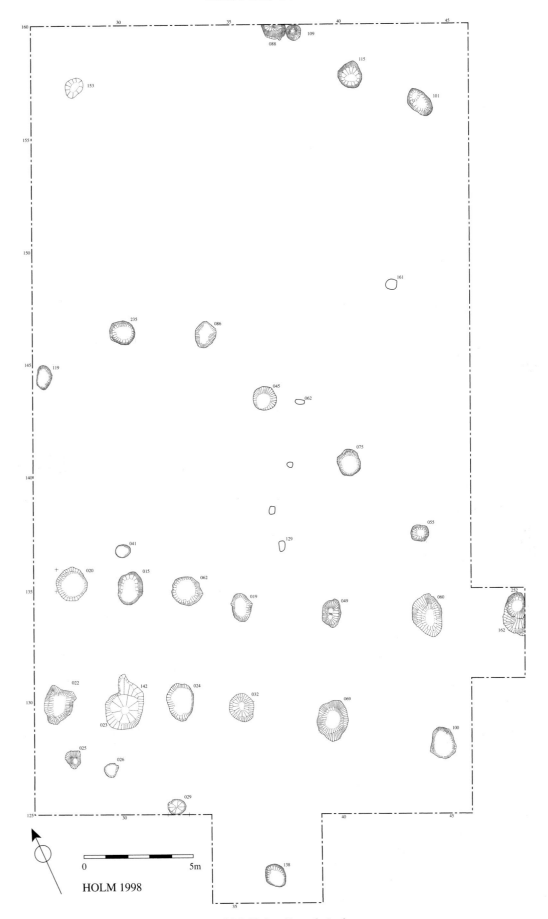

Fig. 22.2 Holm: Trench A plan.

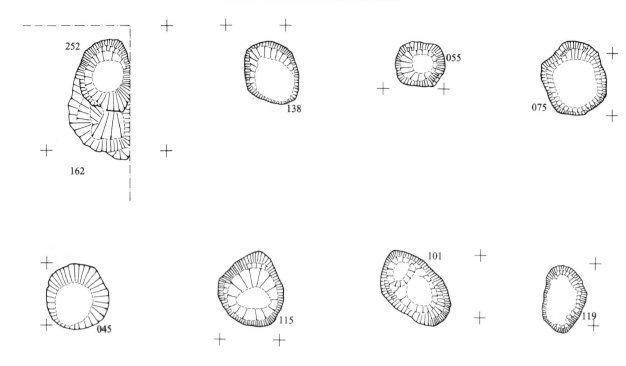

Fig. 22.3 Holm: 'Cursus' feature plans.

and reached the base of that cut in the centre. A loose dark brown sandy matrix with a high proportion of stones (217) was apparently packing material for a second post which itself did not survive. The post void was filled with a tenacious dark reddish brown sandy loam with much charcoal which is best understood as material from the burning of the post which fell into the void. This material was recorded as contexts 102 and 151 since it in turn was truncated by a second recut (context 185) which destroyed the base and upper portion of the eastern side of the first recut. Context 218 (a tenacious dark brown sandy clay with a large proportion of stones) again seems to have been packing, whilst context 089 (a loose dusky red loamy sand) represented the fill of the third post void. There was no direct evidence of this third post having been burnt.

Immediately to the east of 088, another feature (109) with a single fill (091) may have represented another post, replacing or replaced by one of the posts in 088. In other words, four separate posts may have stood at different times in the general area of 088.

Post-hole 115 (Plate 22.3)

Cut 115 was a steep-sided, oval pit with a slightly rounded base, which had been disturbed by later cuts. Across the base of this cut on the western side was a thin layer of loose dark brown sand within which were very large pieces of charcoal (context 198, 0.10 metres deep), most probably representing the base of the original post. This material produced a radiocarbon date of 3970–3780 Cal. BC at 95.4 % probability (SUERC-2131). Subsequent to the burning of this post, the pit began to fill with a loose dark reddish brown loamy sand (context 179), again only seen on the western side of the feature since its putative eastern portion (along with the eastern portion of 198)

was subsequently cut away by cut 195 – the first recut of this post-hole.

This recut had a vertical east side, but sloped much more gradually on the west, and removed much of the fill of the original feature. The base was flat, but narrow compared to the diameter of the cut at the top (1.10 m; 0.69 m deep). After the cutting of this socket, a post was presumably placed against the vertical eastern face and then packed in place with a loose, dark reddish brown loamy sand (fill 196) with a high content of very large (up to 0.25 m) rounded stones. The post-pipe (0.50 m diameter, 0.36 m deep) was filled with a tenacious, very dark brown silt loam (139). Toward the bottom of this deposit, roughly 50% of the material was made up of charcoal, suggesting that the post had at least partially been burned out, although the section may indicate that a portion of the timber rotted, and was replaced by silting.

The second recut of this feature (cut 194) again had a near-vertical east side, a more gradual west side and an undulating base. The recut was 0.55 m diameter and 0.44 m deep. A post had been inserted into this cut and packed in place with a friable, dark reddish brown sandy clay matrix with a medium stone content (fill 145). The post was subsequently burnt and its base survived as a substantial piece of charcoal 0.32 by 0.05 by 0.30 metres (context 227). Two radiocarbon determinations were acquired from this material: 3820–3690 Cal. BC (SUERC-2129) and 3950–3700 Cal. BC (SUERC-2130), both at 95.4 % probability. After the destruction of the post the packing began to collapse and the sides of the cut weathered into the pipe (fill 197 – a friable dark brown sandy silt loam; and 084 – a tenacious dark brown sandy clay, the uppermost fill).

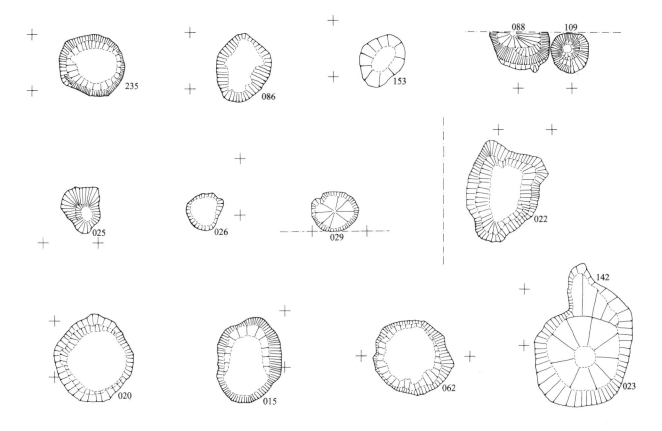

Fig. 22.4 Holm: 'Cursus' and pit avenue feature plans.

Plate 22.3 Post-hole 115.

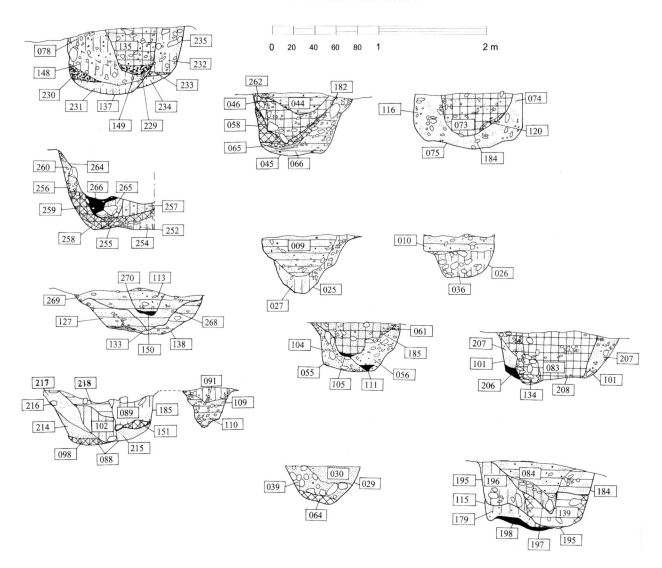

Fig. 22.5 Holm: 'Cursus' feature sections, features 235, 045, 075, 252, 138, 025, 026, 055, 101, 088, 029 and 115.

Post-hole 101 (Plate 22.4)

Cut 101 was an oval, steep-sided pit with a flat base. The surviving depth was 0.50 metres; the diameter was unreconstructable as a result of later cuts. A thin layer of burnt material (a friable dark brown gravelly sand with a high charcoal content – fill 206) lined the base of this cut on the western side, probably deriving from the destruction of the post. Subsequent to this destruction the sides of the cut began to weather into the post void (fill 207 – a friable dark yellowish brown sand with pebbles).

This weathered layer was then cut by context 208, an oval feature steeper on the east than the west and generally flat-bottomed (1.15 metres diameter; 0.30 metres deep). On the north-west side of this cut a friable dark brown/black sandy clay loam with frequent large stones represented packing (134) for a post which either rotted or was withdrawn: the fill of the post void (083) was a tenacious dark brown clay loam with no evidence of burning.

Post-hole 235

Only the western half of the primary cut 235 survived. It was 1.10 metres north-south, 0.43 metres east-west, and 0.55 metres deep, with a sharp upper break of slope to a steeply sloping side and bowl-shaped base. The base of this cut was lined with an apparently natural layer (0.08 metres deep) of loose dark brown loamy sand which seemed to derive from the collapse of the pit side almost immediately upon its being dug (context 234). Above this was a 0.04 metres deep layer of friable, very dark brown sandy silt loam with a high charcoal content which most probably represented the remains of a burnt primary post falling into the void left by its destruction (context 233). This charcoal was sealed by a substantial quantity of friable dark brown loamy sand (context 232) representing the filling of the post void either deliberately or through natural weathering processes.

The pit was then recut (cut 137) at 0.70 metres diameter and to 0.60 metres deep by a steep sided pit with

Plate 22.4 Post-hole 101.

a gradually sloping to flat base. This cut destroyed the entire eastern side of the original cut and fills. Again, the base of this cut was lined by a thin layer of weathered brown loamy sand (context 231), which was in turn sealed by a charcoal-rich dark grey silt loam representing the burning of a second post (230). Above and east of 230 was a loose, dark yellowish brown loamy sand which seems to have been packing material which collapsed once the post it held had been destroyed (148). This collapsed packing was then sealed by a second loose dark yellowish brown loamy sand distinguishable by a higher stone content and the presence of some charcoal, which seems to be weathered infill of the remains of the second post void (078).

Cut 229 cut this material. This third cut was 0.50 metres in diameter and 0.42 metres deep with steep sides and a bowl-shaped base. At the base of this cut was a very dark grey-brown sandy silt loam containing an appreciable quantity of charcoal (149) which may have been burnt material derived from the final post. This was sealed by context 135, a friable, very dark brown sandy clay loam which was the uppermost fill of the surviving feature.

Post-hole 045 (Plate 22.5)

The primary cut 045 had a slightly sloping side and a flat base, and measured 1.00 metre by 1.00 metre. The basal fill, 066, was a dark reddish brown mixture of sandy gravel and clayey sand with patches of small rounded pebbles, and seemed to be the remains of the original post packing which had collapsed subsequent to the des-

truction of the post. Above this was a bright orange sandy gravel (065) which was most probably a burnt material washed into the primary post void. More direct evidence of the burning of this first post was provided by context 058 (sealing 065) – a friable black silty clay with a high charcoal content.

Cut 182, the first recut of this post-hole, was 0.80 by 0.80 metres in extent. The fill of this recut (046) was a compact to friable dark reddish brown sandy clay loam with a very high stone content, and most probably packing for a withdrawn second post.

Cut 262 was the tertiary cut of this feature, 0.60 by 0.70 metres in extent. It was filled by a tenacious dark reddish brown sandy clay with some charcoal flecks (044).

Post-hole 075

Cut 075 (1.25 metres in diameter, 0.65 metres deep) was filled by contexts 074 and 116: friable dark reddish brown sandy gravels with a high stone content. These are most probably the collapse of the pit sides after the (putative) primary post had been destroyed by burning or removed (there is no direct evidence of this first post other than these two contexts).

Recut 184 cut these two fills (strengthening the argument for an ostensibly invisible primary post). In diameter 0.66 metres, in depth 0.73, the recut was lined by a thin layer of friable, very dark grey sandy clay loam (120) with some charcoal, probably from the burning of the second post. This was sealed by a substantial deposit of tenacious dusky red sandy clay loam, which contained

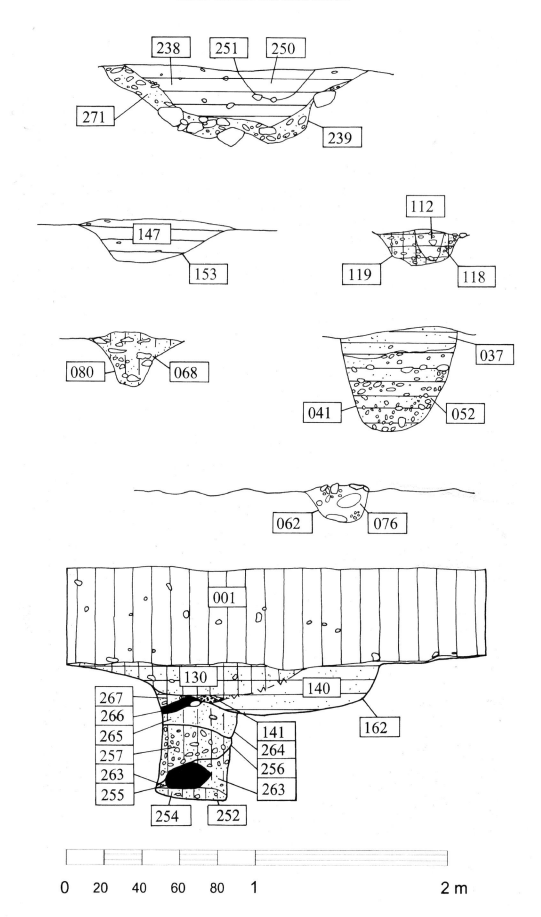

Fig. 22.6 Holm: 'Cursus' and miscellaneous feature sections, features 239, 153, 119, 080, 041, 062 and 252/162.

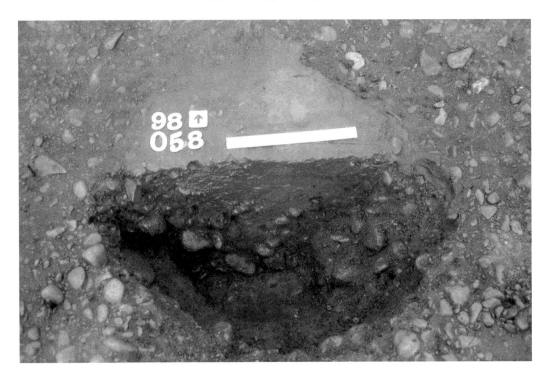

Plate 22.5 Post-hole 058/045.

Plate 22.6 Post-hole 061/055.

a great deal of stone and some charcoal, and which filled the remaining void (073). Charcoal from context 073 produced two radiocarbon dates, 3970–3790 Cal. BC (SUERC-2124) and 3990–3770 Cal. BC (SUERC-2126), both at 95.4 % probability.

Post-hole 055 (Plate 22.6)

Pit 055 (0.80 metres diameter; 0.56 metres deep) was steep-sided with a flat base. A post (not surviving) had been packed in place with context 104: a loose to friable reddish-brown sand with a high proportion of large stones. Subsequent to the destruction of the primary post (see below) this packing material collapsed. Above this slumped packing was a layer of dusky red sandy clay loam with a high charcoal content, representing the remains of the primary post after its burning (111). The fill of the post void (056) was a firm yellowish-red sand with much stone and some charcoal.

183 was the first recut of this post-hole, 0.70 metres diameter and 0.30 metres deep. The south side of this cut was near vertical, the north much more gradual and irregular. Lining this cut was 105, a firm dusky red sandy clay loam with a 50% charcoal inclusion, representing the burnt second post. This was sealed by 061, a soft dark brown silty clay loam filling the second post void and most probably a mixture of collapsed packing and weathered material from the sides of the pit.

063 cut into 061 and was more likely to be a stake than post hole (its dimensions 0.17 by 0.24 metres at the top and only 0.13 metres deep make a post-hole interpretation unlikely). It is possible that this stake (if such it was) marked the location of the post-hole in preparation for an episode of recutting which never took place. The fill of this cut (054) was a firm dark brown clay loam with a high charcoal content and some stone.

Post-hole 252 (Plate 22.7)
Pit 252 had been cut and a light silting of loose yellowish-red sandy material had formed within it (254). A post was then inserted and packed with a loose dark brown loamy sand with a high stone content (263). The post was then burnt, and a compact, dark reddish-brown sandy silt loam with a high charcoal content (255) fell into the void.

This material was then cut by the first recut (256), which destroyed the western part of the original cut completely. A post had then been inserted against the western side and packed with 257 – a friable dark brown sandy loam. This post was then burnt and the below-ground portion was withdrawn or rotted. The void weathered somewhat (258 – a loose dark brown loamy sand) before a friable dark brown silty clay loam with a high charcoal content fell in. This material (259) derived from the destruction of the second post. The upper portion of the post void then weathered, and was filled by a loose dark brown loamy sand (260).

A third post-hole was then cut (cut 264). A post was packed in (265 – a loose dark brown loamy sand was the collapsed packing), was burnt (266 – a friable dark brown sandy silt loam with much charcoal), and then filled with 267 – a friable strong brown sandy clay loam. At this point, avenue pit 162 was cut through the top of this post-hole (see below for details of avenue posts). This strati-graphic relationship demonstrated the priority of the cursus posts over the post avenue.

Post-hole 025
Pit 025 was 0.53 metres deep and 0.93 metres in diameter. The sides were near vertical, breaking gently to a flat base. Lining the base and sides was a layer of weathered material (027): a friable dark reddish brown loamy sand with a very high stone content. Above this was a very densely packed layer of large stones (packing 040; a minimum of 0.70 metres diameter). The post held in this socket was probably burned out: the tenacious, very dusky red sandy clay which had fallen into the post-pipe, 009,

Plate 22.7 Post-hole 252 and avenue pit 162.

contained some charcoal (presumably derived from this burning). There were no recuts to this feature.

Post-hole 026 (Plate 22.8)

Pit 026 was 0.61 metres diameter by 0.65 metres deep. The lowest fill (036) was a compact, yellowish-red loamy sand with a very high stone content which may have been collapsed packing. Above this was 010 – a compact dusky red sandy clay sealing 036 and filling the top of the pit but also containing some charcoal flecks. In profile it appeared that the post had been withdrawn rather than burnt, in which case the charcoal flecks in 010 may have blown in from another burnt post episode in another pit nearby.

Post-hole 029

Pit 029 was 1.00 metre in diameter and approximately 0.50 metres deep. The sides were near vertical and the base saucer-shaped. Fill 064 – a tenacious dark black/grey matrix on the south side – was most probably burnt material derived from the post. Above this was context 039 (a very stony black silty sand) which was most probably collapsed material from the side of the pit (it is unlikely to have been packing since it sealed 064). 030 (a tenacious dark reddish brown silty sand) was the uppermost fill of the pit above these.

Post-hole 138

Cut 138 (1.05 by 0.47 metres) was steep sided with a gradual break of slope to a bowl-shaped base. 133 (a friable dark brown sandy clay) was the primary fill probably deriving from weathering of south edge. 127 (a friable, very dark brown sandy clay) was a secondary fill

deriving from burnt post material. This was followed by a recut (268) and its fill (269), and a second recut (270) filled by context 150, the friable black clay and charcoal of a burnt post, and context 113, an upper fill of tenacious, very dark brown sandy clay.

The pit avenue (see Fig. 22.2)

The pit avenue consisted of two lines of features, generally occurring in pairs, running at an angle across the line of the cursus. From the air the avenue can be recognised over a length of some 50 metres. This orientation points toward the more easterly of the two ring ditches, a further fifty metres to the south-east. There is no indication that the ends of the avenue were closed, but within Trench A the pairs of posts appeared to be progressively further apart toward the south-east, while the air photographs suggest that they may converge again further on, so that the overall configuration is somewhat cigar-shaped.

The avenue pits (Figs. 22.7 and 22.8)
Pit 020 (Plate 22.9)

The cut of this pit was 1.60 metres in diameter and 0.75 metres deep. Lining its base was a thin (0.04 metres deep) layer of friable yellow-brown gravelly sand with a high stone content, most probably weathering of the edges of the pit (context 021). Above this, layer 017 was a friable, dark reddish grey sandy clay with pebbles, sealed by 003 (a tenacious dark brown sandy clay). This pit had no evidence of a post, or any *in situ* burning, and most probably stood open for a short time before being back-filled.

Plate 22.8 Post-hole 026.

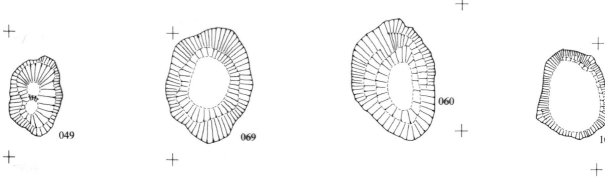

Fig. 22.7 Holm: Pit avenue feature plans.

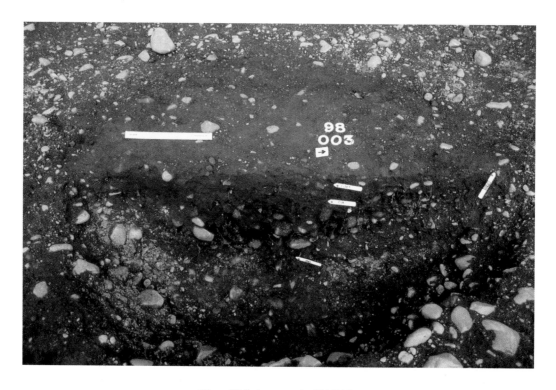

Plate 22.9 Avenue pit 003/020.

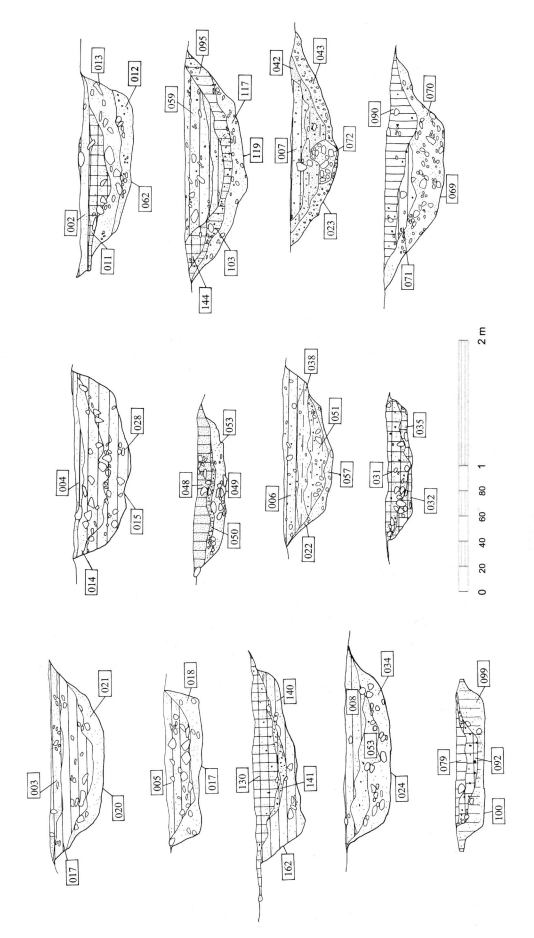

Fig. 22.8 Holm: Pit avenue feature sections, features 020, 017, 162, 024, 100, 015, 049, 022, 032, 062, 119, 023 and 069.

Pit 015

Cut 015 was a steep-sided pit with a gradual break of slope to a rounded base, 1.22 by 1.18 metres, and 0.49 metres deep. The primary fill (028) was a friable, very dark brown sandy clay of 0.17 metres depth, above which (on the northern side) was a layer of tenacious, very dark brown sandy clay with a high charcoal content throughout (context 014; maximum depth 0.18 metres). Both 028 and 014 were sealed by 004, a tenacious dark brown sandy clay with a medium stone content but no evidence of burnt material, to a depth of 0.14 metres.

Pit 062

Cut 062 was 0.42 metres deep and 1.49 by 1.50 metres in diameter, with sides ranging from near-vertical to gradual, and a flat base. The basal fill (012) was a friable dark yellowish brown gravelly sand, weathered from the sides of the pit. It was sealed by a second dark yellowish brown sandy gravel (013) which was in turn overlaid by a tenacious, very dark brown sandy clay loam 0.16 metres deep (context 011). The uppermost fill (002) was a tenacious dark brown sandy clay with charcoal flecks.

Pit 019

Cut 019 was 1.24 by 1.10 metres in plan, and 0.30 metres deep. The sides sloped steeply to a flat base. The primary fill was a friable reddish-brown coarse sand with a medium stone content and some charcoal (concentrated in the centre of the feature), 0.10 metres deep (context 018). This material appears to have been a mixture of weathered gravel from the pit sides and material washed in from elsewhere. The upper fill was context 005, a tenacious dark brown sandy clay with more charcoal than 018, which was 0.20 metres deep and had a low stone content.

Pit 049

Oval in plan (1.50 by 0.82 metres), cut 049 had a near vertical western slope but was more gradual on the east. The base was slightly concave. A loose, very dark grey-brown gravel (053), 0.01 to 0.02 metres deep and containing occasional charcoal flecks, covered the base. This was sealed by context 050, a tenacious black silt loam, which contained more frequent flecks of charcoal, which occurred in distinct concentrations in the fill. The uppermost fill was a friable dark brown silt loam 0.06 metres deep (048) with occasional charcoal flecks and some stone.

Pit 060

Pit 060 was a steep-sided pit, 1.65 by 1.80 metres in plan, with a flat base. The primary fill was a loose dark reddish-brown sand with a very high gravel content which covered the entire base and was probably the product of a weathering event (117). Above this, 114 was a compact, dark reddish-brown sandy clay sealed by 106, a compact dark brown clay loam. Both of these contexts appeared to have been material washed into the pit. Context 103, above these layers, was a tenacious reddish brown sandy loam with a small amount of charcoal, and which might conceivably have represented a post-pipe. If so, then the preceding contexts must be packing. This is perhaps unlikely. 103 was sealed by 095, a compact, mottled dark brown sandy loam containing no charcoal, which appears to have been a further wash of material caught in the top of the pit. Above this, layer 085 was a charcoal-rich, dark reddish-brown sandy clay, sealed by 059, a second sandy clay containing less charcoal, very dark brown in colour.

Pit 162

Pit 162 cut away the uppermost fills of post-hole 252 in the southern cursus alignment (see above). The sides sloped steeply at the top, but became more gradual, merging into a rounded uneven base. On the north the sides were steeper than on the south. Cut 162 was 0.42 metres deep, and 1.55 metres north-south (the east-west extent was unobtainable since the eastern edge was beneath the trench edge).

The basal fill (140) consisted of a tenacious, dark reddish brown clay with sand and a low stone content. This layer was a maximum of 0.40 metres deep and was overlain by a second tenacious dark reddish brown sandy clay (141, depth 0.25 metres maximum) with less stone and a few charcoal flecks. The uppermost fill, 130, was a tenacious dark brown sandy clay loam with more charcoal flecks and a very low stone content.

Pit 022

Cut 022 was 1.40 metres diameter and its base was covered with a loose yellowish-brown sand with a high stone content (057) which was probably a weathering layer. Above this, tenacious, very dark brown sandy clay 051 contained large quantities of charcoal and large stones. Compact very dark brown sandy clay 038 and tenacious dark brown sandy clay 006 were similar: 006 contained charcoal and large stones (this was the uppermost fill); 038 (the penultimate fill) had a greater sand content. Both contained quantities of charcoal. Charcoal from layer 038 produced a radiocarbon date of 2210–2020 Cal. BC (95.4% probability) (SUERC-2119). 006 produced a date of 1320–1040 Cal. BC (95.4% probability) (SUERC-2123).

Pit 023 (Plate 22.10)

Cut 023 was one of the most sizeable in the pit alignment at 2.10 by 1.80 metres, with a depth of 0.35 metres. The sides sloped gently to a pointed base, and on the north were apparently cut by a narrow linear slot-like feature (cut 142, 1.71 metres long by 0.80 metres wide), the compact brown clay fill of which (097) contained charcoal flecks.

The basal fill of 023 was context 043, a loose dark reddish-brown sandy gravel, 0.02 metres deep, and containing a small amount of charcoal. Above this, a small concentration of medium to large stones was recorded amongst soil matrix 072, a loose dark reddish-brown sand. This concentration was 0.60 metres dia-

Plate 22.10 Avenue pit 023.

meter. Context 042 (1.20 metres by 1.10 metres, 0.76 metres deep) sealed this context. This was a friable, very dark brown silty clay with a large stone concentration and a large quantity of charcoal flecking and staining, (suggestive of the packing and burning of a small post). This was sealed by tenacious dark brown sandy clay 007, which also contained much charcoal.

Pit 024

This cut was 1.48 metres north-south and 0.40 metres deep. In plan it was sub-circular with fairly steep sides and a saucer-shaped base. The basal fill (034) was a friable dark reddish-brown sand 0.22 metres deep with a low stone content. Above this was a tenacious dark reddish-brown clay (033) with less stone and some charcoal in a distinct concentration, sealed by a tenacious dark brown sandy clay (008).

Pit 032

Cut 032 was 1.13 metres north-south and 0.20 metres deep. It was filled by 035, a tenacious dark brown sandy clay loam with a high stone content, 0.10 metres deep; and 031, a firm dark reddish-brown sandy clay loam with less stone and some charcoal flecks, also 0.10 metres deep.

Pit 069 (Plate 22.11)

Cut 069 was a bowl shaped feature 1.8 metres in diameter. The primary fill was a firm reddish-brown sand with a high gravel content which filled the majority of the pit (070). Above this was a firm dark reddish brown clay loam, 0.90 by 0.50 metres, with a low stone content (071) and patches of charcoal and apparently burnt sandstone.

This was sealed by 090 – a tenacious reddish-brown loamy sand with few pebbles and a small quantity of charcoal flecks.

Pit 100

Cut 100 was a bowl-shaped pit with near vertical upper sides, 1.28 by 0.91 metres in extent. The primary fill (099) was a friable dark reddish-brown loamy sand 0.80 by 0.40 metres in plan, with a very high stone content. Some of these stones appeared burnt. Above this, 092 was a tenacious, very dark brown clay loam, almost stone free, with considerable quantities of charcoal throughout. The uppermost fill was dark brown sandy clay loam 079.

Other features (Fig. 22.6)

A number of other features were examined which did not form parts of either the post-hole or pit alignments. All initially appeared on the surface as subsoil variations similar to the features described above. Towards the northern end of the trench, post-hole 239 was a relatively broad shallow cut, 1.40 m NE-SW by 0.37 m deep. The primary fill (271) was an extremely stony sand which was most probably a weathered deposit. This was overlain by 238, a strong brown sandy clay which had been cut by a small recut (251) 0.55m in diameter by 0.13m deep. This was filled by 250, a tenacious dark yellowish-brown clay. This feature was most probably a post-hole.

Cut 153 was a small pit 0.83m E-W with a single fill 147, a tenacious dark yellowish brown clay. The low stone content of this fill differentiated it from the surrounding natural.

Plate 22.11 Avenue pit 069.

Between the northern and southern lines of the cursus, three features were investigated. 086, 161 and 093 were most probably natural subsoil variations, since no hard edges to the cuts were discernable, and the fills were sandy gravels.

In the area between the southern line of the cursus and the northern side of the pit alignment six features were investigated. Of these, 131 and 129 were probably natural, being very poorly defined. Cut 119 seemed to be a post-hole 1.08 m by 0.75 m and 0.36 m deep, filled by context 118, a firm dark yellowish-brown clay, with a post-pipe 0.35 m in diameter and 0.30 m deep. Cuts 062, 080 and 041 were similar (if slightly smaller) features, without evidence of post-pipes, but with good edges and profiles. These were probably small pits.

Trench B: the ring ditch (Figs. 22.9 and 22.10)

The smaller cutting, Trench B, was laid out in order to investigate a ring ditch visible from the air (Plate 23.12). In the western part of the trench this ditch was immediately visible (cut 158).

In the south-east corner of Trench B, the ring ditch was visible as a curving line of stones (173), yet before excavation this area was somewhat confused, and it was clear that the ditch had been somewhat disturbed. In practice, the sequence of stratigraphic events was somewhat complex. The cut of the ring ditch (240) cut through an earlier post-hole (cut 241), evidently part of the southern line of the 'cursus'. This post-hole contained a very stony gravel as its primary fill (199), which had been recut (cut 246) and filled with a pebbly dark brown sandy

clay loam (247) which became redder and more clayey toward the surface (175). This makes it clear that the ring ditch was later than some of the posts of the cursus phase. However, the ring ditch had itself apparently been cut through by another post-hole (cut 220), immediately adjacent to 241, to the east. Post-hole 220 was very large, vertically-sided and flat-bottomed, and contained a complex filling (Plate 22.13). This commenced with a loose sandy gravel packing (243/244), above which was a dark, charcoally layer (261), which might represent the remains of a burnt wooden post. Above this was a lens of clean gravel (242) and larger deposit of dirty gravel (228), which together suggest the slumping of the higher levels of packing and/or the collapse of the post-hole edge, after the burning of the post. These layers were cut through by a large recut (225), which contained a spread of burnt post material in its bottom (223). The fill of the recut above this charcoally deposit showed no clear layering, but was arbitrarily divided into a lower fill (222) and an upper (219). This simply reflects a gradual change in the depositional regime over the period in which the recut was filling up: a change from a slightly sticky dark brown sandy clay containing much charcoal to a more friable dark reddish brown sandy clay, with charcoal flecks.

Another large post-hole (172) was contained within the ring ditch. This contained burnt matter in its primary fill (180), and a single recut with further burnt matter (210), suggesting two successive burnt posts.

The ring ditch itself was complex, in that a series of distinct structures had been present within the area investigated in Trench B. The roughly circular feature

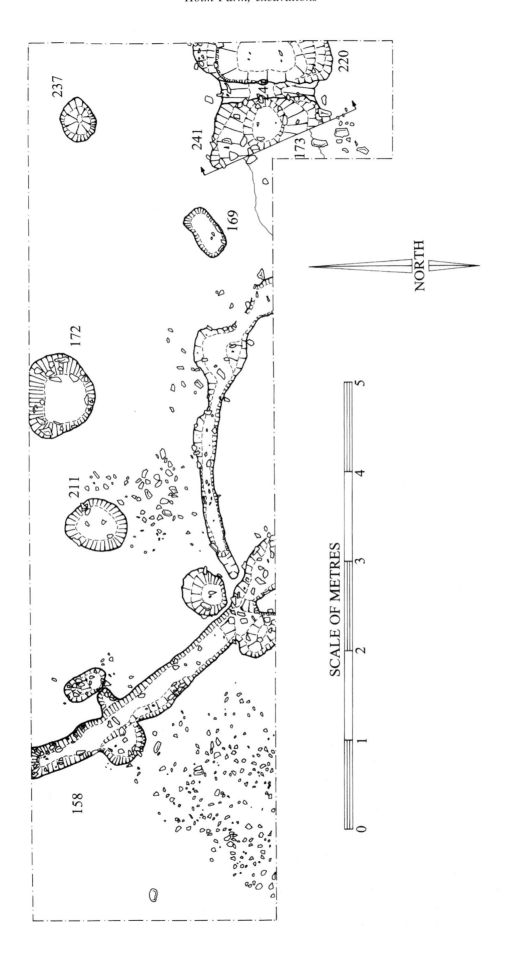

Fig. 22.9 Holm: Trench B plan.

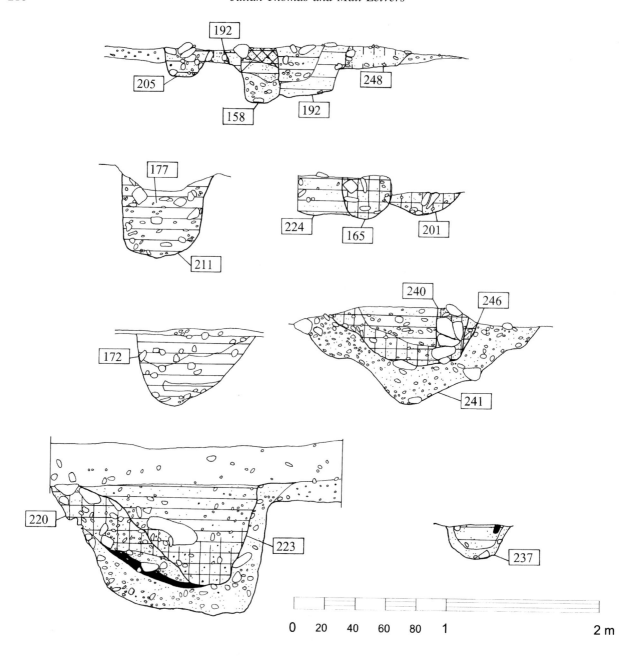

Fig. 22.10 Holm: Trench B feature sections, features 158, 211, 224, 172, 241, 220 and 237.

visible on air photos of the site was the last of three distinct constructions. The cut of the main ring ditch, 158, was narrow and straight-sided, with a sharp break of slope at the top and a flat base. The earliest fill in the ditch was 157, a loose reddish-brown gravel, which appeared to be material that had weathered from the ditch sides. Above this was a dense dark brown sandy clay, 156, which contained numerous medium-sized pebbles. These appeared to have been deliberately packed into the ditch. Above this, the uppermost fill of the ditch was 155, a dark reddish brown silty clay with fewer stones, and occasional charcoal flecks. If 156 had been a deliberate packing of the ring ditch, 155 appeared to be material

that had washed in above. Layer 155 produced a piece of alder charcoal which gave radiocarbon determination SUERC-2128, 120 Cal. BC – 60 Cal. AD. This, in theory, should date the packing of the stony ring ditch fill.

The arc of what was probably another, less substantial ring ditch, cut 170, was present in the south of Trench B. It appeared to be earlier than ring ditch 158, but the point at which they met was complicated by the presence of earlier features, and it is possible that 170 was broken at this point, giving no direct stratigraphic relationship between the two features. This lesser ring ditch was filled by context 160, a tenacious, very dark brown silty clay. From this fill came a further piece of alder charcoal which provided radiocarbon date SUERC-2127, 1420–1210 Cal. BC.

Trench B also contained a number of small, sub-circular cut features. While features 172, 220 and 241 were comparable with the cursus post-holes, these were somewhat smaller, and had less indication of recutting or multiple posts. Of these, 211 was the largest, and might conceivably have been a cursus post. This feature was roughly oval, with a principal fill of loose, dusky red gravely clay (177), capped by a group of quite large stones (176). The remaining features appeared to be small post-holes forming a rough arc that coincided with ring ditch 158. Features 192 (filled by sandy clays 193 and 202) and 224 (filled by sandy clay 213) had been cut by 158, while features 169 (filled by sandy gravel 168), 201 (filled by sandy clay loam 200), 205 (with sandy clay 204 and packing stones 203) and 237 (sandy gravel 236 below silty clay 226) had no stratigraphic relationships. Most of these features contained what appeared to be packing stones, but post-pipes were not evident. They could arguably represent a small post circle, pre-dating the ring ditch.

Overall, the features revealed in Trench B are somewhat perplexing. There appear to have been two ring ditches, constructed in sequence and later than a small post circle. In its manifestation as the stony material 173 in cut 240, which appear equivalent to 156 and 158, the major ring ditch seemed to cut through 241 and be cut by 220. These two large post-holes were similar to those of the post cursus. Yet the two ring ditches produced

Plate 22.12 Holm Trench B from the east.

Plate 22.13 Post-hole 220.

radiocarbon dates that were much later than those from the post structure. This suggests a number of possibilities, none of them entirely satisfactory. It is possible that the alder charcoal that produced SUERC-2127 and 2128 is intrusive. Alternatively, cut 200, while similar to the cursus post-holes, might have been a much later feature. Or perhaps the relationship between 240 and 220 was incorrectly observed. The loose gravely fills in this part of the site were not at all easy to read, and it may be that post-hole 220 was actually earlier than the ring ditch. This would appear to be the most likely alternative, but it still leaves the problem of the apparently late date of the ring ditches, which would ostensibly appear to have had some connection with the post cursus, even if they simply represented an opportunistic re-use of an ancient and hallowed location. Still more problematic is the presence of the putative post circle, which might be identified as either an integral element within the early Neolithic timber structure, or a precursor of the ring ditches. Were it not for the late dating of the ring ditches, both could be the case, but if the latter belong to later prehistory, this seems unlikely.

23

Prehistoric ceramics

Rick Peterson and Julia Roberts

Introduction

Thirty-eight separate finds of pottery were made during the Holywood excavations. All of the material is Neolithic in date and belongs to six different vessels. Where it is possible to reconstruct vessel forms two distinct styles of pottery appear to be present. These correspond to the distinction noted by Cowie (1993, 15–17) between fine carinated bowls and associated pottery, and simpler 'heavy bowls'.

The material was examined using a hand lens of ×10 magnification and placed in fabric groups on this basis. The classification of the fabric is based the categories suggested by Orton, Tyers and Vince (1993, 231–241), but slightly modified to take into account the more variable nature of prehistoric pottery. While Orton, Tyers and Vince use 'feel' as a category of classification we felt that the surface damage to much of the pottery precluded such a division. We also added a classification of fabric thickness on a three point scale of thin (10 mm or less), moderate (10–15 mm) and thick (15 mm or more).

Carinated bowls

The only unambiguous carinated bowl is vessel 1 from Holywood South (Fig. 23.1, 1). This is a finely made and burnished bowl. It is unusual in being ripple fluted as this is usually considered representative of a 'north-eastern' style (Henshall in Burl 1984, 61). The fine fabric and burnishing of vessel 4 from Holywood North (Fig. 23.1, 3) indicate that it was either carinated or belongs with this group as an associated early form. The fragmentary nature of many of the sherds of this vessel make it difficult to be certain about form. This vessel had at least one perforation, bored after firing, just below the rim.

Heavy bowls

Vessel 2 from Holywood South (Fig. 23.1, 2) is a simple, undecorated example of a heavy bowl, with a relatively simple rim, with only a slight external groove. A seed impression survives on one rim sherd from this vessel. The exterior of the base of this vessel shows considerable secondary oxidisation, indicating prolonged or repeated contact with direct heat after the vessel had been fired, presumably during use. This feature is also present on vessel 5 from Holywood North, which is probably also a heavy bowl, although only base sherds of this vessel survive.

Chronology

Radiocarbon dates associated with these two traditions are summarised by Cowie (1993, 19). He suggests that the carinated bowls belong to the first half of the 4th millennium BC and should not be dated later than c. 3500 BC. On the basis of two dates from the Balfarg Riding School (3474–3378 Cal. BC: 3691–3625 Cal. BC) Cowie would see the heavy bowls as dating to the mid to late 4th millennium BC.

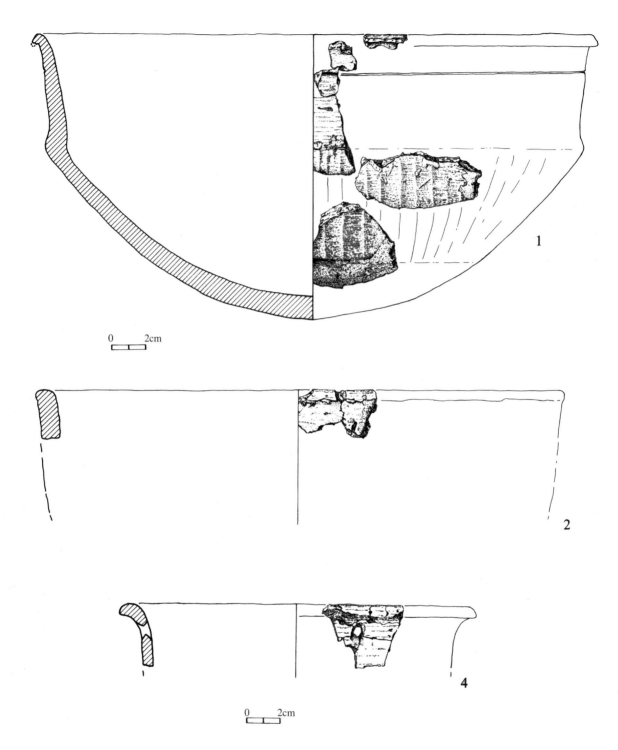

Fig. 23.1 Holywood pottery.

24

Lithics

Gilbert Marshall

Holywood North

The assemblage consisted of 14 pieces, of which two were considered diagnostic; a double backed side scraper or fabricator, and a single edge retouched fragment. The small flake number 47 is typical of waste generated through Mesolithic small platform core use, in particular maintenance of core edge angle.

Raw materials

The assemblage consisted of six (42.9%) pieces of basalt, four pieces (28.6%) of flint, two pieces (14.3%) of rhyolite, one piece (7.1%) of pitchstone, and one piece (7.1%) of what was probably a small chip of coal.

Basalt

Of the six pieces of basalt, only number 101 may have been deliberately struck although it lacked either platform or any evidence of secondary working. Similar surface polishing of all basalt pieces may suggest that they had a similar natural origin. Numbers 19, 28, 102, and 001 were probably natural pebbles, although 19 and 001 were split and number 32 was a chunk. All, apart from 32 and including 101, were polished suggesting a probable natural origin within river derived deposits.

Flint

The flint component of the assemblage consisted of four pieces, numbers 18, 38, 47, and 100. All were fine grained and of good quality, with colours ranging from grey through to a greyish green. The latter, number 18, appeared similar to greenish examples from Holm Cursus (see below). This material tends to be atypical of flint found along the west coast of Scotland north of Kintyre, suggesting local origin in the region of the site. The small size of the pebble, lightly rolled cortex and lack of obvious working points to a natural origin for this small pebble.

Piece number 47 was small and patinated and was probably generated through platform core working, either during platform maintenance or attempted blade removal.

It retained both platform and diffuse bulb with lip, suggestive of soft hammer working. Extensive dorsal scarring indicates intensive use of the core.

Piece number 100 was in a fresh condition with semi-abrupt retouch along the left hand edge, initiated from the ventral surface. The proximal and distal ends as well as the right hand edge were missing.

Piece number 38, a long blade of 59 mm was patinated although unrolled, with slightly irregular semi-abrupt retouch along both edges, and all initiated from the ventral surface. Retouch was most intensive along the mid sections of each edge. A platform was present, indicating removal from a platform core although the bulb of percussion was missing. Dorsal scarring points to previous removals although there appears to have been only limited edge maintenance. In addition, crushing of the platform is suggestive of hard hammer working. No cortex was present and it is therefore unclear as to how the flint was derived, although the blade length of 59mm suggests that the original raw material would have been of at least 70mm. There was some possible edge damage, a result of use along the lower right hand corner and the upper left hand side.

Rhyolite

Numbers 103, a pebble fragment or possible flake, is probably of natural origin. Flake number 003 on the other hand appears to have been struck from a large water rolled boulder although any platform or bulb of percussion was absent. There was no obvious retouch or edge damage. It may be natural or the result of fracturing during use as either a hammer or anvil.

Pitchstone

A single pitchstone chip was present, number 20. It was extremely fine grained and glassy and in a fresh condition. It terminated in a hinge fracture and lacked either platform or bulb of percussion. On the basis of its fine grained matrix it probably derived from sources along the south coast of Arran.

Coal

Piece number 40 was shiny, laminar and fragile, splitting into two laminar fragments on examination. On the basis of this it was defined as coal.

Technology (n=14)

Flakes	(either deliberate or natural)		5 (35.7%)
Blades	(deliberately struck, twice as long as wide)		1 (7.1%)
Chips	(flaked pieces less than 10mm maximum dimension)		2 (14.3%)
Chunks	(amorphous pieces as a result of knapping)		1 (7.1%)
Pebble	(unworked or with less than two deliberate removals)		5 (35.7%)

The volcanics, in particular the basalt and rhyolite, appear on the whole to be of natural origin although the rhyolite flake number 003 may have been deliberately struck from either a hammer or anvil. The pitchstone is undiagnostic and could have resulted from a range of working situations. Three pieces of flint were the result of deliberate working. The small flake number 47 is typical of platform core maintenance waste and suggests a Mesolithic origin. This may be supported by its more patinated nature, although number 38 is similarly patinated but looks later prehistoric in origin, probably Neolithic. Unfortunately, as with the other two collections (see below), small size makes it difficult to say anything more about either the chronology or character of the assemblage.

Holywood South cursus

The assemblage consisted on one undiagnostic flake.

Raw Materials

The assemblage consisted of a single piece of coarse grained quartz, number 43, which appears to have been derived as a water rolled cobble.

Technology (n=1)

The flake appears to have been either accidentally or deliberately struck as a spall from either a hammer or anvil.

Holm Cursus

The assemblage consisted of 24 pieces, none of which were particularly diagnostic apart from a single complete platform core, and a platform core fragment. Small cores of this type are regularly found within Mesolithic assemblages in the area. However, although similarly patinated, it cannot be assumed that the rest of the collection has the same chronology. The small size of the assemblage and lack of diagnostic elements apart from the cores limits its value. At present all that can be said

is that it probably represents low level background activity from the Mesolithic onwards.

Raw materials

The assemblage was dominated by flint with nineteen pieces (79.2%), followed by chert and flint/chert with three pieces (12.5%), and then by two pieces of quartz (8.3%).

Quartz (nos. 27 and 104)

Neither of the quartz pieces appear to have been either deliberately struck or worked and are probably naturally present in the soil.

Flint (nos. 1 to 4, 6 to 13, 15, 17, 18, 20, 23, 24, 105)

The flint component of the assemblage was fine grained and of good quality, with colours ranging from orange through green to black. A small collection of pieces, in particular numbers 7, 9, 10, 24 and 105 were of a greenish grey colour. This is atypical of flint present along the west coast of Scotland north of Kintyre where nodules generally range in colour from grey to brown. These few pieces along with the chert, point as expected to sourcing south of Kintyre. A single piece of flint, number 6, retained diagnostic cortex. Light percussion marks and polishing of the surface are both suggestive of nodular flint derived from a low energy beach or river environment.

Chert and ambiguous flint/chert (nos. 14, 16, 22)

The chert was dark greenish grey in colour, with hairline fractures and a coarse black fill. The angular nature of the material used for the platform core number 22 is suggestive of sourcing from *in situ* deposits rather than as derived water rolled pebbles. Pieces 14 and 16 were ambiguous and were therefore defined as flint/chert.

Technology (n=24)

Flakes	(deliberately struck)		
Blades	(deliberately struck, twice as long as wide)		12 (50%)
Chips	(flaked pieces less than 10mm maximum dimension)		1 (4.2%)
Chunks	(amorphous pieces as a result of knapping)		4 (16.7%)
Core	(with two or more deliberate secondary removals)		5 (20.8%)
Pebble	(unworked or with less than two deliberate removals)		1 (4.2%)
			1 (4.2%)

Both quartz pieces appear to be unworked. Removing them from the assemblage reduced chunks to four and pebbles to zero and the complete assemblage to only 22 pieces. Flakes and blades appear to have been struck from small platform cores. Of the seven proximal pieces with platforms, numbers 2, 3, 6, 7, 10, 23 and 24 all retained pronounced bulbs of percussion suggestive of hard hammer working.

The two blade cores, numbers 22 and 17, the former complete and the latter a fragment, were small and appear to have been intensively worked. The complete core was of chert and retained two platforms. It was probably abandoned due to its small size and awkward shape which would have made holding difficult. Multiple platforms and small size suggest a degree of raw material stress.

The fragmentary flint core would have derived from a very small example, suggesting attempted rejuvenation or reuse, again pointing to raw material stress.

Retouch was absent from the assemblage, although some limited edge damage consistent with light scraping was present on the distal right hand corner of piece number 12.

25

Carbonised remains from Holywood cursus complex

Ciera Clarke
with contributions by Mike Cressey and Ruth Pelling

Holywood cursus – charred plant macrofossil analysis

Introduction

A series of 35 samples taken during excavation of the Holywood Cursus complex were provided. All samples were processed for the extraction of charred plant remains. Recovered remains were identified and catalogued. The methods and results are presented below. Original sample volumes are presented in Table 25.4.

Methodology

Samples ranging in volume from 0.2 to 27.5 litres were processed using a bulk water flotation method (Siraf System) and collected onto nested 1 mm and 300 μm meshes. The residues were washed through a 1 mm mesh. Flots were air-dried in tissue paper wraps and the residues were placed in trays to air-dry. Samples were sorted at Centre for Field Archaeology, University of Edinburgh. Flots were first put through a stack of sieves ranging from 4 mm to 300 μm. Each fraction greater than 2 mm was sorted by eye, whilst the 300 μm and 1 mm fractions were sorted under a binocular miscroscope at ×10 to ×20 magnification. The residues were scanned for charred plant remains and any artefacts. Any wood charcoal, charred seed or chaff were extracted and submitted for identification. The identification of the charcoal material was assisted by the wood anatomy keys of Schweingruber (1990) and reference material held by Centre for Field Archaeology. The identification of non-charcoal charred plant remains, made on morphological characteristics and by comparison with modern reference material, was made at the Oxford University Museum.

The charcoal assemblage

Introduction

The assemblage was scanned predominantly for species composition. The potential for AMS dating has also been recorded. The results are presented in Table 25.1.

Methodology

Identifications were made using a binocular microscope at magnifications ranging between ×10–200. Generally identifications were carried out on transverse cross-sections on charcoal pieces of 4–6 mm dimension. Anatomical keys listed in Schweingruber (1990), in-house reference charcoal, and slide-mounted microsections were used to aid identifications. Asymmetry and morphological characteristics were recorded. Large samples of charcoal (over 100g) were split in a riffle-box to produce sub-samples. Extraneous non-charcoal material such as cinder and modern plant debris was removed during analyses. Heavily mineralized and vitrified charcoal was discarded on account of the difficulties in its identification. In this report "roundwood" is used as a term of reference for branch wood and non-timber material (squared-off or blocky in shape).

Observations on this assemblage

In general the charcoal is in a fairly good state of preservation with a limited amount of serious abrasion. Seventeen samples were found to be below the limit of identification.

The taxa represented within this assemblage are:

Prunus type (probably blackthorn or cherry)
Corylus avellana (Hazel, including nut shell)
Quercus type (Oak)
Betula sp. (Birch)
Pinus sylvesteris (Scots Pine – excellent preservation)

Sample No.	Context	Species	Wgt (gms)	Comment
1	4	-------	------	below limit of ID
1	61	Quercus	16.4	well preserved (10)
2	8	------	------	Indet 1 seed
2	135	Quercus	0.24	Non-roundwood
2	135	Betula	0.19	(3)
2	135	Corylus	0.04	(2)
3	9	Quercus	<0.05	(1)
4	7	Quercus	------	(5)
4	177	Pinus	2.72	(10) small frags
6	16	------	------	Below limit of ID
7?	13	------	------	Below limit of ID
8	14	------	------	Below limit of ID
9	22	Quercus	1.95	Non roundwood (10)
9	22	Corylus	0.78	Abraded (5)
10	21	Quercus	0.04	(3)
10	21	Corylus	0.05	(1)
11	30	------	------	Below limit of ID
12	37	------	------	Below limit of ID
13	15	barren		
14	38	------	------	Below limit of ID
15	31	Quercus	1.07	angular frags, well formed (10)
16	23	Corylus nut	0.05	3 fragments
17	40	barren		
18	40	------	------	Below limit of ID
19	24	Quercus	0.05	(4)
20	47	------	------	Below limit of ID
21	35	------	------	Below limit of ID
21	49	------	------	Below limit of ID
23	35	------	------	Below limit of ID
24	27	------	------	Below limit of ID
25	59	------	------	Below limit of ID
26	57	------	------	Below limit of ID
27	63	Quercus	0.50	(5)
28	64	barren		
29	39	------	------	Below limit of ID
30	93	------	------	Below limit of ID
31	92	Quercus	0.13	(5)
32	95	Quercus	0.27	(3)
47	85	Prunus type	0.55	4 mm fraction roundwood (10)
47	85	Corylus	0.03	(1)
47	85	------	12.77	1 m fraction indet-round and angular frags

Table 25.1 Results of charcoal assessment.

In general terms there is sufficient material for AMS dating with sample 1 context 61 having sufficient material for a conventional date.

Non-wood charcoal charred plant remains

Results

Of the 35 samples four produced small quantities of charred remains (HWN contexts 085, 061, 135 and 177; HWS context 009). Cereal grains were recorded in two samples (contexts 061, 135). Both free-threshing and hulled wheats were represented. The preservation of the grain was poor, thus the hulled wheat has been recorded as *Triticum spelta/dicoccum* (spelt/emmer wheat). A single large (3.5 mm), possibly cultivated, legume was also present, which given the absence of the characteristic hila and testa, is recorded as *Vicia/Pisum* sp. (bean/pea). Several smaller legume seeds all with diameters of less than 2 mm were recorded as wild *Vicia/lathyrus* sp. (vetch/vetchling). Hazel nut shell fragments (*Corylus avellana*) were frequent in context 135 and present in two more samples (contexts 177 and 009). Occasional weed seeds included the vetches and several seeds of *Chenopodium album* (fat hen) a species found in charred archaeological deposits in association with cereal remains from the Neolithic period onwards. Results of recoveries are presented in Tables 25.2 and 25.3.

Sample	Context	Site	Charred remains
1	004	HWS	absent
1	061	HWN	present
2	008	HWS	absent
2	135	HWN	occasional
3	009	HWS	present
4	007	HWS	absent
4	177	HWN	occasional
6	016	HWS	absent
7?	013	HWS	absent
8	014	HWS	absent
9	022	HWS	absent
10	021	HWS	absent
11	030	HWS	absent
12	037	HWS	absent
13	015	HWS	absent
14	038	HWS	absent
15	031	HWS	absent
16	023	HWS	absent
17	040	HWS	absent
18	040	HWS	absent
19	024	HWS	absent
20	047	HWS	absent
21	035	HWS	absent
21	049	HWS	absent
23	035	HWS	absent
24	027	HWS	absent
25	059	HWS	absent
26	057	HWS	absent
27	063	HWS	absent
28	064	HWS	absent
29	039	HWS	absent
30	093	HWS	absent
31	092	HWS	absent
32	095	HWS	absent
47	085	HM	occasional

Table 25.2 Charred macroplant remains recovered through the suite of samples.

	Sample:	47	01	02	04	03
	Context:	085	061	135	177	009
	Site:	HWN	HWN	HWN	HWN	HWS
Triticum spelta/dicoccum	Spelt/emmer wheat			2		
Triticum sp.	free-threshing wheat grain		1	1		
Triticum sp.	wheat grain			2		
Cerealia indet.	indeterminate grain			1		
Vicia/pisum sp.	Bean/Pea	1				
Corylus avallana	Hazel nut shell fragment			17	2	2
Chenopodium album	Fat Hen	10				
Vicia/lathyrus	Vetch/Vetchling	10			2	
Indet. weed					3	
Indet. bud		2		3	2	

Table 25.3 Catalogue of taxa recovered.

Sample	Context	Site	Volume (litres)
1	004	HWS	1.5
1	061	HWN	6.1
2	008	HWS	4.5
2	135	HWN	22.6
3	009	HWS	3.4
4	007	HWS	1.3
4	177	HWN	5.0
6	016	HWS	2.1
7?	013	HWS	2.9
8	014	HWS	2.7
9	022	HWS	3.4
10	021	HWS	2.1
11	030	HWS	4.0
12	037	HWS	2.1
13	015	HWS	3.0
14	038	HWS	3.6
15	031	HWS	3.3
16	023	HWS	2.9
17	040	HWS	2.1
18	040	HWS	2.7
19	024	HWS	3.6
20	047	HWS	2.8
21	035	HWS	1.5
21	049	HWS	3.7
23	035	HWS	3.0
24	027	HWS	1.0
25	059	HWS	2.5
26	057	HWS	4.0
27	063	HWS	0.2
28	064	HWS	1.2
29	039	HWS	? recording error
30	093	HWS	3.5
31	092	HWS	3.0
32	095	HWS	0.4
47	085	HM	27.5

Table 25.4 Sample volumes.

26

Soil phosphate studies at Holywood

John Crowther

Introduction

Phosphate analysis, complemented by loss-on-ignition (LOI) and some pH and particle size determinations, was undertaken on 34 samples from the Holywood Cursus sites (South and North) in the hope of gaining additional insight into the nature and pattern of human activity. The samples are from a wide range of contexts, and were selected by Julian Thomas as being potentially important to an understanding of various phases in the development of the two sites. This study closely parallels the more extensive phosphate survey recently undertaken at the nearby henge site at Pict's Knowe. Details of the methods employed and the difficulties of interpreting results from acidic sandy soils/sediments are presented in the Pict's Knowe phosphate report (Chapter 9).

Results

General character of the soils/sediments

As at Pict's Knowe, the two sites are located on fluvio-glacial sands and gravels. The soils/sediments analysed do, however, differ in four important respects from those sampled at Pict's Knowe. First, there is a generally higher proportion of silts and clays in the mineral fraction (Table 26.1) – giving a sandy loam to loamy sand texture. Secondly, they are much less acidic (pH range, 5.6–6.3; Table 26.1), which may to some extent reflect recent liming of pasture and arable land, depending on the depth of sampling. Thirdly, they appear to be quite rich in iron, with fewer 'bleached' sand grains. Finally, the samples are all essentially minerogenic (cf. presence of peats at Pict's Knowe), with LOI in the range 2.00–6.39%, and the organic matter that is present is fully integrated with the mineral fraction as clay-humus complexes, etc. Under these circumstances, variations in organic matter content are unlikely to exert a major influence over phosphate-P concentrations. Variations in the proportions of silt+clay may be significant, though the degree of textural variability at Holywood is by no means as pronounced as in some fluvio-glacial deposits (Crowther, 1997).

Phosphate survey

Analytical results from the two sites are presented in Tables 26.2 and 26.3. As would be anticipated in view of their higher silt+clay and iron content (and possible enhancement through fertiliser applications?) phosphate-P concentrations at the Holywood sites (range, 0.276–

	Context	Sample	Coarse sand* (%)	Medium sand* (%)	Fine sand* (%)	Silt+Clay (%)	pH (1:2.5, water)
S. Cursus							
	11	5	23.6	54.2	9.4	12.8	5.6
	30	11	17.7	32.3	18.6	31.4	6.0
	38	14	16.1	30.3	18.3	35.3	6.0
	64	28	14.7	29.6	18.0	37.7	5.7
N. Cursus							
	177	4	15.1	46.7	14.8	23.4	6.3

* Coarse sand = 2.00–0.600 mm; Medium sand = 0.600–0.200 mm; Fine sand = 0.200–0.060 mm

Table 26.1 Particle size and pH determinations on selected samples.

Context	Description	Sample	LOI(%)	Phosphate-P (mg g⁻¹)	Possible phosphate enrichment (**)
4	ditch fill in entrance terminal	1	4.25	0.799	
7	ditch fill in entrance terminal	4	5.13	0.723	
8	ditch fill in entrance terminal, incl. charcoal flecks	2	5.98	0.959	
9	ring-ditch top fill, sw quad	3	4.30	1.05	**
11	ditch fill in entrance terminal	5‡	4.45	0.820	
13	ditch fill in entrance terminal, incl. charcoal flecks	7	5.98	1.06	**
14	ring-ditch fill, incl. some charcoal staining, sw quad	8	2.19	0.554	
15	ring-ditch fill, incl. some charcoal staining, sw quad	13	2.63	1.20	**
16	ring-ditch fill, ne quad	6	5.17	0.846	
21	fill of possible post-hole, incl. 5 pot sherds	10	4.51	1.02	**
22	fill of possible post-hole, incl. abundant charcoal	9	4.94	0.971	
23	ring-ditch fill, sw quad	16	2.33	0.444	
24	second fill of post-hole beneath 21, incl. 2 post sherds	19	3.03	0.351	
27	ring-ditch fill, ne quad	24	2.96	0.757	
30	fill of possible post-hole	11‡	2.83	1.75	**
31	fill of possible post-hole, incl. pottery	15	3.21	0.619	
34	ring-ditch fill, sw quad	12	3.69	1.58	**
35	ring-ditch fill, ne quad	23	4.94	0.777	
38	ditch fill in entrance terminal	14‡	4.38	1.77	**
40	ring-ditch fill, ne quad	17	3.17	0.439	
47	ditch fill in entrance terminal	20	4.42	0.640	
49	fill of possible pit	21	5.64	0.755	
57	fill of pit	26	3.05	0.633	
59	fill of pit	25	3.63	0.793	
63	fill of possible post-hole	27	6.33	1.11	**
64	fill of possible post-hole	28‡	6.39	0.896	
92	fill of feature, incl. many rounded stones	31	5.13	0.810	
93		30	2.91	0.572	
95	fill of postpit (pipe 081)	31	4.45	0.584	

‡Particle size and pH determinations made (see Table 26.1)

Table 26.2 Analytical data from Holywood South cursus.

Context	Description	Sample	LOI (%)	Phosphate-P (mg g⁻¹)	Possible phosphate enrichment (**)
61	ditch fill	1	4.87	0.448	
74	ditch fill incl. seeds etc.	7	2.31	0.523	
135a	charcoal in pit 102 incl. charcoal and nutshells	2	2.19	1.00	**
135b	charcoal in pit 102 incl. charcoal and nutshells	2	2.00	0.850	
177	fill of post-hole 167 incl., charcoal	4‡	3.27	0.276	

‡Particle size and pH determinations made (see Table 26.1)

Table 26.3 Analytical data from Holywood North cursus.

1.77 mg g^{-1}) are generally higher than those recorded at Pict's Knowe. Given the inevitable variations in phosphate retention capacity between the different contexts, caution must be exercised in interpreting the results. For present purposes it is assumed that samples with phosphate-P concentrations >1.00 mg g^{-1} exhibit some degree of phosphate enrichment, and these are highlighted in the tables. Of these, the three samples (contexts 30, 34 and 38) from the South Cursus with concentrations >1.50 mg g^{-1} would appear to be significantly enriched.

Acknowledgements

The laboratory analysis was undertaken by Ian Clewes.

27

Holywood and Holm: discussion

Julian Thomas

The diverse group of cursus-related monuments in south-west Scotland are concentrated in the Nith valley, and are in most cases directly associated with watercourses (Brophy 2000; Chapter 20 above). Fourmerkland is positioned above Cluden Water, while the Eskdalemuir bank barrow crosses the White Esk, for instance. This dense concentration of cursus-like structures is remarkable in itself, but there is also an interesting absence of megalithic tombs and long mounds in the immediate area (Gregory 2000, 10). The nearest mortuary monuments are the long cairns of Slewcairn and Lochill, away to the south in the vicinity of the prominent hill of Criffel (Masters 1973; 1981, 103–4). This could suggest either that the cursus monuments had a role in funerary practice that was complementary to that of tombs and barrows, or that the area of modern Dumfries was socially distinct from that which contained the mortuary structures, used in different ways or by different communities. There are other indications that the social landscape of Neolithic south-west Scotland was not homogeneous. Cummings (2001: 219) notes that all kinds of monuments appear to be mutually exclusive with concentrations of rock art, while lithic scatters dating to the period are found mostly in coastal and riverine locations. The implication is that distinct zones of land were understood in different ways, and were used for quite distinct kinds of activities. The alternative possibility, that cursus monuments, long cairns, and rock art are to be associated with separate Neolithic population groups, is perhaps less likely.

All of the structures that have been described in this volume are connected with rivers or streams to some extent, most notably Holm Farm, where the linear timber structures run parallel with the Nith, along a stretch of flat gravel terrace. All of this is in keeping with the general pattern for cursus monuments in Scotland, England and Wales, which are overwhelmingly concentrated on well-drained flat river gravel terraces (Harding & Barclay 1999, 5). To some extent this reflects the topographical requirements for a long, linear monument, although it is clear that in some cases cursuses were laid out with scant regard for the lie of the land. This suggests that the close association with water may be a consequence either of the way in which these structures were used, or of the particular significance that they held for those who made and used them. In the case of the group of cursuses located on the Thames gravels, the suggestion has been made that the monuments were connected with the seasonal movements of communities who pastured cattle on the floodplains, and were located in expanding clearances which were generated by and for grazing (Barclay & Hey 1999, 68). The Holywood and Holm monuments are all located on relatively flat expanses of gravel, and yet demonstrate an extreme sensitivity to the variations of the local landscape: the northern terminal of Holywood North encloses a small knoll; Holywood South runs out across a small promontory; Holm Farm sits neatly on its terrace.

This pattern brings to mind the recent concern with the experiential aspects of cursus monuments (Tilley 1994; Brück 1998). A number of authors have argued that since cursuses are linear enclosures which often cut across landscape zones and connect together significant locations they can best be understood as ceremonial pathways along which processions would have passed. In this connection it is interesting to note that both of the Holywood cursuses have multiple entrances through their ditches, and yet in neither case are these entrances set in the ends of the enclosure. As we have noted already the two northernmost entrances at Holywood South are so positioned as to allow unimpeded progress between the northern cursus and the Twelve Apostles stone circle. In many cursuses the entrances are in the sides of the monument, near to one end (Harding & Barclay 1999, 3). In this respect the site of Curriestanes (west of Dumfries), which has an entrance at one end, is quite unusual. In some cases, as perhaps with the Greater Stonehenge Cursus and the Dorset Cursus, it is possible that these constructions elaborated and monumentalised (or even enclosed and sanctified) a route or pattern of movement that was already of importance (Johnston 1999; Thomas 1999a: 171). The causeways in the sides of the monuments may have been true entrances, but they may also have been a means of allowing passage *across* spaces that were otherwise not intended to be entered.

As Brophy (Chapter 20 above) points out, the history of investigation into cursus monuments is one that has been dominated by aerial photography. Cursuses are rarely visible on the ground, and small-scale excavation has seldom yielded illuminating results beyond what can be learned from a ditch section. Artefactual assemblages derived from cursus monuments have generally been small and uninformative, for instance. As a consequence, much research effort has been invested into typologies based upon the overall morphology of sites viewed from the air. This has often meant that particular monuments have been understood as representatives of a class, and the virtue of the experiential approach has lain in the attempt to address their specificity as elements of a human landscape. The excavations reported here can hopefully build on this framework, by establishing the particular histories of a series of locations, within which the recognisable 'cursus' may be only one element. The fieldwork at Holywood, for instance, has demonstrated that the two cursuses had rather different structural sequences. In either case it may be that post-holes or pits were present on site before the construction of the ditched monument, so that both natural topographic features and the traces of human activity were being bound together and encapsulated within the cursus ditch.

In the case of Holywood North, the precise sequence in which the various structural elements of the monument were put together has proved to be problematic. The combination of ditch, bank, and wooden uprights set in pits is unusual if not unique, and on the basis of the excavated evidence it is not immediately clear whether the earthwork and posts were contemporary or formed entirely separate phases of construction. In attempting to resolve this question, we can first address the stratigraphic evidence, before placing this into the context of the independent radiometric dating. There are a number of stratigraphic relationships which constrain possible interpretations. The large post-pit 224 presented a complicated sequence of at least three, probably four, and perhaps five timber uprights, which were put in place at the northernmost point of a large timber structure, which was potentially more than 300 metres in length. Of course, not all of the posts in 224 need have been elements in such a structure, and one or more may have stood in isolation. However, the circumstantial evidence is that the timber architecture was itself multi-phase, and this implies that each post at 224 was associated with a larger structure. It is possible that some of the posts in 224 were larger than the other uprights, and that end post was an impressive focal entity, occupying a prominent location on a slight topographic rise. Perhaps two or three of these

apical posts were burnt down, the earliest providing the spectacular evidence of charcoal deposit 053.

Eleven of the other postholes provided definite stratigraphic evidence for recutting, while another three showed the more equivocal trait of a stepped – and potentially multiple – base (Fig. 27.1). Other than 224, four post-holes showed direct evidence for burning, and a further seven contained fills of the characteristic dark reddish-brown colour which suggests that the gravel has been subject to the effects of fire, potentially indicating that burning had taken place at a higher level (Fig. 27.2). Wherever burning or discolouration was present in a post-hole with multiple cuts, they were found in a secondary position. Thus if there were two or more phases of timber construction, it was probably the second or later that was burned. Eight posts presented an elongated or 'ramped' morphology, which we have argued is an indication of a post having been removed, with consequent disruption of the subsoil surface to one side of the cut. In several cases, this feature was associated with deposits bedded in a way that again suggested the withdrawal of a post. Such evidence of post-removal was not associated with either post-burning or recutting.

Unfortunately, there was little direct stratigraphic evidence linking the internal features with the ditch. Post-hole 217 appeared to have been cut by the ditch, but this relationship was not secure, as both features were shallow at the point of their intersection. The cut of the ditch itself was followed by a short episode of silting, after which the bank material was returned into the cut; then the ditch was recut. In Trench 2, the 'screen' of smaller posts may have been earlier or later than the initial cut of the ditch, but it is not clear that it was constructed late enough to be contemporary with the ditch recut. Strictly speaking, the various imponderables involved in the site's stratigraphy allow a series of putative sequences for the development of the monument.

Firstly, it is possible that the principal arrangement of post-holes formed an integral structure with the primary ditch. This was the sequence proposed in the interim report on the site (Thomas *et al.* 1999, 110). It was suggested at that time that the very large post-hole 244 was the earliest feature on site, cut into the small hillock before the cursus was built, in order to hold a single massive post. This being the case, the terminal ditch (when it was finally dug) would have been slightly askew from the medial line of the cursus in order to precisely enclose the hillock and the post. The ditch recut would then represent the latest phase of activity, perhaps associated with the Trench 2 post screen, or perhaps later. If the ditch, the internal bank, and the main series of posts were contemporary the uprights would necessarily have occupied the same general area as the bank. This might mean that the free-standing uprights rose up through the bank – presumably with considerable visual impact – or that they might constitute part of a revetment structure, probably with hurdling between them. In the

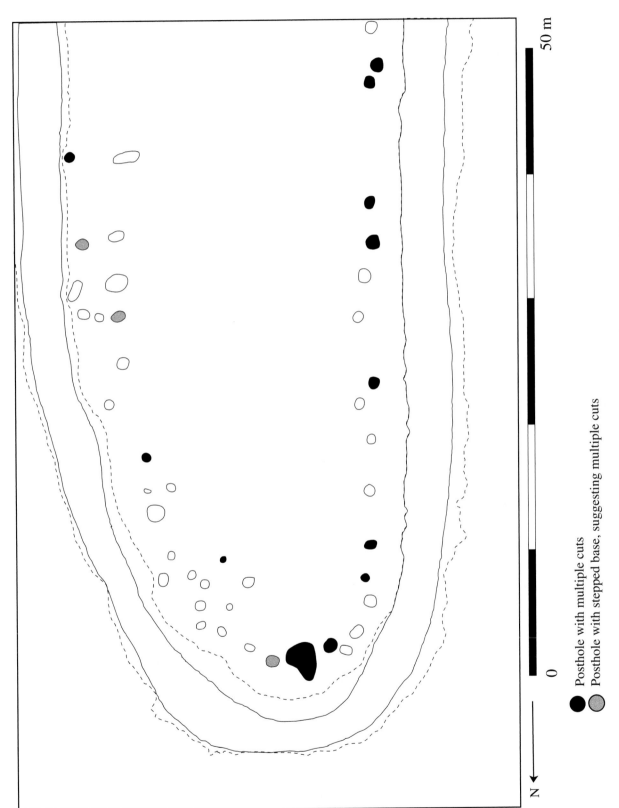

Fig. 27.1 Holywood North: post-holes with evidence for burning or post-withdrawal.

● Posthole with multiple cuts
● Posthole with stepped base, suggesting multiple cuts

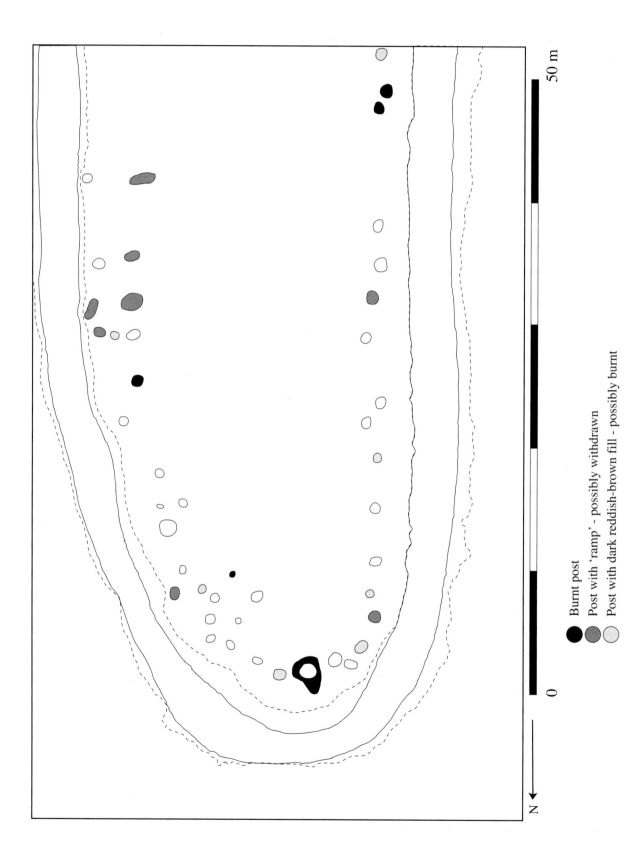

Fig. 27.2 Holywood North: post-holes with evidence for recutting.

Burnt post

Post with 'ramp' - possibly withdrawn

Post with dark reddish-brown fill - possibly burnt

N

0   50 m

latter case, the burning of the posts might result in the collapse of the bank structure, and the filling of the ditch. However, it is arguable whether a bank of gravel that had been compacted by rain and general weathering would actually collapse in a catastrophic fashion when its revetment was removed (I am grateful to Alex Gibson for this observation). If this is so, then the filling of the ditch can only possibly be attributed to deliberate backfilling. The whole of the bank must have been shovelled back into the ditch, whether this took place at the same time as the burning of the timbers or not. This means that the evidence from the ditch cannot definitively tell us whether or not the bank had been revetted. Furthermore, the interim report laid little emphasis on the complexity of the timber structure. While a single-phase timber architecture might have served as the revetment for a bank, it is considerably less likely that a bank would have been associated with timbers that were renewed or replaced on a number of occasions.

The interim evaluation of the site also relied upon an overly straightforward account of post-pit 224 and its relationship with the other post arrangements. The sequence that was proposed for feature 244 was one in which a single large post stood in the initial cut, was burned and toppled, and later cut through by post-hole 015, which was understood as forming an element of a single-phase timber structure. This demands that the large post had been the earliest structure on the site, and that it had stood in isolation, pre-dating the rest of the timber architecture. For this reason, the relatively late radiocarbon date from the burnt post material (SUERC-2116) was somewhat surprising, given the earlier date (SUERC-2115) derived from context 135 in post-hole 102.

The version of events now preferred is one in which as many as four or five posts were erected in sequence in feature 224, and this post-hole represented an important point from which the rest of the structure was laid out. Moreover, the post-structure was clearly multi-phase, and not a single build contemporary with 015, and later than the post represented by 053. It is thus highly likely that *all* of the posts in 224 were integral to one or other phase of a larger structure, and no single free-standing post preceded the timber monument. On the western side of the cursus there were numerous examples of recut postholes, indicating that at least two phases of construction were represented. On the eastern side there were fewer recuts, as it seems that the different phases of construction ran *parallel* with each other, rather than maintaining the same axis. This would mean that at different times the width of the post cursus would have been broader or narrower.

In the south-east part of the site, the configuration of post-holes is particularly informative. At one point, three post-holes were located side by side: 037, 039 and 041. It is unlikely that all three posts were contemporary, and probable that they represent successive phases of construction. 037 had a stepped base, and may have been recut, so it is possible that a total of four posts had been raised at this point in the structure. 041 had arguably been withdrawn, while 039 had a reddish-brown fill suggesting that its post may have been burned. To the south of these three posts were two potentially withdrawn posts, 094 and 217. Further south again were 087, which may have been withdrawn, and 108, which was stepped. Finally, in the extreme south were 106, which had been recut, and 104, which may have been withdrawn. In each case, then, two, three or four posts were indicated at specific points around the circuit of the timber cursus.

At no point other than in feature 224 was more than a single episode of burning documented, and we have seen that this burning had probably not affected the earliest structure on the site, except in the case of feature 102, where both fills 101 and 135 contained considerable quantities of charcoal. It is therefore possible that the first build of the timber structure was dismantled, with a number of posts being withdrawn, but only a small minority including 224 and 102 being selectively burnt out. This 'selection' may have been based on the relative importance of the posts concerned, in that 224 was the 'laying-out post' at the extreme north of the structure, while the packing of 102 (101) contained a significant cultural deposit, including sherds of carinated bowl. This was the only post-hole excavated that contained such a deposit. At a later stage it is possible that a more general burning of the post-structure took place, involving fill 135 of post-hole 102, together with features 184, 057, 167, 211, 129, 131, 220, 031, 196 and 039, as well as either fill 152 or fill 014/012 in feature 224. Such a generalised episode of burning, while not necessarily affecting all of the posts in the structure, would have been more comparable with the events documented at the Holm site (see below).

We have already argued that it is unlikely that the post-structure and the cursus ditch at Holywood North were contemporary, and that they probably did not represent complementary elements of a single monument. It is strictly possible that the post-cursus succeeded the ditched monument, following the return of the bank material into the ditch. The limited evidence of feature 217 suggests the opposite, as does the artefactual material. For while sherds of carinated bowl were recovered from post-hole 102, portions of a heavy, round-based bowl came from the ditch, although admittedly in a secondary position. If the post-defined cursus monument were the first structure on the site, preceding the ditched enclosure, it is possible that this was not as large as the final monument. We have noted that on the poorer-definition aerial photographs of the southern portion of Holywood North there is no indication of the presence of post-holes. But in addition, there seem to be no post-holes in the portion of the cursus immediately south of the two breaks or entrances in the ditch, one of which was investigated in Trench 2 (see Fig. 27.3). Moreover, it appears that immediately south of Trench 1 the width of the post-

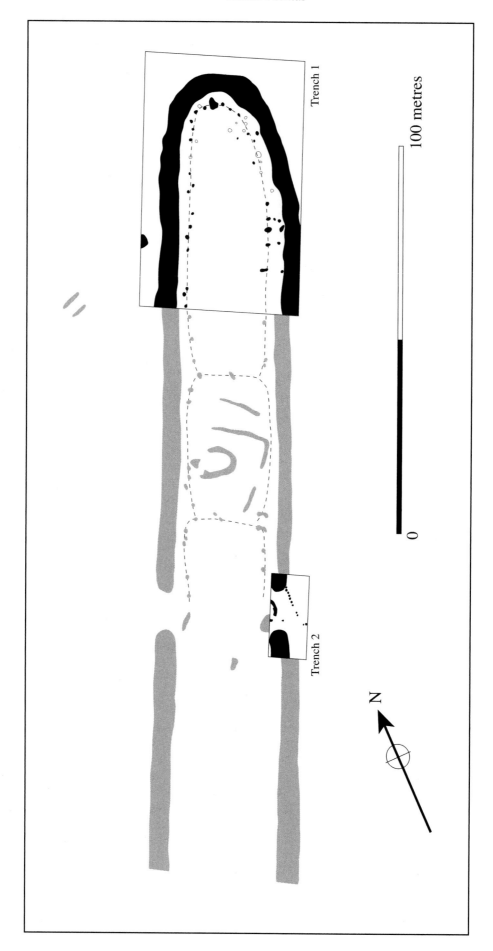

Fig. 27.3 Holywood North: excavated areas and features visible from the air, demonstrating potential 'modular' character of the timber structure.

structure narrowed, and that a transverse line of posts may have run across the enclosure at this point. A further combination of narrowing and transverse 'blocking' posts may have existed around fifty metres to the south. If this arrangement could be demonstrated, it recalls structural features demonstrated at Douglamuir and Castle Menzies (see Fig. 27.6). Moreover, it implies that the post-structure was composed of a series of distinct enclosed areas, and had a 'modular' character. These 'modules' need not all have existed in each of the three or four phases of the structure's existence, and it is possible that at different times the post-cursus was larger or smaller.

Much of the discussion of the timber structures at Holywood North to this point has been framed in terms of distinct 'phases' of construction. While as many as three or four posts were erected (presumably in sequence) in some places within the overall monument, at others only a single post was identified. We have argued on this basis that the precise configuration of the post-structure would have been different in successive phases. However, it is worth considering the possibility that the process of erecting, withdrawing, burning and replacing timber uprights was sporadic rather than concentrated into a small number of events. Perhaps only a single post was raised or brought down at a time, so that the overall morphology of the structure was continually in flux and being added to. In such a scenario, each constructional episode might have been associated with a visit to the site, or may have marked other social events (births, initiations, funerals). The possibility that single posts may have been burned at particular points in the history of the site invites this kind of interpretation. However, the possibility that a series of posts may have been burned simultaneously (possible at Holywood North and probable at Holm) suggests a more concerted intention to renew the monument as a whole, and this implies that a significant performance or event required a specific form of closure.

The available radiocarbon dates do not entirely resolve the constructional sequence for Holywood North. The date of 3800–3650 Cal. BC (SUERC-2115) from fill 135 is the earliest reliable determination from the site (SUERC-2114 being presumably residual). It would provide an appropriate date for the carinated bowl in the underlying fill 102, and given that hazelnut shells were present in 102, it is arguable that the shell that provided SUERC-2115 was redeposited from that context. This would then give a reasonable date for the first construction of the timber cursus. The determination of 3640–3490 Cal. BC (SUERC-2113) from fill 014 in cut 015 within feature 224 would then provide a date for the end of the timber phase, in stratigraphically the latest cut in the post sequence. However, the date of 3640–3490 Cal. BC (SUERC-2116) from layer 053 in the same feature is perplexing. Ashmore (chapter 28 below) suggests that SUERC-2113 may relate to material ultimately derived from the same event as SUERC-2116, and used as

packing around the later post. This would mean that cut 015 was actually later than this date. We have noted that it is entirely possible that layer 053 does not represent the earliest timber upright within the 224 complex (and that fill 154 was the packing for an even earlier post), and it may be that the history of the timber structure was played out over as much as two or three centuries. The ditch recut, dated at 2310–2120 Cal. BC (SUERC-2117), would appear to have been much later than all of this activity, and might easily be connected with the construction of one or more ring-ditches in the area surrounding the cursus in the Early Bronze Age. However, this date conflicts with the developed early Neolithic pottery from the recut.

If we consider these dates in the context of the assembled radiocarbon evidence for other cursus monuments in Scotland, England and Wales, the interpretation of the Holywood North sequence can be strengthened. On the basis of dates from the Dorset Cursus, the Lesser Stonehenge Cursus, Dorchester on Thames and Drayton, Barclay and Bayliss (1999, 25) have suggested that earthwork cursus monmuments, defined by a ditch and bank, can be assigned to a chronological horizon between 3600 and 3000 BC. That is to say, they belong to the later part of the Earlier Neolithic. By contrast, the dates from post and pit cursuses such as Holm (see below), Douglasmuir (Kendrick 1995), Bannockburn (Rideout 1997), Castle Menzies (Halliday 2002) and Dunragit (3759–3638 Cal. BC at 95.4% confidence level: SUERC-2103) are generally earlier, ranging between 4000 and 3600 BC (see Fig. 27.5). A case can therefore be made that pit and post monuments, spatially restricted to lowland Scotland, were replaced by a more widespread distribution of ditched cursuses in the period around 3600 BC. If so, the dates for Holywood North would seem to bracket the transition between the two forms of cursus architecture, and the model of a post structure replaced by a ditch-and-bank enclosure becomes the most likely option. This would be an interesting possibility in the light of Johnston's (1999) argument that the Dorset Cursus enclosed and commemorated a long-established processional way that was effectively taken out of use by its construction. A ceremonial pathway of the living became the prerogative of spirits, deities or the dead. One might suggest that at Holywood North an accessible structure in which some form of performance took place was either destroyed or fell into disrepair, and then enclosed by a ditch that transformed it into a place of memory and veneration. In the process, any remaining traces of the timber architecture would have been sealed and rendered inaccessible by the construction of the bank.

At both Holywood North and Holywood South the primary ditch fills produced no finds at all. This is very much the usual pattern for cursus monuments (Harding 1999: 33). In the case of Holywood North, both pottery sherds and worked flint were recovered from secondary positions in the ditch sequence, although given the dating

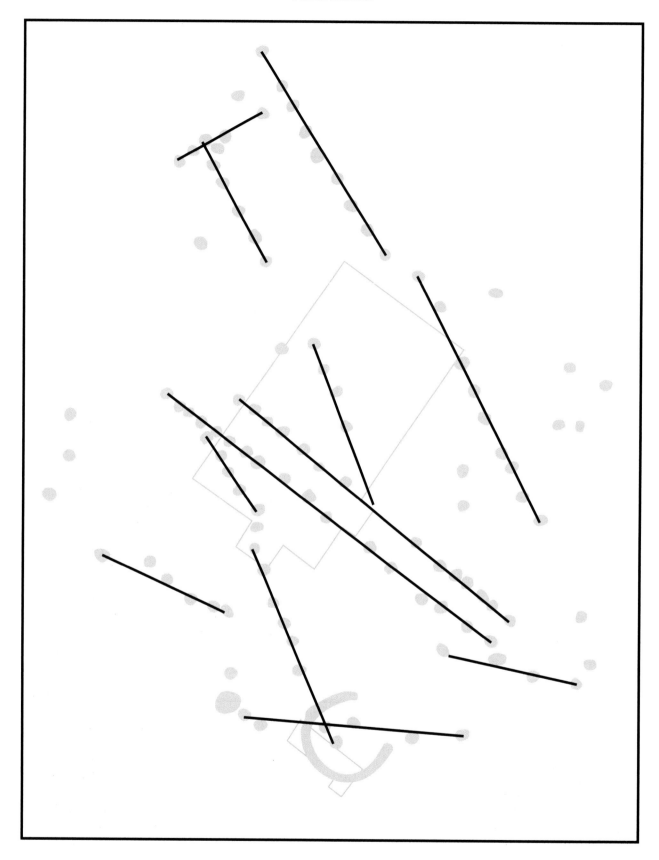

Fig. 27.4 Holm: principal alignments suggested by the features visible from the air.

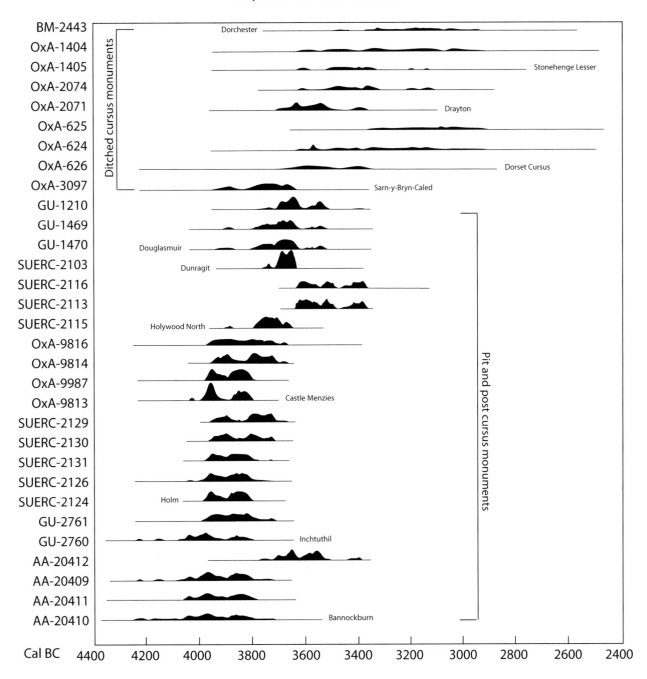

Fig. 27.5 Calibrated radiocarbon dates for pit/post and earthwork cursus monuments.

of the recutting event it is unlikely that they were contemporary with this activity. At Holywood South all of the pottery came from the pits inside the enclosure. Pit 091 contained numerous sherds from the large carinated bowl, Vessel 1, which bore ripple fluting on its lower body. Since such vessels are conventionally dated to before 3500 BC, this supports the notion that the pits pre-date the cursus bank.

Given that the stratigraphic priority of the pits at Holywood South appears to be assured, the sequence is one that fits into a broader pattern in which cursus monuments enclosed or incorporated already important

places or structures, from the pit containing human bones which pre-dated the Dorchester on Thames cursus (Bradley & Chambers 1988), to the long barrows which were encapsulated by the Dorset Cursus (Barrett, Bradley and Green 1991). As Harding puts it, cursus monuments provided a structure which bound together outstanding topographic features and existing places of significance (Harding 1999, 35–6). Harding goes on to suggest that cursuses may have had a general connection with the dead (1999, 35), echoing Bradley's (1983) suggestion that there was a broad affinity between cursus monuments, later long mounds and bank barrows. Equally, we could note the way that the Brampton, Godmanchester and Dorchester on Thames cursuses were all built onto existing long mortuary enclosures (Malim 1999, 80). However, it may be that this connection between cursus monuments and long mounds only applies to the ditched earthwork structures. The post-defined cursuses such as Holm, Douglasmuir, Bannockburn and the putative first phase at Holywood North are perhaps more comparable with the large timber halls of the earlier Neolithic. In Scotland and Northern England, such timber buildings were generally deliberately destroyed by fire, as at Claish, Balbridie and Lismore Fields (Barclay, Brophy & McGregor 2002, 102; Fairweather & Ralston 1993; Garton 1991). This purposeful burning provides a clear connection with the timber cursuses. We might argue that the shift from pit and post to ditch-and-bank cursus monuments amounted to a change from a monumentalisation of the 'house of the living' to a monumentalisation of the 'house of the dead'.

Both the Holywood monuments appear to have stood for a comparatively short period of time before the bank material began to return to the ditch. Possibly, the southern cursus had a dump bank which started to erode back into the ditch quite quickly. In the case of the northern cursus the levelling of the bank may have been deliberate, whether this took the form of collapse or backfilling, yet here there are strong indications that this did not bring the use of the site to an end. The post façade across the eastern entrance may post-date the slighting of the bank, and may or may not have been contemporary with the recutting of the ditch, and the deposit of pottery and stones in the entrance terminal. Furthermore, there are ring-ditches on both sites, located in both cases in direct association with an entrance through the cursus ditch, positioned so as to dominate the point of access into the monument, or perhaps the route by which the monument was to be crossed. So, although both structures may have had a principal phase of use which was very short, this formed part of a history of the use and modification of the immediate landscape that was much more extensive.

The contrasting structural histories of the two cursuses are complemented by two very different assemblages of carbonised plant remains (see Clarke, Chapter 25 above). At Holywood South the charcoals were dominated by oak, and despite extensive sampling only two fragments of hazelnut shell were recovered. Conversely, the material from Holywood North included a wider range of charcoals. This is curious, for the structural evidence indicates the use of oak posts at Holywood North, and their absence at Holywood South. The diverse plant material at Holywood North might suggest that twiggy wood species were used in hurdling, used either as a revetment for a gravel bank or as shuttering between free-standing uprights. But alternatively, if the massive, free-standing oak posts *were* burned in situ, they would not easily have caught alight. The burning would have been a major

undertaking, and would have required considerable quantities of brushwood to be piled up against each post and lit. It may be the burning of this material and its eventual penetration of the post-voids that the diverse charcoals at Holywood North represent. Also at Holywood North, spelt wheat and numerous hazelnut shells came from post-hole 102, which also produced sherds from a carinated bowl and the highest soil phosphate values on the entire site (which may indicate the presence of some organic material). It is possible that the contents of this feature represent a rather special deposit.

Another point that is worthy of consideration concerns the unusual use of stones within the features associated with both monuments at Holywood. In the northern cursus, numerous pebbles were deposited together with pottery and flint waste in the northern terminal of the eastern entrance, subsequent to the collapse or backfilling of the bank. Neither stones nor cultural material were found in the southern terminal. In the southern cursus, angular gritstone pebbles were found in pit 091, another large feature with a singularly complex series of fillings. Moreover, a group of cobbles was located at the bottom of the cursus ditch at the entrance terminal, echoing the terminal deposit at the northern cursus. In all of these examples, the stones concerned were quite distinct from those found in the surrounding subsoil, and they were certainly more numerous. Recently, a number of authors have pointed out the importance of materials and substances drawn from the earth (chalk, soil, stone, wood) to Neolithic architecture and cosmology (e.g. Bender 1992). I have used the term 'cosmological engineering' (Thomas 1999b) to describe the way in which the use of these materials involves not simply the manipulation of their substance, but of their meanings and connotations as well. In building monuments and placing deposits in the earth, people were able to re-organise the landscape in microcosm. At Holywood, the massive feat of constructing the ditched cursus monuments, re-creating places and transforming patterns of movement across the local topography, was complemented by more intimate events, which reconfigured the land in subtler ways.

The complex of structures at Holm Farm has evident similarities with the cursus monument at Holywood North, where lines of posts were set inside and parallel with the ditch surrounding the monument. At both sites it is possible that a complex structural sequence was involved in generating the existing archaeological evidence. Moreover, at both sites the timber uprights may have been deliberately burned, perhaps on a number of separate occasions, although this is less clear at Holywood. Further afield, post-defined cursus monuments have recently been excavated at Bannockburn, Castle Menzies and Douglasmuir (see Fig. 27.6). Douglasmuir was early in date, giving values of 3930–3510 Cal. BC (Brophy 1999, 126), and arguably had a sequence involving more than one phase of construction. Castle Menzies was earlier still, at 4040–3660 Cal. BC, but lacked the

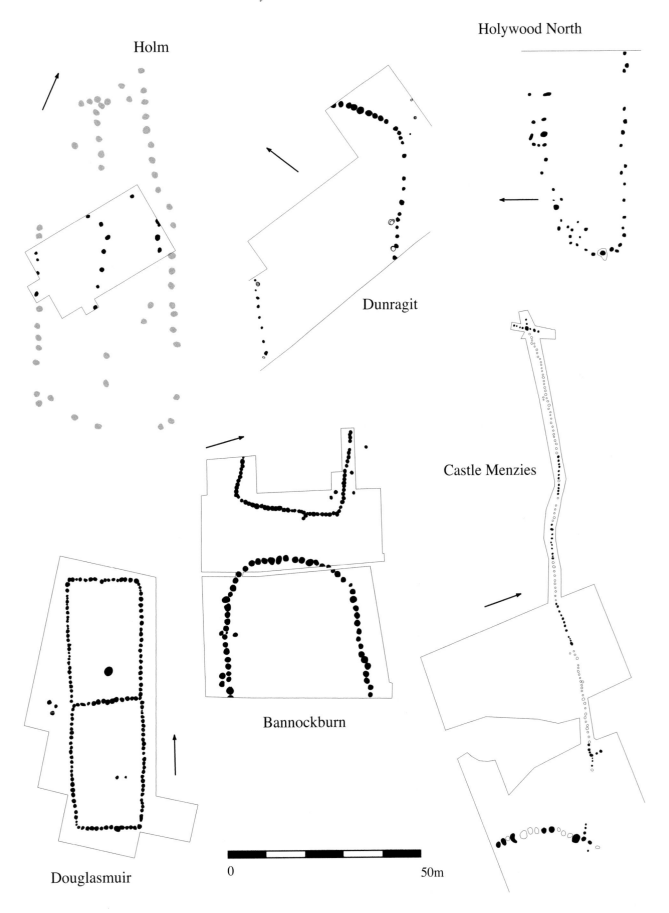

Fig. 27.6 Comparative plans of pit and post cursus monuments in Scotland.

evidence for deliberate burning found at the other sites (Halliday 2002, 14). At Bannockburn, the pit-defined Enclosure 1, dated to a little after 4000 Cal. BC, was earlier than the post structure of Enclosure 2, dated to 3300–3000 Cal. BC (Ridout 1997, 52). Interestingly, this reverses the sequence at Holm Farm, where the pit avenue was later than the post structure. The radiocarbon dates for the post-holes at Holm are consistently early. Five dates (SUERC-2124, 2126, 2129, 2130 and 2131) all fall into the bracket between 3990 and 3660 Cal. BC. Although these were all dates on charcoal, and an old wood effect may have been in operation, this none the less strengthens the case that post-defined cursus structures or alignments represented an early form of public architecture.

As at Holywood, material culture of any kind was extremely scarce at Holm. Yet the carbonised assemblage was different again, including blackthorn or cherry, hazel, pea/bean, fat hen and vetch from layer 085 in Avenue pit 060. What is most distinctive about the site is the clear indication that it was reused and the structures reconfigured on a number of occasions. At different times, at least three separate circular monuments stood on the location investigated in Trench B. The final ring ditch, cut 158/240, was possibly both preceded *and* succeeded by multiple phases of upright timbers, forming the structural elements of the 'cursus'. These structural relationships are baffling in the context of the two very late radiocarbon dates from the ring-ditch, 1420–1210 Cal. BC (SUERC-2127) and 120 Cal. BC – 60 Cal. AD (SUERC-2129). Possibly the final phase of the ring-ditch was indeed very late, but if so the posts that cut it must relate to some phase of activity quite separate from the cursus. Alternatively, if the ring-ditch had originally been associated with a bank or mound, it is conceivable that the dates are associated with recutting that took place long after the structure was originally built. It is also possible that the relationship between the ring-ditch and the cursus posts was incorrectly identified in the field, given the extreme difficulties involved in reading the gravel fills of the site. In any case, the post structures were finally replaced by the double pit alignment, leading toward another ring ditch, on a new alignment which none the less continued to lead along the river terrace. Luckily, the relationship between post-hole 252 and avenue pit 162 was clear enough to establish the overall sequence for the entire site. This was confirmed by the two dates of 2210–2020 Cal. BC (SUERC-2119) and 1320–1040 cal. BC (SUERC-2123) from layers 038 and 006 in avenue pit 022.

This potentially gives us at least eight structural phases, although their absolute sequence and duration is very difficult to elaborate. The precise details of the settings at each stage in the process are hard to ascertain, as neither regularities in soil colour, nor texture, nor the shape of post holes, nor depth, nor diameter appear to indicate coherent plans for distinct monumental phases.

For the most part, the post-holes within the two northern lines of the 'cursus' contain a greater number of recuts, and this suggests that they may have formed a distinct rectangular structure at some point. This suggestion is supported by the observation that almost all of the post-holes that were greater than one metre in diameter belonged to these two alignments. On the other hand, the greatest stratigraphic depth was demonstrated in Trench B, where post holes 201 and 241 arguably bracketed the digging of the ring ditch, thus suggesting the presence of four successive phases of posts at this point. The three relatively small post holes, 025, 026 and 029, which make up the westerly part of the southern post line each had only one cut and filling, suggesting that this part of the monument was quite short-lived. Moreover, post 138 and the others to the south-east of it lie on a different alignment, implying a separate phase of construction. Overall, the features visible from the air suggest a number of kinks and changes of direction in the various alignments (Fig. 27.4). The implication is that at different points in its history, the timber setting may have been laid out in rather different ways. Sometimes there may have been two lines of posts, sometimes three, and the length and orientation of each line may have varied. Transverse lines and arcs of postholes are visible on the air photograph plots, and these indicate that during at least some of these phases of construction the monument had been a trapezoidal enclosure, rather than simply an avenue or series of alignments.

An explanation for the complexity of the post arrangements can be found in the sequence of events that generated the complex stratigraphic sequence. After being constructed and used (perhaps over a quite short period of time), the timbers of the cursus appear to have been deliberately burnt, removed, or simply allowed to rot away. It does not appear that there was any uniform sequence in which whole groups of posts were burnt, removed or left standing: the succession in each post hole bears no particular relationships with its neighbours. After this destruction, the site was apparently abandoned for a time, yet it could have been recognised at a later point by the presence of burnt stumps or rotting timbers. However, if some time had elapsed, only a proportion of the original plan of the monument might be recoverable, and a structure would have been 'reconstructed' on the basis of the recognisable posts. This would explain why in some cases individual posts seem to have 'missed' the original post socket that they were intended to replace, and why numerous minor changes of alignment seem to have occurred. It is even possible that at some point the whole of one side of the monument was lost, so that the three main alignments of posts represent a cursus which has 'slipped' to one side, the southern side having become the northern, or vice-versa.

Alternatively, the structure may genuinely have consisted of three lines of posts at some point in its history. In this case, the parallels that we might wish to invoke might have to be drawn from further afield. The timber rows certainly appear to become wider apart to the south and east: an arrangement which suggests either the stone fans of Caithness, or the megalithic alignments of southern Brittany. In the latter case there is a further point of comparison in the way in which the uprights lead toward (or away from) an enclosed space, in the form of the ring ditch. This is very similar to the alignments at Carnac, several of which terminate with a stone enclosure.

If we can accept that the post-alignments or post-cursus had been reconstructed on a number of occasions, the statistical indistinguishability of all of the radiocarbon dates from these features suggests that these events need not have been spread over a very long period of time. A single year, or perhaps ten years, might have elapsed between each re-use. The chronological relationship between the posts and the pit alignment is more difficult to explain, since it appears that this was of the order of 1800 years later. While in the case of the post arrangements it is easy to imagine that the details of a particular configuration of architectural space might be preserved in oral tradition for months or even decades, the construction of the avenue on the same spot after such a long elapse of time is simply remarkable. What kind of awareness of the earlier structure did the people who dug the avenue pits and their associated ring-ditch have? Was it simply coincidence that caused them to construct a linear monument that terminated in a circular space, or had the importance of the place been maintained for generations? This is very similar to the questions which are raised by the similar, spatially juxtaposed, yet seemingly temporally remote enclosures at Bannockburn.

The work undertaken at the Twelve Apostles stone circle was largely negative in its outcome, but can potentially contribute something to our understanding of the monumental complex constituted by Holywood and Holm. As far as can be seen without undertaking more invasive excavations, it seems that no earlier structures existed at the Twelve Apostles, and that the stone circle was a single-phase monument. However, as we have seen, the circle has a complicated spatial relationship with both of the cursus monuments – a relationship that implies a pattern of movement between the stones and the northern cursus, passing through the southern cursus. If we hypothesise that this pathway pre-dated the construction of the ditched cursus enclosures, then it is possible that the location of the Twelve Apostles was one that had been important for some considerable while, even if it had not been marked by any structure. It might, for instance, simply have been a clearing that had been maintained over a period. Interestingly, there is an account of 1837 which states that there had been another 'Druidical temple' (that is, a stone circle) at Holm, which consisted of 'nine large stones' that has been 'broken and applied to the purposes of building' (Stell 1996, 170). Recently, Richard Bradley (2002, 96) has argued that stone circles were often the last element to be built on sites which had been host to complex sequences of Neolithic structures. Stone circles might thus represent a kind of 'closing statement', which drew a series of events and performances to an end, while at the same time commemorating them. We have noted that this seems to be the case with timber circles like those at Machrie Moor, but Bradley points to the sequences at the Clava Cairns and at recumbent stone circles like Tomnaverie, where the construction of a stone circle may have been a termination of activities that was intended from the beginning. It is interesting to hypothesise that the Twelve Apostles and the putative Holm stone circle were the closing elements of the two groups of earth and timber structures. As such, they would not simply have replaced timber circles on the same site, but actively signalled the conclusion of building and deposition in the immediate area. The Twelve Apostles referenced the cursus monuments, and effectively memorialised them, but it equally signalled that they were no longer in use.

PART THREE
CONCLUSION

28

Radiocarbon dates from the Pict's Knowe, Holywood and Holm

Patrick Ashmore

Introduction

The radiocarbon dating strategy for Holm, Holywood and the Picts Knowe was designed to determine the absolute dates for their various phases. In addition, many dates were measured from peat and other materials in the landscape surrounding the Picts Knowe, to allow an understanding of changes in the local environment from place to place and over time. These latter are considered in Chapter 2 and will not be further analysed here.

The excavations produced many fragments of charcoal from diverse contexts spanning nearly four millennia. It was expected from the observations made during excavation that some residual charcoal would be present, particularly at Holm and Holywood. Where no samples from short-lived species were available pieces of oak charcoal were dated, in the belief that this would give at least a broad indication of date, even though it was recognised that they might come from heartwood, and be centuries older than the context in which they were found. It was expected that the interpretation of dates from fragments of oak would be aided through comparisons with recently excavated similar sites, such as those at Upper Largie, Castle Menzies and Crathes, where both oak and shorter lived species had been dated. It was also anticipated that some information about the age and size of the oak trees used might be deducible.

Thirty-five dates were obtained including two from peat beneath the bank at the Pict's Knowe. In retrospect, that was far too few for sites with deeply interesting complexity. The problem was a lack of suitable samples and, probably, a model in which there were fewer construction phases than now seems likely. The dates suggest many more episodes of activity than Occam's Razor had demanded from the stratigraphic and artefactual evidence alone. The opportunity remains for a further dating programme based on the abundant charred material remaining from the sites (see Appendix 9).

In what follows I shall provide only the laboratory codes and associated calibrated dates as references in the text. Other details can be found in the diagrams and in Appendix 9.

Traces of forager activity

The earliest date from the sites, by far, is SUERC-2114 at 7530 to 7190 Cal BC, from a piece of birch charcoal from Holywood North Cursus, in layer 104 which may reflect deliberate backfilling of the ditch. It is clear from the other dates at Holywood North and elsewhere in Scotland that it does not relate to the period of construction of the cursus. It may represent the prior presence of foragers at the site, assuming that the birch was not charred naturally. Belonging a millennium or more after the first evidence for foragers in Scotland, it falls in the earlier third of a thousand-year long period when forager population sizes in Scotland seem to have been fairly stable judging by the radiocarbon dated sites (Ashmore 2004a, 87). Again judging by radiocarbon-dated sites, people were by then active throughout Scotland (except perhaps the extreme north and the Western Isles).

The early dates from Holm

The next five earliest dates come from Holm, where avenues of posts were constructed more than three millennia later (Fig. 28.1). The abundant charcoal in early pits suggested that extensive burning had taken place in the area, and that the resulting material had contributed to the primary silting of the cut features.

SUERC-2126 and 2124 are each from a piece of oak charcoal from a fill within pit 075, one of the cursus postholes (this supersedes the context description in Thomas 2004c, 161). SUERC-2131, 2130 and 2129, indistinguishable in age from each other, were also taken from individual oak charcoal fragments. SUERC-2131 came from the earliest of three posts and the other two came from the latest of three posts within cursus posthole 115.

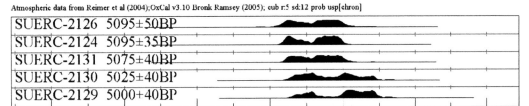

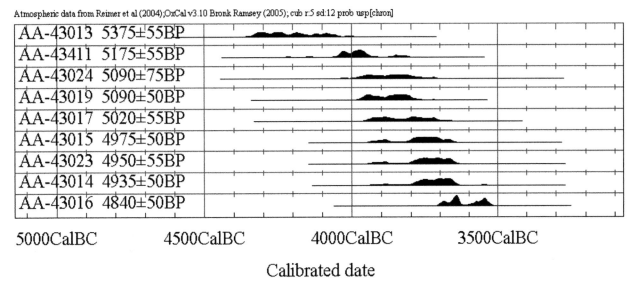

Fig. 28.1 The early construction-related dates from the pits and postholes related to the cursus at Holm.

Fig. 28.2 Dates from oak charcoal fragments in the pits of the cursus at Nether Largie, Kilmartin.

Stratigraphic evidence suggests that cursus posthole 115 should be of a broadly similar date to pit 075. SUERC-2129, the stratigraphically latest and radiocarbon youngest age, dates to between 3950 and 3690 cal BC, and, slightly more probably than not (55.7%), dates to between 3800 and 3700 Cal. BC. Given that it comes from the stratigraphically latest of the contexts in posthole 115, it is not at all surprising that SUERC-2129 cannot be combined satisfactorily with all of the other four dates at once (Agreement test: A= 55.6%(<A'c= 60.0%)), suggesting that there is a significant amount of chronological depth in the sequence of early events at Holm. It is frustrating that, because they cannot be shown to be of precisely the same true date as each other, none of the sample measurements can be combined with others to provide greater precision (Ward and Wilson 1978). Even if SUERC-2126 and 2124 were from the same tree, they may come from very different sets of tree rings.

The earlier three dates all suggest that the charred oak wood used for dating last exchanged carbon with the atmosphere before c. 3800 BC. All five oak charcoal fragments may have come from outer tree rings of trees cut down shortly before the fragments reached the contexts in which they were found. However, the perfectly acceptable possibility that some at least of the posts and pits at the cursus date to before 3800 Cal. BC has to be treated with some caution. There is abundant evidence from similar sites elsewhere in Scotland for the presence of oak heartwood charcoal fragments with radiocarbon ages older than the contexts in which they were found.

Comparanda

At the Upper Largie cursus, Kilmartin nine ages were obtained from the cursus postholes, ranging from 5375±55 BP (AA-43013) to 4840±50 (AA-43016). The younger dates suggest a true date for cutting down of trees for the cursus timbers some time in the first half of the 4th millennium BC, perhaps most probably between about 3800 and 3650 cal. BP (Ellis in prep.).

Such robust evidence is not available from the dates from the pit-defined enclosure at Cowie Road,

Bannockburn, (Rideout 1997, 52–3). Nevertheless it does seem to indicate presence of oak charcoal fragments considerably older in radiocarbon terms than the contexts in which they were found. Very little charcoal survived from Phase 1 deposits in the pits, and none was dated. Three oak charcoal dates from Phase 2 deposits in Pit 6 suggested wood of about 4000 to 3800 cal BC, but the other phase 2 date, from hazel charcoal in Pit 25, lay between 3780 and 3385 cal. BC (AA-20412 4830 ± 60). It seems quite likely from the apparent rarity of charcoal from Phase 1 and the difference in date between the oak and hazel assigned to Phase 2 that the oak charcoal fragments were from wood one or two centuries old at the time of Phase 2 of the enclosure.

Less directly comparable, perhaps, is the range of dates from the timber hall at Crathes Warrenfield (Murray & Murray 2005: 155). The hall lies close to an alignment of pits which may, provisionally, be interpreted as having contained fires, and has produced a date (SUERC-4031: 5025+/35 BP) from an oak charcoal fragment of 3950 to 3700 Cal. BC (Murray pers. comm.). The hall itself has produced both three oak charcoal dates and nine dates from short-lived species. Of these latter, SUERC-4033 and 4044 came from contexts sealed below post-pipes while other samples appeared to line the sides of post-pits. Thus the two older oak dates seem to represent wood dating to the centuries around 4000 BC while the short-lived species belong between 3800 and 3650 cal. BC, implying that oak timbers a few centuries old had been used. Similar but slightly more ambiguous evidence could be adduced from the nearby hall at Balbridie (Fairweather & Ralston 1993) and that at Claish (Barclay *et al.* 2002, 98).

The pattern of dates from the large hall-like timber burial enclosure, at Littleour, Perth and Kinross, is much the same, although the site belongs to a later period, with oak charcoal from post-holes dating considerably earlier than pot encrustations and birch (Barclay & Maxwell 1998, 59).

Interpretation of the early fourth millennium dates from Holm

All this suggests that the early Holm dates must be treated with some restraint. The evidence from Upper Largie and Crathes shows fairly unambiguously that large oak trees a few centuries old were used for substantial timber structures at about this time. The pattern of dates at other early 4th millennium sites is similar. That, of course, does not mean that the oak charcoal dated at Holm must also be from heartwood. It could be from sapwood or from small branches used to fire the main posts. Nevertheless, it seems likely that at least some of the oak charcoal found in the cursus contexts at Holm was from mature trees used to provide wood for substantial posts. Overall, and in an informal sense, it seems to me that there is a better than evens chance that Holm dates to 3800 BC or later. Nevertheless, the abundance of charcoal from early contexts suggests that it may be feasible to test this interpretation further. Careful macroplant analysis of potential samples may reveal charcoal likely to represent tree rings which were young at the time they were charred.

Whatever its precise date of construction, the cursus and associated timbers at Holm are broadly similar in date to a set of substantial timber monuments, alignments, avenues and halls, which appeared from Aberdeenshire in the north-east to Dumfries and Galloway the south-west of Scotland in the first or second quarter of the fourth millennium BC. Fine carinated pottery occurs at many of those sites, as discussed below.

The earliest date from Holywood North potentially related to its construction

The earliest date from Holywood potentially related to its construction is SUERC-2115, measured at 3890 to 3650 cal BC from a hazel nut shell from a fill (135) of pit 102. The fill is probably the contents of a collapsed primary post-pipe. Pit 102 is one of the main line of post-holes

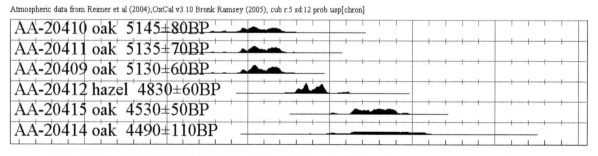

Atmospheric data from Reimer et al (2004);OxCal v3.10 Bronk Ramsey (2005); cub r:5 sd:12 prob usp[chron]

| AA-20410 oak 5145±80BP |
| AA-20411 oak 5135±70BP |
| AA-20409 oak 5130±60BP |
| AA-20412 hazel 4830±60BP |
| AA-20415 oak 4530±50BP |
| AA-20414 oak 4490±110BP |

5000CalBC 4500CalBC 4000CalBC 3500CalBC 3000CalBC 2500CalBC 2000CalBC

Calibrated date

Fig. 28.3 Dates from Cowie Road, Bannockburn.

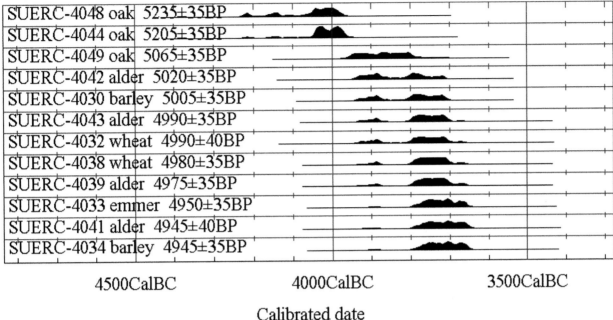

Fig. 28.4 Dates from the timber hall at Crathes Warrenfield.

inside the ditched cursus. With its packing 101, it is interpreted as primary. It formed part of either a free-standing post-enclosure or a timber revetment for an internal bank of the ditched enclosure. The packing (101) contained large amounts of charcoal, as well as numerous fragments of carinated bowl and some fragments of burnt nut shell. Stones in the packing appeared to have been exposed to fire, but there was no indication that burning had taken place in the pit itself.

Given the amount of modern truncation of the site, it may be that hazelnuts and carinated pottery sherds were lying on the surface of the site when the posthole was dug. If so the contents of fill 101 may represent earlier (but archaeological invisible) activity very close to the posthole. However, the lack of similar material in adjacent features could also suggest that the pottery and charcoal was added purposefully to this particular posthole when the post was set up. The material in the packing may thus have come from a different site, local or distant, and it may be curated ancestral material or material dug up from an ancestral site. Further, because of the lack of charred hazel in adjacent contemporary features, it does not seem likely that there was a fresh flux of material like the charred hazel nut shell which provided the date. Admittedly, the possibility that the nut shell was part of combustible material brought in to fire the posts cannot be rejected, because not much of that material need have been visible in the highly truncated features at Holywood North. All this said, it seems most likely that the charred hazel nut shell in post pipe 135 derived immediately from its associated post-packing 101. If it be accepted that the immediate origin of the nut shell was indeed the set of

potsherds and charred material in the packing which had collapsed or silted into the empty post-pipe, it provides an indication of the date of the carinated pottery. Indeed, the chain of argument above is supported by the fact that the date for the piece of hazel in the filling of the post pipe at Holywood is similar to the earliest dates from the Picts Knowe, from material also associated with carinated pottery.

The date of activities associated with carinated pottery at the Picts Knowe, and other sites with carinated pottery

The earliest group of dates from the Picts Knowe (SUERC-2093 to 2096) relates to activities conducted by people using carinated pottery. The dates were measured from two fragments of alder charcoal, one of hazel charcoal and a charred hazel nut shell, all from pits sealed by peat below the enclosure bank. Although these ages are statistically indistinguishable from each other there is no a priori reason why they should all have exactly the same true date, so they cannot be combined. They may represent activities lasting less than a year or many decades.

Comparanda for the dates associated with carinated pottery at the Picts Knowe

Several settlements and structures with carinated pottery have been dated to about 3800 cal. BC and later. In what follows I have used only a selection of early dates from contexts with carinated pottery, omitting most of those

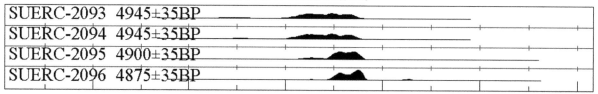

Atmospheric data from Reimer et al (2004);OxCal v3.10 Bronk Ramsey (2005); cub r:5 sd:12 prob usp[chron]

SUERC-2093	4945±35BP
SUERC-2094	4945±35BP
SUERC-2095	4900±35BP
SUERC-2096	4875±35BP

4200CalBC 4000CalBC 3800CalBC 3600CalBC 3400CalBC 3200CalBC

Calibrated date

Fig. 28.5 Dates from pits containing carinated pottery at the Picts Knowe.

with problems (Ashmore 2004c, 131). A forthcoming study by Alison Sheridan will cover a wider chronological and geographical range of sites (Sheridan forthcoming). I shall rest some suggestions on combinations of dates for short-lived material from destruction deposits, but the exact contemporaneity required in each case for valid combination can merely be suggested, not demonstrated (Ward and Wilson 1978).

The earliest date (3960 to 3660 cal. BC) from a Scottish site with carinated pottery comes from a pit at Carzield, Dumfriesshire (Maynard 1993 Beta-68480: 5010±70 BP). However no charcoal identification to species was reported, and the dated material may have included several pieces of charcoal. That increases the likelihood that the sample included charcoal old at the time that the pit was filled and thus the date has to be treated with caution (Ashmore 1999). The earliest non-oak date (3970 to 3640 cal. BC) from the timber hall with carinated pottery at Balbridie, Deeside came from a crab apple in destruction deposits (Fairweather and Ralston 1993; OxA-1769 5010±90 BP). Combining that measurement with two other ages of short-lived samples from destruction levels, on the basis that they may have died in the same year because they should not have survived more than a year before being charred, produces a date range of 3790 to 3630 cal. BC. A similarly early date (3950 to 3700 cal. BC) comes from a charred naked barley grain found in a post-pit of the nearby timber hall at Crathes, at which carinated pottery was also present (Murray 2004; SUERC-4030 5005±35 BP). If that measurement is combined with four other ages of short-lived samples from destruction levels, again on the basis that the samples probably died in the same year, they suggest a date range of 3785 to 3705 cal. BC.

Four of the five dates from short-lived samples of grain and hazel nut shell from an ovoid structure at Garthdee Road, Aberdeen, with well-sealed surviving occupation deposits and hearths, including carinated pottery, suggested a date between 3780 and 3650 BC. The other, although probably of much the same date, also had a roughly one in twenty chance of lying between 3910 and 3870 cal. BC (Murray 2005, 165).

A complex pit at the timber hall at Claish Farm, Stirling included a piece of hazel dating to between 3950 to 3660 cal. BC (Barclay *et al.* 2002; AA-49645 5000 ± 50 BP). Combining that measurement with four other hazel nut shell ages from destruction levels, on the basis that they may have died in the same year, produces a date range of 3705 to 3645 cal. BC.

Hazel charcoal from one of a cluster of large pits at Dubton farm, Brechin, Angus was dated to between 3890 and 3710 cal. BC. The pit included parts of 3 vessels including Impressed Ware and carinated bowl pots. The large plant assemblage included naked and hulled barley, emmer and bread wheat and weed seeds (Cameron 2002, 68; AA-39951 4990±45 BP).

Recent excavations in East Lothian in advance of the construction of the A1 Expressway between Haddington and Dunbar have revealed two early sites with mortuary structures, Eweford and Pencraig Hill, which belong early in the fourth millennium BC. The earliest dates associable with structures at Eweford (all from single pieces of short-lived material) are SUERC-5280 at 3950 to 3780 cal. BC, SUERC-5290 at 3950 to 3770 cal. BC and SUERC-5298 at 3940 to 3710 cal. BC (MacGregor 2005, 169–70); those at Pencraig Hill are SUERC-7663 at 3950 to 3710 cal. BC and SUERC-7657 at 3950 to 3700 cal. BC (McLellan 2005, 171). Although not directly related to major timber components at Eweford, these dates suggest an earlier horizon of activity than that indicated by the dates for timber halls and alignments. There are two apparently later pit alignments near the Eweford enclosure. A piece of willow charcoal from a post-pipe within the northern pit alignment may represent portions of a linear arrangement comprising uprights holding wattle. It suggests a date between 3520 and 3360 cal BC (SUERC-5347: 4685 +/-40 BP). A piece of willow charcoal from a post-pipe fill in the southern pit alignment dated to between 2870 and 2580 cal BC (SUERC-5340: 4140+/-35) was interpretable in a similar way (MacGregor 2005, 169–70).

The cursus and the ditch at Holywood North

At the north end of the cursus was a shallow pit (224),

about 3 metres long, with a complex set of fills. A large post, packed with large stones, had been set into it, in posthole 238. Cut by this posthole, at the base of the large pit, was a 2.6m long layer of oak charcoal (053) which produced a date SUERC-2116 of 3640 to 3370 cal. BC.

Once Pit 224 had filled up, it was cut by posthole 015 of the timber setting inside the cursus enclosure ditch. The fill 014 of this posthole was very similar to that of other postholes of the setting in this area. It contained oak charcoal which produced a date (SUERC-2113) between 3640 and 3370 cal BC.

The two dates are indistinguishable. It seems possible that the charcoal in fill 014 of posthole 015 derived from (potentially much earlier) burning events. In other words, charcoal from the burnt post in 238 or the spread of charcoal 053 was included in the soil dug out to create the posthole 015 for the timber setting. Soil containing this charcoal was then packed round the new post. The main alternative is that the oak charcoal came from burning of the new post in 015. But unlike posthole 184 of the setting, which contained a great deal of charcoal in the pipe, the fill of 015 was homogenous with no charcoal concentrations. It therefore seems less likely that the stray pieces of charcoal in it derived from burning of the post than that they derive at second hand from the fills of the large shallow pit. It is of course possible that the charcoal was associated with some other event during the setting of successive posts into the large shallow pit 224.

A pit or more likely the end of a small ditch was found outwith the enclosing ditch of the cursus. A piece of oak charcoal from the fill 185 of this cut feature 186 produced a date (SUERC-2118) of between 2580 and 2340 cal. BC. In future it may be possible to date one of the hazel nut fragments from the same context to reduce the uncertainty introduced by the use of non-roundwood oak charcoal. It was not clear whether 186/185 was a re-cut of 666/221, or a distinct and later feature cutting through the former purely by chance.

A piece of oak roundwood charcoal from a shallow recut of the cursus ditch itself produced a date (SUERC-2117) of between 2310 and 2030 cal. BC. While on purely stratigraphic grounds the small ditch which produced SUERC-2118 and the cursus ditch might have fallen into a single archaeological phase there seems to be no

pressing reason why they cannot have been very different in date from each other. So although it may be that the difference between the two dates reflects a considerable age at death for the oak charcoal from the small recut feature outside the cursus, it is equally possible that the difference is an indication of long-continued activities in the area.

These slight features at Holywood may not seem very exciting, but the more easily interpreted date SUERC-2117 falls into a distinctly interesting period when old ways had given way to new ones in many parts of Scotland, but had not replaced them everywhere. This seems to be a period when ancestral rights and identities are likely to have been challenged. Such concerns may provide a context for re-establishment of the cursus ditch at Holywood.

Various activities at by then ancient sites have been recorded. In what follows, I shall exclude weak dates (Ashmore 2004c, 125–7). For convenience, I shall consider those dated samples whose central ages fall into the 95% confidence span of the age from Holywood (thus between 3845 BP and 3705 BP). A preferable approach, including only those dates which are not significantly different from SUERC-2117 in a statistical sense, would take far longer and produce results not very different at the level of generalisation I am attempting here.

At Machrie Moor on Arran it seems almost as if traces of a ceremonial centre were purposefully obliterated. Cultivation succeeded timber circles. Charcoal from features associated with fence lines and well-fertilised ard-cultivated fields was dated to between 2300 and 2000 cal. BC (GU-2319 3770±50 BP; GU-2317 (3780± 50 BP) and GU-2322 (3840± 50 BP). The ceremonial identity of the place was subsequently reasserted, when stone circles were built in identical positions to the timber circles (Haggarty 1991).

At Littleour, Perth and Kinross, oak charcoal from a posthole immediately to the west of a major timber structure 22m long by 7–8m broad and associated with use of grooved ware, provided a date between 2500 and 1850 cal. BC. This and other dates from the site suggest that grooved ware was still being deposited in pits at a time when beakers were in common use (Barclay & Maxwell 1998, 59; GU-4829: 3730±90).

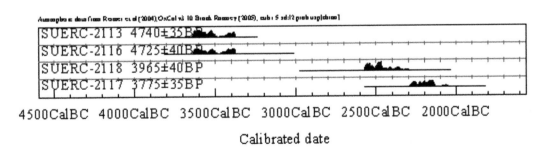

SUERC-2113 4740±35BP					
SUERC-2116 4725±40BP					
SUERC-2118 3965±40BP					
SUERC-2117 3775±35BP					

4500CalBC   4000CalBC   3500CalBC   3000CalBC   2500CalBC   2000CalBC

Calibrated date

Fig. 28.6 Dates from pits and the ditch at Holywood North.

In the north of Scotland, chambered tombs were still in use, albeit perhaps not generally for burials. A token burial was inserted into that at Embo, near Dornoch, on the east coast of Highland. Two human vertebrae were tucked behind a stone. The pottery associated with this phase of activity was dominated by beaker. Elsewhere single inhumation was common; but single cremation in pits was far from rare. There is a communal burial of six bodies in a cist at Mill Road, Linlithgow (Cook 2000, 81) and a small inhumation cemetery at Dryburn Bridge in East Lothian (Dunwell forthcoming); and cremation cemeteries of rather different type to each other have been found at Pencraig Wood (McLellan 2005) and Eweford in East Lothian (MacGregor 2005). Many of the dated inhumation burials were accompanied by insular beakers, 10 of which are nominally earlier than SUERC-2117 and 10 later.

Beaker sherds were also found in a pit in a probable settlement site Fox Plantation, Dunragit, dating to 2460 to 2040 cal. BC (AA-28050 3795±55 BP). There is more evidence for agriculture than for preceding periods. At Sligeanach, South Uist a soil overlay ard-marks of the earliest cultivation level containing beaker sherds. A cattle metapodial from the soil dated to between 2280 to 1950 cal. BC (Parker Pearson, Sharples & Symonds 2004, 21-2; OxA-8920 3710±45). The earliest large caches of charred grain are found at Eweford, near Dunbar in East Lothian dating to between 2200 and 2020 cal. BC (Macgregor 2005; SUERC-5296: 3735±35 BP), and the well-known cache from Ness of Gruting falls only slightly later than this period (Barcham 1980, 504). Metal objects make their first appearance; a burial at Rameldry Farm, Fife was accompanied by a fancy dagger (Baker 2003) and that at Tavelty Farm, Kintore, Aberdeenshire, dating between 2300 and 1880 cal BC, included a beaker, part of a small copper dagger and other grave goods (Ralston 1996: 149; GU-2169: 3710 ±70).

Some of this diversity was probably due to regional differences. Some similarities in radiocarbon age may be due to the probabilistic nature of radiocarbon dating. Nevertheless, it does suggest a period in which the reactivation of by then ancient monuments at Holm and Holywood may have been felt necessary to refresh memories of land rights and status (Campbell 2006, 102) during a period of significant change.

Peat growth at the Picts Knowe

The site of the by then ancient settlement at the Picts Knowe was covered by peat in the last quarter of the third millennium, or very slightly later. The base of the peat was dated by AA-21249 to between 2400 and 1850 cal. BC. The top was dated by AA-21250 to between 2350 and 1970 cal. BC. The age for the top of the peat was thus slightly earlier, radiometrically, than that of the bottom. Analysis with OxCal 3.10 using a simple sequence model suggests that the true date of the upper peat slice probably lay between 2280 and 1960 cal. BC. The favoured interpretation is that peat growth ceased because of burial by a freshly constructed bank. The significance of this is discussed below.

Later activities at Holm

At Holm, a piece of hazel charcoal (SUERC-2119) from the penultimate fill 038 of pit 022 of the pit avenue has been dated to between 2280 and 1970 Cal. BC. The double pit alignment or avenue succeeded the post avenues on the site. Another and very significantly later terminus post-quem for filling up of this pit is provided by a piece of heather charcoal from its final (surviving) fill 006, dating (SUERC-2123) to between 1380 and 1040 Cal. BC. Various fills in the pits of the avenue contained charcoal. Most commonly it occurred as flecks or stray pieces. The charcoal rich layers included the primary fill of Pit 015, a high fill of Pit 060 and the upper fills of Pit 023. The Pit 069 primary fills were sterile, but the penultimate fill included patches of charcoal and apparently burnt sandstone. Only in one case is it suggested that the charcoal might relate to burning in situ, fill 042 of Pit 023 suggesting a small post. Fill 103 of Pit 060 resembled a post-pipe although there was no evidence of burning in situ. Given that the two dates from

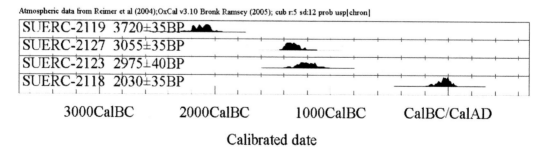

Atmospheric data from Reimer et al (2004);OxCal v3.10 Bronk Ramsey (2005); cub r:5 sd:12 prob usp[chron]

SUERC-2119	3720±35BP
SUERC-2127	3055±35BP
SUERC-2123	2975±40BP
SUERC-2118	2030±35BP

3000CalBC   2000CalBC   1000CalBC   CalBC/CalAD

Calibrated date

Fig. 28.7 Dates from later activities at Holm.

Pit 022 were so different from each other, it seems possible that some or all of the pits remained open for many centuries, filling up gradually or sporadically. The lower fills of these pits were commonly loose and friable, and except in the case of Pit 015 fairly charcoal free suggesting rapid erosion of the pit sides. Higher fills tended to be tenacious clays, suggesting waterborne silts from a vegetation-poor landscape. One explanation might be episodes of cultivation in the immediate vicinity, perhaps commonly preceded by burning of the ground-cover. If so the heather in the upper fill of Pit 022 may represent the start of an episode of cultivation, and possibly the hazel in the penultimate fill (also clayey) represents an earlier one. However, allowing for the fact that the hazel might have been residual, which means that its chronological relationship to the original digging of the pits is completely ambiguous, neither date need relate to creation of the pit avenue.

In the area of Trench B at the end of the post alignments there was a series of inter-cutting structures. A piece of alder charcoal (Sample 058) from the principal fill 160 of a ring-ditch slot 170 within the complex was dated (SUERC-2127) to between 1420 and 1210 Cal. BC. This was a less substantial ring ditch than the main ring ditch and appeared to be earlier than it, although the point at which they met was complicated by the presence of yet earlier features, and it is possible that the slot 170 was broken at this point, leaving no direct stratigraphic relationship between the two ring ditches.

The main ring ditch in this area was narrow and straight-sided, with a sharp break of slope at the top and a flat base. The earliest fill in the ditch was a loose reddish-brown gravel, which appeared to be material that had weathered from the ditch sides. Above was what appeared to be a deliberately packing of dense pebbly clay and above that again was a silty clay 155, with fewer stones and occasional charcoal flecks which produced a piece of alder charcoal with a date (SUERC-2128) of 160 cal. BC to cal. AD 60. Layer 155 appeared to be material that had washed in from above. Therefore the charcoal may have lain in the source of that material for a long time before it was incorporated in the deposit in which it was found. However, no old ground surface was recorded between the pebbly fill and the in-washed material, so it seems unlikely that the washed-in deposit formed a considerable time after the pebbly fill was put into the ditch.

The terminus post quem of between 1420 and 1210 Cal. BC provided for the smaller, earlier ring ditch by SUERC-2127 is broadly similar to that for small ring cairns and other small structures which appear to represent re-use of much earlier ceremonial complexes in several parts of Scotland (Ashmore 2001, 4). As at the beginning of the second millennium BC at Holywood and Holm, so at some time in the second half of the millennium there was a renewed interest in the area for what appear to be non-domestic activities. It is not impossible that the late date from the main ring ditch, allied to the extremely complex inter-cutting of many features, hints at some sort of continuity. The implications of such long-term continuity are discussed in Chapter 29 below.

The Pict's Knowe in the first millennia BC and AD

Six samples from the bank and primary ditch fills at the Pict's Knowe produced a range of ages (AA-17475, AA-17476, SUERC-2098, SUERC-2097, AA-17473 and AA-17474). They could not all have been of identical date (T=35.98; 5% = 11.1). Although the three oldest dates could all have been from wood grown in a single year, the next oldest could not have been from the same year (T=13.59 5% 7.8). The latest date (AA-17474) is significantly later than the others. What is more, the two dates from the upper core of the bank (SUERC-2098 at between 120 cal BC and cal AD 70 from a piece of hazel charcoal and SUERC-2097 at between cal AD 30 and 240 from an oak twig) were significantly different from each other. These two dates came from orange sandy loams with large fragments of sandstone which capped the main body of the bank. Overlying them was a series of inter-leaved hard sandy layers which appeared to be individual dumps of material. Each will have had a radiocarbon age similar to that of the atmosphere at their time of death. The likeliest explanation for the difference between them is that the hazel at between 120 cal. BC and cal. AD 70 was residual. The oak twig dated to between 30 and 240 cal. AD probably provides a safe terminus post quem (of 30 AD) for the sandstone-rich layer of the main inner bank and the overlying dumps of material. However, caution is required, because this close to the entrance all of the deposits were thin, and potentially compromised by animal disturbance.

One obvious question is whether the bank is best dated by the top of the underlying peat (which lacked any evidence for the soil formation which might have been expected if it had stopped growing naturally and lain open for nearly two millennia) or by these two dates for charcoal in this sandstone-rich layer of the bank make-up. The layer seems to have been broadly similar to other layers below it (red loams with sandstone). There does not seem to have been a relic land surface between any layers in this section of the bank, as might be expected if it was built in two widely separated phases. In other words, it seems to have been of unitary construction. However, it is possible that there were longitudinal variations in the bank. If a bank had been created between 2280 and 1960 cal. BC, as the cessation of underlying peat growth suggests (see above), there may have been gaps in it or it may have degraded severely in some areas through a combination of natural erosion, animal trampling and ploughing. Also or instead, the original entrance may have been reduced in size during the late first millennium BC when the bank was refurbished. It is thus possible that in parts of its circuit it was in effect of unitary construction because recognisable traces of the early bank were absent, particularly near to the original entrance or entrances.

Two of the samples (AA-17475 and AA-17476) from primary ditch fills also seem to have been residual. They belong between 350 cal. BC and cal. AD 50. They came from pieces of wood incorporated in the gradual build up of primary ditch silts by collapse or discard of wood into the ditch: not a deliberate deposition. Two later dates from wood and charred wood near the upper surface of slightly higher primary fill 0119 (AA-17473 at cal. AD 60 to 330 and AA-17474 at cal. AD 130 to 440) could suggest that the primary silting was a long drawn out process. However the fragments used for dating were revealed by the removal of the recut fill (0122) in the western ditch cutting, and it was recognised during excavation that they may have originated during the process of recutting itself. What seemed to be evidence of trampling was observed at the base of the recut, which may have resulted in little bits of wood penetrating the fills below. It seems most economical then to suppose that the fragments dated by AA-17473 and AA-17474 are to be associated with the recut rather than the primary ditch fills. Alternatively, this part of the ditch near the entrance may have been recut completely: the earliest silts in this area may have formed after the main recut for which evidence survived and probably after subsequent partial cleaning. In broad terms the difference between these two possible explanations is not important: what is important is that there are two perfectly rational ways of explaining the late dates, both involving cleaning or recutting of the ditch near the entrance. Indeed, it would not be surprising if this part of the ditch was more carefully maintained than others.

The piece of wood dated by AA-17472 to between 160 cal. BC and cal. AD 220 came from a different recut to that containing green clay, and while its date is not statistically different from that of the objects in the green

clay-filled recut when it and they are considered as a group, it is the earliest date in the group. It is probably a casual inclusion rather than having been deposited purposefully.

The dates from the wooden artefacts and other pieces of wood in the green clay fill of the main recut of the ditch are not, as a group, significantly different to each other. If deposition of the other dated objects were a unitary event, and involved pieces of wood with outer rings all of the same age, it could be argued that the dates can be combined. However, there are really too many imponderables to allow combination in this way to be valid, and because it is possible that they were deposited over a considerable period, one should say only that they were deposited some time in the early first to early fourth century AD range allowed by the individual dates.

Comparanda for the enclosure at the Picts Knowe

There are few radiocarbon dates unambiguously related to the construction of Scottish henges. There are rather more for activities conducted in their interiors. It can rarely be shown whether the henges were built round existing structures (in this I include burials) or the structures were created within pre-existing henges. Further, there is a general consensus that the term itself, along with 'hengiform structure', covers a wide range of sites many of which lack obvious links to one another apart from one or two of their physical attributes.

There are few reliable dates directly relevant to construction of a large enclosure with a ditch inside a bank. The earliest and indeed the only fairly reliable Scottish dates come from the primary ditch fills of the Stones of Stenness in Orkney. They suggest that the bank and ditch were constructed around 3000 BC (Ritchie 2000, 125; 2001, 125). The henge (in the sense of bank and ditch) at Balfarg in Fife is not dated; all of the dates relate to structures now inside the ditch. There is a fairly

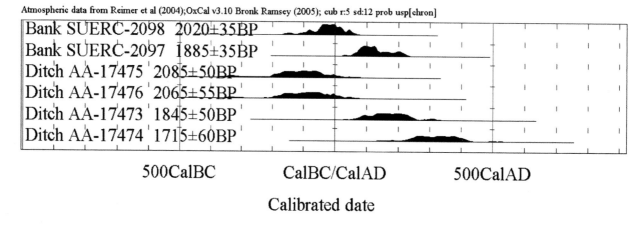

Fig. 28.8 Dates from the bank and early ditch silts at the Picts Knowe.

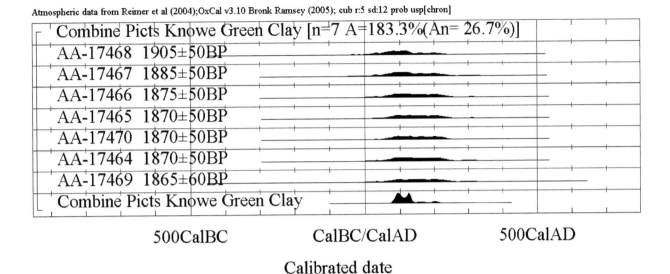

Atmospheric data from Reimer et al (2004);OxCal v3.10 Bronk Ramsey (2005); cub r:5 sd:12 prob usp[chron]

Combine Picts Knowe Green Clay [n=7 A=183.3%(An= 26.7%)]
AA-17468 1905±50BP
AA-17467 1885±50BP
AA-17466 1875±50BP
AA-17465 1870±50BP
AA-17470 1870±50BP
AA-17464 1870±50BP
AA-17469 1865±60BP
Combine Picts Knowe Green Clay

500CalBC   CalBC/CalAD   500CalAD

Calibrated date

Fig. 28.9 Dates from wood in the green clay at the Picts Knowe.

large corpus of dates related to burials and other features inside a ditched enclosure (often with no information about the relationship of bank to ditch). It is extremely difficult to point to Scottish structures with the bank outside the ditch dating to around the time (between 2280 and 1960 cal. BC) that the peat underlying the bank at the Pict's Knowe ceased to grow.

It was not until two millennia later that a broadly comparable site appears to have been constructed. A comparison can be drawn with the settlement at Shiels Farm, near Glasgow, originally interpreted as a henge from air photographs. It measured about 42m E–W by 36m N–S, with a single entrance in the east. There may have been round structures in the interior. Set across the entrance to the enclosure there was a curious rectangular structure measuring 5 by 3m, the longer sides consisting of upright timbers close-set in stone-lined holes. The open end of the building faced the interior of the enclosure, and clearly there was a relationship between the two. On the south side it seems that an attempt had been made to stabilise the side of the ditch by applying a clay lining. The ditch bottom was filled with waterlogged silts some 0.75m deep. Wooden objects in the silts included a small dome-shaped piece of wood and a stick with deliberately charred ends (Alexander 2000, 163–4; Scott 1974, 82–3).

The ages (SRR-576, 1930± 100 BP, and SRR-577, 1640±80) from alder wood in this organic layer at Shiels are unsatisfactory for most modern purposes because of their large errors, for both are probably best treated as having a greater error than that quoted by the laboratory (Ashmore et al 2000). Once their errors are increased to ±140 and ±100 respectively, they suggest dates between cal. AD 100 and 650, and between 400 cal. BC and cal AD 550. The earlier date is not distinguishable from those for the wood in the green clay fill of the ditch at the Picts Knowe, although the later date remains distinct (an

attempt to combine it with the others shows that SRR-577 fails the agreement test (A= 18.0%(<A'c= 60.0%)). However, truncation at Shiels had removed all the layers of the bank and those underlying it. Without the survival of peat under the bank the bank and ditch at the Picts Knowe could easily have been interpreted as belonging exclusively to the late first millennium BC and later. Conversely, Shiels may have had an earlier phase, which means that it should not be adduced as support for any suggestion that the Picts Knowe enclosure was of a single, late phase. It does however show that first millennium creation or refurbishment of Scottish enclosures with banks outside the ditch was not restricted to the Picts Knowe. It is all too easy to suppose that enclosures with this feature reflect a desire to resuscitate the ancient importance of the location. However there is another possibility. In areas of high rainfall, low-lying enclosures with banks inside the ditch may have been susceptible to flooding. The earlier peat growth at the Pict's Knowe demonstrates that its drainage was impeded. The re-cut ditch may therefore have served a practical function as a drain.

Discussion

The radiocarbon dating record does not suggest any particular growth in non-farming populations in any area of Scotland in the period from about 4200 to about 3800 cal BC. Indeed the current picture is that the number of sites displaying evidence of forager lifestyles remained remarkably constant from before 7000 BC to perhaps as late as 3400 BC, apart from two peaks around 6500 and 4400 cal. BC. What the currently available evidence suggests is that practises associated with farmers appeared over a period of at most a few generations in several parts of Scotland south of the Highlands. Various models including at one extreme demic expansion and at the other trait adoption-diffusion have been suggested for the introduction of farming lifestyles into areas previously dominated by foragers (Gkiasta *et al.* 2003, 45–7; Bentley *et al.* 2003, 63, 65). Thomas (2003, 72–3) preferred a model involving strengthened social networks and exchanges of ideas in a heterogeneous change from foraging-dominated to farming-dominated lifestyles. The radiocarbon dating evidence from Scotland, taken on its own, precludes neither demic diffusion (Ashmore 2004a, 2004b) nor trait-adoption models (Thomas 2003). It is hard to think of any evidence other than from DNA and stable isotopes from human remains which could securely distinguish between them (Bentley *et al.* 2003). Thus the traces of settlement with carinated pottery at the Picts Knowe and at or near Holywood, dating to within at most a few centuries from the time when farming practises enter the archaeological record in Scotland and northern England, may represent people whose recent ancestors were incomers or foragers. My own preference is for a model incorporating major influences at around 3800 cal. BC, or, at least, significantly after 4000 BC, from incoming farmers (without precluding the possibility that some foragers took up farming, but with the strong suggestion that if they did so then they learnt these practices from close neighbours rather than distant farming groups) basically because I see no evidence for forager-style artefacts at any of the early timber structure sites, nor any sign of pre-farming communities settled most of the year round in one location, nor for strengthening long distance social networks amongst foragers. The most probable origins of new social practises are the countries facing the north sea (Barclay *et al.* 2002, 127–129) although it is possible that the East Lothian structures, at least, have a more immediate origin in NE England.

The timber halls and the early timber avenues and alignments are not the earliest forms of expression of people who relied to some extent on agriculture. That honour appears to fall to pits and structures at Eweford and Pencraig Hill in East Lothian. Pencraig Hill mortuary enclosure, in particular, has charcoal from short-lived species which implies that the contexts containing them are earlier than those at Holm and Holywood can be shown to be. The East Lothian sites are comparable to similar mortuary sites in NE England, which may be compared with the timber halls (Barclay *et al.* 2002, 12).

The creation of the Eweford alignments close to the long-lasting mortuary focus is of considerable interest. It provides an interesting analogy to the apparently repeated replacements and destructions of timbers settings at Holm and Holywood over a similarly long period. It is conceivable that some of the later post alignments at Holm and Holywood reflect a somewhat different motive than those of the earliest phases of the cursuses. At very least, the Eweford complex reinforces the impression provided

by Holm and Holywood that activities of fourth and early third millennium farmers in Scotland were probably far more complex than present evidence can demonstrate.

The presence of another potentially fourth millennium BC landscape element in the Dunbar area, the timber post-built hall at Doon Hill (Hope-Taylor archive, NMRS), has not been generally recognised. Attention has instead been focused on the two halls there with continuous wall-slots, which are probably aspects of Anglian settlement in the area. The Doon Hill timber post-built hall has not been scientifically dated, and it appears to be simpler in plan than the examples at Balbridie and Crathes. It may on further study be better compared to later enclosures such as Littleour or Balfarg Riding School (Barclay & Maxwell 1998; Barclay & Russell-White 1993).

The chronologically and spatially complex structures at Holm and Holywood North seem to have been initiated not long after farming became prevalent in Scotland. Judging by their date the two cursuses and their associated standing timbers seem to be of much the same period as the timber halls in Aberdeenshire and Stirling. In this context, the proximity to each other and similar dates of a timber alignment and hall at Crathes Warren Field is of particular interest. The dates from Balbridie, Garthdee, Crathes and Claish are a reflection of social changes starting about 3800 BC and continuing for up to six generations, but perhaps much less. They suggest a fairly rapid spread of practices which led to the charring of grain and use of carinated pottery, and of building both substantial timber halls and (at least in Aberdeenshire) slighter ovoid structures. More generally, the dating evidence suggests the presence of people using carinated pottery and cereals through much of mainland Scotland south of the Moray Firth before the end of the first quarter of the fourth millennium BC. There is insufficient evidence to demonstrate whether these practices had multiple points of origin in Scotland or a single one.

It is tempting to interpret Holm and Holywood as sites where bursts of activity lasting a few decades were interspersed with long periods of inactivity. However, even with the small number of radiocarbon dates currently available another interpretation is possible. After all, on sites without much surviving bone or peat layers the radiocarbon record is one of fire, thinned out by subsequent destruction of evidence. Indeed it is a very partial history of fires which took place in conditions suitable for charring of organic material. That is, it reflects fires in reducing rather than oxidising conditions. It may be, then, that from the fourth millennium through to the first millennia, the radiocarbon record from Holm and Holywood reflects long periods of activity interspersed with relatively short hiatuses. It may be productive to reconsider complexes like North Mains (Barclay 1983), Balfarg / Balbirnie (Barclay & Russell-White 1993) and Eweford (MacGregor 2005) from this perspective.

The early enclosure at the Pict's Knowe remains something of an enigma. It is easy enough to explain the dating evidence in terms of two phases of activity separated by two millennia. All it requires is longitudinal variations in the bank particularly at entrances, allowing the bank to appear primary at different periods in different parts. Nonetheless, it would be helpful in sustaining this interpretation if there were careful re-examination of the peat layer and its underlying deposits, sealed by parts of the bank. The enclosure of the first few centuries BC or AD is well attested by the radiocarbon dates. The existence of the morphologically similar enclosure of probably overlapping date at Shiels, Govan, with wooden objects in its ditch (Alexander 2000), suggests that this enclosure type and the practises which they sheltered may have been more common than previously supposed (at least in SW Scotland).

29

Conclusion: the Dumfries monuments and the archaeology of place

Julian Thomas

The Pict's Knowe henge, the Holywood cursus monuments and the pit and post alignments at Holm are small parts of a phenomenon that characterised the Neolithic of north-west Europe, and which was perhaps most pronounced in the British Isles. The building of large structures from earth, stone and timber took place over hundreds of years and over enormous geographical areas, but explanations that have operated at this grand scale have often proved unsatisfactory. It is clear that these structures placed a human imprint on the landscape, and established conditions under which places could be encountered and understood. But it seems unlikely that the relationships between people and place that they engendered or transformed were either uniform or static. There was no single universal Neolithic way of life in Atlantic Europe, and both the character of subsistence activities and the degree of mobility of human populations would have varied from place to place. Those geographical areas for which we have evidence of good quality give us an impression of the kind of variability that existed in patterns of residence and economy. These range from the village settlements of Orkney, which appear to have been involved in sedentary agriculture, to the situation in central Wessex, where communities may have been much more mobile, concentrating on the herding of domesticated animals. Of course, there is no reason to suppose that all Neolithic groups in Britain should have adhered to one or other of these patterns. We should anticipate that as our knowledge of the period grows, so will our appreciation of the distinctiveness of local Neolithic societies and their ways of life. In the case of the south-west of Scotland, that awareness is not yet well developed. There are sites like Beckton Farm, near Lockerbie, or Chapelfield, Cowie, where concentrations of stake-holes, hearths, sporadic post-holes and spreads of clay suggest occupation (Pollard 1997, 75–6), but its character is far from resolved.

For most Neolithic communities in Atlantic Europe, everyday life will have involved a series of superimposed and interlocking cycles of activity, whether these were played out across a landscape or concentrated around a more or less permanent domestic focus. It will be in explicating the details of these cycles that many of the advances in Neolithic archaeology will be made in the coming years. As Fowler (2003: 48) points out, many of the practicalities of life for Neolithic communities would have involved the combination of slowly repeating seasonal events, and the slow linear temporality of the decay and decomposition of materials, organisms and structures. The periodic cycles of Neolithic existence would have included the movement of cattle between pastures, the seasonal harvesting of wild and tended resources, the production of pottery and extraction of stone for chipped tools, the intermittent exchange of gifts between groups, the circulation of the remains of the dead between sites of different kinds, and the coming and going of people between communities and of communities between locations (Thomas 1999b; 2000). Interwoven with these rhythms would be the critical junctures of the human life-cycle: birth, initiation, marriage and death. In this way the biographies of people (living and dead), animals and artefacts would have been braided into the recurring temporalities of Neolithic life-worlds.

Where everyday life involved the recurrent return to particular locations, it is to be expected that the shared history of Neolithic communities would have been highly spatialised. Events would have been recalled as much in terms of where they took place as of when they happened. Paul Connerton (1989, 72) points out that memory can be sustained both through explicit recollection and through bodily performance. This latter would include the repetition of both quotidian tasks and ceremonial performances that dwelt on the past, in the process drawing it into the present. In this sense, Neolithic landscapes were 'landscapes of memory'. The experience of living, travelling and labouring within expanses of countryside, tracks and pathways, as well as more delimited spaces continually brought the past back to mind. All of this would have been equally true of the foraging communities of the Mesolithic, whose way of life would have been similarly seasonal and cyclical. In the course of the year, Mesolithic groups would have re-encountered many locations and landmarks whose significance would have been cosmological or mythological as much as economic. This would have meant that as the necessary tasks of acquiring food, fuel and raw materials were achieved, so myths and meanings embedded in the landscape would have been recreated and renewed. Where the Neolithic differed from this lay in the introduction of a series of new material technologies, all of which initiated and sustained memory in new and perhaps more explicit ways. This effectively meant that the character of people's engagement with the material world was altered. For instance, the preparation, serving and shared consumption of food are all memorable activities, and these were transformed by the introduction of pottery, not least in that new kinds of food were made possible through the mixing of ingredients and their sustained heating in a container. New stone artefacts, such as polished stone axes, and new forms of lithic procurement involving mines and quarries, expanded the significance of acts of exchange as memorable events, and increased the potential of artefacts to operate as reminders of social relationships and shared histories. Domesticated animals also transformed the character of social memory, for while hunted creatures only enter into social relationships when they are encountered and killed, herded beasts have bloodlines that descend into the past. The division of game carcases is a means by which relationships can be maintained within a community, but the exchange of bloodstock forms an enduring record of the connections between social groups.

Yet public architecture was the material innovation of the Neolithic that is most obviously connected with memory. There were, to be sure, large structures built during the Mesolithic, as in the case of the alignments of colossal post-holes of eighth millennium BC date discovered in the construction of Stonehenge car-park (Allen and Gardiner 2002). But it appears that the occurrence of constructions not primarily intended for dwelling increased dramatically with the beginning of the Neolithic, at around 4000 BC. Just as Connerton argues, memory can take a number of forms, but it is important to note that built structures can be memorable in a variety of different ways simultaneously. In the first place, as the 'stages' or arenas in which ritual activity took place, monumental architecture orchestrated bodily performance in ways that often connected actions in the present with the past. This was clearly the case with funerary structures of one kind or another, in which the observances of the living took place in spatial proximity to the remains of the dead. But this also applies to post-defined cursus monuments, which as we have seen were constructed in such a way as to evoke already ancient architectural forms, particularly timber halls and perhaps mortuary

structures as well. Furthermore, the configuration of banks, ditches, stone and timber uprights, and other symbolic elements which characterised Neolithic monuments could act as a series of reminders in 'reconstructing' ritual performances and social relationships. The architecture would prompt people to move from one place to another, to stand in certain ways in relation to others, and so on (e.g. Barrett 1994, 58). Effectively, the endurance of the architectural elements between one event and another laid down conditions that demanded repetition, reiteration and citation of past performances: the same acts, in the same sequence, in the same location (see Jones 2001, 343 on some of these themes).

However, the arguments that we have made concerning the rhythms and temporality of Neolithic ways of life suggests that at another level specific places (including monuments) would also have been identified with the particular events that had taken place in them. These would especially have been events central to the genealogies and life-crises of particular people, and to the shared histories of communities: births, initiations, marriages, funerals, feasts, important exchanges, and the forging of alliances. In other words, the perceived map of the landscape, and of people's pathways and life-histories threaded through it, would have been congruent with the 'mapping' of social relationships, in terms of kinship, descent, alliance and exchange. At a number of different levels, remembering the past would have had a role in maintaining or recreating social ties. And of course, in many traditional societies the knowledge of descent, genealogy, alliance and inheritance is an important form of power. So places that drew critical events back to mind would also have been a significant element of social strategy: they would have been reminders of who was descended from whom, and of who could call on the assistance or indebtedness of whom. Funerary structures, which actually contain the remains of the dead are again the most obvious example of this phenomenon. Occupying particular spaces within these monuments, and speaking from them at auspicious times, would have been a means of securing the legitimacy of one's authority. However, while we habitually associate 'the monumental' with the colossal scale of some Neolithic constructions, we do well to remember that some enduring structures owe their importance to the particular events that they commemorate, rather than to their scale. War memorials and Holocaust memorials are contemporary cases in point. They may be more humble and intimate, but they may be much more affecting than monuments that rely on their immensity for their impact. None the less, they rely for their effect on a familiarity with the past that they evoke. In other words, their appreciation arises out of sharing a particular cultural tradition, at some level. This is a theme to which we will return below.

In the modern landscape, stone circles and megalithic tombs represent an enduring reminder of the ancient past. It is reasonable to argue that this reflects the intentions of their builders: to create structures that would remain in place for many generations, continuing to be witnessed long after their construction. As Richard Bradley (1998, 99) argues in the case of Stonehenge, monuments that survive unchanged for centuries, and the rituals that they facilitate, can constitute a powerful force for stability and conservatism in a society. This might mean that as social change took place in the landscapes surrounding them a kind of negotiation would have to take place, accommodating monuments to the new circumstances. However, the survival of prehistoric works into the present has been uneven, and can lead us to focus preferentially on stone structures that can be construed as 'architecture' in a contemporary sense. This is to say that we sometimes think of them as *buildings*, which have been made by transforming natural raw materials into cultural artefacts, which are imposed on their surroundings as if from outside. This may be a mistaken view, for two reasons.

In the first place, understanding monuments as buildings gives the impression that they are *products*, entirely separate from the natural world. A very different perspective is suggested by Christopher Tilley (1996), who argues that in the Neolithic stone may not have been looked on as an inert substance, but may have been recognised as having an inherent power. He argues that this helps to explain the Neolithic preoccupation with rock outcrops and caves, and that such a power of rock would have been appropriated and redirected through its incorporation into megaliths and stone circles. The implication is that archaeologists need to attend more closely to the materials from which monuments are constructed, and to their potential significance, as much as to their structural organisation. In a similar vein, Colin Richards (1996, 331) has considered the architecture of henges, suggesting that their ditches and banks embodied the relationship between water and hills, thereby representing a microcosm of their surrounding landscapes. Just as portable artefacts in the Neolithic were not so much alienated commodities as things that were embedded in flows of substance that linked persons, places and abstract ideas (Thomas 1999a), so monuments were combinations of significant materials which brought together meanings that were already well established before any event of construction. As Kenneth Brophy points out in the case of cursus monuments, a monumental structure can enclose space, but it also does a great deal more through the way that it re-orders a set of materials into a specific relationship with hills, streams, rivers and woodland (Brophy 2000, 68). We have already argued (Chapter 27 above) that the introduction of small stones into significant locations at Holywood represented an aspect of this reorganisation of the material world and its meanings. All of this suggests that our efforts to typologise Neolithic architecture occlude as much as they enlighten, neglecting both the materiality of built structures and the contextual topographic relationships which contributed so much to their meaning.

Secondly, much of the public architecture that was constructed during the Neolithic was anything but permanent and enduring. This was perhaps first explicitly discussed by Francis Pryor (1984, 10), who contrasted the substantiality and longevity of henges and cursus monuments in Wessex with the brief use and rapid abandonment of a group of sites that he had investigated at Maxey in East Anglia. If monuments are not intended to survive more than a few seasons, it seems unlikely that they can serve a mnemonic function, their material presence helping to encourage future generations to dwell on the past. Yet while the 'timelessness' of stone monuments operates as a way of anchoring memory in space, sites that have an entirely different temporal structure can be made memorable in entirely different ways. As Suzanne Küchler (1987, 240) has pointed out, one of the means by which the memory of an object can be secured is through its deliberate destruction. Recently, many archaeologists have drawn a parallel between the 'lives' of human beings and those of artefacts and structures. In that an object is produced, passes through a series of contexts and events, and is finally destroyed, it has a 'biography'. In these terms, if a stone circle can sustain its significance because it is in a sense 'immortal', the memorability of other monuments can be secured through a spectacular or premature 'death'. This is true of many objects and buildings in the modern world. The twin towers of the World Trade Centre in New York are probably more widely known and recognised since their destruction on 11th September 2001, for instance. In its absence, an object can enjoy a fame or notoriety that is far greater than it had when it physically existed. However, this kind of memorability depends upon cultural tradition: people must keep the memory alive by telling stories about the thing. It is also important that destroying a thing (by burning, or breaking, or burying it) takes it out of circulation – something that has been recognised in the study of Bronze Age metalwork, for example (Bradley 1990). This consumption of objects in destructive acts stops them flowing from person to person in exchange networks, and where the latter are understood as central to the continuance of social life the 'death' of the object is again comparable with that of a human being (Munn 1986, 15). The 'stopping of flows' causes a rupture in social relations, which is in itself a memorable event. Monuments and buildings, being non-portable artefacts, are obviously not exchangeable. But in using and inhabiting them, people create ties with structures that are analogous with those that arise from passing things from hand to hand.

The foregoing discussion should hopefully have demonstrated how themes of memory and materiality can help us to illuminate several aspects of the evidence from the Pict's Knowe, Holywood and Holm. There are two particular phenomena which occur at some or all of these sites, and which can be explained in these terms. These are early Neolithic pits, and burnt timber structures.

Neither of these left a conspicuous trace on the ground, but it is arguable that they both had a significant role in structuring the remembrance of place. As Gordon Barclay has pointed out, there is a recurring pattern in lowland Scotland and beyond of early Neolithic pits being discovered at sites that later had large monuments built on them, so that the 'special' character of particular locations, once established, was maintained over very long periods (Barclay 1999, 28). The implication is that the act of digging a pit and depositing particular kinds of artefacts and materials in it conferred a singular character upon a place. This is a phenomenon that appears to be quite widespread in Scotland, England, and Wales. In many cases, the isolated pits that have been discovered in close proximity to later monuments have contained the plain carinated Grimston bowls that Andrew Herne (1988) has identified as the earliest pottery in Britain, or sometimes more developed forms of carinated vessels. At Machrie Moor on Arran, for instance, one pit contained a rich assemblage of Grimston Ware, while four other features held individual sherds, on a site which would later see the construction of a series of timber and, eventually, stone circles (Haggarty 1991, 57). At Flagstones House in Dorset, the middle Neolithic enclosure was preceded by two pits which produced sherds of thirteen carinated vessels (Smith *et al.* 1997, 30). At Dyffryn Ardudwy in north Wales a pit was found immediately in front of the portal of a megalithic chamber. The bottom of this pit was spread with rounded stones, with nested groups of sherds lying amongst them. It is at least arguable that the pit may have predated the dolmen (Powell 1973: 12). Finally, at Balfarg in Fife, the earliest phase of activity on a site which was later to contain timber structures and a henge monument consisted of the digging and deliberate backfilling of a number of pits. In at least one case, sherds of a Grimston vessel had been used to line the sides of the pit (Barclay and Russell-White 1993, 60).

Many further examples of the association between earlier Neolithic pits and large monuments that may have been constructed generations later are to be found in the literature. The principal point is clear though: monuments were often constructed in locations that had been distinguished by much earlier acts of deliberate deposition. The contents of the pits are strikingly similar, consisting of sherds of carinated vessels in a matrix which may include rounded stones and burnt material. The pottery has generally been selected from a larger assemblage, suggesting that the deposit is representative of a more extensive set of activities, which presumably involved the breaking of the pots. The sherds were frequently drawn from the upper parts of vessels, principally rims and carinations. In other words, sherds were chosen that would most clearly identify them as standing for, or being representative of, a particular class of vessels. Burying these things in a pit more explicitly linked an event that involved conspicuous consumption with a particular site.

My suggestion is that such activities gave places an identity that became embedded in memory and tradition, and that this is why they were chosen as the sites for much later tombs and henges. The construction of these monuments drew upon and transformed the existing meanings of these places. While the pattern is clearest where early Neolithic pits are concerned, there are indications that pits containing material culture continued to have a transformitive role in the landscape over a longer period. For instance, at Meldon Bridge in Peebleshire, the late Neolithic palisaded enclosure was preceded by a large number of pits containing middle Neolithic Impressed Wares (Speak and Burgess 1999, 101).

Of course, we should not give the impression that all of the places where earlier Neolithic pit-digging took place were later chosen as the locations for monumental structures. Cleal (2004, 176) points to a group of rich pit sites from the initial Neolithic in Wessex which seem to be connected with major episodes of food consumption, having ceramic assemblages dominated by large open vessels and smaller cups or bowls. Cleal suggests that these might have represented the sites of substantial social gatherings in the period prior to the construction of causewayed enclosures (generally considered to have commenced around 3650 BC). These include Cannon Hill in Berkshire, Roughridge Hill in north Wiltshire, and the Coneybury 'Anomaly' in south Wiltshire. Only the last of these was succeeded by a major monument, the Coneybury henge (Richards 1990, 123–58). Throughout the Neolithic in Britain, pit-digging took place in lowland areas, and often this appears to have commemorated or 'marked' episodes of settlement activity, which may have involved the cyclical re-occupation of particular locations (Garrow, Beadsmoore and Knight 2005). The relationship between pit-digging and the construction of monumental architecture in Neolithic Britain was thus a complicated one: in some cases they were complementary practices, and in some cases they formed separate stages in the biography of a single place.

Similar themes of performance, memorability, and consumption are raised by the deliberate burning of timber structures of one kind or another. It has long been recognised that the wooden façades, avenues and mortuary enclosures which preceded the construction of many earthen long barrows were sometimes fired before the raising of the mound (e.g. Morgan 1959; Manby 1963; Hodder & Shand 1988; Evans and Simpson 1991). These structural arrangements were generally in place while the mortuary deposit in the chamber was gradually accumulating: the flesh rotting away from the bodies, and the bones being reorganised or actually removed. So it seems that burning the timbers marked the cessation of a particular phase of activity, during which the monument had been open to exchanges of bodily matter. Following the firing and the building of the mound, the barrow was severed from patterns of circulation. Just to underline the point, in the north of Britain some long barrows contained timber chambers which were effectively crematorium structures, and which were burned after the construction of the mound. Flues were left through the mound material to enable combustion to take place (Manby 1963).

Recent excavations have demonstrated that this pattern of activity extends to a variety of other timber enclosures and alignments. Throughout much of Scotland and northern England in the earlier Neolithic it appears to have been commonplace to build rectilinear timber structures and then to burn them down. This practice applied to post-defined cursus monuments, as at Douglasmuir (Kendrick 1995), rectangular mortuary enclosures, as at Inchtuthil (Barclay and Maxwell 1991), and roofed timber buildings, as at Claish (Barclay, Brophy & MacGregor 2002). In some cases the firing of the monument demonstrably took place soon after its construction. At Dunragit in Galloway the burning of the uprights of the cursus had been sufficiently intense to scorch the gravel surface around the post-holes and redden the packing-stones (Thomas 2004b). Clearly, firing such a structure would involve an enormous amount of effort, as brushwood would have to be piled up around the free-standing uprights in order to make them burn at all (see Chapter 27 above). Indeed, in the case of thick oak posts it is possible that more than one episode of burning would have been required to char the timbers through to the core. In other cases, post-defined enclosures were simply allowed to rot away, without the renewal of any uprights, as at Bannockburn and Castle Menzies (Taverner 1987; Rideout 1997; Halliday 2002). In a recent article, Michael Parker Pearson and Ramilisonina (1998) have drawn attention to the contrast between timber and stone monuments, arguing that the former were generally used for gatherings of the living, while the latter were set aside as the prerogative of the dead. While reservations have been raised concerning the analogies used in this argument (Barrett and Fewster 1998), the distinction that they make between the transience of wooden structures in comparison with stone is useful. If we think of enclosures and alignments as the temporary settings for processions, ceremonies, initiations, funerals or the like, then their deliberate destruction becomes more comprehensible. Rather than remaining in the landscape, susceptible to re-use and reappropriation of whatever kind, the construction, use and consumption of the monument become parts of a continuous performance. They form parts of a single event, which is immediately consigned to memory, in the strong sense.

To return to an earlier theme, monuments that are constructed of different kinds of substance have different potential temporalities, and this conditions the character of their insertion into memory. Stone monuments change imperceptibly from one generation to the next, and are their own memorial. Timber monuments decay at a rate that can be recognised over the decades, and the derelict state of wooden structures can serve as the guarantee of their authenticity. Alternatively, the destruction of timber constructions by fire can remove them from the landscape at a stroke, while simultaneously rendering their destruction memorable.

We can now recapitulate the evidence from the three sites discussed in this volume in the context of these ideas. To begin with the Pict's Knowe, we have seen that the probable henge monument was constructed in a low-lying valley a little inland from the Solway Firth, which was inundated by a rise of sea level after the last Ice Age. The valley drained slowly, and would have been boggy throughout much of prehistory. The enclosure stood at one end of a low sand ridge, which would have stood between the damp heathland of the upper terrace and wetter country with standing water to the north and east. Seemingly, the site saw sporadic activity over more than four thousand years. We have argued that in a general sense it remained a place of importance throughout much of this duration, although it is not claimed that either the meaning of the location or the ways in which it was used remained stable over the centuries. The details of the interior of the henge monument have been lost to rabbit burrowing, but the profusion of features on the entrance causeway suggest that access to the enclosed area was carefully regulated, and that entry had to be achieved by passing across damp ground, but not necessarily though water. The combination of the liminal location and the architectural arrangements, including whichever of the stake-hole structures were contemporary with the enclosure, indicate that the actions performed inside the henge were intended to be somewhat secluded. The ditches were filled with very layered deposits which seem to indicate that they were laid down in wet conditions, but eventually they appear to have stabilised and a turf formed on top. Some time later, substantial recuts were dug into the ditches, at the two entrance terminals and at the back of the enclosure. This apparently took place in the first few centuries AD, and the extensive deposits of waterlogged wood found within these recuts included bucket-staves, hurdles, perforated pegs and bundles of twigs. Much of this material was wood-working debris, but a good deal may have resulted from the collapse or dismantling of some kind of timber structure inside the enclosure. Some of the larger wooden objects appear to have been deliberately placed, along with fragments of smashed quernstones. Moreover, a timber platform seems to have been constructed over the top of the recut at the back of the enclosure, and there were sparse traces of metal-working on site during this final phase of activity. What we can take this to mean is that during the late Iron Age the enclosure represented something other than a simply a domestic settlement, and that over an extremely long period of time the Pict's Knowe had maintained a particular distinction.

It is in relation to this sustained importance that we should evaluate the earliest activity on the site, which pre-dated the construction of the henge. Beneath the henge bank, within the old land surface an extensive scatter of early Neolithic pottery and chipped stone was identified. This might conceivably document the use of the sand island and its marshy surroundings for economic activities, such as the taking of wildfowl. However, nearby was small pit 6724, which contained sherds from eight earlier Neolithic vessels, and numerous chipped stone fragments. The pottery included six different fabrics, as opposed to only two amongst the sherds in the old land surface. This pit is obviously comparable with the earlier Neolithic pits discussed above, and while its presence does not contradict the possibility that the earliest activity at the Pict's Knowe was domestic or logistic in character, it does represent an indication that some aspects of this occupation went beyond the purely mundane. Stratigraphically equivalent with the pit was the small oval mound. This mound covered a large pit and was flanked by two substantial withdrawn post-holes. While soil conditions would not have allowed the preservation of bone, it is just conceivable that the pit was a grave, in which case burial activity on a site later occupied by a henge would find parallels at North Mains and Cairnpapple (Barclay 1983, 180). When the henge was constructed, probably at the very end of the Neolithic (but see Ashmore this volume, Chapter 28 above), its entrance was positioned over the oval mound, and maintained precisely the orientation that had been established by the mound and its attendant post-holes, all of which were covered by the levelling layer. It is hard to escape the conclusion that the henge deliberately maintained something of the spatial organisation of the earlier structures, while at the same time hiding their remains from view. This is perhaps comparable with the situation at Balfarg Riding School, where a hengiform enclosure was preceded by two rectangular timber structures, which the excavator interprets as unroofed enclosures used for the exposure of the dead (Barclay and Russell-White 1993: 169). Structure 2 was covered by an 'obscuring layer' containing sherds of Grooved Ware, and it is possible that some kind of low mound was also built over Structure 1 after its collapse. In any case, the later ring-ditch and ring-cairn complex was built with its central point located precisely on the extension of the axis of Structure 1, and the ring-ditch actually clipped the end of the building (*ibid.*, 176). This suggests that precise details of the building were known for some while after its destruction, even though they had been hidden in a manner similar to the Pict's Knowe oval mound.

The digging of pits also emerged as an important aspect of the cursus complex at Holywood. Inside the northern terminal of the southern cursus we noted the presence of a group of pits with elaborate burnt fills. These produced an assemblage of early Neolithic pottery, dominated by rim-sherds and carinations, and their position in the area that would have been occupied by the cursus bank suggests their stratigraphic priority. So as at Balfarg, Machrie Moor and Dyffryn Ardudwy, it is probable that these pit deposits lent a special character to a particular place, which in turn

influenced the location and spatial organisation of the cursus. The Holywood North cursus, by contrast, had a flat-bottomed ditch which had apparently filled in a single episode of bank collapse or backfilling, following a short period of silting. Once again there were features in the area enclosed by the ditch, but in this case they were post-holes, and some of the posts had been burnt or withdrawn. Perhaps as many as four or five separate timber structures were successively built and destroyed, or perhaps construction was piecemeal and ongoing. The precise sequence is unclear, but it is evident that a number of different events of construction and destruction were represented at Holywood North, and that in its initial form the ditched enclosure may not have been extant for more than a year. So although the cursus would have been an imposing construction, it may have been intended for a single episode of use: a particular event.

At the northern end of the north cursus, the rounded terminal curved in a slightly asymmetrical fashion in order to enclose the small hillock where post-hole 224 was located. The primary filling of this pit consisted of a dump of water-worn cobbles, quite different in character from the stones in the surrounding gravel. These had apparently served as packing for the earliest of a series of posts at the apex of the linear timber structure. On top of these stones, there was a great mass of disturbed burnt organic material, which probably represented the remains of a colossal wooden post: either the first or the second in the series. This had been burned, and then collapsed. The great timber had probably been integral to one of the builds of the post-defined cursus enclosure, but it is not clear whether other elements of this initial structure were also burned. The construction, use and destruction of the post structures may have been played out over a number of centuries, and is comparable with the pit-digging at Holywood South, which might have been contemporary. Both the pits and charred post-stumps were sealed beneath the earthen banks of the two ditched cursus enclosures, rendering them inaccessible. This recalls the fate of the oval mound and two large post-holes at the Pict's Knowe, sealed beneath the 'levelling layer' in front of the henge entrance.

The post- and pit-complex at Holm, which might be identified (in part) as a post-defined cursus, lay only a kilometre to the east of Holywood, and we have argued that they can be seen as related and broadly contemporary groups of structures. Like Holywood, Holm was originally identified by aerial photography. At Holm, the series of alignments of pits and post-holes ran along a gravel terrace overlooking the River Nith, while two ring ditches lay immediately to the south of these features. On excavation, three lines of post-holes were identified. Most of the posts had been burnt out and replaced by new posts within the same feature, often on more than one occasion. However, the sequence of cutting, burning and recutting varied from one feature to another, so that it is clear that not all of the posts would have been standing at any one time. Indeed, the two northernmost post lines appear from the air to be closed by another line of features running at right-angles to them, and it is this that identifies them as a post-defined cursus.

One of the ring ditches was partially excavated (Trench B), and the feature visible from the air proved to be the last of three distinct structures on the same site, another of which had been a small timber circle. The stratigraphic relationship between the ring ditch and the post-holes was not entirely clear. In all, a maximum of eight phases of activity can potentially be defined at Holm, the final one consisting of an avenue of pits which cuts across the post hole alignments on a different orientation, heading for the more easterly of the two ring ditches. Unlike the post structures, the pit-avenue gives no indication of having been closed, and indeed the area between the two lines of pits was very narrow. Aside from this contrast, it seems that the same basic structure was maintained throughout the sequence. In every phase, a linear monument ran along the terrace, parallel with the course of the river, toward (or away from) an enclosed space in the form of a ring-ditch or post-circle.

It is arguable that the post- and pit-settings at Holm maintained their fundamental form through numerous phases of rebuilding because they were intended to facilitate a particular kind of performance. Presumably, this involved some combination of procession parallel with the route of the river and (in some cases) gathering in a circular space. However, looked at in detail, the alignments and avenues at Holm reveal numerous kinks and changes of orientation (Fig. 27.4). The complex as a whole appears to be made up of a number of smaller modules. This is plausibly a product of the multiple burnings and rebuildings. If each structure was burnt immediately after its use, what would have been left behind would have been a series of burnt-out stumps. If any amount of time elapsed before the site was re-occupied and the alignments reconstructed, only a minority of the posts might have been relocated. The

monument would then have been reconstructed through a combination of a memory of what had been there, the remaining traces of the posts, and a particular under-standing of the way in which the structure had to be used, the requirements that it had to fulfil. Bradley (2002, 87) makes an interesting comparison between the burning and replacement of posts at sites like Holm and the recutting and backfilling of the ditches at causewayed enclosures. In both cases, monuments were reinstated, possibly on a cyclical basis. Quite possibly the sites of causewayed enclosures and cursus monuments would have been recognised as being significant throughout the year, but the recutting of ditches or erection of posts re-established the temporary conditions under which specific activities could take place.

This suggests that the architecture of posts and ring-ditches was absolutely integral to the ritual or ceremonial practiced at Holm. The cycle of reiteration involved not only repeated processions in the alignments and gather-ings in the enclosures, but also numerous episodes of construction and burning. The sequence at Holm demon-strates an extraordinary attentiveness to the details of almost vanished structures on the part of the builders. This is again comparable with the relationship between the oval mound and the henge at the Pict's Knowe, and the pits, posts and cursus monuments at Holywood: considerable effort was expended in re-establishing spatial configurations that may already have been quite ancient. It is arguable that this kind of continuity arose from the repetition of ritual acts over time in fixed locations, and the need to incorporate them into new structures as these were brought into being. At all of these sites the longevity of the monument was connected with the various ways in which the activities that took place within it were made memorable. This point is amplified by the possibility that at both Holywood and Holm the sequence of construction was brought to an end by the building of a stone circle, which replaced the transient earth and timber structures with a permanent marker.

Appendix 1
Catalogue of pottery from the Pict's Knowe 1994/1995 excavations

Rick Peterson and Julia Roberts

Find No.	Context	Location	Sherd Length	No.	Type	Fabric Group	Vessel
1	0001	475.81/ 131.54/ 11.03	16	1	body	3	V
2	0001	475.56/ 131.92/ 11.08	<10	1	frag.	indet.	
3	0001	475.51/ 131.92/ 11.08	<10	1	frag.	indet.	
4	0001	475.01/ 133.59/ 10.92	12	1	body	2	IV
7	0001	461.08/ 125.78/ 10.64	11	1	body	mod.	
8	0001	461/ 125	<10	1	frag.	indet.	
24	0014	438/ 138	26	1	body	2	IV
25	0014	438/ 138	<10	1	frag.	indet.	
32	0002	469/ 130.3/ 9.95	22	1	rim?	7	IX
36	0002	468.87/ 125.9/ 10.18	23	1	body	3	V
38	0002	469.04/ 125.23/ 10.15	11	1	body	3	V
39	0002	466.65/ 124.30/ 10.31	25	1	body	5	VII
44	0002	466/ 133/ 10.91	82	1	rim	1	I
58	0122	455.6/ 128.6/ 9.36	26	1	body	8	X
81	0385	455/ 130.12/ 9.76	23	1	body	mod.	
143	0393	not recorded	<10	1	frag.	indet.	
192	0003	471.11/ 132.48/ 9.94	15	1	body	1	I
192	0003	471.11/ 132.48/ 9.94	<10	1	frag.	indet.	
none	0001	479/ 129	10-20	2	body	mod.	
none	0001	477/ 129	<10	20	body	3	V
			10-20	36	body	3	V
			10-20	1	body	2	IV
			10-20	1	body	6	VIII
none	0001	475/ 129	10-20	1	body	6	VIII
193	0001	473/ 129	<10	7	body	2	IV
			10-20	4	body	2	IV
195	0001	478/ 128	<10	5	body	3	V
			10-20	5	body	3	V
196	0001	476/ 128	<10	1	body	2	IV
			10-20	3	body	2	IV
none	0001	474/ 128	10-20	2	body	2	IV
197	0001	477/ 127	<10	3	body	3	V
198	0001	475/ 127	<10	2	body	2	IV
			10-20	3	body	2	IV
199	0001	473/ 127	<10	1	body	2	IV
			10-20	3	body	2	IV
			20-30	1	body	2	IV
200	0001	471/ 127	10-20	1	body	3	V
202	0001	476/ 126	<10	1	body	2	IV
203	0001	477/ 125	<10	2	body	2	IV
204	0001	475/ 125	<10	1	body	mod.	
206	0001	471/ 125	<10	2	body	2	IV
			10-20	2	body	2	IV
207	0001	474/ 124	<10	3	body	2	IV
			10-20	3	body	2	IV
208	0001	473/ 123	10-20	1	body	2	IV
			20-30	1	body	2	IV
			<10	1	body	2	IV

Find No.	Context	Location	Sherd Length	No.	Type	Fabric Group	Vessel
209	0001	471/ 123	<10	2	body	2	IV
			10-20	4	body	2	IV
			10-20	1	body	3	V
210	0001	472/ 122	10-12	1	body	mod.	
none	0001	474/ 122	10-20	3	body	2	IV
211	0001	473/ 121	10-20	1	body	2	IV
212	0001	471/ 121	10-20	2	body	3	V
213	0001	474/ 120	<10	1	body	2	IV
214	0001	472/ 120	<10	2	body	2	IV
			10-20	2	body	2	IV
			10-20	1	body	2	IV
215	0002	477/ 129	20-30	6	body	3	V
			30-40	2	body	3	V
216	0002	475/ 129	20-30	3	body	3	V
			61	1	base/ collar	3	V
			10-20	1	rim	mod.	
217	0002	473/129	<10	12	body	3	V
			10-20	9	body	3	V
			20-30	2	body	3	V
218	0002	471/ 129	<10	2	body	3	V
			10-20	2	body	3	V
			13	1	body	3	V
219	0002	478/ 128	<10	17	body	3	V
			10-20	26	body	3	V
			20-30	3	body	3	V
221	0002	478/ 128	61	1	body	2	IV
220	0002	476/ 128	<10	1	body	3	V
			10-20	3	body	3	V
			20-30	6	body	3	V
			30-40	1	body	3	V
			40-50	2	body	3	V
222	0002	474/ 128	<10	9	body	3	V
			10-20	9	body	3	V
			20-30	2	body	3	V
223	0002	472/ 128	42	1	body	5	VII
225	0002	477/ 127	10-20	2	body	2	IV
226	0002	475/ 127	<10	9	body	3	V
			10-20	26	body	3	V
			20-30	4	body	3	V
224	0002	473/ 127	<10	3	body	3	V
			10-20	3	body	3	V
227	0002	471/ 127	<10	3	body	2	IV
			10-20	9	body	2	IV
			10-20	1	body	3	V
			20-30	1	body	3	V
			20-30	1	body	mod.	
228	0002	478/ 126	22	1	rim?	3	V
229	0002	476/ 126	<10	2	body	3	V
			10-20	2	body	3	V
230	0002	474/ 126	10-20	1	body	3	V
			20-30	1	body	3	V
			20-30	1	rim	5	VII
231	0002	472/ 126	<10	3	body	3	V
			10-20	5	body	3	V
			10-20	1	body	5	VII
			20-30	2	body	3	V
			17	1	body	1	I
234	0002	471/ 125	20-30	1	body	2	IV

Find No.	Context	Location	Sherd Length	No.	Type	Fabric Group	Vessel
303	0977	not recorded	47	1	body	5	VII
311	1316	495.39/ 125.86/ 10.03	20	1	rim	mod.	
430	0888	not recorded	20-30	2	body	5	VII
487	0966	474.16/ 138.76/ 9.83	<10	1	frag.	indet.	
502	0888	424.24/ 122.05/ 9.88	<10	1	frag.	indet.	
536	1960	457.18/ 121.95/ 9.92	<10	1	frag.	indet.	
540	1900	459.75/ 121.22/ 9.76	24	1	body	mod.	
548	0699	484.80/ 120.00/ 10.21	<10	1	frag.	indet.	
566	0524	495.84/ 137.80/ 10.22	58	1	whole profile	4	VI
577	0524	not recorded	<10	3	body	2	IV
			10-20	3	body	5	VII
584	0524	495.75/ 134.79/ 10.21	58	1	base	2	
585	0524	495.47/ 139.92/ 10.28	34	1	body	mod.	
600	2081	Grid 3 & 4, Sieve	22	1	rim	7	IX
674	2002	480.62/ 120.01/ 9.57	35	1	body	1	II
			17	1	body	1	II
750	0888	483.15/ 126.61/ 9.75	37	1	rim?	7	IX
782	2202	496.56/ 133.70/ 10.18	<10	1	frag.	indet.	
784	1959	481.75/ 134.91/ 9.38	38	1	body	2	IV
807	0001	488.15/ 120.79/ 10.43	<10	1	frag.	indet.	
834	1901	465.10/ 112.75/ 9.60	22	1	body	1	III
842	2298	463.95/ 118.48/ 9.86	<10	1	frag.	indet.	

Catalogue

Fabric Group I   **Vessel 1**

An open S-profiled bowl, in a thin fabric, with a simple, slightly everted, rim. The vessel is around 150mm in diameter at the rim and has been burnished externally.

Colour

Core	Inner Margin	Inner Surface	Outer Margin	Outer Surface
7.5YR 4/0 (dark grey)	7.5Y 5/3 (brown)	7.5YR 5/6 (yellowish red)	7.5YR 4/3 (dark brown)	7.5YR 4/3 (dark brown)

Hard hackly fabric

Inclusions

Class	Size	Frequency	Sorting	Roundness
limestone	very coarse	sparse	poor	sub-angular
quartz	fine	sparse	fair	sub-rounded

Sherd List

Finds No.	Context	Description	East	North
44	0002	1 rim sherd	466	133
231	0002	1 body fragment	472	126
2650	6725	1 body fragment	471.571	103.085
2670	6725	3 body fragments	471.915	103.046

Fabric Group I   **Vessel 2**
2 plain body sherds of fine thickness

Colour

Core	Inner Margin	Inner Surface	Outer Margin	Outer Surface
5 YR 3/1 (very dark grey)	7.5 YR 5/2 (brown)	7.5 YR 5/2 (brown)	7.5 YR 6/2 (pinkish grey)	7.5 YR 6/2 (pinkish grey)

Soft irregular fabric

Inclusions

Class	Size	Frequency	Sorting	Roundness
limestone	coarse	moderate	poor	angular
quartz	fine	sparse	good	sub-angular

Sherd List

Finds No.	Context	Description	East	North
674	2002	2 body sherds and frags.	480.62	120.01
2680	6725	1 body sherd	471.568	103.031

Fabric Group I   **Vessel 14**
Carinated bowl with simple upright rim. It is of thin fabric and the surfaces of all the sherds have been affected by the acidic soil

Colour

Core	Inner Margin	Inner Surface	Outer Margin	Outer Surface
10 YR 3/1 (very dark grey)	10 YR 4/1 (dark grey)	10 YR 4/1 (dark grey)	10 YR 4/2 (dark greyish brown)	10 YR 4/2 (dark greyish brown)

Soft irregular fabric

Inclusions

Class	Size	Frequency	Sorting	Roundness
limestone	coarse - very coarse	moderate	poor	sub-rounded
quartz	fine	sparse	fair	rounded

Sherd List

Finds No.	Context	Description	East	North
no s/f No.	6480	3 frags.	-	-
no s/f No.	6480	1 frag.	sieve	sieve
no s/f No.	2404	4 frags.	sieve	sieve
2436	6120	body sherd	517.869	100.280
2441	6120	3 sherds, 2 frags.	479.509	97.43
2458	6270	3 sherds, 3 frags.	sieve	sieve
2467	2404	2 body sherds, 2 frags.	474.869	96.895
2470	6471	1 sherd	478.782	96.973
2478	2404	2 body sherds, 1 frag.	481.817	98.273
2486	2404	body frag.	482.394	97.303
2494	6486	1 frag.	482.115	96.216
2495	2404	2 frags.	480.055	99.732
2501	6486	1 body sherd, 1 frag.	481.148	97.276
2502	6486	2 frags.	483.689	98.326
2509	6486 (register, on bag 2404)	10 frags.	483.746	99.598
2517	6486	6 + frags.	477.956	96.897
2518	2404	1 rim sherd, 3 frags.	482.419	98.661
2522	6486	carination	484.127	101.379
2531	6486	3 frags.	481.327	99.191
2534	6486	4 body frags.	477.347	99.183
2535	6486	2 frags.	477.603	98.764
2537	6486	2 body sherds, 1 frag.	477.157	99.970
2542	6486	2 body sherds, 4 frags.	481.789	98.718
2543	6486	6 frags.	sieve	sieve

Finds No.	Context	Description	East	North
2545	6486	1 body sherd	477.567	100.403
2548	6486	6 + frags.	478.308	99.862
2551	6486	5 frags	sieve	sieve
2553	6486	large body sherd	477.520	100.529
2559	6486	1 frag.	474.64	99.272
2563	6486	body sherd	474.259	100.197
2572	2404	body sherd	480.266	100.739
2583	6480	2 frags.	sieve	sieve
2590	6486	2 sherds	471.304	101.040
2594	6120	1 frag.	480.070	96.569
2595	6486	4 body sherds, 3 frags.	471.920	101.402
2599	6486	1 body sherd, 2 frags.	471.650	101.981
2604	2160	1 frag.	480.638	96.805
2606	6486	4 sherds, 9 frags.	471.567	101.158
2611	2404	1 frag.	sieve	sieve
2616	6270	1 body sherd	479.293	96.715
2619	2404	9 frags. +	481.356	102.444
2624	6486	body sherd	470.681	101.413
2626	6486	2 frags.	469.983	101.479
2632	6486	11 body frags.	471.615	101.821
2633	6486	2 sherds, 1 frag.	471.116	102.755
2635	6486	9 frags. +	471.288	102.319
2665	6725	1 frag.	471.660	103.153

Fabric Group IV   **Vessel No. 6**

Large piece of a lamp with two additional small fragments all of thin to moderate thickness

Colour

Core	Inner Margin	Inner Surface	Outer Margin	Outer Surface
10 YR 5/3 (brown) 10 YR 4/2 (dark greyish brown)	10 YR 5/3 (brown) 10 YR 4/2 (dark greyish brown)	10 YR 5/3 (brown) 10 YR 4/2 (dark greyish brown)	10 YR 6/3 (pale brown)	10 YR 6/3 (pale brown)

Hard laminated fabric

Inclusions

Class	Size	Frequency	Sorting	Roundness
grog	medium	sparse	fair	rounded
limestone	coarse	very sparse	1 piece	sub-angular

Sherd List

Finds No.	Context	Description	East	North
0566	0524	lamp	495.84	137.80
2656	6725	fragment	471.475	103.099
2666	6725	fragment	471.761	102.956

Fabric Group IX   **Vessel No. 11 (incorporating Vessel 3 of 1995)**
Four plain body sherds of thin fabric

Colour

Core	Inner Margin	Inner Surface	Outer Margin	Outer Surface
10 YR 5/3 (brown)	10 YR 5/3 (brown)	10 YR 5/3 (brown)	10 YR 5/3 (brown)	10 YR 5/3 (brown)

Hard laminated fabric

Inclusions

Class	Size	Frequency	Sorting	Roundness
limestone	coarse	very sparse	poor	sub-angular

Sherd List

Finds No.	Context	Description	East	North
834	1901	body sherd	465.10	112.75
2657	6725	1 body frag.	471.660	103.233
2672	6725	1 body sherd, 1 frag.	471.840	103.004

Fabric Group X   **Vessel No. 12**
Two pieces of the rim and one from the body, the thickness of the pot is unclear

Colour

Core	Inner Margin	Inner Surface	Outer Margin	Outer Surface
10 YR 4/1 (dark grey) to 10YR 6/4 (light yellowish brown)	10 YR 4/1 (dark grey)	10 YR 4/1 (dark grey)	10 YR 4/1 (dark grey)	10 YR 4/1 (dark grey)

Soft fine fabric.

Inclusions

Class	Size	Frequency	Sorting	Roundness
metasediment	fine	sparse	poor	sub-angular
quartz	very fine	moderate	fair	sub-angular
limestone	fine	sparse	good	sub-angular

Sherd List

Finds No.	Context	Description	East	North
2006	2605	rim frag.	462.75	62.20
2634	2404	rim sherd (top of)	480.88	107.320
2659	6725	body frag.	471.752	102.905

Fabric Group XIII   **Vessel No. 15**
One small sherd of very thin fabric

Colour

Core	Inner Margin	Inner Surface	Outer Margin	Outer Surface
7.5 YR 32 (dark brown)	7.5 YR 32 (dark brown)	7.5 YR 32 (dark brown)	7.5 YR 32 (dark brown)	7.5 YR 32 (dark brown)

Hard, hackly/laminated fabric

Inclusions

Class	Size	Frequency	Sorting	Roundness
limestone	medium coarse	moderate	fair	angular
grog / metasediment	coarse	moderate	good	very angular

Sherd List

Finds No.	Context	Description	East	North
2669	6725	1 frag.	471.851	103.149

Fabric Group XIV   **Vessel No. 16**

An open carinated bowl of moderate thickness with a simple rim. The surfaces of these sherds has also been badly affected by the acidic soil

Colour

Core	Inner Margin	Inner Surface	Outer Margin	Outer Surface
7.5 YR 2/0 (black)	7.5 YR 3/2 (dark brown)	7.5 YR 3/2 (dark brown)	7.5 YR 3/3 (dark brown)	7.5 YR 3/3 (dark brown)

Very soft irregular fabric

Inclusions

Class	Size	Frequency	Sorting	Roundness
limestone	very coarse	moderate	very poor	sub-rounded

Sherd List

Finds No.	Context	Description	East	North
2438	6120	1 sherd, 3 frags.	518.180	108.96
2448	6120	5+ frags.	479.125	96.935
2453	2404	1 sherd	482.940	96.925
2457	2404	5 sherds, 14 frags.	483.088	97.545
2459	6431	8+ frags.	483.418	97.608
2460	6431	1 frag.	483.380	97.265
2461	6270	1 sherd	480.148	96.879
2463	6431	1 sherd	sieve	sieve
2468	2404	2 sherds	478.576	97.391
2469	6471	1 frag.	478.647	96.989
2472	2404	2 frags.	483.709	98.916
2475	2404	2 frags.	482.333	98.259
2476	6480	1 rim sherd	-	-
2479	6480	2 frags.	-	-
2480	2404	1 frag.	481.370	97.416
2481	2404	1 frag	481.689	98.402
2482	2404	2 frags.	481.417	97.318
2484	2404	4 sherds, 2 frags.	479.873	101.095
2485	2404	1 frag.	481.759	98.786
2488	2404	2 body sherds	482.261	98.225
2492	6486	4 frags.	480.903	96.853
2493	6486	3 sherds, 4 frags	481.272	96.708
2496	6480	2 sherds, 5 frags	481.818	96.349
2497	6486	3 frags.	482.762	97.041
2498	6486	6 + frags.	482.269	99.776
2503	6480	3 sherds (1 carinated)	480.861	99.258
2504	2404	1 sherd, 2 frags.	482.023	99.732
2505	6486	1 sherd	480.062	97.946
2507	2404	2 frags.	481.696	99.134
2508	2404	3 frags.	481.297	98.528
2510	2404	2 sherds, 5 frags.	479.567	97.916
2511	2404	2 frags..	478.951	98.816
2512	6486	4 frags.	484.180	99.919
2513	2404	1 frag.	482.170	99.045
2521	6486	6 frags.	477.413	96.856
2523	6486	1 frag.	476.771	97.523
2524	6486	6 frags.	477.564	99.043
2525	6486	1 frag.	478.442	98.60
2526	6486	1 sherd	477.360	98.188
2527	6486	1 sherd, 1 frag.	477.423	99.167
2528	2404	2 sherds, 3 frags	481.276	99.570
2540	6486	many frags.	481.469	98.685
2544	6486	1 sherd, 5 frags.	481.139	98.583
2550	6486	many frags.	481.430	97.850
2552	6486	2 frags	481.302	97.943
2554	2404	2 sherds, 6 frags.	478.750	100.517
2557	6486	1 sherd, 2 frags	482.389	97.298
2560	6486	3 sherds	477.520	100.529

Finds No.	Context	Description	East	North
2562	6486	2 sherds	474.393	100.867
2565	6486	1 frag.	473.761	97.428
2566	6486	1 body sherd, 2 frags.	474.113	99.883
2568	6486	1 sherd, 4 frags.	478.116	101.481
2569	2404	4 sherds, 5 frags	497.060	101.196
2570	2404	1 sherd, 3 frags.	481.681	101.277
2573	2404	1 sherd	sieve	sieve
2574	2404	7 frags.	sieve	sieve
2574*	2404	6 frags. (tiny)	481.342	100.416
2575	4480	2 sherds, 1 frag.	480.180	99.276
2576	6486	1 sherd	481.008	101.302
2579	6486	2 sherds	480.725	98.440
2589	2404	1 sherd, 5 frags.	472.117	97.344
2592	6486	4 sherds, 2 frags.	482.926	103.254
2601	6120	2 frags.	481.112	96.838
2602	6486	2 frags.	480.654	97.818
2608	2404	1 sherd, 2 frags.	479.801	102.396
2610	6486	2 sherds	471.725	101.698
2615	6486	2 sherds, 2 frags.	472.692	99.078
2627	2404	1 frag.	478.383	101.684
2628	2404	5 frags.	479.870	101.783
2637	6486	3 sherds, many frags.	470.419	101.761
2641	6270	1 sherd	480.601	96.839
2644	6486	1 sherd, 3 frags.	474.417	98.861
2655	6486	1 sherd, 1 frag.	478.773	101.210
2662	6486	2 frags.	sieve	sieve
2663	6486	1 sherd, 3 frags.	481.970	100.880
2688	6480	1 sherd, 2 frags	480.94	99.15
2679	6486	1 body sherd	480.784	100.068
2684	6486	1 body sherd	478.148	96.835
-	2404	4 sherds, 2 frags.	sieve	sieve
-	6416	1 frag.	sieve	sieve
No number	Topsoil PK 1997	1 abraded body sherd	---	---

Fabric Group XI   **Vessel No. 13**
A body sherd from a pot of moderate thickness

Colour

Core	Inner Margin	Inner Surface	Outer Margin	Outer Surface
7.5 YR 6/4 (light brown)	10 YR 5/4 (yellowish brown)	10 YR 5/4 (yellowish brown)	10 YR 6/3 (pale brown)	10 YR 6/3 (pale brown)

Very hard laminated fabric

Inclusions

Class	Size	Frequency	Sorting	Roundness
limestone	medium - very coarse	moderate	poor	angular
quartz	very coarse	sparse	very poor	sub-rounded

Sherd List

Finds No.	Context	Description	East	North
2674	6725	body sherd	471.743	103.036

There are also some unstratified pottery fragments found in the topsoil of trench A in 1997, these are too badly abraded to identify and date. The fragments are soft black material with quartzite inclusions, possibly relating to a vessel of fabric group one but there is too little pottery for this identification to be certain.

Appendix 2
The Pict's Knowe – wood measurements

Anne Crone, Rob Sands and Theo Skinner

All measurements shown in this section are in millimetres.

Table 1: Perforated pegs

Number	Context	Total Length	Length of head	Width of head	Depth of head	Length of shank	Width of shank	Depth of shank
0384	1953	455	100	80	56	355	52	27
0385	1953	350	85	90	70	265	54	34
0169	0130	365	100	90	75	265	55	36

Number	Context	Length of hole in shank	Width of hole in shank	Distance from head to hole
0384	1953	58	25	120
0385	1953	39	20	110
0169	0130	42	15	105

Table 2: Wedge shaped pieces

Find	Context	Maximum length	Minimum length	Maximum width	Minimum width	Maximum depth	Minimum depth
0852	2326	445	445	70	42	35	12
0853	2268	92	92	60	42	26	4

Table 3: Oblong shaped pieces

Find	Description	Context	Length	Width	Thickness
0317	Oblong timber	0698	750	110	0
0400	Oblong timber	0888	350	75	16
0454	Oblong timber	1959	180	35	28
0801B	Oblong timber	0888	455	70	12
0817	Oblong timber	2232	242	23	12
0818	Oblong fragment	2232	81	22	11
0821	Oblong fragment	2232	129	57	18
0840	Oblong timber	2168	225	43	9

Table 4: roundwood

Find	Context	Length	Diameter	Cutting style	Cutting angle
0352a	0888		32	na	
0402	1960	98	19	na	
0436	0501		24	na	
0448	0888	565	18	chisel	23
0450A	0880	230	32	na	
0450B	0880	20	26	chisel	32
0463	0888	77	13		
0464	0888		22		
0485	0888		24		
0489	0888	175	41	pencil	
0522	1953	177	46		
0525	0888	87	27	polygonal	
0530A	0888	94	21	chisel	14
0545	1953	75	21	polygonal	
0549	1953		18	chisel	10
0556	1953	75	30	chisel	32
0569	1953	114	29	chisel	29
0587	1953	225	17	pencil	
0608	2037	72	21	pencil	
0624	1971		20	na	
0639	1971	213	27	pencil	
0675	0888		15		
0704	1960	85	24	chisel	24
0755	2002	440	19	chisel	13
0798	0888		11	na	
0800	0888	85	74	wedge	
0801	0888	335	30	pencil	
0816	2222	210	27	chisel	20
0847	2268	1585	30	chisel	
0851	2248	285	43	chisel	29
0860	1953	280	24	chisel	29

Table 5: Turning Waste

Find	Context	Maximum diameter top	Maximum diameter bottom	Length	Complete	Pre-turning marks	Mounting hole	Mandrel socket
0453	1959	19	23	47	no	yes	absent	absent
0521	1953	27	32	53	yes	yes	cylindrical	absent
0611	2037	32	24	48	yes	yes	cylindrical	absent
0679	0888	28	23	23	no	no	absent	absent
0823	2232	33	22	65	no	yes	absent	absent

Table 6: Woodchips and offcuts (continued p.278)

Find	Context	Description	Length	Width	Thickness	Form
0352B	0888	woodchip	100	35	12	chisel
0354a	0888	woodchip	98	47	13	oblique parallelogram
0354b	0888	woodchip	125	40	11	oblique parallelogram
0375	0888	woodchip	106	51	19	irregular-squared end
0427	0888	offcut	83	82	66	wedge
0448b	0888	woodchip	165	40	11	
0459	0888	offcut	78	73	31	irregular
0460	0888	woodchip	133	54	11	flat
0462	0888	woodchip	99	38	11	chisel
0488	0888	woodchip	127	46	25	oblong
0490	0888	woodchip	113	45	11	oblique parallelogram
0499	0888	offcut	160	76	58	oblong
0506a	0888	woodchip	96	46	10	oblique parallelogram
0508b	0888	woodchip	70	31	14	chisel
0508c	0888	woodchip	45	44	43	irregular
0508d	0888	woodchip	106	24	20	oblique parallelogram
0509a	0888	offcut	97	48	14	wedge
0509b	0888	woodchip	105	43	29	chisel
0512.1	0888	offcut	106	97	36	uncertain
0512.3	0888	woodchip	48	29	7	chisel
0512.6	0888	woodchip	92	56	17	chisel
0526	0888	woodchip	83	68	17	chisel
0529	0888	offcut	151	70	69	chisel
0529A	0888	woodchip	240	45	12	sliver
0530	0888	offcut	68	58	44	chisel
0533	0888	woodchip	120	76	11	flat-faceted upper
0546	1953	offcut	48	45	21	chisel
0555	1953	woodchip	82	17	18	chisel
0563	1953	woodchip	44	34	15	na
0592	1953	woodchip	47	24	11	oblique parallelogram
0602	2071	offcut	74	17	13	oblong
0606	2037	woodchip	65	37	9	oblique parallelogram
0607	2037	woodchip	32	28	6	chisel
0610	0888	woodchip	85	42	11	chisel
0614	2041	woodchip	85	48	11	chisel
0616	2037	offcut	122	55	47	irregular
0627	2041	woodchip	60	53	13	chisel
0634	2041	offcut	56	54	17	irregular
0642	1971	offcut?	103	66	21	uncertain
0676	0888	woodchip	150	70	21	wedge
0681	2039	woodchip	39	39	12	oblique parallelogram
0695	1960	offcut	255	100	75	oblong
0722	0888	offcut	134	69	23	oblong
0728	1971	woodchip	23	27	11	oblique parallelogram
0730	1971	woodchip	66	28	12	chisel
0741	2039	offcut	75	55	12	flat oblong
0744	2039	woodchip	50	36	11	oblique parallelogram
0745	2039	woodchip	100	25	8	
0748	2039	woodchip	30	19	6	oblique parallelogram

Find	Context	Description	Length	Width	Thickness	Form
0752	2039	woodchip	35	22	5	oblique parallelogram
0762	2117	woodchip	60	25	11	oblique parallelogram
0765	2117	woodchip	50	28	4	oblique parallelogram
0768A	1971	woodchip	35	40	12	oblique parallelogram
0768B	1971	woodchip	27	33	11	oblique parallelogram
0785	1959	offcut?	65	33	30	irregular
0786	2189	offcut	140	86	67	oblong
0787	2087	offcut	74	23	18	irregular
0790	2087	woodchip	65	55	11	
0791	2087	offcut	76	32	27	chisel
0792	2087	woodchip	145	40	24	chisel
0794	2087	woodchip	72	24	14	chisel?
0803	0000	offcut?	200	92	31	irregular
0804A	2232	woodchip	64	31	19	oblique parallelogram
0806	2232	woodchip	66	42	8	
0811	0222	offcut	125	67	20	oblong
0812	0222	woodchip	75	80	20	trapezium
0813	0222	woodchip	90	80	25	trapezium
0819	2232	offcut	84	19	15	oblique parallelogram
0826	2190	offcut	79	56	33	steep sided trapezium
0831	2273	chip without	107	68	16	
0839	2168	woodchip	100	58	8	oblong
0845	2232	woodchip	54	31	12	oblique parallelogram
0856	1953	woodchip	82	31	11	chisel
0857	1953	woodchip	50	45	17	oblique parallelogram
0858	1953	woodchip	65	65	27	trapezium

Appendix 2a
The Pict's Knowe – catalogue of wood finds

Anne Crone, Rob Sands and Theo Skinner

Find No.	Context	Description	Identification
47 (=861)	122	part of round vessel	Alnus sp.
48	122	"ard"	Quercus sp.
50	122	stake cut to point	Corylus avellana
52	122	stake tip	Corylus avellana
54	122	stake tip	Corylus avellana
61	119	small chip	Quercus sp.
66	119	sliver	Quercus sp.
67	119	Peg tip with oval hole	Quercus sp.
72	285	roundwood fragment	Corylus avellana
93.1	123	roundwood stake	Corylus avellana
93.2	123	roundwood stake	Corylus avellana
93.3	123	roundwood stake	Corylus avellana
94	123	roundwoood fragments	Corylus avellana
116	392	chip	Quercus sp.
118	392	chip	Quercus sp.
128	285	twig eroded to point	Corylus avellana
130	285	2 fragments	Quercus sp.
130	285	roundwoood	Corylus avellana
135	285	stake	Corylus avellana
145	130	shaped but eroded timber	Quercus sp.
160	412	split roundwood fragment	Corylus avellana
164	412	twig	Alnus sp.
168	412	small roundwood (twig)	Prunus avium?
169	130	perforated peg	Quercus sp.
170	130	fragmented wood chip	Quercus sp.
175	412	roundwood	Corylus avellana
178	392	fragmented wood chip	Quercus sp.
179.1	130	degraded split fragment	Quercus sp.
179.2	130	large roundwood	Alnus sp.
179.3	130	small roundwood	Salix sp.
180	130	chip	Quercus sp.
184.1	130	stake tip	Alnus sp.
184.2	130	stake tip	Alnus sp.
186	130	point	Fraxinus excelsior
188	130	stake tip	Corylus avellana
188.1	130	roundwood	Castanea sativa
188.2	130	roundwood	Betula sp.
188.3	130	roundwood	Corylus avellana
235	130	plank	Quercus sp.
310.1	524	roundwood	Corylus avellana
310.2	524	chip	Quercus sp.
310.3	524	roundwood	Corylus avellana

Find No.	Context	Description	Identification
315.1	698	chip	Quercus sp.
315.2	698	roundwood	Corylus avellana
317.1	698	oblong timber	Quercus sp.
317.2	698	chip	Quercus sp.
318.1	698	chip	Quercus sp.
318.2	698	chip	Quercus sp.
318.3	698	roundwood	Corylus avellana
318.4	698	roundwood	Corylus avellana
323	698	Roundwood fragments	Betula sp.
324	698	roundwood	Corylus avellana
333.1	698	peg head?	Quercus sp.
333.2	698	chip	Quercus sp.
333.3	698	chip	Quercus sp.
333.4	698	amorphous fragment	Quercus sp.
333.5	698	amorphous fragment	Quercus sp.
334.1	698	chip	Quercus sp.
334.2	698	chip	Quercus sp.
335	501	Crushed roundwood fragments	Corylus avellana
338	501	roundwood	Corylus avellana
341	888	roundwood fragments	Corylus avellana
341	888		Quercus sp.
347	888	amorphous fragment	Quercus sp.
352.1	888	roundwood fragment	Alnus sp.
352.2	888	sliver	Quercus sp.
360	501		Corylus avellana
361.1	501	thin sliver	Quercus sp.
361.2	501		Alnus sp.
363	Unstrat.		Quercus sp.
373	888	roundwood with facet	Corylus avellana
375	888	large chip	Quercus sp.
376	888	thin sliver	Quercus sp.
377	888	chip	Quercus sp.
383	1975	Roundwood with cut end	Salix sp.
384	1953	perforated peg	Quercus sp.
385	1953	perforated peg	Quercus sp.
388	1953	Split roundwood fragment	Quercus sp.
391.1	888	chip	Quercus sp.
391.2	888	chip	Quercus sp.
393	888	Roundwood fragments	Corylus avellana
400	888	oblong timber	Quercus sp.
402	1960	roundwood, possibly cut	Corylus avellana
403	823	fragment of wood with bark	Quercus sp.
411	501	roundwood fragments	Corylus avellana
415	888	2 roundwood fragments	Alnus sp.
417	888	roundwood	Salix sp.
418	888	roundwood	Corylus avellana
419	888		Betula sp.
420	888	Split roundwood fragment	Taxus baccata
425	888	wood chip	Quercus sp.
427	888	offcut	Quercus sp.
429	888	?stave	Quercus sp.
444	888	roundwood	Castanea sativa
445	888	Roundwood fragments	Corylus avellana

Find No.	Context	Description	Identification
448	888	Roundwood cut to point	Alnus sp.
448.1	888	chip	Alnus sp.
449	888	carved object	?Alnus sp.
450.1	888	Roundwood, possibly gnawed	Betula sp.
450.2	888	Roundwood with facet	Corylus avellana
452	1959	amorphous fragment	Quercus sp.
453	1959	multi-facetted object	Quercus sp.
454	1959	oblong timber	Quercus sp.
456.1	1959	fragment	Quercus sp.
456.2	1959	stake tip	Pirus/Crataegus/Malus
456.3	1959	roundwood	Betula sp.
458.1	888	Amorphous fragment	Quercus sp.
458.2	888	Amorphous fragment	Quercus sp.
459	888	offcut	Quercus sp.
460	888	chip	Fraxinus excelsior
462	888	chip	Quercus sp.
463.1	888	roundwood	Corylus avellana
463.2	888	roundwood	Quercus sp.
464	888	roundwood	Corylus avellana
464.1	888	chip	Alnus sp.
464.2	888	roundwood	Corylus avellana
465.1	888	large chip	Fraxinus excelsior
465.2	888	chip	Quercus sp.
465.3	888	chip	Quercus sp.
465.4	888	roundwood	Salix sp.
485	888	roundwood	Corylus avellana
488	888	chip	Alnus sp.
489	888	roundwood	Quercus sp.
490	888	chip	Alnus sp.
491	888		Fraxinus excelsior
499	888	offcut	Quercus sp.
506.1	888	chip	Quercus sp.
506.2	888	chip	Alnus sp.
507.1	888	4 chips/offcuts	Quercus sp.
507.2	888	roundwood, 2	Corylus avellana
507.3	888	2 amorphs	Quercus sp.
508.1	888	offcut	Quercus sp.
508.2	888	offcut	Quercus sp.
508.3	888	offcut	Quercus sp.
508.4	888	offcut	Betula sp.
508.5	888	offcut	Quercus sp.
508.6	888	offcut	Alnus sp.
508.7	888	offcut	Quercus sp.
509.1	888	offcut	Quercus sp.
509.2	888	chip	Quercus sp.
509.3	888	offcut	Quercus sp.
509.4	888	offcut	Quercus sp.
512.1	888	roundwood fragment	Corylus avellana
512.2	888	fragments	Quercus sp.
512.3	888	chip	Quercus sp.
512.4	888	amorphous, possibly worked	Quercus sp.
512.5	888		Quercus sp.
520	1953		Alnus sp.

Appendix 2a

Find No.	Context	Description	Identification
522	1953	worked roundwood	Alnus sp.
522	1953	worked roundwood	Corylus avellana
525	888	possible peg	Quercus sp.
526	888	chip	Quercus sp.
529	888	offcut	Quercus sp.
529.2	888	slat	Quercus sp.
530.1	888	offcut	Alnus sp.
530.2	888	chip	Quercus sp.
530.3	888	roundwood	Corylus avellana
531	888	roundwood	Corylus avellana
532	888	2 joining worked fragments	Quercus sp.
533	888	chip with facets	Quercus sp.
541	1953	roundwood	Corylus avellana
542	1953	Roundwood fragment	Alnus sp.
543	1953	Roundwood fragment	Salix sp.
543.1	1953	point	Salix sp.
543.2	1953	roundwood	Quercus sp.
543.3	1953	point	Quercus sp.
545	1953	multi-facetted roundwood	Fraxinus excelsior
546	1953	offcut	Quercus sp.
549	1953	roundwood	Salix sp.
550	1953	roundwood	Alnus sp.
551	1953	roundwood	Corylus avellana
552	1953	roundwood fragments	Quercus sp.
554	1953	roundwood, cut at one end	Corylus avellana
555	1953	small offcut	Quercus sp.
556	1953	roundwood, cut to point, 2cm	Corylus avellana
558	1953	Twig	Alnus sp.
560	1953	roundwood fragments with facet	Corylus avellana
562	1953	chip	Quercus sp.
563	1953	chip	Quercus sp.
567.1	1985	roundwood, cut to point, 3cm	Corylus avellana
567.2	1985	roundwood cut to point	Corylus avellana
568	1953	roundwood fragments	Corylus avellana
570	1953	Roundwood	Corylus avellana
571	1953	round wood fragments	Alnus sp.
574	1953	root?	Corylus avellana
586	1985	charred wood	Quercus sp.
587	1953	worked roundwood	Betula sp.
588	1953	roundwood	Betula sp.
589	1953	roundwood	Castanea sariva
595	1953	roundwood fragments	Alnus sp.
596	1953	roundwood	Corylus avellana
597	1953	?object	Alnus sp.
598	1953	roundwood	Corylus avellana
602	2071	offcut	Quercus sp.
603	2071		Quercus sp.
606	2037	chip	Quercus sp.
608	2037	roundwood	Salix sp.
610	888	chip	Quercus sp.
614	2041	chip	Fraximus excelsior
616	2037	offcut	Fraximus excelsior
617	2041		Alnus sp.

Find No.	Context	Description	Identification
623	2041	roundwood	Corylus avellana
624.1	2041	roundwood	Salix sp.
624.2	2041	3 chips	Quercus sp.
627	2041	chip	?Quercus sp.
633	1971	roundwood fragment	Corylus avellana
637	2041		Quercus sp.
639	1971	roundwood	Quercus sp.
642	1971	offcut?	Quercus sp.
643	1971		Quercus sp.
647	1971	roundwood twig	Corylus avellana
649	1971		Quercus sp.
653	1971	roundwood	Corylus avellana
654	1971	Roundwood, cut to point	Corylus avellana
655	1971	Roundwood	Corylus avellana
656	1971		Quercus sp.
659	1971		Fraxinus excelsior
660	1971	roundwood	Corylus avellana
661	1971	chip	Quercus sp.
664	1971	amorphs	Quercus sp.
672	1971		Quercus sp.
675	888	roundwood	Corylus avellana
676	888	chip	Quercus sp.
679	888	?turning waste	Betula sp.
680	2039	Twig	Corylus avellana
681	2039	chip	Alnus sp.
682	2039	Perforated peg	Quercus sp.
685	2039	roundwood fragment	Betula sp.
686	2039	fragment of ? worked wood	Quercus sp.
687	2039	chip	Quercus sp.
688	2039	chip	Quercus sp.
689	888	chip	Quercus sp.
689	888	4 chips	Quercus sp.
692	1960		Salix sp.
693	1960	amorph	Quercus sp.
695	1960	roundwood	Quercus sp.
696	1960		Quercus sp.
700	1960	fragments	Quercus sp.
701	1960	amorph	Quercus sp.
702	1960	roundwood	Quercus sp.
703	1960	?stave for handled bucket	Alnus sp.
704.1	1960	Charred roundwood fragment	Alnus sp.
704.2	1960	roundwood	Corylus avellana
704.3	1960	roundwood	Corylus avellana
704.4	1960	roundwood	Corylus avellana
722	888	offcut	Quercus sp.
723	1971	amorphous fragment	Quercus sp.
725	1971	amorphous fragments	Quercus sp.
726	1971		Alnus sp.
727	1971	2 roundwood fragments	Alnus sp.
728	1971	wood chip	Alnus sp.
729	1971	4 chips	Quercus sp.
737	1971	Roundwood fragment	Corylus avellana
741	2087	offcut	Quercus sp.

Find No.	Context	Description	Identification
744	2039	chip	Quercus sp.
745	2039	chip	Quercus sp.
746	2039	roundwood	Corylus avellana
748	2039	chip	Salix sp.?
751	1971	roundwood fragments	Corylus avellana
752	2039	2 chips	Quercus sp.
753	2086	roundwood fragment	Corylus avellana
755	2002	roundwood	Corylus avellana
756	1971		Quercus sp.
757	2039	Amorphous sliver	Quercus sp.
758	2039	Roundwood, possibly cut to point	Corylus avellana
762	2117	chip	Quercus sp.
765	2039	chip	Quercus sp.
768	1971	2 chips	Alnus sp.
770	1971	Amorphous worked wood	Quercus sp.
771	1971	twig fragments	Corylus avellana
772	1971	twisted roundwood	Corylus avellana
778	2190	Roundwood fragment	Corylus avellana
780	888	chip	Quercus sp.
781	888	amorphous fragment	Quercus sp.
785	1959	offcut?	Quercus sp.
786	2189	offcut	Quercus sp.
787	2087	offcut	Quercus sp.
788	2087	offcut	Quercus sp.
790	2087	chip	Quercus sp.
791	2087	Worked offcut	Quercus sp.
792	2087	axe chip	Quercus sp.
792	2087	chip	Quercus sp.
793	2087	8 "chips"	Alnus sp.
793.1	2087	roundwood	Corylus avellana
793.2	2087	Small worked fragment	Quercus sp.
794	2087	chip	Alnus sp.
796	2087	Split sliver	Quercus sp.
797	2087	chip	Quercus sp.
798	888	Roundwood fragments	Corylus avellana
799	2232	Roundwood, possibly cut to point	Corylus avellana
799	2232	roundwood	Corylus avellana
800	888	roundwood	Quercus sp.
801	888	roundwood	Castanea sativa
803	Unstrat.	offcut	Quercus sp.
804.1	2232	chip	Alnus sp.
805	2232	fragments	Quercus sp.
806	2232	chip	Quercus sp.
808	1953	peg	Alnus glutinosa
811	2222	offcut	Quercus sp.
812.1	2222	offcut	Quercus sp.
812.2	2222	offcut	Quercus sp.
813	2222	offcut with bark	Alnus sp.
817	2232	oblong timber; lathe	Quercus sp.
818	2232	oblong fragment	Quercus sp.
819	2232	offcut	Quercus sp.
820	2232	chip	Quercus sp.
821	2232	oblong fragment	Corylus avellana

Find No.	Context	Description	Identification
821.1	2232	wood chip	Quercus sp.
822	2232	Roundwood with cut end	Corylus avellana
823	2232	turning waster	Pirus/Crataegus/Malus
824	2191	forked charred timber	Prunus sp.
827	2191		Alnus sp.
832	Unstrat.		Quercus sp.
833	Unstrat.	peg top?	Quercus sp.
835	2222	part of round vessel	Alnus sp.
837	2169	large rw timber, charred on inside	Quercus sp.
838	2169	Roundwood fragment; 36 mm	Salix sp.
839	2168	chip	Quercus sp.
840	2168	oblong timber	Quercus sp.
843	2232	slat	Quercus sp.
844	1953	stake tip	Alnus sp.
845	2232	chip	?Quercus sp.
846	2232	amorphous fragment	Quercus sp.
851	2248	roundwood	?Salix sp.
852	2326	amorphous fragment	Quercus sp.
853	2268	peg point?	Quercus sp.
856	1953	2 chips	Quercus sp
858	1953	chip	Quercus sp.
859	1953	chip	Quercus sp.
860	1953	roundwood	Corylus avellana
571/531	Unstrat.		Alnus sp.
572/592	Unstrat.	2 chips	Quercus sp.
747 ?0797	1971	amorphous fragment	Alnus sp.

Appendix 3
The Pict's Knowe – soil analyses

John Crowther

Appendix 3.1

Particle size determination on selected samples

Soil column (Column 1) through bank

Depth (cm)	Coarse sand* (%)	Medium sand* (%)	Fine sand* (%)	Silt (%)	Clay (%)	Texture class
20 - 22	2.1	53.3	30.1	11.7	2.8	Sand
28 - 30	0.4	52.4	37.2	7.5	2.5	Sand
38 - 40	0.4	52.3	38.0	6.5	2.8	Sand

Entrance causeway

Grid reference	Coarse sand* (%)	Medium sand* (%)	Fine sand* (%)	Silt (%)	Clay (%)	Texture class
481/130	0.6	55.4	38.0	5.6	0.4	Sand
484/133	0.7	47.6	40.7	7.6	3.4	Sand
487/131	0.6	53.0	39.9	6.2	1.3	Sand
489/128	0.9	54.5	34.6	7.0	3.0	Sand

Miscellaneous contexts

Context number	Sample number	Coarse sand* (%)	Medium sand* (%)	Fine sand* (%)	Silt (%)	Clay (%)	Texture class
123?	47	0.7	65.3	31.0	1.8	1.2	Sand
123?	65	0.5	56.8	33.9	5.4	3.4	Sand
139	17	0.6	51.4	37.4	6.6	4.0	Sand
164	34	0.6	52.9	35.7	7.4	3.4	Sand
203	39	1.8	45.7	35.7	12.1	4.7	Sand
234	45	0.6	58.2	34.9	3.8	2.5	Sand
285	62	0.6	66.2	31.7	1.2	0.3	Sand
309	48	1.6	45.2	38.6	9.2	5.4	Sand
327	53	0.6	49.8	37.8	8.3	3.5	Sand
413	75	0.4	49.9	39.3	7.5	2.9	Sand
417	77	0.7	53.1	36.7	5.5	4.0	Sand
421	78	0.8	55.0	37.6	4.2	2.4	Sand

*Coarse sand=2.00-0.600mm; Medium sand=0.600-0.200mm; Fine sand=0.200-0.060

Appendix 3.2

Analytical data for Soil Column 1

Sample depth (cm)	LOI (%)	Phosphate-P (mg g^{-1})	Possible phosphate enrichment (**)	χ (μm^3 kg^{-1})	pH (1:2.5, water)
TOPSOIL					
8-10	50.2	1.216	**	0.013	4.1
BANK					
18-20	34.7	0.363		0.003	
20-22*	3.98	0.112		0.064	4.0
22-24	2.89	0.122		0.046	
24-26	2.75	0.106		0.069	
26-28	2.50	0.111		0.055	
28-30*	3.21	0.137		0.056	4.1
30-32	3.34	0.137		0.068	
32-34	3.82	0.146		0.062	
34-36	4.37	0.148		0.061	
36-38	4.50	0.181		0.068	
38-40*	5.36	0.191		0.048	4.1
40-42	8.76	0.241		0.063	

* Particle size analysis undertaken (see Appendix 3.1)

Appendix 3.3

Analytical data for Column 3 (Trench A, Section 138) through ditch deposits of Neolithic age

Sample depth (cm)	Context*	LOI (%)	Phosphate-P (mg g^{-1})	Possible phosphate enrichment (**)
0-2	1049	52.7	1.25	**
4-6	1049	63.0	0.842	
8-10	1049	65.3	0.719	
12-14	1049	66.9	0.985	**
16-18	1049	67.1	0.762	
18-20	1049	75.7	0.784	
22-24	1049	89.6	0.740	
26-28	1049/1050	93.9	1.01	**
30-32	1050	93.8	1.13	**
34-36	1050	82.7	1.08	**
38-40	1050	94.8	0.962	**
46-48	0698	7.34	0.570	
50-52	0698	2.94	0.199	
54-56	0698/1082	2.64	0.343	
58-60	1082	2.58	0.333	
62-64	1985	2.52	0.224	
66-68	2037	2.45	0.052	
70-72	2037	2.34	0.071	
74-76	2117	1.94	0.056	
78-80	2040	2.36	0.100	
82-84	2198	1.81	0.087	
86-88	natural	3.69	0.211	
90-92	natural	3.63	0.162	
94-96	natural	4.05	0.215	
98-100	natural	1.85	0.172	
102-104	natural	0.689	0.292	

* Based on Section drawing 138

Appendix 3.4 (continued p. 289)

Analytical data for grid across entrance causeway

Grid Reference	LOI (%)	Phosphate-P (mg g⁻¹)	Possible phosphate enrichment (**)	χ (µm³ kg⁻¹)	pH (1:2.5, water)
480/128	2.43	0.269	**	0.096	
481/128	3.92	0.166		0.096	
482/128	5.36	0.238		0.098	
483/128	4.82	0.310		0.066	
484/128	7.96	0.365		0.087	
485/128	7.00	0.289		0.048	
486/128	9.65	0.334		0.075	
487/128	9.23	0.318		0.060	
488/128	8.12	0.279		0.066	
489/128*	6.42	0.250		0.046	3.4
490/128	1.51	0.092		0.031	
480/128	1.76	0.157	**	0.000	
481/129	2.61	0.159		0.080	
482/129	4.51	0.266		0.072	
483/129	3.59	0.180		0.030	
484/129	3.42	0.248		0.084	
485/129	2.85	0.276		0.054	
486/129	3.75	0.255		0.056	
487/129	3.21	0.192		0.054	
488/129	3.64	0.218		0.050	
489/129	1.16	0.067		0.025	
490/129	1.33	0.084		0.034	
480/130	2.02	0.157		0.048	
481/130*	1.05	0.056		0.032	4.0
482/130	1.04	0.077		0.034	
483/130	1.39	0.061		0.025	
484/130	2.20	0.066		0.015	
485/130	1.74	0.126		0.016	
486/130	2.23	0.113		0.031	
487/130	2.71	0.120		0.033	
488/130	1.25	0.049		0.099	
489/130	1.00	0.046		0.020	
490/130	1.52	0.047		0.025	
480/131	2.57	0.222		0.002	
481/131	1.02	0.055		0.041	
482/131	1.08	0.089		0.025	
483/131	1.42	0.085		0.032	
484/131	1.17	0.060		0.026	
485/131	2.69	0.107		0.034	
486/131	0.903	0.052		0.014	
487/131*	1.41	0.090		0.025	3.9
488/131	2.58	0.269	**	0.043	
489/131	1.21	0.063		0.014	
490/131	4.55	0.197		0.059	
480/132	2.55	0.167		0.066	
481/132	2.05	0.126		0.033	
482/132	1.34	0.088		0.026	
483/132	3.24	0.204		0.048	
484/132	3.74	0.179		0.050	
485/132	1.78	0.118		0.031	
486/132	1.82	0.104		0.015	
487/132	1.58	0.116		0.048	
488/132	1.41	0.054		0.024	
489/132	1.81	0.056		0.023	
490/132	1.58	0.054		0.016	
480/133	missing				
481/133	6.38	0.211		0.001	

Grid Reference	LOI (%)	Phosphate-P (mg g-1)	Possible phosphate enrichment (**)	χ (µm³ kg⁻¹)	pH (1:2.5, water)
482/133	5.51	0.122		0.068	
483/133	6.45	0.313		0.066	
484/133*	8.34	0.472	**	0.072	3.7
485/133	5.24	0.294		0.062	
486/133	4.31	0.194		0.066	
487/133?	4.70	0.282		0.054	
488/133	2.51	0.105		0.031	
489/133	1.88	0.078		0.020	
490/133	1.10	0.050		0.014	

*Particle size analysis undertaken (see Appendix 3.1)

Appendix 3.5 (continued p. 290)

Analytical data from other contexts

Ctxt	Description	Sample	LOI (%)	Phosphate-P (mg g⁻¹)	Possible phosphate enrichment (**)	χ (µm³ kg⁻¹)	pH
063	Black peat beneath bank	72	86.6	0.296		0.000	4.1
120*	Bank material	60	2.49	0.091		0.032	4.1
123?*	Ditch silt	47	2.34	0.128		0.071	4.8
123?*	Bank material	65	7.73	0.052		0.068	4.1
131	Stakehole fill	15	2.47	0.170		0.063	4.0
133	Stakehole fill	16	2.87	0.210		0.064	4.0
139*	Stakehole fill	17	3.20	0.177		0.002	4.3
145	Stakehole fill	18	7.19	0.233		0.068	4.1
147	Stakehole fill	19	5.30	0.081		0.029	4.0
152	Stakehole fill	20	5.85	0.091		0.054	3.9
154	Stakehole fill	21	2.56	0.142		0.084	4.4
156	Stakehole fill	22	7.12	0.209		0.001	3.9
164*	Stakehole fill	34	2.75	0.090		0.035	4.2
178	Stakehole fill	35	5.18	0.311		0.054	3.9
179	Stakehole fill	36	5.25	0.278		0.042	3.9
194	Stakehole fill	37	11.6	0.685	**	0.001	3.8
195	Stakehole fill	38	27.2	1.10		0.001	4.0
203*	Stakehole fill	39	14.1	0.258		0.001	3.7
223	Stakehole fill	40	6.21	0.444		0.047	3.7
227	Stakehole fill	41	5.19	0.470	**	0.001	3.6
234*	Ditch silt	45	4.45	0.155		0.001	4.6
272	Stakehole fill	42	6.82	0.245		0.055	4.1
278	Stakehole fill	43	3.55	0.164		0.062	4.3
285*	Ditch silt	62	1.77	0.094		0.001	4.7
309*	Stakehole fill	48	10.4	0.495		0.091	3.6
315	Stakehole fill	49	4.92	0.355		0.083	3.6
317	Stakehole fill	50	4.75	0.236		0.001	4.2
318	Stakehole fill	51	4.08	0.276		0.002	4.3
324	Stakehole fill	52	10.7	0.792	**	0.092	3.8
327*	Stakehole fill	53	6.50	0.349		0.079	3.7
339	Stakehole fill	54	4.30	0.283		0.040	4.0
341	Stakehole fill	55	8.17	0.215		0.087	3.7
343	Red peat associated with tree roots	57	93.7	0.237		0.012	3.6
397	Stakehole fill	68	3.77	0.222		0.001	4.0
408	Stakehole fill	74	6.70	0.341		0.091	3.7
413*	Posthole fill	75	6.07	0.239		0.023	3.8
417*	Slot trench fill	77	5.64	0.323		0.001	4.1
421*	Stakehole fill	78	1.83	0.170		0.063	4.3
441	Stakehole fill	79	2.31	0.151		0.043	5.0

Ctxt	Description	Sample	LOI (%)	Phosphate-P (mg g⁻¹)	Possible phosphate enrichment (**)	χ (µm³ kg⁻¹)	pH
465	Stakehole fill	82	4.21	0.124		0.066	4.2
501	Red organic peat:post- recut fill of upper part of ditch	31/A	90.0	1.24	**		
1149	Stakehole fill	8/F	12.2	0.0331			
1731	Burnt ashy material from top of bank	45/C	13.7	0.723	**		
1732	Burnt ashy material from top of bank	46/C	9.69	0.549	**		
1792	Stakehole fill	30/F	18.3	0.227			
1960	Post-recut ditch fill (close to one of large wooden objects)	49/B	96.4	0.933			
1965	Bank make-up	79/F	5.03	0.273			
2040	Ditch fill	98/E	2.36	0.079			
2130	Post-recut ditch fill	113/A	21.4	1.11	**		
2134	Basal fill of oval pit	146/F	4.08	0.099			
2216	Top of oval mound	151/F	2.04	0.049			
2223	Dark deposit on OGSin front of entrance	111/F	2.52	0.174			
2303	Posthole fill	168/F	3.04	0.078			
6444	Pre-bank tree-throw hole?	1017/G	4.35	0.304			
6444	Pre-bank tree-throw hole?	1018/G	5.71	0.264			
6469	Pre-bank tree-throw hole?	1015/G	5.11	0.378			
6725	Pre-bank tree-throw hole?	1021/G	5.19	0.507	**		

* Particle size analysis undertaken (see Appendix 3.1)

Appendix 4
The Pict's Knowe – archaeobotanical data

Penny Johnson

Appendix 4.1 Assessment of sample contents

Context No.	36	93	520	520	520	524	524	524	524	528	1731	1732	1943	1953	1954
Sample No.	3	****	84	85	87	58	68	69	70	83	45	46	41	172	100
Fraction of <1 mm sorted															
Modern seeds			R				R		R		F	A		O	O-F
Cenococcum geophylum		O	A	A	F	F	F	O	O	A	R	R	R	O	O
Weed seeds					R		R		R	R				R	R
Cereals							F		O		R		R		R

Context No.	1960	1965	1971	1988	2038	2039	2081	2081	2081	2097	2109	2118	2130	2170	2190
Sample No.	49	79	71	66	63	94	77	80	81	72	75	73	113	105	119
Fraction of <1 mm sorted															
Modern seeds	R			O		R			R	O	O			O	
Cenococcum geophylum	R		R	F	R	O	O	O	O-F	R	F	R	R	A	F
Weed seeds								R				R	R		
Cereals															

Context No.	2201	2217	2218	2218	2221	2232	2240	2254	2286	2296	2316	2327	2328
Sample No.	102	161	112	171	****	106	110	147	159	156	160	****	****
Fraction of <1 mm sorted													
Modern seeds				R		O		O		R			
Cenococcum geophylum	F	R	O	O	O	F	R	O	O	O	R	F	O
Weed seeds						R			R				
Cereals						R							

D = dominant, A = abundant, F = frequent, O = occasional, R = rare

Appendix 4.2 Summary of contextual information and plant remains for relevant samples

Context No.	Sample No.	Context description	Plant remains found
520	87	Tr F, grid 3A, brown peat layer beneath topsoil	undetirmined seed
524	68	Tr F, grid 3B, upper layer of bank material	cereals, one weed
524	70	Tr F, grid 3B, upper layer of bank material	cereals
528	83	Tr F, grid 2A, modern drainage feature	one weed
1731	45	Tr C, burnt ashey material	cereal
1943	41	Tr F, layer in bank, C524	cereal
1954	100	Tr D. Primary ditch silts incorporated into recut fills	cereal and some weeds
1953	172	stakehole fill/green clay deposit from recut ditch silts	one weed
2081	80	Tr F, grid 3, slump from bank incorporated into ditch fill	one weed
2118	73	Tr D, black clay	one weed
2130	113	Tr A, clay lens in fill of recut	one weed
2232	106	Tr D, ditch fill, primery fills redeposited in recut	cereals and some weeds
2286	159	Tr A, ditch silting in sondage 3	one weed

Appendix 4.3 Archaeobotanical remains from the Pict's Knowe

Context number	520	524	524	528	1731	1943	1954	1953	2081	2118	2130	2232	2286
Soil sample number	87	68	70	83	45	41	100	172	80	73	113	106	159
Fraction of <1 mm flot sorted	all	all	all	*	**1/2	all	all	all	all	all	all	all	all
Volume of earth floated (litres)	3	3	3	3	3	3	3	3	3	3	3	3	3
Triticum monococcum/dicoccum													
1 grained seed			1				1						
glume base			1										
Triticum indet grain		1										1	
Hordeum sativum													
var hulled grain		5	3		1							1	
indet grain		2	1									1	
Cereal indet grain		6	1										
Large undetermined seed	1												
Cyperaceae type 1		1											
Cyperaceae type 2								1					
cf Ubmillifer type									1				
Polygonaceae type											1		
Undet seed type 1				1									
Undet seed type 2							3						
Undet seed type 3										1			
Undet seed type 4												4	1

*Context 528 is a modern feature, sorting the entire fine flot would not benefit archaeobotanical interpretation.
**No plant remains were found during sorting of half of the <1mm flot for this sample.
Undetermined seeds were badly preserved and undiagnostic.

Appendix 5
The Pict's Knowe – plant macrofossils

Paula Milburn and Richard Tipping

Appendix 5.1
The Pict's Knowe macrofossils and their most common habitats

Taxa	Macrofossil type	Number found	Wetland	Woodland	Heath	Arable/ Grassland
Alnus gelutinosa	fruit	1	+	+	.	
Anthemis arvensis	achene	1	.	.	.	+
Callitriche stagnalis	drouplet	232	+	.	.	
Calluna vulgaris	capsule	18	+	.	+	.
	seed	16	+	.	+	.
	leafy stem	3	+	.	+	.
	leaf	1	+	.	+	.
Carex curta	nutlet	1	+	.	.	.
Carex echinata	nutlet	1	+	.	+	.
Carex panicea	nutlet	1	+	.	+	+
carex rostrata	nutlet	5	+	.	.	.
Carex sp.	nutlet	3	.	.	.	.
Cerastium fontanum	seed	1	.	.	.	+
Dicranum scoparium	leafy stem	1	+	+	+	+
Eleocharis palustris	nutlet	14	+	.	.	.
Eleocharis cf.*palustris*	nutlet	24	+	.	.	.
Eurhynchium praelongum	leafy stem	1	+	+	.	+
Glyceria fluitans	caryopsis	24	+	.	.	.
Hylocomium splendens	leafy stem	several	.	+	+	.
Juncus bufonius	seed	2	+	.	.	+
Juncus effusus/conglomeratus type	seed	many	+	+	.	.
Lemna cf.*minor*	seed	4	+	.	.	.
Leotodon autumnalis/hispidus	achene	1	.	.	.	+
Lycopus europaeus	nutlet	1	+	.	.	.
Prunella vulgaris	nutlet	1	.	+	.	+
Prunus pardus	fruit stone	1	.	+	.	.
Ranunculus flammula	achene	1	+	.	.	.
Ranunculus repens	achene	1	+	.	.	+
Rubus fruticaosus	fruit stone	2	.	+	+	.
Rumex acetosella	fruit	3	.	.	+	+
Sagina procumbens	seed	1	.	.	.	+
Salix cinerea	leaf	many	+	+	.	.
Salix sp.	fruit	1	+	+	.	.
	bud	few	+	+	.	.
	twig	few	+	+	.	.
Sparganium erectum	fruit	116	+	.	.	.
Tripleurospermum inodorum	achene	1	.	.	.	+
Viola subg. Melanium	seed	1	.	.	.	+

Appendix 5.2
The Pict's Knowe pollen results

	Pollen Type	Sample from below wood % Total Pollen	Sample from amongst leaves % Total Pollen
Trees	*Alnus*	3.7	6.0
	Betula	8.5	13.1
	Quercus	0.4	2.0
	Ulmus	0.2	0.4
Tall shrubs	*Salix*	48.2	25.8
	Coryloida	3.1	8.7
Heaths	*Calluna vulgaris*	7.5	17.1
Herbs	*Anthemis* type	0.2	----
	Atremisia	0.2	0.5
	Aster type	----	0.2
	Chenopodiaceae	----	0.2
	Cyperaceae	1.5	1.3
	Filipendula	----	0.4
	Galium type	0.2	----
	Lemna	1.5	1.6
	Liguliflorae	0.4	----
	Plantago lanceolata	2.0	2.9
	Plantago sp.	----	0.4
	Poaceae	10.8	14.1
	Potentilla type	0.2	0.2
	Ranunculaceae	0.2	0.5
	Rumex acetosella type	1.7	1.8
	Sparganium erectum	7.4	0.2
	Succisa	0.2	----
Ferns	*Polypodium*	1.1	----
	Pteridium	0.4	0.5
	Filicales	0.6	----
Moss	*Sphagnum*	0.2	0.2
	total pollen grains counted	544	551

Appendix 5.3
Common names and families of macrofossil and pollen types

Taxa	Common name	Family
Alnus glutinosa	alder	Betulaceae
Anthemis arvensis	corn chamomile	Asteraceae
Anthemis type		Asteraceae
Artemisia	mugwort	Astereceae
Aster type		Astereceae
Betula	birch	Betulaceae
Callitrichae stagnalis	common water-star wort	Callitrichaceae
Calluna vulgaris	heather	Ericaceae
Carex curta	white sedge	Cyperaceae
Carex echinata	star sedge	Cyperaceae
Carex panicea	carnation sedge	Cyperaceae
Carex rostrata	bottle sedge	Cyperaceae
Carex sp.	sedge	Cyperaceae
Cyperaceae	sedge	Cyperaceae
Cerastium fontanum	common mouse-ear	Caryphyllaceae
Chenopodiaceae	goosefoot	Chenopodiaceae
Coryloid	hazel/bog myrtle	Corylaceae/Myricaceae
Dicranum scoparium		Dicranaceae
Eleocharis palustris	spike-rush	Cyperaceae
Eleocharis cf. *palustris*	spike-rush	Cyperaceae
Eurhynchium praelongum		Brachytheciaceae
Filicales	Ferns	
Filipendula	meadow sweet	Rosaceae
Galium type	bedstraw	Rubiaceae
Glyceria fluitans	floating sweet-grass	Poaceae
Hylocomium splendens		Hypnaceae
Juncus bufonius	toad rush	Juncaceae
Juncus effusus/ conglomeratus type	soft rush/ compact rush	Junaceae
Lemna cf. *minor*	common duck weed	Lemnaceae
Leontodon autumnalis/ hispidus	autumn/ rough hawkbit	Asteraceae
Liguliflorae		Asteraceae
Lycopus europaeus	gypsy-wort	Lamiaceae
Plantago Lanceolata	ribwort plantain	Plantaginaceae
Plantago sp.	Plantain	Plantaginaceae
Poaceae	grass	Poaceae
Polypodium	pollypody fern	Polypodiaceae
Potentilla type	cinquefoil	Rosaceae
Prunella vulgaris	selfheal	Lamiaceae
Prunus padus	bird cherry	Rosaceae
Pteridium	bracken	Dennstaedtiaceae
Quercus	oak	Fagaceae
Ranunculaceae	buttercup	Ranunculaceae
Ranunculus flamumula	lesser spearwort	Ranunculaceae
Ranunculus repens	creeping buttercup	Rannunculaceae
Rubus fruticosus	bramble	Rosaceae
Rumex acetosella	sheep's sorrel	Polygonaceae
Sagina procumbens	procumbent pearlwort	Caryophyllaceae
Salix cinerea	grey willow	Salicaceae
Salix sp.	willow	Salicaceae
Sparganium erectum	branched bur-reed	Sparganiaceae
Sphagnum	bog moss	Sphagnaceae
Succisa	devil's-bit scabious	Dipsacaceae
Tripleurospermum inodorum	scentless mayweed	Asteraceae
Ulmus	elm	Ulmaceae
Viola subg. Melanium	violet	Violceae

Appendix 6
The Pict's Knowe – petrological examination of lithic artefacts

Diane Dixon

The petrological identification of early Neolithic artefacts from the Pict's Knowe, near Dumfries

The provenance of cherts, devitrified glassy volcanic rock and pitchstone:

Chert is a common occurrence in the Lower Palaeozoic rocks of the Southern Uplands, plus the widespread Pleistocene (Ice Age) fluvio-glacial deposits contain quantities of cobbles derived from them. Chert artefacts, therefore, easily could have been found 'locally'.

Devitrified glassy volcanic rocks [dgv]
Small quantities of glassy volcanic rock could have been found at many of the outcrops of acidic lava in the Southern Uplands, and further afield, but cannot be specifically linked to known sites.

Pitchstone is only found at a few very specific and well known localities, the nearest to Dumfries being Arran, Mull, Sgurr of Eigg, Ben Hiant on Ardnamurchan. Pitchstones characteristically are devitrified, containing crystallites. Thus Pitchstone artefacts must have been imported ready-made in the absence of a flake industry identified at the site.

Silicified siltstone, i.e. very fine grained sandstone saturated with silica from ground water.

Context	Finds No.	Identification
0001	9	devitrified pitchstone
0001	10	chert
0001	209	sub-pitchstone,~glassy volcanic
0002	11	devitrified glassy volcanic [pitchstone]
0002	19	chert*
0002	20	chert
0002	233	chert
0001	2002	chert blade
0500	300	chert
2110	665	chert
2110	332	chert
2402	2424	chert
2404	2008	chert
2404	2010	chert
2404	2012	devitrified pitchstone
2404	2013	devitrified pitchstone
2404	2014	devitrified pitchstone
2404	2046	devitrified pitchstone
2404	2051	chert
2404	2059	chert
2404	2067	chert
2404	2070	devitrified pitchstone
2404	2408	devitrified glassy volcanic
2404	2433	chert
2404	2414	silica cemented siltstone
2404	2447	partly devitrified pitchstone

Context	Finds No.	Identification
2404	2483	glassy pitchstone
2404	2506	chert
2404	2555	'crazed' chert
2404	2561	chert
2404	2567	chert
2404	2578	devitrified glassy volcanic
2404	2605	chert
2404	2629	'crazed' chert
2404	2631	chert
2404	2690	>8 individs, 6 cherts, 2 devit pitchst, 2 'crazed' chert
2404	2799	chert, crazed white
2404	2964	devitrified pitchstone
2407	2414	silicified siltstone
2801	2017	chert*
3883	2691	'crazed' chert
4486	2692	chert, dark
6228	2466	chert
6230	2456	chert, surround of silicified siltstone*
6486	2516	devitrified pitchstone
6486	2530	devitrified pitchstone
6486	2532	chert
6486	2533	chert
6486	2538	chert
6486	2539	devitrified pitchstone
6486	2541	devitrified pitchstone
6486	2558	devitrified pitchstone
6486	2577	chert
6486	2585	devitrified pitchstone
6486	2596	devitrified pitchstone
6486	2613	pitchstone, not devitirified
6486	2618	chert**
6486	2623	glassy devitrified pitchstone
6486	2630	vein quartz
6486	2636	'crazed' chert
6486	2638	?'crazed' chert
6486	2642	fine grained volcanic, very weathered
6486	2646	chert
6486	2647	chert
6486	2649	chert
6486	2652	chert
6486	2689	chert
6725	2651	chert
6725	2653	chert
6725	2661	chert including cortext
6725	2676	chert
6725	2682	chert, darkish brown
6725	2664	totally devitrified, kaolinised volcanic[1]
6725	2675	totally devitrified, kaolinised volcanic
6725	2678	totally devitrified, kaolinised volcanic
6725	2681	totally devitrified, kaolinised volcanic

*sent to M. Roy
**sent to M. Hall

[1] Separated out 4 similar fragments opaque, soft, white, does not react with HCl i.e. not calcareous; feels 'light' i.e. low density ~?clay, probably kaolinised rotted in ground, totally devitrified.

Appendix 7
The Pict's Knowe – catalogue of worked stone finds

Graeme Brown and Mike Roy

Context	Finds No.	Material	Colour	Reduc-tion	Length	Width	Thick-ness	Attributes	Type & Comments
001	9	pitchstone	grey/green; opaque	-	12	8	2	lightly patinated; missing proximal & distal; visible ripples	broken bladelet
001	10	chert	honey; translucent	3	24	16	3	missing distal; linear butt; diffuse bulb; visible ripples; (medium/ soft percussion); shallow discontinuous direct retouch on right edge; partial direct abrupt retouch on left edge	broken retouched bladelet
001	209	dgv	black; opaque	?					chunk
001	2002	chert	light grey; opaque	3	37	11	6	heavily patinated; missing proximal; hinge termination	broken bladelet
002	11	dgv	grey/; opaque	3	12	6	2	pronounced bulb; visible ripples; (hard percussion); hinge termination	bladelet
002	19	chert	dark grey/brown; translucent	3	16	12	3	broken piece; tip remaining; irregular invasive bifacial retouch; macroscopic damage on both edges	tip of projectile point
002	20	chert	grey; opaque	3					chip
002	233	chert	dark grey; opaque	2	14	9	2	cortical butt; diffuse bulb; visible ripples (medium/ hard percussion); plunging distal termination	irregular flake
500	300	chert	brown; translucent	3	13	7	2	lightly patinated; linear butt; platform lip; diffuse bulb; visible ripples; (indirect percussion); plunging distal termination	regular flake
?	332	chert	white; opaque	3	5	5	1	strongly patinated; punctiform butt; diffuse bulb; (soft percussion)	irregular flake
2110	665	chert	mottled grey; translucent	3	26	17	4	lightly patinated; missing proximal part; pronounced hackles; (hard percussion?); partial semi-abrupt edge retouch on left lateral; notched on left edge; bifacial retouch on right and left distal edges forming a point	notched flake
2402	2424	chert	grey/ brown; translucent	2	22	14	3	lightly patinated; missing proximal part; visible ripples & hinge fracture; short semi- abrupt direct retouch along right edge; retouch has produced a straight edge; an intentional break (?) has produced a point at the proximal end	retouched bladelet
2404	2008	chert	light grey; opaque	2	8	6	1	irregular shape; punctiform butt; diffuse bulb; bulbar scar; (soft/ medium percussion)	irregular flake

Context	Finds No.	Material	Colour	Reduc-tion	Length	Width	Thick-ness	Attributes	Type & Comments
2404	2010	chert	light grey; translucent	3	10	6	2	linear butt; prepared platform margin; platform lip; diffuse bulb; (indirect percussion); plunging distal termination	irregular flake
2404	2012	pitchstone	mottled grey; opaque	3	20	11	5	patinated; missing proximal; visible ripples; (hard percussion?) plunging distal termination	core basal trimming flake
2404	2013	pitchstone	grey; translucent	2	13	10	8	patinated; weathered surface	chip
2404	2014	pitchstone	light grey; opaque	3	12	12	2	patinated; part of distal end missing; winged butt; pronounced bulb; visible ripples (hard percussion)	broken bladelet
2404	2046	pitchstone	brown/ grey opaque	3	15	15	3	missing proximal and distal parts; visible ripples & hackles; (hard percussion?); macroscopic edge damage on right	segment
2404	2051	chert	grey/ brown; translucent	3	14	7	2	damaged proximal; visible ripples; macroscopic edge damage on right	bladelet
2404	2059	chert	light grey; translucent	3	5	4	1	linear butt; diffuse bulb; (soft percussion)	irregular flake
2404	2067	chert	light grey; translucent	2	10	7	2	missing proximal part; visible ripples	irregular flake
2404	2070	pitchstone	dark grey; opaque	3	15	6	1	patinated; missing proximal & distal; visible ripples; macroscopic edge damage to right side	irregular flake
2404	2408	dgv	dark grey; opaque	3	17	10	2	patinated; missing distal; flat butt; diffuse bulb; visible ripples; pronounced bulbar scar (medium/ hard percussion)	broken bladelet
2404	2433	chert	grey; translucent	2	7	8	1	linear butt; diffuse bulb (soft percussion)	irregular flake
2404	2447	pitchstone	dark grey; opaque	3	17	9	2	linear butt; diffuse bulb; bulbar scar; visible ripples (medium/ hard percussion)	bladelet
2404	2483	pitchstone	grey/ black; opaque	3	25	14	8	irregular shape; punctiform butt; diffuse bulb; visible ripples; bulbar scar (medium/ hard percussion); plunging distal termination; multiple irregular flake scars on dorsal.	core basal trimming flake
2404	2506	chert	light grey; translucent	2	7	6	1	punctiform butt; diffuse bulb; (soft percussion)	irregular flake
2404	2555	chert	grey/ blue; opaque	3	25	23	7	burnt with crazed surfaces; triangular shaped; missing base/ distal end; short abrupt retouch on left edge; semi- abrupt invasive retouch on right; macroscopic edge damage on left inverse	broken preform for projectile point
2404	2561	chert	light grey; translucent	3	8	8	1	corticated; winged butt; diffuse bulb	irregular flake
2404	2567	chert	honey; translucent	3	14	8	2	missing distal; linear butt; diffuse bulb; visible ripples; (medium/ soft percussion); macroscopic edge damage on right inverse distal	broken bladelet
2404	2578	dgv	grey/ brown; opaque	3	5	9	1	missing proximal & distal; visible ripples	segment
2404	2605	chert	brown; translucent	3	9	7	2	cortical butt; pronounced bulb; visible ripples (hard percussion).	irregular flake
2404	2629	chert	light grey; opaque	3	10	9	3	burn piece; crazed surfaces	chip

Context	Finds No.	Material	Colour	Reduc-tion	Length	Width	Thick-ness	Attributes	Type & Comments
2404	2631	chert	honey; translucent	3	7	10	2	missing distal; flat butt; prepared platform margin; diffuse bulb; platform lip (indirect percussion)	broken bladelet
2404	2690	pitchstone	dark grey; opaque	3	8	7	3	patinated	chip
2404	2690	pitchstone	grey; opaque	3	10	10	3	patinated; missing distal; flat butt; pronounced bulb; visible ripples; bulbar scar (hard percussion)	irregular flake
2404	2690	chert	dark grey; opaque	3	14	6	3	lightly patinated	chip
2404	2690	chert	blue/ grey; translucent	3	12	5	4	-	chip
2404	2690	chert	grey; translucent	3	9	6	2	missing proximal	irregular flake
2404	2690	chert	light grey; opaque	3	22	12	4	-	chunk
2404	2690	chert	grey/ brown; translucent	2	9	6	1	missing proximal	irregular flake
2404	2690	chert	light grey; opaque	3	10	6	2	heavily patinated	chip
2404	2690	chert	dark grey; translucent	3	12	7	3	linear butt; diffuse bulb (soft percussion); plunging distal termination	regular flake
2404	2690	chert	light grey; translucent	3	10	9	1	linear butt; diffuse bulb; bulbar scar (soft/ medium percussion)	irregular flake
2404	2799	chert	light grey; opaque	1	26	19	11	burn piece(?); crazed surfaces	chunk
2404	2964	pitchstone	grey; opaque	3	11	16	2	patinated; missing distal; winged butt; pronounced bulb; visible ripples (hard percussion)	regular flake
2407	2414	silicified siltstone	dark grey; opaque	3	20	13	2	-	chunk
2801	2017	chert	honey; translucent	3	20	22	3	roughly triangular in shape; missing tip; shaped with shallow continuous invasive bifacial retouch	bifacially flaked (leaf shaped) point
3883	2691	chert	grey/ blue; opaque	3	25	20	4	burnt piece; irregular shape; post- depositional break; flat butt; prepared platform margin; pronounced bulb; visible ripples (hard percussion); macroscopic edge damage on left dorsal; crazed surfaces	irregular flake
4486	2692	chert	dark grey; translucent	3	24	13	5	flat butt; pronounced bulb; bulbar scar; visible ripples (hard percussion); overshot distal termination	overshot bladelet
6228	2466	chert	light grey; opaque	3	4	4	1	missing distal; flat butt; diffuse bulb; (soft percussion)	irregular flake
6230	2456	chert	grey/ brown; translucent	2	43	23	7	sharp point; straight sides; irregular base; visible ripples; semi- abrupt sub- parallel & scaled retouch on right and left edges to form point; macroscopic edge damage on inverse; cortical base	borer
6486	2516	pitchstone	grey mottled; opaque	3	14	6	1	patinated; missing proximal; surviving part split into two; visible ripples	broken bladelet
6486	2530	pitchstone	grey; opaque	3	11	9	2	patinated; missing distal; damaged proximal; pronounced bulb (hard percussion)	irregular flake
6486	2532	chert	light grey; opaque	3	9	8	2	heavily burn; crazed surfaces; missing proximal	irregular flake

Context	Finds No.	Material	Colour	Reduc-tion	Length	Width	Thick-ness	Attributes	Type & Comments
6486	2533	chert	brown; translucent	2	21	22	3	cortical butt; pronounced bulb; visible ripples (hard percussion)	irregular flake
6486	2538	chert	light brown; translucent	2	11	8	2	missing proximal; visible ripples; plunging distal termination	irregular flake
6486	2539	pitchstone	light grey; opaque	3	14	9	2	patinated piece; missing proximal	irregular flake
6486	2541	pitchstone	light grey; opaque	3	18	10	2	patinated piece	chunk
6486	2558	pitchstone	green/ light grey; opaque	3	22	13	7	patinated; flat butt; pronounced bulb; visible hackles; plunging distal termination (hard percussion)	regular flake
6486	2577	chert	light brown; translucent	2	11	16	5	diffuse bulb; plunging distal termination (medium/ hard percussion); macroscopic edge damage on distal end	core rejuvenation flake
6486	2585	pitchstone	blue/ grey; opaque	3	16	11	2	patinated	chunk
6486	2596	pitchstone	dark grey; opaque	2	21	13	5	patinated; flat butt; pronounced bulb; visible ripples; bulbar scar; plunging distal termination (hard percussion)	regular flake
6486	2613	pitchstone	black/ grey; opaque	3	16	13	7	missing distal; flat butt; diffuse bulb; visible ripples; bulbar scar; hinged distal termination (hard percussion)	irregular flake
6486	2618	chert	grey; opaque	3	21	13	3	patinated; curved base; shallow semi- abrupt invasive retouch on right edge; irregular shallow retouch on base and inverse left	bifacially flaked (leaf shaped) projectile point
6486	2623	pitchstone	grey; opaque	3	12	12	5	flat butt; pronounced bulb; bulbar scars; visible ripples (hard percussion); macroscopic edge damage on proximal	irregular flake
6486	2630	vein quartz	translucent	-	14	9	4	-	chip
6486	2636	chert	light grey; opaque	3	11	7	1	burn; crazed surfaces	chip
6486	2636	chert	light grey; opaque	3	11	8	2	burn; crazed surfaces	chip
6486	2636	chert	light grey; opaque	3	16	12	2	burn crazed surfaces; missing proximal; visible ripples; short section of semi- abrupt retouch on right distal	retouched bladelet
6486	2636	chert	dark grey; opaque	3	16	8	3	burnt piece; crazed surfaces	chunk
6486	2638	chert	grey; opaque	3	17	19	6	burn prominent crazing, thermal cracks and spalls; flat butt; diffuse bulb; visible ripples (medium/ hard percussion)	irregular flake
6486	2642	fgv	grey; opaque	3	32	15	4	very weathered piece; punctiform butt; diffuse bulb; platform lip (indirect percussion)	bladelet
6486	2646	chert	grey; opaque	3	44	35	13	pronounced bulb; flat butt (hard percussion)	irregular flake
6486	2647	chert	grey; translucent	2	24	20	6	cortical butt; pronounced bulb; plunging distal termination (hard percussion)	regular flake
6486	2649	chert	dark grey; opaque	2	53	18	12	visible ripples; macroscopic edge damage	columnar spall
6486	2652	chert	grey/ brown; translucent	2	9	6	2	flat butt; pronounced bulb; visible ripples; plunging distal termination (hard percussion)	irregular flake
6486	2689	chert	light grey; translucent	3	10	10	2	linear butt; diffuse bulb; platform lip; plunging distal termination (indirect percussion)	regular flake

Context	Finds No.	Material	Colour	Reduc-tion	Length	Width	Thick-ness	Attributes	Type & Comments
6725	2651	chert	blue/ grey; opaque	3	14	6	1	burn?; missing proximal; visible ripples; macroscopic edge damage on left	broken bladelet
6725	2653	chert	grey/ brown; translucent	3	26	11	8	extensive edge damage	chunk
6725	2661	chert	light grey; translucent	2	14	13	3	weathered piece; damaged proximal; flat butt; visible ripples (hard percussion)	irregular flake
6725	2664	kv	light brown; opaque	3	13	11	1	modern breakage creating 5 pieces from the original chip	chip
6725	2675	kv	brown/ grey; opaque	3	20	14	7	-	chunk
6725	2676	chert	dark grey; opaque	3	27	19	5	weathered	chunk
6725	2678	kv	grey/ brown; opaque	3	38	47	13	flat butt; pronounced bulb; hinge termination (hard percussion); macroscopic edge damage to right distal	irregular flake
6725	2681	kv	white/ brown; opaque	3	18	14	10	-	chunk
6725	2682	chert	grey/ brown; opaque	3	20	8	6	-	chunk

Appendix 8
Holywood pottery catalogue

Rick Peterson and Julia Roberts

1. Holywood South

Fabric Group I   **Vessel 1**

Vessel 1 is a fine slightly open carinated bowl (see Fig. 23.1, 1). It has a hooked rim. The top of the rim has been burnished. There is a horizontal incised line approximately 20mm below the rim, below this line the exterior of the vessel has been burnished. Below the carination the body of the vessel has been fluted, although this fluting does not continue under the base of the vessel. The base of the vessel does not appear to be burnished. There are some traces of a deposit on the inside of the vessel. The vessel was around 330mm in diameter at the rim.

Colour

Core	Inner Surface	Outer Surface
ranges from light brown (7.5YR 4/2) and light brownish grey (10YR 6/2) through reddish brown (5YR 5/3) to very dark grey (5YR 3/1) and black (7.5YR 2/0)	ranges from brown (10YR 5/3: 7.5YR 5/2) through dark greyish brown (10YR 4/2) to very dark grey (5YR 3/1: 10YR 3/1)	ranges from light brown (7.5YR 6/3) through brown (10YR 5/3: 7.5YR 5/3) and dark greyish brown (10YR 4/2) to very dark grey (10YR 3/1: 7.5YR 3/0)

Hard hackley-laminated fabric of moderate thickness

Inclusions

Class	Size	Frequency	Sorting	Roundness
rock fragments[1]	medium-very coarse	moderate-abundant	poor	sub-angular

Sherd List

Finds No.	Context	Description	East	North	Elevation
4	021	1 body sherd	531.489	122.366	9.386
5	024	1 body sherd	531.444	122.367	9.346
6	024	2 fragments	531.444	122.367	9.346
8	021	1 body sherd with finger fluting, burnished	531.562	122.079	9.388
13 & 14	022	2 joining body sherds with finger fluting, burnished	529.931	123.266	9.347
16	031	1 carinated sherd with finger fluting, burnished	531.216	122.314	9.361
17 - 25	031	8 body fragments 1 incised rim sherd fragment, burnished	531.210	122.314	9.361
26	031	1 rim sherd, burnished & joins sf 27	531.154	122.305	9.355
27	031	burnished rim fragment joins sf 26	531.154	122.305	9.355
28 - 30	031	1 burnished rim sherd & 4 body fragments	531.154	122.305	9.355
34	024	1 burnished body sherd, possible fluting	531.737	121.994	9.309
35	024	5 burnished body sherds, possible fluting	531.520	121.974	9.359
36	024	1 body sherd	531.592	122.044	9.290
40	069	1 body sherd joins sf 52	531.778	122.478	9.228
48	091	1 body sherd, possibly burnished	section	----	----
50	031	1 body sherd	531.752	122.407	9.329
52	069	1 body sherd joins sf 40	531.770	122.384	9.241

[1] The rock fragments appear to be heterogeneous very small sandstone pebbles

Fabric Group II   **Vessel 2**

Simple plain hemispherical bowl with a slight external rim groove (see fig. 23.1, 2). The vessel is undecorated except for the top of the rim, which is burnished. The fabric is quite badly abraded. A seed impression survives on one rim sherd. The vessel is around 320mm in diameter at the rim. There are traces of a deposit on the inside of many base sherds and quite extensive secondary oxidisation of the exterior of the base sherds.

Colour

Core	Inner Surface	Outer Surface
dark grey (10YR 4/1) or dark greyish brown (10YR 4/2)	ranges from pale brown (10YR 6/3) to very dark grey (10YR 3/1) and black (7.5YR 2/0)	ranges from pale brown (10YR 6/3) to very dark grey (10YR 3/1)

Hard laminated thick fabric

Inclusions

Class	Size	Frequency	Sorting	Roundness
grog	very coarse	abundant	fair	sub-rounded
quartzite	medium-coarse	sparse	poor	sub-angular
mica	fine	sparse	good	sub-angular

Sherd List

Finds No.	Context	Description	East	North	Elevation
7	021	2 body sherds which join	531.562	122.079	9.388
9	021	1 body sherd	531.562	122.079	9.388
10	021	1 body sherd	531.562	122.079	9.388
33	031	1 body sherd	531.332	122.204	9.342
44	039	2 joining rim sherds, one with cereal impression, top of rim sherds are burnished	531.446	121.888	9.236
53	024	4 body sherds , fragments of possible rim	532.213	122.213	9.315

Fabric Group II   **Vessel 3**

A single very badly abraded sherd which may possibly be an unrepresentative piece of vessel 2.

Colour

Core	Inner Surface	Outer Surface
grey brown (10YR 5/2)	not present	brown (10YR 5/3)

Hard fine-irregular fabric

Inclusions

Class	Size	Frequency	Sorting	Roundness
grog	coarse	moderate	fair-poor	angular
quartzite	medium	sparse	fair-poor	angular

Sherd List

Finds No.	Context	Description	East	North	Elevation
51	031	1 sherd	531.749	122.140	9.304

2. Holywood North

Fabric Group III **Vessel 4**

A fine bowl with an out-turned rim (see Fig. 23.1. 4). The vessel is burnished internally and externally. There is a 5mm diameter perforation just below the rim. The vessel is approximately 210mm in diameter at the rim. The fragmentary state of the surviving sherds makes it very difficult to determine whether this vessel was carinated or not.

Colour

Core	Inner Surface	Outer Surface
ranges from light brown (7.5YR 6/3) to very dark grey (7.5YR 3/0)	dark grey (10YR 4/1: 7.5YR 4/0) and dark brown (7.5YR 3/2)	dark grey (10YR 4/1: 7.5YR 4/0) and dark brown (7.5YR 3/2)

Hard fine thin fabric

Inclusions

Class	Size	Frequency	Sorting	Roundness
quartzite	medium-coarse	moderate-abundant	poor	sub-rounded
grog	coarse-very coarse	sparse	fair	sub-angular

Sherd List

Finds No.	Context	Description	East	North	Elevation
8	101	1 burnished rim sherd; 1 unburnished body sherd; 1 fragment	137.94	113.46	10.80
13	135	3 upper body sherds; some fragments, all burnished on both sides	137.94	113.46	10.85
14	135	1 body sherd burnished on both sides	137.94	113.46	10.78
17	101	1 rim sherd; 1 rim sherd and body sherd in 3 pieces; many fragments, all burnished on both sides. Perforation.	137.94	113.46	10.82
31	156	1 fragment & 1 sherd burnished on both sides	137.69	115.05	10.87

Fabric Group IV **Vessel 5**

Base sherds from a round based bowl. There has been considerable secondary oxidisation of the exterior surface of these sherds.

Colour

Core	Inner Surface	Outer Surface
light brown (7.5YR 6/4)	very dark greyish brown (10YR 3/2)	light brown (7.5YR 6/4)

Hard hackley laminated thick fabric

Inclusions

Class	Size	Frequency	Sorting	Roundness
grog	very coarse	abundant	fair	sub-angular

Sherd List

Finds No.	Context	Description	East	North	Elevation
21	074	6 body sherds	2.39	18.00	9.75
44	074	1 sherd	2.30	19.59	9.58
46	074	3 fragments	2.02	19.25	9.76
50	074	3 fragments	2.82	18.81	9.54
51	074	1 sherd & 1 fragment	2.83	18.86	9.54
53	074	9 sherds & many fragments	? 2.10	19.36	9.81

Fabric Group V   **Vessel 6**

Single very badly abraded fragment.

Colour

Core	Inner Surface	Outer Surface
black (7.5YR 2/0)	---	----

Soft fabric

Inclusions

Class	Size	Frequency	Sorting	Roundness
quartzite	medium	abundant	fair	sub-rounded

Sherd List

Finds No.	Context	Description	East	North	Elevation
41	140	1 fragment	158.45	130.10	10.02

Appendix 9
Calibrated radiocarbon determinations from Holm, Holywood and the Pict's Knowe

Patrick Ashmore

These dates are sorted by site followed by Age (descending). They are calibrated using atmospheric data from Reimer *et al.* (2004); and OxCal v3.10 (Bronk Ramsey 2005); the model used was cub r:5 sd:12 prob usp[chron]. Only the 95.4% limits are presented, giving a roughly 19 out of 20 chance that the true date falls in the range quoted. Given the number of dates quoted here it is likely that a few of the true dates (but we cannot know which) fall outside the quoted range.

Holm

Description	Code	Calibrated date	Age	Error	d13c
A piece of oak charcoal (Sample 030) from fill 073 within pit 075 of the post cursus. It was securely sealed in a gravel fill of a feature cut into gravel.	SUERC-2126	3990 to 3770 Cal BC	5095	50	-25.6
A piece of oak charcoal (Sample 026) from fill 073 within pit 075 of the post cursus. It was securely sealed in a gravel fill of a feature cut into gravel.	SUERC-2124	3970 to 3790 Cal BC	5095	35	-27.4
A piece of oak charcoal (Sample 069) from an in situ post in fill 198 within a cursus post-hole 115. This is the earliest of three posts within this post-hole. It is possible that the post was from a large split timber and therefore the dated sample may be significantly earlier than the death of the tree which supplied the post, or of much the same date, or some date in between. See also samples 067 (1) and 067 (2).	SUERC-2131	3970 to 3780 Cal BC	5075	40	-24.8
A piece of oak charcoal (Sample 067 (Bag 2)) from an in situ post from a fill 227 within cursus post-hole 115. This is the third of three posts within this post-hole. It is possible that the post was from a large split timber and therefore the dated sample may be significantly earlier than the death of the tree which supplied the post, or of much the same date, or some date in between.	SUERC-2130	3950 to 3700 Cal BC	5025	40	-24.5
A piece of oak charcoal (Sample 067 (Bag 1)) from an in situ oak post from fill 227 within a cursus post-hole (cut number 115). This is the third of three posts within this post-hole. It is possible that the post was from a large split timber and therefore the dated sample may be significantly earlier than the death of the tree which supplied the post, or of much the same date, or some date in between.	SUERC-2129	3950 to 3660 Cal BC	5000	40	-25.5
A piece of hazel charcoal (Sample 007) securely sealed in gravel layer 038 of the fill of pit 022 of the double pit avenue which succeeded the post avenues on the site. The fills of each of the pits in the pit avenue contained a great quantity of burnt material. This did not relate to burning in situ, but suggested that extensive burning had taken place in the area, and that the resulting material had contributed to the primary silting of the cut features. Given that these were pits cut into gravel, and that much of this silting would have been very rapid, and that the quantities of burnt material are very substantial, it is likely that the burning event(s) and the cutting and filling of the pits are near contemporary, but given the succession of burning events on the site it may be residual.	SUERC-2119	2280 to 1970 Cal BC	3720	35	-27.4
A piece of alder charcoal (Sample 058) from the principal fill 160 of a slot within the ring-ditch complex in Trench B. This is part of a series of ring-ditch structures which seem to terminate the post alignments. This is the principal fill of a feature cut into natural gravel. The slot	SUERC-2127	1420 to 1210 Cal BC	3055	35	-25.7

Description	Code	Calibrated date	Age	Error	d13c
appears to represent a structural element of the ring-ditch complex. Assuming this to be a part of the avenue/cursus, it is likely that burnt matter here relates to one of the phases of the burning of the monument. Its incorporation into this deposit is unlikely to post-date this activity by a significant number of years, but given the succession of burning events on the site it may be residual.					
Heather charcoal (Sample 020) from fill 006 within pit 022 of the double pit avenue, which succeeded the post avenues on the site. Securely sealed, in a gravel fill of a feature cut into gravel. The fill of all the pits in the pit avenue contained a great quantity of burnt material. This did not relate to burning in situ, but suggested that extensive burning had taken place in the area, and that the resulting material had contributed to the primary silting of the cut features. Given that these were pits cut into gravel, and that much of this silting would have been very rapid, and that the quantities of burnt material are very substantial, it is likely that the burning event(s) and the cutting and filling of the pits are near contemporary.	SUERC-2123	1380 to 1040 Cal BC	2975	40	-24.8
A piece of alder charcoal (Sample 061) from layer 155, the principal fill within the ring-ditch in Trench B. This is part of a series of ring-ditch structures which seem to terminate the post alignments. Assuming this to be a part of the avenue/cursus, it is likely that burnt matter here relates to one of the phases of the burning of the monument. Its incorporation into this deposit is unlikely to post-date the burning by a significant number of years but given the succession of burning events on the site it may be residual.	SUERC-2128	160 Cal BC to 60 Cal AD	2030	35	-27.3

Holywood

Description	Code	Calibrated date	Age	Error	d13c
A piece of birch charcoal (Sample 07) from layer 104 in the North Cursus ditch, which apparently relates to its deliberate backfilling. The material in the layer may have been part of the bank prior to its collapse or destruction.	SUERC-2114	7530 to 7190 Cal BC	8330	40	-23.7
A hazel nutshell (Sample 09) from the post-pipe fill 135 of one of the post-holes of a post setting within the ditch of the North Cursus. This fill 135 was composed of compact black silt containing fragments of charcoal. It is possible that it represented the filling of the lower part of a post-pipe. The lower and side fill 101 of the posthole was a compact dark red silt, which contained larger quantities of charcoal, carinated bowl, a piece of burnt bone and some fragments of burnt nut-shell.	SUERC-2115	3890 to 3650 Cal BC	4960	35	-25
A piece of oak charcoal (Sample 02) from fill 014 of one of the post-holes of the post setting within the ditch of the North Cursus. This post-hole cut through the earlier large post-hole (224), which seems to pre-date the cursus. The charcoal seemingly represents the burnt post within the post-hole.	SUERC-2113	3640 to 3370 Cal BC	4740	35	-26.2
A piece of oak charcoal (Sample 15 (Bag 2)) from a sealed layer 053 within the very large post-hole 224 at the north end of the North Cursus. Burning took place in situ, and the charcoal may come from the post. The post-hole pre-dated the cursus, and held a very large upright. It was cut into natural gravel.	SUERC-2116	3640 to 3370 Cal BC	4725	40	-25.1
A piece of oak charcoal (Sample 42) from primary ditch fill 185, a sealed layer in a ditch terminal revealed in the same trench as the terminal of the North Cursus. The ditch was cut into natural gravel. The date should reveal whether this feature forms part of the same monumental complex.	SUERC-2118	2580 to 2340 Cal BC	3965	40	-26.5
A piece of oak roundwood charcoal (Sample 34) from fill 155 of a cut into gravelly ditch fills in the top of the North Cursus ditch, sealed by the top silty layer of the ditch. This relatively narrow feature would have filled very quickly, especially given that it was cut into loose gravely ditch fill. It potentially dates the refurbishment of the monument after deliberate backfilling of the ditch.	SUERC-2117	2310 to 2030 Cal BC	3775	35	-25.8

The Pict's Knowe

Description	Code	Calibrated date	Age	Error	d13c
A piece of alder charcoal (Sample 2687) from an early Neolithic pit 6270, sealed by a layer of peat running beneath the henge bank, cut into sandy subsoil and filled with sandy material. The pit contained worked flints and carinated bowl pottery. The fragments of charcoal were incorporated into the (deliberate?) backfilling of the pit. If this were from firewood, it is unlikely that it was very old when it entered this matrix.	SUERC-2093	3790 to 3650 Cal BC	4945	35	-26.9
A piece of alder charcoal (Sample 2491) from an early Neolithic pit 6471, sealed by a layer of peat running beneath the henge bank, cut into sandy subsoil and filled with sandy material. The pit contained worked flints and carinated bowl pottery. The fragments of charcoal were incorporated into the (deliberate?) backfilling of the pit. If this were from firewood, it is unlikely that it was very old when it entered this matrix.	SUERC-2094	3790 to 3650 Cal BC	4945	35	-28.2
A charred hazel nutshell (Sample 2655 (date1)) from an early Neolithic pit fill 6725, sealed by a layer of peat, and located directly beneath the henge bank. The pit was cut into sandy subsoil and filled with sandy soil. It contained a rich artefact assemblage, including sherds from several vessels, flints, and a flake from a stone axe. The backfilling of the pit was deliberate and if the fragments of charcoal and nut shell were from firewood, it is unlikely that they were very old when they entered this matrix.	SUERC-2095	3770 to 3630 Cal BC	4900	35	-24.4
A piece of hazel charcoal (Sample 2655(date2)) from an early Neolithic pit fill 6725, sealed by a layer of peat, and located directly beneath the henge bank. The pit was cut into sandy subsoil and filled with sandy soil. It contained a rich artefact assemblage, including sherds from several vessels, flints, and a flake from a stone axe. The backfilling of the pit was deliberate and if the fragments of charcoal and nut shell were from firewood, it is unlikely that they were very old when they entered this matrix.	SUERC-2096	3720 to 3530 Cal BC	4875	35	-26.1
Amorphous peat 55.05-55.09cm from ground surface. This sample will date the top of the peat, probably the time that peat growth ceased through burial by upcast. The sample is demonstrably in situ, laterally extensive and securely sealed.	AA-21250	2454 to 2030 Cal BC	3760	60	-30.0
Amorphous peat 61.2-61.5cm from ground surface. This sample will date the base of the peat and the onset of peat growth over highly permeable late glacial marine sands. The sample is demonstrable in situ, laterally extensive and securely sealed.	AA-21249	2452 to 1900 Cal BC	3715	80	-29.7
Wood from a sandy layer 285 right on the bottom of the primary ditch. The wood was incorporated in the gradual build up of primary ditch silts by collapse or discard of wood into the ditch: not a deliberate deposition.	AA-17475	350 cal BC to cal AD 50	2085	50	-29.9
Wood from a primary ditch fill 123 from the west ditch cutting. The sediment was probably laid down in standing water. It contains numerous wood fragments and pre-dates the major recut from whose fill came the more substantial wood. Incorporated in the gradual build up of primary ditch silts by collapse or discard of wood into the ditch: not a deliberate deposition.	AA-17476	350 cal BC to cal AD 60	2065	55	-26.2
A piece of hazel charcoal (Sample 2077) from a sealed layer 2813/4 of sand within the makeup of the henge bank. These layers represented the 'capping' of the bank, and produced two radiocarbon determinations on charcoal fragments, of 50 – 240 AD (SUERC-2097) and 120 BC – 170 AD (SUERC-2098) (both at 95.4 % probability). At this level the full extent of two of the field drains excavated in Trench F were revealed, along with a large amount of animal disturbance.	SUERC-2098	120 Cal BC to 70 Cal AD	2020	35	-25.8
Hazel 412 from a silt on the inner side of the ditch representing a secondary but still major recut; the wood was incorporated in the gradual build up of pre recut ditch silts by collapse or discard of wood into the ditch. Not a deliberate deposition.	AA-17472	160 cal BC to cal AD 220	1970	65	-28.7

Hazel roundwood from green clay in the north ditch terminal, thought to represent the fill of a major ditch recut. Rich in finds of relatively substantial wooden artefacts.	AA-17468	cal AD 0 to 240	1905	50	-29.2
Roundwood from green clay in the north ditch terminal, thought to represent the fill of a major ditch recut. Rich in finds of relatively substantial wooden artefacts.	AA-17467	cal AD 0 to 250	1885	50	-28.4
A twig of oak charcoal (Sample 2057) from a sealed layer 2813/4 of sand within the makeup of the henge bank. These layers represented the 'capping' of the bank, and produced two radiocarbon determinations on charcoal fragments, of 50 – 240 AD (SUERC-2097) and 120 BC – 170 AD (SUERC-2098) (both at 95.4 % probability). At this level the full extent of two of the field drains excavated in Trench F were revealed, along with a large amount of animal disturbance.	SUERC-2097	30 to 240 Cal AD	1885	35	-24.5
Birch twigs and roundwood from green clay in the north ditch terminal, thought to represent the fill of a major ditch recut. Rich in finds of relatively substantial wooden artefacts.	AA-17466	cal AD 20 to 320	1875	50	-28.6
Oak wood from green clay in the north ditch terminal, thought to represent the fill of a major ditch recut. Rich in finds of relatively substantial wooden artefacts.	AA-17465	cal AD 20 to 320	1870	50	-28.1
Willow leaves 122 from a compact green clay thought to represent the fill of a major ditch recut in west ditch cutting opposite site entrance. See also AA-17471.	AA-17470	cal AD 20 to 320	1870	50	-29.9
Oak wood from green clay in the north ditch terminal, thought to represent the fill of a major ditch recut. Rich in finds of relatively substantial wooden artefacts.	AA-17464	cal AD 20 to 320	1870	50	-27.5
Oak (122) from a post in compact green clay thought to represent the fill of a major ditch recut in west ditch cutting opposite site entrance. Post dates primary ditch fill 123&207 above 122 is 024: red peat.	AA-17469	cal AD 0 to 330	1865	60	-29.5
Wood (119) from compact silty sand from near site entrance forming the primary fill of the ditch. Incorporated in the gradual build up of primary ditch silts by collapse or discard of wood into the ditch: not a deliberate deposition. See also AA-17474.	AA-17473	cal AD 60 to 330	1845	50	-30.6
Charred wood from compact silty sand 119 from near the site entrance forming the primary fill of ditch. The wood was incorporated in the gradual build up of primary ditch silts by collapse or discard of wood into the ditch: not a deliberate deposition. See also AA-17473.	AA-17474	cal AD 130 to 440	1715	60	-28.3
'Ard-like' round-headed wooden peg FN48 from green clay 122 in west ditch cutting.	AA-16250	cal AD 20 to 340	1835	65	

Bibliography

Aaby, B. and Tauber, H. 1975. Rates of peat formation in relation to degree of humification and local environment, as shown by studies of a raised bog in Denmark. *Boreas* 4, 1–17.

Aaby, B. 1986. Palaeoecological studies of mires. In: B. E. Berglund (ed.) *Holocene Palaeoecology and Palaeohydrology*, 145–64. Chichester: Wiley.

Aberg, F. A. and Bowen, H. C. 1960. Ploughing experiments with a reconstructed Donneruplund ard. *Antiquity* 34, 144–7.

Alexander, D. 2000. Later prehistoric settlement in west central Scotland. In: Harding, J. and Johnston, R., *Northern Pasts: Interpretations of the Later Prehistory of Northern England and Southern Scotland*. Oxford: British Archaeological Reports 302.

Allen, M. J. and Gardiner, J. 2002. A sense of time: cultural markers in the Mesolithic of southern England. In: B. David and M. Wilson (eds.) *Inscribed Landscapes: Marking and Making Place*, 139–53. Honolulu: University of Hawaii Press.

Andersen, S. Th. 1979. Identification of wild grass and cereal pollen. *Danmarks Geologiske Undersogelse Arbog* 1978, 69–92.

Anderson, J. 1885. Notice of a bronze cauldron found with several small kegs of butter in a moss near Kyleakin in Skye: with notes of other cauldrons of bronze found in Scotland. *Proceedings of the Society of Antiquaries of Scotland* 19, 309–315.

Andrew, R. 1984. *A Practical Pollen Guide to the British Flora. Technical Guide One*. Cambridge: Quaternary Research Association.

ApSimon, A., Musgrave, J. Sheldon, J., Tratman, E. K. and Wijngaaden-Bakker, L. 1976. Gorsey Bigbury, Cheddar, Somerset: radiocarbon dating, human and animal bones, charcoals and archaeological reassessment. *Proceedings of the University of Bristol Spaeleological Society* 14, 155–183.

Armit, I. 1993. Drylawhill, East Lothian – cursus and associated features. *Discovery and Excavation in Scotland 1993*, Council for Scottish Archaeology, 57.

Ashbee, P., Bell, M., and Proudfoot, E. 1989. *The Wilsford Shaft: Excavations 1960–62*. London: Historic Buildings and Monuments Commission.

Ashmore, P. J. 1998 Single Entity Dating. *Actes du colloque <<C14 Archéologie>>*, 1998, 65–71.

Ashmore, P. J. 1999a. Radiocarbon dating: avoiding errors in dating by avoiding mixed samples. *Antiquity* 73, 124–130.

Ashmore, P. J. 2001. Settlement in Scotland during the second millennium BC, In: Bruck, J. (ed.) 2002 *Bronze Age Landscapes: Tradition and Transformation*, 1–8. Oxford: Oxbow Books.

Ashmore, P. J. 2004a. Dating forager communities in Scotland. In: A. Saville, (ed.), *Mesolithic Scotland and its Neighbours: The Early Holocene Prehistory of Scotland, its British and Irish Context, and some Northern European Perspectives*, 83–94. Edinburgh: Society of Antiquaries of Scotland.

Ashmore, P. J. 2004b. Date list (to October 2002) for early foragers in Scotland. In: Saville, A. (ed.) *Mesolithic Scotland and its Neighbours: The Early Holocene Prehistory of Scotland, its British and Irish Context, and some Northern European Perspectives*, 95–158. Edinburgh: Society of Antiquaries of Scotland.

Ashmore, P. J. 2004c. Absolute Chronology. In: I. A. G. Shepherd and G. J. Barclay (eds.) 2004 *Scotland in Ancient Europe: The Neolithic and Early Bronze Age of Scotland in their European Context*, 125–38. Edinburgh: Society of Antiquaries of Scotland.

Ashmore, P. J., Cook G. T. and Harkness D. D. 2000. A Radiocarbon Database for Scottish Archaeological Samples. *Radiocarbon* 42, 41–48.

Atkinson, R. J. C. 1951. The henge monuments of Great Britain. In: Atkinson, R. J. C., Piggott, C. M. and Sandars, N. 1951 *Excavations at Dorchester, Oxon*. Oxford: Ashmolean Museum.

Avery, B. W. and Bascomb, C. L. (eds.) 1974. *Soil Survey Laboratory Methods*. Harpenden: Soil Survey

Bachmann, H. G. 1982 *The Identification of Slags from Archaeological Sites*. London (= Inst. Archaeol. Univ. London Occasional Paper 6).

Baker, I. 2003. An Early Bronze Age 'dagger grave' from Rameldry Farm, near Kingskettle. *Proceedings of the Society of Antiquaries of Scotland* 133, 85–123.

Ball, D. F. 1964. Loss-on-ignition as an estimate of organic matter and organic carbon in non-calcareous soils. *Journal of Soil Science* 15, 84–92.

Banks, I. B. J. 2002. Always the bridesmaid: the Iron Age of south-west Scotland. In: B. Ballin Smith and I. B. J. Banks (eds.) *In the Shadow of the Brochs: The Iron Age in Scotland*, 27–34. Stroud: Tempus.

Barber, J. W. 1982. A wooden bowl from Talisker Moor, Skye. *Proc Soc Antiq Scot* 112, 578–9.

Barber, J. W. 1981. Excavations on Iona, 1979. *Proceedings of the Society of Antiquaries of Scotland* 111, 282–380.

Barber, K. E., Chambers, F. M. and Maddy, D. 1994a. Sensitive high-resolution records of Holocene palaeoclimate from ombrotrophic bogs. In: Funnell, B. M. and Kay, R. L. F. (eds.) *Palaeoclimate of the Last Glacial/Interglacial Cycle*, 57–60 London: NERC Earth Sciences Directorate Special Publication No. 94/2.

Barber, K. E., Chambers, F. M. and Maddy, D. 2002. Holocene palaeoclimates from peat stratigraphy: macrofossil proxy climate records from three oceanic raised bogs in England and Ireland. *Quaternary Science Reviews* 22, 521–539.

Barber, K. E., Chambers, F. M., Maddy, D., Stoneman, R. and Brew, J. S. 1994b. A sensitive high-resolution record of late Holocene climatic change from a raised bog in northern England. *The Holocene* 4, 198–205.

Barcham, R. C. 1980. A lost radiocarbon date for Shetland Islands. *Proceedings of the Society of Antiquaries of Scotland* 110, 502–6.

Barclay, A. and Bayliss, A. 1999. Cursus monuments and the radiocarbon problem. In: A. Barclay and J. Harding (eds.) *Pathways and Ceremonies: The Cursus Monuments of Britain and Ireland*, 11–29. Oxford: Oxbow Books.

Barclay, A. and Hey, G. 1999. Cattle, cursus monuments and the river: the development of ritual and domestic landscapes in the Upper Thames Valley. In: A. Barclay and J. Harding (eds.) *Pathways and Ceremonies: The Cursus Monuments of Britain and Ireland*, 67–76. Oxford: Oxbow Books.

Barclay, G. J. 1983. Sites of the third millennium bc to the first millennium ad at North Mains, Strathallan, Perthshire. *Proceedings of the Society of Antiquaries of Scotland* 113, 122–281.

Barclay, G. J. 1989. Henge monuments: reappraisal or reductionism? *Proceedings of the Prehistoric Society* 55, 260–2.

Barclay, G. J. 1997. The Neolithic. In: Edwards, K. J. and Ralston, I. B. M. R. (eds.) *Scotland: Environment and Archaeology, 8000BC–AD1000*, 63–82. Chichester: John Wiley and Sons.

Barclay, G. J. 1999. Cairnpapple revisited: 1948–1998. *Proceedings of the Prehistoric Society* 65, 17–46.

Barclay, G. J. 2000. Croft Moraig reconsidered. *Tayside and Fife Archaeological Journal* 6, 1–7.

Barclay, G. J. 2003. 'The Neolithic'. In: Edwards, K. J. and Ralston, I. B. M. (eds.) *Scotland after the Ice Age*, 127–50. Edinburgh: Edinburgh University Press.

Barclay, G. J., Brophy, K. and McGregor, G. 2002. Claish, Stirling: an early Neolithic structure in its context. *Proceedings of the Society of Antiquaries of Scotland* 132, 65–137.

Barclay, G. J. and Fojut, N. 1990. The site at Pict's Knowe, Troqueer, near Dumfries: a south-western henge rediscovered. *Transcations of the Dumfriesshire and Galloway Natural History and Antiquarian Society* 65, 69–72.

Barclay, G. J. and Maxwell, G. S. 1991. The excavation of a

Neolithic long mortuary enclosure at Inchtuthill, Perthshire. *Proceedings of the Society of Antiquaries of Scotland* 121, 27–44.

Barclay, G. J. and Maxwell, G. S. 1998. *The Cleaven Dyke and Littleour: Monuments in the Neolithic of Tayside*. Edinburgh: Society of Antiquaries of Scotland.

Barclay, G. J. and Russell-White, C. J. 1993. Excavations in the ceremonial complex of the fourth to second millennia BC at Balfarg/Balbirnie, Glenrothes, Fife. *Proceedings of the Society of Antiquaries of Scotland* 123, 43–210.

Barnes, I. 1983. The analysis and recreation of bronzes and brass mould residues. In: Bryce, T. and Tate, J. (eds.) *The Laboratories of the National Museum of Antiquities of Scotland* 2, 40–4. Edinburgh.

Barrett, J. C., Bradley, R. J. and Green, M. 1991. *Landscape, Monuments and Society: The Prehistory of Cranborne Chase*. Cambridge: Cambridge University Press.

Barrett, J. C. 1994. *Fragments from Antiquity*. Oxford: Blackwell.

Barrett, J. C. and Fewster, K. J. 1998. Stonehenge: is the medium the message? *Antiquity* 72, 847–52.

Battarbee, R.W. 1986. Diatom analysis. In: Berglund, B. E. (ed.) *Handbook of Holocene Palaeoecology and Palaeo-hydrology*, 527–570. Chichester: Wiley and Sons.

Bayley, J. 1985. What's what in ancient technology: an introduction to high temperature processes. In: Phillips, P. (ed.), *The Archaeologist and the Laboratory*, 41–4. London (= Council British Archaeology Research Report 57).

Bayley, J. 1990. The production of brass in antiquity with particular reference to Roman Britain. In: Craddock, P. T. (ed.), *2000 Years of Zinc and Brass*, 7–24. London (= British Museum Occasional Paper 50).

Bell, M., Caseldine, A. and Neumann, H. 2000. *Prehistoric intertidal archaeology in the Welsh Severn Estuary*. York: CBA Research Report 120.

Bell, M. 1991. *Goldcliff Excavation 1991*. Lampeter: Severn Estuary Levels Research Committee Annual Report 1991.

Bender, B. 1992. Theorising landscapes, and the prehistoric landscapes of Stonehenge. *Man* 27, 735–56.

Bengtsson, L. and Enell, M. 1986. Chemical analysis. In: B. E. Berglund (ed.) *Handbook of Holocene Palaeoecology*, 423–51. Chichester: Wiley.

Bennett, K. D. and Birks, H. J. B. 1990. Postglacial history of alder (*Alnus glutinosa* (L. Gaertn.) in the British Isles. *Journal of Quaternary Science* 5, 123–134.

Bennett, K. D. 1984. The post-glacial history of *Pinus sylvestris* in the British Isles. *Quaternary Science Reviews* 3, 133–155.

Bennett, K. D. 1994. *Annotated Catalogue of Pollen and Pteridophyte Spore Types of the British Isles*. Cambridge: Department of Plant Sciences.

Bennett, K. D., Simonson, W. D. and Peglar, S. M. 1990. Fire and man in post-glacial woodlands of eastern England. *Journal of Archaeological Science* 17, 635–642.

Bentley R. A., Chikhi, L. and Price, T. D. 2003. The Neolithic Transition in Europe: comparing broad scale genetic and local scale isotopic evidence. *Antiquity* 77, 63–6.

Bethel, P. and Máté, I. 1989. The use of phosphate analysis in archaeology: a critique. In: J. Henderson (ed.) *Scientific Analysis in Archaeology*, 1–29. Oxford: Oxford University Committe for Archaeology.

Birks, H. J. B. 1973. *The Present and Past Vegetation of the*

Isle of Skye – A Palynological Study. Cambridge: Cambridge University Press.

Birks, H. H. 1972. Studies in the vegetational history of Scotland. II Two pollen diagrams from the Galloway Hills, Kirkcudbrightshire. *Journal of Ecology* 60, 183–217.

Birks, H. J. B. 1989. Holocene isochrone maps and patterns of tree-spreading in the British Isles. *Journal of Biogeography* 16, 503–540.

Birley, R. E. 1977. *Vindolanda: a Roman frontier post on Hadrian's Wall*. London: Thames and Hudson.

Bishop, W. W. and Coope, G. R. 1977. Stratigraphical and faunal evidence for Lateglacial and early Flandrian environments in South-West Scotland. In: Gray, J. M. and Lowe, J. J. (eds.) *Studies in the Scottish Lateglacial Environment*, 61–88. Oxford: Pergamon Press.

Blackford, J. J. 1993. Peat bogs as sources of proxy climatic data: past approaches and future research. In: F. M. Chambers (ed.) *Climate Change and Human Impact on the Landscape*, 49–55. London: Chapman and Hall.

Blackford, J. J. and Chambers, F. M. 1991. Proxy records of climate from blanket mires: evidence for a Dark Age (1400 BP) climatic deterioration in the British Isles. *The Holocene* 1, 63–67.

Blackford, J. J. and Chambers, F. M. 1993. Determining the degree of peat decomposition for peat-based palaeoclimatic studies. *International Peat Journal* 5, 7–24.

Blackford, J.J. 1990. *Blanket Mires and Climate Change: A Palaeoecological Study based on Peat Humification and Microfossil Analyses*. Unpublished Ph.D. Thesis, University of Keele.

Bonny, A. P. 1972. A method for determining absolute pollen frequencies in lake sediments. *New Phytologist* 71, 393–405.

Bonsall, C. 1981. The coastal factor in the Mesolithic settlement of north-west England. In: Gramsch, B. (ed.) *Mesolithikum in Europa*, 451–472. Berlin: Deutscher Verlag der Wissenschaften.

Bormann, F. H. and Likens, G. 1979. *Pattern and Process in a Forested Ecosystem*. Heidelberg: Springer-Verlag.

Boyd, W. E. and Dickson, J. H. 1986. Patterns in the geographical disribution of the early Flandrian Corylus rise in southwest Scotland. *New Phytologist* 102, 615–23.

Boyd, W. E. 1982. Archaeological implications of a new palaeoenvironmental model for part of the Ayrshire coast. *Glasgow Archaeological Journal* 9, 15–18.

Boyd, W. E. 1984. Environmental change and Iron Age land management in the area of the Antonine Wall, central Scotland: a summary. *Glasgow Archaeological Journal* 11, 75–81.

Boyd, W. E. 1987. Cereals in Scottish antiquity. *Circaea* 5, 101–110.

Bradley, R. J. 1983. The bank barrows and related monuments of Dorset in the light of recent fieldwork. *Proceedings of the Dorset Natural History and Archaeology Society* 105, 15–20.

Bradley, R. J. 1990. *The Passage of Arms; An Archaeological Analysis of Prehistoric Hoards and Votive Deposits*. Cambridge: Cambridge University Press.

Bradley, R. J. 1993. *Altering the Earth: The Origins of Monuments in Britain and Continental Europe*. Edinburgh: Society of Antiquaries of Scotland.

Bradley, R. J. 1994. The philosopher and the field archaeologist: Collingwood, Bersu, and the excavation of King Arthur's Round Table. *Proceedings of the Prehistoric Society* 60, 27–34.

Bradley, R. J. 1998. *The Significance of Monuments: On the Shaping of Human Experience in Neolithic and Bronze Age Europe*. London: Routledge.

Bradley, R. J. 2002. *The Past in Prehistoric Societies*. London: Routledge.

Bradley, R. J. and Chambers, R. A. 1988. A new study of the cursus complex at Dorchester on Thames. *Oxford Journal of Archaeology* 7, 271–90.

Bradshaw, R. 1988. Spatial scale in the pollen record. In: Harris, D. R. and Thomas, K. D. (eds.) *Modelling Ecological Change*, 41–52. London: University College.

Brann, M. 2003. *Curriestanes Cursus, Dumfries. Archaeological Monitoring of Cargenbridge Sewerage Scheme*. Unpublished Report held in NMRS.

Bronk Ramsay, C. 2005. *OxCal 3.10* Oxford: University Of Oxford Radiocarbon Accelerator Unit.

Brooks, D. and Thomas, K. W. 1967. The distribution of pollen grains on microscope slides. I The non-randomness of the distribution. *Pollen et Spores* 9, 621–9.

Brophy, K. and Cowley, D. 2005. *From the Air* – an introduction. In Brophy, K. and Cowley, D. (eds.) *From the air. Understanding Aerial Archaeology*, 11–23. Stroud: Tempus.

Brophy, K. and RCAHMS in press. *The Neolithic Cursus Monuments of Scotland*. Edinburgh: Society of Antiquaries of Scotland Monograph.

Brophy, K. 1995. *The Landscape Archaeology of Scotland's Cursus Monuments*. Unpublished BSc Dissertation, University of Glasgow.

Brophy, K. 1999. The cursus monuments of Scotland. In: Barclay, A. and Harding, J. (eds.) *Pathways and Ceremonies: the Cursus Monuments of Britain and Ireland*, 119–129. Oxford: Oxbow Books.

Brophy, K. 2000a. Excavations at a cropmark site at Milton of Rattray, Blairgowrie, with a discussion of the pit-defined cursus monuments of Tayside. *Tayside and Fife Archaeological Journal* 6, 8–17.

Brophy, K. 2000b. Water Coincidence: cursus monuments and rivers. In: Ritchie, A. (ed.) *Neolithic Orkney in its European Context*, 59–70. Cambridge: McDonald.

Brophy, K. 2005. Not my type. Discourses in monumentality. In: Cummings, V. and Pannett, A. (eds.), *Set in Stone: New Approaches to Neolithic Monuments in Scotland*, 1–13. Oxford: Oxbow Books.

Brück, J. 1998. In the footsteps of the ancestors: a review of Christopher Tilley's 'A Phenomenology of Landscape: Places, Paths and Monuments'. *Archaeological Review from Cambridge* 15, 23–36.

Brunning, R. 1996. *Waterlogged Wood – Guidlines on the Recording, Sampling, Conservation and Curation of Waterlogged Wood*. London: English Heritage.

Buckland, P. C. and Edwards, K. J. 1984. The longevity of pastoral episodes of clearance activity in pollen diagrams: the role of post-occupation grazing. *Journal of Biogeography* 11, 243–249.

Bullock, P., Federoff, N., Jongerius, A., Stoops, G. and Tursina, T. 1985. *Handbook for Soil Thin Section Description*. Wolverhampton: Waine Research Publications.

Burgess, C. 1986 'Urnes of no small variety': Collared Urns

reviewed. *Proceedings of the Prehistoric Society* 52, 339–51.

Burl, H. A. W. 1969. Henges: internal structures and regional groups. *Archaeological Journal* 126, 1–28.

Burl, H. A. W. 1984. Report on the excavation of a Neolithic mound at Boghead, Speymouth Forest, Fochabers, Moray, 1972 and 1974. *Proceedings of the Society of Antiquaries of Scotland* 114, 35–73.

Cameron, K. 2002. 'The excavation of Neolithic pits and Iron Age souterrains at Dubton Farm, Brechin, Angus'. *Tayside and Fife Archaeological Journal* 8, 19–76.

Campbell, M. 2006. 'Memory and Monumentality in the Rarotongan landscape' *Antiquity* 80, 102–117.

Chambers, F. M., Barber, K. E., Maddy, D. and Brew, J. S. 1997. A 5500-year proxy-climate and vegetational record from blanket mire at Talla Moss, Borders, Scotland. *The Holocene* 7, 391–400.

Charman, D. J., Hendon, D. and Packham, S. 1999. Multi-proxy surface wetness records from replicate cores on an ombrotrophic mire: implications for Holocene palaeoclimatic records. *Journal of Quaternary Science* 14, 451–464.

Childe, V. G. 1940. *Prehistoric Communities of the British Isles*. London: W. and R. Chambers.

Clapham, A. R., Tutin, T. G. and Moore, D. M. 1989. *Flora of the British Isles* (3rd Edition). Cambridge: Cambridge University Press.

Clark, J. G. D. 1936. The timber monument at Arminghall and its affinities. *Proceedings of the Prehistoric Society* 2, 1–51.

Cleal, R. 2004. The dating and diversity of the earliest ceramics in Wessex and south-west England. In: R. Cleal and J. Pollard (eds.) *Monuments and Material Culture: Papers on Neolithic and Bronze Age Britain in Honour of Isobel Smith*, 164–92. East Knoyle: Hobnob Press.

Coles, F. R. 1892–93. The motes, forts and duns of Kirkcudbright. *Proceedings of the Society of Antiquaries of Scotland* 27, 92–182.

Coles, F. R. 1893. The motes, forts, and doons in the east and west divisions of the stewartry of Kirkudbright. *Proceedings of the Society of Antiquaries of Scotland* 27, 92–182.

Coles, J. M. 1971. The early settlement of Scotland: excavations at Morton, Fife. *Proceedings of the Prehistoric Society* 37, 284–366.

Collingwood, R. G. 1938. King Arthur's Round Table. Interim report on the excavations of 1937. *Transactions of the Cumberland and Westmorland Antiquarian Society* New Series 38, 1–31.

Connerton, P. 1989. *How Societies Remember*. Cambridge: Cambridge University Press.

Cook, M. J. 2000. An early Bronze Age multiple burial cist from Mill Road Industrial Estate, Linlithgow, West Lothian, *Proceedings of the Society of Antiquaries of Scotland* 130, 77–91.

Cowie, T. 1993. A survey of the Neolithic pottery of eastern and central Scotland. *Proceedings of the Society of Antiquaries of Scotland* 123, 13–41.

Cowley, D. and Gilmour, S. 2003. Discovery from the air: a pit-defined cursus monument in Fife, *Scottish Archaeological Journal* 25, 171–8.

Cowley, D. C. and Brophy, K. 2001. The impact of aerial photography across the lowlands of south-west Scotland, *Transactions of the Dumfries-shire and Galloway Natural History and Archaeology Society* 75, 47–72.

Crone, A. and Barber, J. 1981. Analytical techniques for the investigation of non-artefactual wood from prehistoric and mediaeval sites. *Proceedings of the Society of Antiquaries of Scotland* 111, 510–515.

Crone, B. A. 1993. 'A wooden bowl from Loch a' Ghlinne Bhig, Bracadale', *Proceedings of the Society of Antiquaries of Scotland* 123, 269–75.

Crone, B. A. 2000. *The History of a Scottish Lowland Crannog: Excavations at Buiston, Ayrshire 1989–90*. Edinburgh: STAR Mono. Ser. 4.

Crone, B. A. 2005. The conserved wood assemblage. In Crone, B. A. & Campbell, E. *A crannog of the 1st millennium AD; excavations by Jack Scott at Loch Glasham, Argyll, 1960*, 29–56. Edinburgh: Society of Antiquaries of Scotland.

Crowther, J. 1997. Soil phosphate surveys: critical approaches to sampling, analysis and interpretation. *Archaeological Prospection* 4, 93–102.

Crowther, J. 2002. The Experimental Earthwork at Wareham, Dorset after 33 years: Retention and leaching of phosphate released in the decomposition of buried bone. *Journal of Archaeological Science,* 29, 405–411.

Cummings, V. M. 2001. *Landscapes in Transition? Exploring the Origins of Monumentality in South-west Wales and South-west Scotland*. Unpublished PhD Thesis: University of Wales, Cardiff.

Cunliffe, B. W. 1991. *Iron Age Communities in Britain*. London: Routledge.

Curle, A. O. 1914. Report on the excavation of a vitrified fort at Rockcliffe, Dalbeattie, known as the Mote of Mark, *Proceedings of the Society of Antiquaries of Scotland* 48, 126–168.

Curle, J. 1911. *A Roman Frontier Post and its People. The Fort of Newstead in the Parish of Melrose*. Glasgow: James Maclehose and Sons.

Cushing, E. J. 1967. Late Wisconsin pollen stratigraphy and the glacial sequence in Minnesota. In: E. J. Cushing and H. E. Wright (eds.) *Quaternary Palaeoecology*, 59–88. Connecticut: Yale University Press.

Cushing, E. J. and Wright, H. E. (eds.) 1967. *Quaternary Palaeoecology*. Connecticut: Yale University Press.

Dark, K. and Dark, P. 1997. *The Landscape of Roman Britain*. Stroud: Sutton.

Darvill, T. 1996. *Prehistoric Britain from the Air. A Study of Space, Time and Society*. Cambridge: Cambridge University Press.

David, A., Cole, M., Horsley, T., Linford, N., Linford, P. and Martin, L. 2004. A rival to Stonehenge? Geophysical survey at Stanton Drew, England. *Antiquity* 78, 341–58.

Dawson, A. G. Dawson, S., Cressey, M., Bunting, J., Long, D. and Milburn, P. 1999. Newbie Cottages, inner Solway Firth: Holocene relative sea-level changes. In, Tipping, R. (ed.) *The Quaternary of Dumfries and Galloway. Field Guide*, 98–104. London: Quaternary Research Association.

Delacourt, P. A. and Delacourt, H. R. 1980. Pollen preservation and Quaternary environmental history in the Southern United States. *Palynology* 4, 215–31.

Dick, W. A. and Tabatabai, M. A. 1977. An alkaline oxidation method for the determination of total phosphorus in soils. *Journal of the Soil Science Society of America* 41, 511–4.

Driel-Murray, C. van 1999. 'And did those feet in ancient

time...' Feet and shoes as a material projection of the self. In: P. Baker, C. Forcey, S. Jundi and R. Witcher (eds.) *TRAC 98: Proceedings of the Eighth Annual Theoretical Roman Archaeology Conference*, 131–40. Oxford: Oxbow Books.

Driel-Murray, C. van 2003. The leather trades in Roman Yorkshire and beyond. In: P. R. Wilson and J. Price (eds.) *Aspects of Industry in Roman Yorkshire and the North*, 109–23. Oxford: Oxbow Books.

Driscoll, S. T. 1998. Picts and prehistory: cultural resource management in early Medieval Scotland. *World Archaeology* 30, 142–58.

Dungworth, D. B. 1996. The production of copper alloys in Iron Age Britain. *Proceedings of the Prehistoric Society* 62, 399–421.

Dungworth, D. B. 1998. EDXRF analysis of copper-alloy artefacts. In: Main, L. 1998, 347–355.

Dungworth, D. B. 2000. A note on the analysis of crucibles and moulds. *Historical Metallurgy* 34, 83–6.

Earwood, C. 1988. Wooden containers and other wooden artefacts from the Glastonbury Lake Village. *Somerset Levels Papers* 14, 83–90.

Earwood, C. 1990. The wooden artifacts from Loch Glashan Crannog, Mid Argyll. *Proceedings of the Society of Antiquaries of Scotland* 120, 79–94.

Earwood, C. 1993. *Domestic Wooden Artefacts – In Britain and Ireland from Neolithic to Viking times*. Exeter: University of Exeter Press.

Edwards, K. J. and Hirons, K. R. 1984. Cereal pollen grains in pre-elm decline deposits: implications for the earliest agriculture in Britain and Ireland. *Journal of Archaeological Science* 11, 71–80.

Edwards, K. J. 1988. The hunter-gatherer/agricultural transition and the pollen record in the British Isles. In: Birks, H. H. *et al.* (eds.) *The Cultural Landscape Past, Present and Future*, 255–266. Cambridge: Cambridge University Press.

Edwards, K. J. 1990. Fire and the Scottish Mesolithic: evidence from microscopic charcoal. In: Vermeesch, P. and van Peer, P. (eds.) *Contributions to the Mesolithic in Europe*, 71–79. Leuven: Leuven University Press.

Ellis, C. in prep. Excavations at Upper Largie.

Evans, C., Pollard, J. and Knight, M. 1999. Life in the woods: three-throws, 'settlement' and forest cognition. *Oxford Journal of Archaeology* 18, 241–54.

Evans, J. G. and Simpson, D. D. A. 1991. Giant's Hills 2 long barrow, Skendleby, Lincolnshire. *Archaeologia* 109, 1–45.

Evans, P. 1975. The intimate relationship: an hypothesis concerning pre-Neolithic land use. In: Evans, J. G., Limbrey, S. and Cleere, H. (eds.) *The Effect of Man on the Landscape: the Highland Zone*, 43–48. London: Council for British Archaeology.

Faegri, K. and Iverson, J. 1989. *Textbook of Pollen Analysis* (4th Edition). Chichester: John Wiley and Sons.

Fairweather, I. and Ralston, I. B. M. 1993. The Neolithic timber hall at Balbridie, Grampian Region, Scotland: the building, the date, the plant macrofossils. *Antiquity* 67, 313–24.

Fowler, C. 2003. Rates of (ex)change: decay and growth, memory and the transformation of the dead in early Neolithic southern Britain. In: H. Williams (ed.) *Archaeologies of Remembrance: Death and Memory in Past Societies*, 45–63. The Hague: Kluwer.

Fowler, P. J. 1983. *The Farming of Prehistoric Britain*. Cambridge: Cambridge University Press.

Fox, C. 1947. *The Personality of Britain: Its Influence on Inhabitant and Invader in Prehistoric and Early Historic Times*. Cardiff: National Museum of Wales.

Garrow, D., Beadsmore, E. and Knight, M. 2005. Pit clusters and the temporality of occupation: an earlier Neolithic site at Kilverstone, Thetford, Norfolk. *Proceedings of the Prehistoric Society* 71, 139–57.

Garton, D. 1991 Neolithic settlement in the Peak District: perspective and prospects. In: R. Hodges and K. Smith (eds.) *Recent Developments in the Archaeology of the Peak District*, 3–22. Sheffield: J. R. Collis.

Gkiasta, M., Russell, T., Shennan, S. and Steele, J. 2003. Neolithic transition in Europe: the Radiocarbon record revisited. *Antiquity* 77, 45–62.

Godwin, H. E., Walker, D. and Willis, E. H. 1957. Radiocarbon dating and post-glacial vegetational history: Scaleby Moss. *Proceedings of the Royal Society of London* 147, 352–66.

Gordon, J. E. and Sutherland, D. G. 1993. *Quaternary of Scotland*. London: Chapman and Hall.

Gosden, C. and Lock, G. 1998 Prehistoric histories. *World Archaeology* 30, 2 12.

Gregory, R. 2000. Prehistoric landscapes in Dumfries and Galloway. Part 1. Mesolithic and Neolithic landscapes. *Transactions of the Dumfries and Galloway Natural History and Antiquarian Society* 74, 1–26.

Greig, D. C. 1971. *British Regional Geology: The South of Scotland* (3rd edition). Edinburgh: HMSO.

Grime, J. P., Hodgson, J. G. and Hunt, R. 1988. *Comparative Plant Ecology*. London: Unwin Hyman.

Grimm, E. C. 1991. *TILIA and TILIA.GRAPH*. Illinois: Illinois State Museum.

Groenman-van Waateringe, W. 1983. The early agricultural utilisation of the Irish landscape: the last word on the Elm Decline? In: Reeves-Smyth, T. and Hamond, F. (eds.) *Landscape Archaeology in Ireland*, 217–232. Oxford: British Archaeological Reports 116.

Guilloré, P. 1985. *Methode de Fabrication Mechanique et en Series des Lames Minces*. Paris: Institut National Agronomique.

Haggart, B. A. 1989. Variations in the pattern and rate of isostatic uplift indicated by a comparison of Holocene sea-level curves from Scotland. *Journal of Quaternary Science* 4, 67–76.

Haggart, B. A. 1999. Pict's Knowe: Holocene relative sea-level change. In: Tipping, R. (ed.) *The Quaternary of Dumfries and Galloway. Field Guide*, 62–74. London: Quaternary Research Association.

Haggarty, A. 1991. Machrie Moor, Arran: recent excavations at two stone circles. *Proceedings of the Society of Antiquaries of Scotland* 121, 51–94.

Halliday, S. 2002. Excavations at a Neolithic enclosure at Castle Menzies, Aberfeldy, Perthshire. *Tayside and Fife Archaeological Journal* 8, 10–18.

Hamond, F. W. 1983. Phosphate analysis of archaeological sediments. In: T. Reeves-Smyth and F. W. Hamond (eds.) *Landscape and archaeology in Ireland*, 47–80. Oxford: British Archaeological Reports.

Hanson, W. S. and Macinnes, L. 1991. The archaeology of the Scottish lowlands: problems and potential. In: Hanson, W. S. and Slater, E. A. (eds.) *Scottish Archaeology, New*

Perspectives, 153–166. Aberdeen: Aberdeen University Press.

Harding, A. F. 1981. Excavations in the prehistoric ritual complex near Milfield, Northumberland. *Proceedings of the Prehistoric Society* 47, 87–136.

Harding, J. 1999. Pathways to new realms: cursus monuments and symbolic territories. In: A. Barclay and J. Harding (eds.) *Pathways and Ceremonies: the Cursus Monuments of Neolithic Britain and Ireland*, 30–8. Oxford: Oxbow Books.

Harding, J. and Barclay, A. 1999. An introduction to the cursus monuments of Neolithic Britain and Ireland. In: A. Barclay and J. Harding (eds.) *Pathways and Ceremonies: the Cursus Monuments of Neolithic Britain and Ireland*, 1–8. Oxford: Oxbow Books.

Harris, E. C. 1979. *Principles of Archaeological Stratigraphy.* London: Academic Press.

Haselgrove, C. and McCullagh, R. 1996. Excavations at Fisher's Road, Port Seton, East Lothian, 1994 and 1995. *Transactions of the East Lothian Antiquarian and Field Naturalists' Society* 23, 1–12.

Havinga, A. J. 1984. A 20-year experimental investigation into the differential corrosion susceptibility of pollen and spores in various soil types. *Pollen et Spores* 26, 541–558.

Hedges, J. D. and Buckley, D. G. 1981. *Springfield Cursus and the Cursus Problem.* Essex County Council Occasional Paper No.1.

Helgeby, S. and Simpson, G. 1995. King Arthur's Round Table and Collingwood's archaeology. *Collingwood Studies* 2, 1–11.

Herne, A. 1988. A time and a place for the Grimston bowl. In: J. Barrett and I. Kinnes (eds.) *The Archaeology of Context in the Neolithic and Bronze Age: Recent Trends*, 9–29. Sheffield: Department of Archaeology and Prehistory.

Hibbert, F. A. and Switsur, V. R. 1976. Radiocarbon dating of Flandrian pollen zones in northern England. *New Phytologist* 77, 793–807.

Higham, N. 1986. *The Northern Counties to AD 1000.* London: Longman.

Hingley, R. 1996 Ancestors and identity in the later prehistory of Atlantic Scotland: the reuse and reinvention of Neolithic monuments and material culture. *World Archaeology* 28, 231–43.

Hingley, R. 1999. The creation of the later prehistoric landscape and the context of the reuse of Neolithic and earlier Bronze Age monuments in Britain and Ireland. In: B. Bevan (ed.) *Northern Exposure: Studies of the Iron Age of Northern and Western Britain.* Leicester: Leicester University Press.

Hirons, K. R. and Edwards, K. J. 1986. Events at and around the first and second Ulmus declines: palaeoecological investigations in Co. Tyrone, Northern Ireland. *New Phytologist* 104, 131–153.

Hodder, I. R. 1999. *The Archaeological Process: An Introduction.* Oxford: Blackwell.

Hodder, I. R. and Shand, P. 1988. The Haddenham long barrow: an interim statement. *Antiquity* 62, 394–353.

Hope-Taylor, B. 1977. *Yeavering. An Anglo-British Centre of Early Northumbria.* London: HMSO.

Hubbard, R. N. L. B. and Clapham, A. 1992. Quantifying macroscopic plant remains. *Review of Palaeobotany and Palynology* 73, 117–32.

Hughes, P. D. M., Mauquoy, D., Barber, K. E. and Langdon, P. G. 2000. Mire-development pathways and palaeoclimatic records from a full Holocene peat archive at Walton Moss, Cumbria, England. *The Holocene* 10, 465–480.

Hunter, F. 1998a. The iron. In: Main, L. 1998, 356–367.

Hunter, F. 1998b. Discussion of the artefact assemblage. In: Main, L. 1998, 393–401.

Hustedt, F. 1957. Die Diatomeenflora des Fluss-systems der Weser im Gebiet der Hansenstadt Bremen. *Abhandlungen herausegegeben vom Naturwissen schaftlichen Verein zu Bremen* 34, 181–440.

Jacobson, G. L. and Bradshaw, R. H. W. 1981. The selection of sites for palaeovegetational studies. *Quaternary Research* 16, 80–96.

Jardine, W. G. 1964. Post-glacial sea levels in south-west Scotland. *Scottish Geographical Magazine* 80, 5–11.

Jardine, W. G. 1971. Form and age of late Quaternary shorelines and coastal deposits of south-west Scotland: critical data. *Quaternaria* 14, 104–114.

Jardine, W. G. 1975. Chronology of Holocene marine transgression and regression in south-western Scotland. *Boreas* 4, 173–96.

Jardine, W. G. 1980. Holocene raised coastal sediments and former shorelines of Dumfriesshire and Eastern Galloway. *Transactions of the Dumfriesshire and Galloway Natural History and Antiquarian Society* 55, 1–59.

Jardine, W. G. 1982. Sea-level changes in Scotland during the last 18000 years. *Proceedings of the Geologists' Association* 93, 25–42.

Johnston, R. 1999. An empty path? Processions, memories and the Dorset Cursus. In: A. Barclay and J. Harding (eds.) *Pathways and Ceremonies: the Cursus Monuments of Neolithic Britain and Ireland*, 39–48. Oxford: Oxbow Books.

Jones, R. 2005. The advantage of bias in Roman studies. In: Brophy, K. and Cowley, D. (eds.) *From the Air. Understanding Aerial Archaeology*, 86–93. Stroud: Tempus.

Jones, V. J. and Stevenson, A. C. 1993. Round Loch of Glenhead. In: Gordon, J. E. and Sutherland, D. G. (eds.) *Quaternary of Scotland*, 609–613. London: Chapman and Hall.

Jowsey, P. C. 1966. An improved peat sampler. *New Phytologist* 65, 245–8.

Kendrick, J. 1995. Excavation of a Neolithic enclosure and an Iron Age settlement at Douglasmuir, Angus. *Proceedings of the Society of Antiquaries of Scotland* 125, 29–67.

Kendrick, T. D. and Hawkes, C. F. C. 1932 *Archaeology in England and Wales, 1914–1931.* London: Methuen.

Kilbride-Jones, H. E. 1936. Late Bronze Age cemetery: being an account of the excavations of 1935 at Loanhead of Daviot, Aberdeenshire. *Proceedings of the Society of Antiquaries of Scotland* 70, 278–310.

Küchler, S. 1987. Malangan: art and memory in a Melanesian society. *Man* 22, 238–55.

Lane, A. 1987. English migrants in the Hebrides: 'Atlantic Second B' revisited. *Proceedings of the Society of Antiquaries of Scotland* 117, 47–66.

Lloyd, J. M. 1999. Priestside Flow: Holocene sea-level record and implications for sea-level change. In: Tipping, R. (ed.) *The Quaternary of Dumfries and Galloway. Field Guide*, 87–98. London: Quaternary Research Association.

Lloyd, J. M. Shennan, I., Kirby, J. R. and Rutherford, M. M. 2000. Holocene relative sea-level changes in the inner Solway Firth. *Quaternary International* 60, 83–105.

Loveday, R. 1985. *Cursuses and Related Monuments of Britain and Ireland*. Unpublished PhD: Leicester University.

Loveday, R. 1998. Double entrance henges – routes to the past? In: Gibson, A. and Simpson, D. (eds.) *Prehistoric Ritual and Religion*, 14–31. Stroud: Sutton.

Loveday, R. and Petchey, M. 1982. Oblong ditches: a discussion and some new evidence. *Aerial Archaeology* 8, 17–24.

Lowe, J. J. 1982. Three Flandrian pollen profiles from the Teith Valley, Scotland. II. Analyses of deteriorated pollen. *New Phytologist* 90, 371–385.

Lucas, G. 2001 *Critical Approaches to Fieldwork: Contemporary and Historical Archaeological Practice*. London: Routledge.

Macadam, W. I. 1882. On the results of a chemical investigation into the composition of the 'bog butters' 'adipocere' and 'mineral resins'; with notice of a cask of bog butter found in Glen Gill, Morvern, Argyllshire and now in the museum. *Proceedings of the Society of Antiquaries of Scotland* 26, 204–23.

MacDonald, G. and Park, A. 1906. *The Roman Forts on the Bar Hill*. Glasgow: James Maclehose and Sons.

MacGregor, G. 2005. Eweford, Dunbar. *Discovery and Excavation in Scotland New Series* 6, 169–70.

MacKie, E. W. 1982 The Leckie broch, Stirlingshire: an interim report. *Glasgow Archaeological Journal* 9, 60–72.

Macleod, D., Monk, M. and Williams, T. 1988. The use of the single context recording system on a seasonally excavated site in Ireland: a learning experience. *Journal of Irish Archaeology* 4, 55–63.

Macphail, R. I., Crowther, J., Acott, T., Bell, M. G. and Cruise, G. 2003. The Experimentsl Earthwork at Wareham, Dorset after 33 years: Changes to the buried LFH and Ah horizons. *Journal of Archaeological Science,* 30, 77–93.

Main, L. 1998. Excavation of a timber round-house and broch at the Fairy Knowe, Buchlyvie, Stirlingshire, 1975–8. *Proceedings of the Society of Antiquaries of Scotland* 128, 293–419.

Malim, T. 1999. Cursuses and related monuments of the Cambridgeshire Ouse. In: A. Barclay and J. Harding (eds.) *Pathways and Ceremonies: The Cursus Monuments of Britain and Ireland*, 77–85. Oxford: Oxbow Books.

Manby, T. G. 1963. The excavation of the Willerby Wold long barrow. *Proceedings of the Prehistoric Society* 29, 173–205.

Manby, T. G. 1988. The Neolithic in Eastern Yorkshire. In: T. G. Manby (ed.) *Archaeology in Eastern Yorkshire*, 35–88. Sheffield: Department of Archaeology and Prehistory.

Mannion, A. M. 1982. Palynological evidence for lake-level changes during the Flandrian in Scotland. *Transactions of the Botanical Society of Edinburgh* 44, 13–18.

Masters, L. 1973. The Lochhill long cairn. *Antiquity* 47, 96–100.

Masters, L. 1981. Chambered tombs and non-megalithic barrows in Britain. In: C. Renfrew (ed.) *The Megalithic Monuments of Western Europe*, 97–112. London: Thames and Hudson.

Mauquoy, D. and Barber, K. E. 1999. A replicated 3000 yr proxy-climate record from Coom Rigg and Felecia Moss, the Border Mires, northern England. *Journal of Quaternary Science* 14, 263–276.

Maxwell, G. S. 1983a. Air Photography 1982: Strathmore. *Popular Archaeology* 5, 33–34.

Maxwell, G. S. 1983b. Recent aerial survey in Scotland. In: Maxwell, G. S. (ed.) *The Impact of Aerial Reconnaissance on Archaeology*, 27–40. London: CBA Research Report No. 49.

Maxwell, G. S. 1979. Air photography and the work of the Royal Commission on the Ancient and Historic Monuments of Scotland. *Aerial Archaeology* 2, 37–43.

May, J. A. 1981. *The Glaciation and Deglaciation of Upper Nithsdale and Annandale*. Unpublished Ph.D thesis: University of Glasgow.

Maynard, D. 1993. Neolithic pit at Carzield, Kirkton, Dumfriesshire, *Transactions of the Dumfriesshire and Galloway Natural History and Antiquarian Society* 68, 25–32.

McDermott, C. 1995. The wetland unit field recording system. *Irish Archaeological Wetland Unit Transactions* 4, 7–15.

McDonnell, G. 1986. *The Classification of Early Ironworking Slags*, unpub. PhD thesis: University of Aston.

McDonnell, G. 1983. How to identify slags, *Current Archaeology* 86, 81–84.

McDonnell G. 1988. Ore to Artefact: A study of early ironworking. In: Slater, E. and Tate, J. (eds.), *Science and Archaeology Glasgow 1987,* 283–293. Oxford: British Archaeological Reports 196.

McDonnell, G. 1991. A model for the formation of smithing slags. *Materialy Archeologiczne* 26 (1991), 23–27.

McDonnell, G. 1995. Ore, Slag, Iron and Steel. In: Crew, P. and Crew, S. (eds.), *Iron For Archaeologists*, 3–7. Plas Tan y Bwlch (= Occas. Pap. 2, Snowdonia National Park).

McGavin, G. C. 1992. *Insects of the Northern Hemisphere*. London: Drangon's World.

McLellan, K. G. 2005. Pencraig Hill. *Discovery and Excavation in Scotland New Series* 6, 171.

Mercer, R. J. 1981. The excavation of a late Neolithic henge-type enclosure at Balfarg, Fife, Scotland. *Proceedings of the Society of Antiquaries of Scotland* 111, 63–171.

Milburn, P. and Tipping, R. 1999a. Pict's Knowe: mid-Holocene vegetation history and groundwater fluctuations. In: Tipping, R. (ed.) *The Quaternary of Dumfries and Galloway. Field Guide*, 75–80. London: Quaternary Research Association.

Milburn, P. and Tipping, R. 1999b. Pict's Knowe: high-resolution depiction of vegetation change and human activities in the early Bronze Age. In: Tipping, R. (ed.) *The Quaternary of Dumfries and Galloway. Field Guide*, 81–83. London: Quaternary Research Association.

Milburn, P. 1996. *Palaeoenvironmental Investigation into Aspects of the Vegetation History of North Fife and South Perthshire*. Unpublished PhD thesis: University of Edinburgh.

Moar, N. T. 1969. Late Weichselian and Flandrian pollen diagrams from south-west Scotland. *New Phytologist* 68, 433–67.

Moore, P. D. and Webb, J. A. 1978. *An Illustrated Guide to Pollen Analysis*. London: Hodder and Stoughton.

Moore, P. D., Webb, J. A. and Collinson, M. E. 1991. *Pollen Analysis* (2nd Edition). Oxford: Blackwell Scientific Publications.

Morgan, F. de M. 1959. The excavation of a long barrow at Nutbane, Hants. *Proceedings of the Prehistoric Society* 25, 15–51.

Morris, C. A. 2000. *Wood and Woodworking in Anglo-Scandinavian and Medieval York*. The Archaeology of York, Vol 17, Fasc 13. York: CBA.

Morris, C. A. 1982. Aspects of Anglo-Saxon and Anglo-Scandinavian Lathe-turning. In: S. McGrail (ed.), *Woodworking Techniques Before A.D. 1500*, 245–261. Oxford: British Archaeological Reports.

Mowat, R. J. C. 1996. *The Logboats of Scotland*. Oxford: Oxbow Books.

Munn, N. 1986 *The Fame of Gawa*. Cambridge: Cambridge University Press.

Murphy, C. P. 1986. *Thin Section Preparation of Soils and Sediments*. Berkhamsted: A. B. Academic Publishers.

Murray, C. and H. 2004. Crathes Warren Field Hill. *Discovery and Excavation in Scotland New Series* 5, 155.

Murray, C. and H. 2005. Garthdee Road, Aberdeen. *Discovery and Excavation in Scotland New Series* 6, 165.

Museum of London 1980. *The Written Record*. London: Museum of London.

Nichols, H. 1967. Vegetational change, shoreline displacement and the human factor in the late Quaternary history of south-weat Scotland. *Transactions of the Royal Society of Edinburgh* 67, 145–87.

Odgaard, B. 1992. The fire history of Danish heathland areas as reflected by pollen and charred particles in lake sediments. *The Holocene* 2, 218–26.

Oldfield, F. 1963. Pollen analysis and man's role in the ecological history of the south-east Lake District. *Geografiska Annaler* 45, 23–40.

Olsen, B. 1990. Roland Barthes: from sign to text. In: C. Tilley (ed.) *Reading Material Culture: Structuralism, Hermeneutics and Post-Structuralism*, 163–205. Oxford: Blackwell.

Ó'Ríordáin, S. P. 1940. Pole lathe from Borrisokane, Co. Tipperary. *Journal of the Cork Historical and Archaeological Society* 45, 28–32.

Orton, C., Tyers, P., and Vince, A. 1993. *Pottery in Archaeology*. Cambridge: Cambridge University Press.

O'Sullivan, A. 1991. *Prehistoric Woodworking Techniques: the Evidence for Excavated Trackways in the Raised Bogs of Co. Longford*. Unpublished MA thesis: University College Dublin.

O'Sullivan, P. E. 1975. Early and Middle-Flandrian pollen zonation in the Eastern Highlands of Scotland. *Boreas* 4, 197–207.

Parker Pearson, M., Sharples, N. and Symonds, J. 2004. *South Uist: Archaeology and History of a Hebridean Island*. Stroud: Tempus.

Parker Pearson, M. and Ramilsonina. 1998. Stonehenge for the ancestors: the stones pass on the message. *Antiquity* 72, 308–26.

Patterson, W. A., Edwards, K. J. and Maguire, D. A. 1987. Microscopic charcoal as an indicator of fire. *Quaternary Science Reviews* 6, 3–23.

Piggott, S. 1951. Excavation in the broch and hillfort of Torwoodlee, Selkirkshire, 1950. *Proceedings of the Society of Antiquaries of Scotland* 85, 92–117.

Piggott, S. and Piggott, C. M. 1939. Stone and earth circles of Dorset. *Antiquity* 13, 138–58.

Pollard, T. 1997. Excavation of a Neolithic settlement and ritual complex at Beckton Farm, Lockerbie, Dumfries and Galloway. *Proceedings of the Society of Antiquaries of Scotland* 127, 69–121.

Powell, T. G. E. 1973. Excavation of the chambered cairn at Dyffryn Ardudwy, Merioneth, Wales. *Archaeologia* 54, 44–6.

Pryor, F. 1984. Personalities of Britain: two examples of long-term regional contrast. *Scottish Archaeological Review* 3, 8–15.

Pryor, F. M. 1992. Current research at Flag Fen. *Antiquity* 66, 239–53.

Pryor, F. M. and French, C. 1985. *The Fenland Project 1: Archaeology and Environment in the Lower Welland Valley*. East Anglian Archaeology 27.

Ralston, I. 1996. Four short cists from north-east Scotland and Easter Ross. *Proceedings of the Society of Antiquaries of Scotland* 126, 121–55.

RCAHMS 1992. Report of the Commission. *Discovery and Excavation in Scotland* 1992.

RCAHMS 1997. *Eastern Dumfries-shire: an archaeological landscape*, Edinburgh: HMSO.

Richards, C. C. 1996 Henges and water: towards an elemental understanding of monumentality and landscape in late Neolithic Britain. *Journal of Material Culture* 1, 313–36.

Richards, C. C. 2005. *Dwelling Among the Monuments: The Neolithic Village of Barnhouse, Maeshowe Passage Grave and Surrounding Monuments at Stenness, Orkney*. Cambridge: McDonald Institute.

Richards, C. C. and Thomas, J. S. 1984. Ritual activity and structured deposition in later Neolithic Wessex. In: R. J. Bradley and J. Gardiner (eds.) *Neolithic Studies*, 189–218. Oxford: British Archaeological Reports.

Richards, J. 1990. *The Stonehenge Environs Project*. London: English Heritage.

Rideout, J. 1997. Excavation of Neolithic enclosures at Cowie Road, Bannockburn, Stirling, 1984–5. *Proceedings of the Society of Antiquaries of Scotland* 127, 29–68.

Rieley, J. and Page, S. 1990. *Ecology of Plant Ccommunities: a Phytosocilogical Account of the British Vegetation*. London: Longman.

Ritchie, J. 1942. A keg of 'bog-butter' from Skye and its contents. *Proceedings of the Society of Antiquaries of Scotland* 75, 5–22.

Ritchie. J. N. G. 2000. Stones of Stenness' Aberdeen. *Discovery and Excavation in Scotland New Series 1*, 125.

Ritchie. J. N. G. 2001. Stones of Stenness' Aberdeen. *Discovery and Excavation in Scotland New Series 2*, 125.

Rowell, T. K. and Turner, J. 1985. Litho-, humic- and pollen stratigraphy at Quick Moss, Northumberland. *Journal of Ecology* 73, 11–25.

Sands, R. J. S. 1997. *Prehistoric Woodworking: the Analysis and Interpretation of Bronze and Iron Age Toolmarks*. London: UCL Institute Archaeol.

Sands, R. J. S. 1994. *The Recording and Archaeological Potential of Tool Marks on Prehistoric Worked Wood – with special reference to Oakbank Crannog, Loch Tay, Scotland*. Unpublished PhD thesis: University of Edinburgh.

Saville, A. 1983. Excavations at Condicote henge monument, Gloucestershire, 1977. *Transactions of the Bristol and Gloucester Archaeological Society* 101, 21–47.

Schweingruber, F. H. 1990. *Microscopic Wood Anatomy*. Davos: Swiss Federal Institute for Forest, Snow and Landscape Research.

Scott, J. G. 1974. Govan, Shiels, ditched enclosure. *Discovery and Excavation in Scotland*, 1974.

Shennan, I. and Innes, J. B. 1986. Late Devensian and Flandrian environmental changes at The Dod, Borders Region. *Scottish Archaeological Review* 4, 17–26.

Shepherd, I. A. G. and Greig, M. K. 1996. *Grampian's Past: its Archaeology from the Air*. Aberdeen: Grampian Regional Council.

Sheridan, A. forthcoming. From Picardie to Pickering and Pencraig Hill? New information on the 'Carinated Bowl Neolithic' in northern Britain. In: A. Whittle and V. Cummings (eds.) *Going Over: the Mesolithic-Neolithic Transition in Europe*. London: British Academy.

Sherratt, A. G. 1981. Plough and pastoralism: aspects of the secondary products revolution. In: I. Hodder, N. Hammond and G. Isaac (eds.) *Pattern of the Past*, 261–306. Cambridge: Cambridge University Press.

Simmons, I. G. and Innes, J. B. 1988. The later mesolithic period (6000–5000 bp) on Glaisdale Moor, North Yorkshire. *Archaeological Journal* 145, 1–12.

Simmons, I. G. and Innes, J. B. 1996. Prehistoric charcoal in peat profiles at North Gill, Yorkshire Moors, England. *Journal of Archaeological Science* 23, 193–197.

Simmons, I. G. 1996. *The Environmental Impact of Later Mesolithic Cultures*. Edinburgh: Edinburgh University Press.

Simpson, G. 1996. Collingwood's philosophy of history: observations of an archaeologist. *Collingwood Studies* 3, 217–25.

Smith, A. J. E. 1978. *The Moss Flora of Britain and Ireland*. Cambridge: Cambridge University Press.

Smith, A. G. 1981. The Neolithic. In: Simmons, I. G. and Tooley, M. J. (eds.) *The Environment in British Prehistory*, 125–209. London: Duckworth.

Smith, D. E., Cullingford, R. A. and Firth, C. R. 2000. Patterns of isostatic land uplift during the Holocene: evidence from mainland Scotland. *The Holocene* 10, 489–502.

Smith, D. E., Haggart, B. A., Cullingford, R. A., Tipping, R., Wells, J. M., Mighall, T. M. and Dawson, S. 2003. Holocene relative sea level changes in the lower Nith valley and estuary. *Scottish Journal of Geology*, 39, 97–120.

Smith, R. J. C., Healy, F., Allen, M. J., Morris, E. L., Barnes, I. and Woodward, P. J. 1997. *Excavations along the Route of the Dorchester By-Pass, Dorset, 1986–8*. Salisbury: Wessex Archaeology.

Speak, S. and Burgess, C. 1999. Meldon Bridge: a centre of the third millennium BC in Peeblesshire. *Proceedings of the Society of Antiquaries of Scotland* 129, 1–118.

Spence, D. H. N. 1964. The macrophytic vegetation of freshwater lochs, swamps and associated fens. In: Burnett, J. H. (eds.) *The Vegetation of Scotland*, 306–425. Edinburgh: Oliver and Boyd.

St Joseph, J. K. 1976. Air reconnaissance: recent results 40. *Antiquity* 50, 55–57.

Stace, C. 1991. *New Flora of the British Isles*. Cambridge: Cambridge University Press.

Stell, G. 1996. *Dumfries and Galloway: Exploring Scotland's Heritage*. Edinburgh: The Stationery Office.

Stewart, M. 1985. The excavation of a henge, stone circles and metal working area at Moncreiffe, Perthshire. *Proceedings of the Society of Antiquaries of Scotland* 115, 125–50.

Stuiver, M. and Reimer, P. J. 1993. Extended ^{14}C data base and revised CALIB 3.0 ^{14}C age calibration program. *Radiocarbon* 35, 215–230.

Sugita, S., Gaillard, M.-J. and Brostrom, A. 1999. Landscape openness and pollen records: a simulation approach. *The Holocene* 9, 409–421.

Tauber, H. 1965. Differential pollen dispersion and the interpretation of pollen diagrams. *Danmarks Geologiske Undersogelse* II 89, 7–69.

Taverner, N. 1987. Bannockburn: the pit and post alignments excavated in 1984 and 1985. *Scottish Development Department Central Excavation Unit and Ancient Monuments Laboratory Annual Report* 1987, 71–6.

Taylor, M. 1981. *Wood in Archaeology*. Aylesbury: Shire Publications.

Thomas, J. S. 1991. *Rethinking the Neolithic*. Cambridge: Cambridge University Press.

Thomas, J. S. 1999a. *Understanding the Neolithic*. London: Routledge.

Thomas, J. S. 1999b. An economy of substances in earlier Neolithic Britain. In: J. Robb (ed.), *Material Symbols: Culture and Economy in Prehistory*, 70–89. Carbondale: Southern Illinois University Press.

Thomas, J. S. 2000. Death, identity and the body in Neolithic Britain. *Journal of the Royal Anthropological Institute* 6, 603–17.

Thomas, J. S. 2003. Thoughts on the 'Repacked' Neolithic Revolution. *Antiquity* 77, 67–74.

Thomas, J. S. 2004a. Materiality and traditions of practice in Neolithic south-west Scotland. In: V. Cummings and C. Fowler (eds.) *The Neolithic of the Irish Sea: Materiality and Traditions of Practice*, 174–84. Oxford: Oxbow Books.

Thomas, J.S. 2004b The later Neolithic architectural repertoire: the case of the Dunragit complex. In: R. Cleal and J. Pollard (eds.) *Monuments and Material Culture: Papers on Neolithic and Bronze Age Britain in Honour of Isobel Smith*, 98–108. East Knoyle: Hobnob Press.

Thomas, J. 2004c. Holm. *Discovery and Excavation in Scotland New Series* 5, 161.

Thomas, J. S., Brophy, K., Fowler, C., Leivers, M., Ronayne, M. and Wood, L. 1999. The Holywood Cursus complex, Dumfries 1997: an interim account. In: A. Barclay and J. Harding (ed.) *Pathways and Ceremonies: the Cursus Monuments of Neolithic Britain and Ireland*, 107–15. Oxford: Oxbow Books.

Thompson, D. A. 1971. Lightning strikes in Galloway – June 1970. *Scottish Forestry* 25, 51–52.

Tight, J. A. 1987. *The Late Quaternary History of the Western Branxholme and Kingside Lochs, South-east Scotland*. Unpublished PhD thesis, University of Reading.

Tilley, C. Y. 1994. *A Phenomenology of Landscape*. London: Berg.

Tilley, C. Y. 1996. The powers of rocks: topography and monument construction on Bodmin Moor. *World Archaeology* 28, 161–76.

Tilley, C. Y. 1999. *Metaphor and Material Culture*. Oxford: Blackwell.

Tipping, R. and Milburn, P. 2000. The mid-Holocene charcoal fall in southern Scotland: spatial and temporal variability. *Palaeogeography, Palaeoclimatology, Palaeoecology* 164, 193–209.

Tipping, R. 1994. The form and fate of Scottish woodlands. *Proceedings of the Society of Antiquaries of Scotland* 124, 1–54.

Tipping, R. 1995a. Holocene evolution of a lowland Scottish landscape: Kirkpatrick Fleming. I Peat- and pollen-stratigraphic evidence for raised moss development and climatic change. *The Holocene* 5, 69–82.

Tipping, R. 1995b. Holocene evolution of a lowland Scottish landscape: Kirkpatrick Fleming. II Regional vegetation and land-use change. *The Holocene* 5, 83–96.

Tipping, R. 1995c. Holocene evolution of a lowland Scottish landscape: Kirkpatrick Fleming. III Fluvial history. *The Holocene* 5, 184–195.

Tipping, R. 1995d. Holocene landscape change at Carn Dubh, near Pitlochry, Perthshire. *Journal of Quaternary Science* 10, 59–75.

Tipping, R. 1996. Microscopic charcoal records, inferred human activity and climate change in the mesolithic of northernmost Scotland. In: Pollard, A. and Morrison, A. (eds.) *The Early Prehistory of Scotland*, 39–61. Edinburgh: Edinburgh University Press.

Tipping, R. 1997a. Environment and environmental change in Eastern Dumfriesshire. In: Royal Commission on Ancient and Historical Monuments (Scotland) *Eastern Dumfriesshire – An Archaeological Landscape*, 10–25. Edinburgh: The Stationery Office.

Tipping, R. 1997b. Medieval woodland history from the Scottish Southern Uplands: fine spatial-scale pollen data from a small woodland hollow. In: Smout, C. (ed.) *Scottish Woodland History*, 49–72. Aberdeen: Scottish Cultural Press.

Tipping, R. 1999a. Quaternary landscape evolution of Dumfries and Galloway. In: Tipping, R. (ed.) *The Quaternary of Dumfries and Galloway. Field Guide*, 6–27. London: Quaternary Research Association.

Tipping, R. 1999b. Rotten Bottom: Holocene upland environments. In: Tipping, R. (ed.) *The Quaternary of Dumfries and Galloway. Field Guide*, 171–181. London: Quaternary Research Association.

Tipping, R. 1999c. Towards an environmental history of the Bowmont Valley and the Northern Cheviot Hills. *Landscape History* 20, 41–50.

Tipping, R. 2000. Palaeoecological approaches to historic problems: a comparison of sheep-grazing intensities in the Cheviot Hills in the Medieval and later periods. In: Atkinson, J., Banks, I. and MacGregor, G. (eds.) *Townships to Farmsteads. Rural Settlement Studies in Scotland, England and Wales*, 30–43. Oxford: British Archaeological Reports 293.

Tipping, R., Carter, S. and Johnston, D. 1994. Soil pollen and soil micromorphological analyses of old ground surfaces on Biggar Common, Borders Region, Scotland. *Journal of Archaeological Science* 21, 387–401.

Tipping, R., Haggart, B. A., Milburn, P. A. and Thomas, J. 2004. Landscape perception in early Bronze Age henge construction at The Pict's Knowe, southern Scotland: a palaeoenvironmental perspective. In: Carver, E. and Lelong, O. (eds.) *Modern Views – Ancient Lands. New Work and Thought on Cultural Landscapes*, 33–40. Oxford: Archaeopress.

Topping, P. 1982. Excavations at the cursus at Scorton, North Yorkshire 1978. *Yorkshire Archaeological Journal* 54, 7–21.

Tratman, E. K. 1970. The Glastonbury Lake Village: a reconsideration. *Proceedings of the University of Bristol Spelaeological Society* 12, 143–67.

Truckell A. E. 1984. Some lowland native sites in western Dumfriesshire and Galloway. In: Miket, R. and Burgess, C. (eds.), *Between and Beyond the Walls. Essays on the Prehistory and History of North Britain in Honour of George Jobey*, 199–205. Edinburgh: Donald.

Tylecote, R. F. 1986. *The Prehistory of Metallurgy in the British Isles.* London: Institute of Metals.

van Geel, B. 1981. *A Palaeoecological Study of Holocene Peat Bog Sections Based on the Analysis of Pollen, Spores and Macro and Microscopic Remains of Fungi, Algae, Cormophytes and Animals.* Amsterdam.

Waddell, J. 1998. *The Prehistoric Archaeology of Ireland.* Galway: Galway University Press.

Waddington, C. 1999. *A Landscape Archaeological Study of the Mesolithic-Neolithic in the Milfield Basin, Northumberland.* Oxford: British Archaeological Reports, British Series 291.

Wainwright, G. J. 1979. *Mount Pleasant, Dorset: Excavations 1970–71.* London: Society of Antiquaries.

Wainwright, G. J. and Longworth, I. 1971. *Durrington Walls: Excavations 1966–1968.* London: Society of Antiquaries.

Walker, B., McGregor, C., and Stark, G. 1996. *Thathches and Thatching Techniques: a Guide to Conserving Scottish Thatching Traditions.* Edinburgh: Historic Scotland.

Walker, D. 1966. The late Quaternary history of the Cumberland lowland. *Philosophical Transactions of the Royal Society of London* B251, 1–210.

Ward G. K. and Wilson S. R. 1978. Procedures for comparing and combining radiocarbon age determinations: a critique. *Archaeometry* 20, 19–31.

Wells, J. 1997. The 'Errol Beds' and 'Clyde Beds': a note on their equivalents in the Solway Firth. *Quaternary Newsletter* 83, 21–26.

Wells, J. 1999a. Late-Glacial and Holocene sea-level changes in the Solway Firth. In: Tipping, R. (ed.) *The Quaternary of Dumfries and Galloway. Field Guide*, 27–32. London: Quaternary Research Association.

Wells, J. 1999b. Brighouse Bay: coastal evolution and relative sea-level change. In: Tipping, R. (ed.) *The Quaternary of Dumfries and Galloway. Field Guide*, 44–50. London: Quaternary Research Association.

Wells, J. M. and Smith, D. E. 1999. The Cree Estuary: Holocene relative sea-level changes. In: Tipping, R. (ed.) *The Quaternary of Dumfries and Galloway. Field Guide*, 33–43. London: Quaternary Research Association.

Wells, J. M., Mighall, T. M., Smith, D. E. and Dawson, A. G. 1999. Brighouse Bay, southwest Scotland: Holocene vegetational history and human impact at a small coastal valley mire. In: Andrews, P. and Banham, P. (eds.) *Late Cenozoic Environments and Hominid Evolution: a Tribute to Bill Bishop*, 217–233. London: Geological Society.

White, K. D. 1970. *Roman Farming.* London: Thames and Hudson.

Whittle, A., Pollard, J. and Grigson, C. 1999. *The Harmony of Symbols: The Windmill Hill Causewayed Enclosure.* Oxford: Oxbow Books.

Williams, B. B. 1978. Excavations at Lough Eskragh, Co. Tyrone. *Ulster Journal of Archaeology* 41, 37–48.

Williams, B. B. 1983. A wooden bucket found near Carrickmore, Co. Tyrone. *Ulster Journal of Archaeology* 46, 150–1.

Woodbury, R. S. 1964. *History of the Lathe.* Cambridge: The Massachusetts Institute of Technology.

Yates, M. J. 1984. *Bronze Age Round Cairns in Dumfries and Galloway: an Inventory and Discussion.* Oxford: British Archaeological Reports 132.

COLOUR PLATES

Colour plate 1. The Pict's Knowe: view of the site under excavation, 1994.

Colour plate 2. The Pict's Knowe, ditch flooded, on the final day of excavation, 1994.

Colour plate 3. The Pict's Knowe: Trench A ditch section.

Colour plate 4. The Pict's Knowe: Trench E under excavation.

Colour plate 5. Holywood North excavations from the air.

Colour plate 6. Holywood North Trench 1 from the north.

Colour plate 7. Holywood South excavations from the air.

Colour plate 8. Holm Trench A under excavation.